AMERICA

BRIEF SECOND EDITION

STUDY GUIDE

TINDALL and SHI

AMERICA

A NARRATIVE HISTORY

STUDY GUIDE

BRIEF SECOND EDITION

—————

THOMAS S. MORGAN
WINTHROP COLLEGE

and

CHARLES W. EAGLES
UNIVERSITY OF MISSISSIPPI

W • W • NORTON & COMPANY • NEW YORK • LONDON

ISBN 0-393-95701-2

W. W. Norton & Company, Inc.
500 Fifth Avenue, New York, N. Y. 10110
W. W. Norton & Company Ltd.
37 Great Russell Street, London WC1B 3NU

1 2 3 4 5 6 7 8 9 0

CONTENTS

Introduction   vii
   Structure of this Study Guide   vii
   Studying History   viii
   How to Read a Textbook   ix
Acknowledgments   x
1. Discovery and Settlement   1
2. Colonial Ways of Life   8
3. The Imperial Perspective   16
4. From Empire to Independence   22
5. The American Revolution   32
6. Shaping a Federal Union   39
7. The Federalists: Washington and Adams   47
8. Republicanism: Jefferson and Madison   55
9. Nationalism and Sectionalism   61
10. The Jacksonian Impulse   68
11. The Dynamics of Growth   78
12. An American Renaissance: Romanticism
    and Reform   84
13. Manifest Destiny   90
14. The Old South: An American Tragedy   99
15. The Crisis of Union   108
16. The War of the Union   116
17. Reconstruction: North and South   126
18. New Frontiers: South and West   136
19. Big Business and Organized Labor   145
20. The Emergence of Modern America   154
21. Gilded Age Politics and Agrarian Revolt   164
22. The Course of Empire   173

23. Progressivism: Roosevelt, Taft, and
        Wilson   180
24. Wilson and the Great War   188
25. Society and Culture Between the Wars   196
26. Republican Resurgence and Decline,
        1920–1932   203
27. Franklin D. Roosevelt and the New
        Deal   210
28. From Isolation to Global War   221
29. The World at War   231
30. The Fair Deal and Containment   238
31. Through the Picture Window: Society
        and Culture, 1945–1960   248
32. Conflict and Deadlock: The Eisenhower
        Years   256
33. Into the Maelstrom: The Sixties   263
34. Rebellion and Reaction: The Nixon
        Years   270
35. Retrenchment: Ford to Reagan   281

INTRODUCTION

This *Study Guide* is designed to help you learn the important concepts in *America: A Narrative History*, Brief Second Edition, by George B. Tindall and David E. Shi. It is not intended as a replacement for the textbook, but as an aid to be used along with the text. When used conscientiously, this *Study Guide* will help you to understand the major themes in American history and to do well on quizzes based on your reading.

STRUCTURE OF THIS STUDY GUIDE

Each chapter of the *Study Guide* contains the following sections:

Chapter Objectives
Chapter Outline
Key Items of Chronology
Terms to Master
Vocabulary Building
Exercises for Understanding:
   Multiple-Choice Questions
   True-False Questions
   Essay Questions
Document(s) or Reading(s)

The purpose of each of the sections, along with instructions for its use, is explained below.

Chapter Objectives

For each chapter you will find about five objectives, or key concepts, on which you should focus your attention as you read. You should read the whole of each chapter, taking in details as well as major themes, but by keeping the chapter objectives in mind you will avoid getting bogged down and missing the key ideas.

Chapter Outline

Skim this outline carefully before you begin reading a chapter. The outline provides a more detailed overview than do the objectives. Often headings in the outline are worded to suggest questions about the material. For example, "Duties of the King" and "Patterns of Colonization" raise the questions "What were the duties of the king?" and "What were the patterns of colonization?" Look for the answers to such questions as you read the text. This approach will help those of you who are new to reading history.

Key Items of Chronology

Each chapter of this *Study Guide* will include a list of dates. You need not learn every date you encounter in the chapter, but if you learn the key ones listed here and any other dates emphasized by your instructor, you will have the sound chronological framework so important for understanding historical events.

Keep in mind that dates, while important, are not the sole subject matter of history. Seldom will any of the quizzes in this *Study Guide* ask for recall of dates. On the other hand, term papers and answers to essay questions should include important dates and show that you are familiar with the chronology of your subject.

Terms to Master

This section of the *Study Guide* gives you a list of important terms to study. (Remember, of course, that your instructor may emphasize additional terms which you should learn.) After reading each chapter, return to the list of terms and write a brief definition of each. If you cannot recall the term readily, turn to the relevant pages in the textbook and reread the discussion of the term. If you need or want to consult another source, go to the annotated bibliography at the end of the relevant chapter, or ask your instructor for suggestions.

Vocabulary Building

This is a section of the *Study Guide* that you may or may not need. If you do not know the meaning of the words or terms listed in Vocabulary Building, look them up in a dictionary before you begin reading a chapter. By looking up such words and then using them yourself, you will increase your vocabulary.

When the terms in Vocabulary Building are not readily found in the standard dictionary or when their use in the Tindall text lends them a special meaning, we have defined them for you. We've used the *American Heritage Dictionary*, Second College Edition, as a guide to determine which terms should be defined here for you.

Exercises for Understanding

You should reserve these exercises to use as a check on your reading after you study the chapter. The multiple-choice and true-false questions included here will test your recall and understanding of the facts in the chapter. The answers to these questions are found at the end of each *Study Guide* chapter.

Essay Questions

The essay questions which come next may be used in several ways. If you are using this *Study Guide* entirely on your own, you should try to outline answers to these questions based on your reading of the chapter. In the early stages of the course you may want to consider writing formal answers to these essay questions just as you would if you encountered them on an exam. The questions will often be quite broad and will lead you to think about material in the chapter in different ways. By reviewing the essay questions in this *Study Guide* before attending class, you will better understand the class lecture or discussion.

Documents and Readings

All the chapters in this *Study Guide* contain a section of documents or readings. The documents are sources from the time period of the chapter (primary sources), chosen to illumine some aspect of the period covered in the text. The readings are excerpts from works of historians (secondary sources), chosen either to illustrate the approach of a master historian or to offer varying interpretations of an event. Study the document or reading after you have completed the chapter, and consult the headnotes given in this *Study Guide* before each document. Then attempt to answer the questions that follow the document.

STUDYING HISTORY

The term "history" has been defined in many ways. One way to define it is "everything that has happened in the past." But there are serious problems with this definition. First, it is simply impossible to recount *everything* that has happened in the past. Any single event, such as your eating dinner, is a combination of an infinite number of subevents, ranging from the cultivation of vegetables to the mechanisms involved in digestion. Each of these is itself composed of an unlimited number of subevents. The past, which includes everything that has happened, is shapeless; history is a way of lending shape to the past by focusing on significant events and their relationships. Your "history" of last night's dinner will include only the significant elements, perhaps who your companions were and why you got together, not where the spinach was grown.

Second, the historical record is limited. As you will discover, there is much we don't know about everyday life in seventeenth-century America. History must be based on fact and evidence. The historian then, using the evidence available, fashions a story in which certain past events are connected and take on special meaning or significance. If we accept this definition, we will recognize that much history is subjective, or influenced by the perspective and bias of the historian attempting to give meaning to events.

This is why there is so much disagreement about the importance of some past events. You may have been taught in high school that it was important simply to learn dates and facts: that the Declaration of Independence was adopted on July 4, 1776, or that Franklin Roosevelt was inaugurated on March 4, 1933. But these facts by themselves are limited in meaning. They gain significance when they become parts of larger stories, such as why the American colonies revolted against England, or how America responded to the Great Depression. When historians construct stories or narratives in which these facts or events take on special significance, room for disagreement creeps in.

Since it is valid for historians to disagree, you should not automatically accept what any one historian writes. You should learn to apply general rules of logic and evidence in assessing the validity of different historical interpretations. This *Study Guide* will at times give you an opportunity to assess different interpretations of events. By doing this you will learn to question what you read and hear, to think critically.

HOW TO READ A TEXTBOOK

Reading a textbook should be both pleasurable and profitable. The responsibility for this is partly the author's and partly yours, the reader's. George Tindall has written a text which should teach and entertain. In order to get the most out of it you must read actively and critically. One way to avoid passive, mindless reading is to write, underline, or highlight material by hand. Thus simply by highlighting or underlining pertinent passages in the textbook you will later be better able to recall what you have read and you will be able to review quickly important material. The key to effective highlighting is to be judicious about what you choose to mark. You should highlight key words and phrases, not whole sentences unless all the words are important. For example, the two paragraphs below show the way we would highlight them:

Even the Tudors, who acted as autocrats, preserved the forms of constitutional procedure. In the making of laws the king's subjects consented through representatives in the House of Commons. By custom and practice **the principle was established that the king taxed his subjects only with the consent of Parliament.** And by its control of the purse strings Parliament would draw other strands of power into its hands. This structure of habit broadened down from precedent to precedent to form a **constitution that was** not written in one place, or for that matter, **not fully written down at all.** The *Magna Carta* (Great Charter) of 1215, for instance, had been a statement of privileges wrested by certain nobles from the king, but it became part of a broader tradition that the people as a whole had rights which even the king could not violate.

A further buttress to English liberty was the **great body of common law** which had developed since the twelfth century in royal courts established to check the arbitrary caprice of local nobles. Without laws to cover every detail, judges had to exercise their own ideas of fairness in settling disputes. **Decisions once made became precedents for later decisions** and over the years a body of judge-made law developed, the outgrowth more of experience than of abstract logic. Through the courts the principle evolved that **a subject could be arrested or his goods seized only upon a warrant issued by a court** and that **he was entitled to a trial by a jury of his peers** (his equals) in accordance with established rules of evidence.

Probably no two persons would agree on exactly what words in the passage should be underlined, but you can readily see that we have emphasized only the major points concerning English justice.

Highlighting like this can be helpful, but even more useful in increasing your retention of the material is to jot down brief notes about what you read. For example, from the passage above you might list some key elements in the development of liberty under the Tudors: the principle that the king could tax his subjects only with the consent of Parliament, the development of an unwritten constitution, the principle that a court order was required for arrest or seizure of property, and the principle of trial by jury.

Taking notes makes it easier to commit important points to memory. This will help especially when you review for a test.

ACKNOWLEDGMENTS

We wish to thank George B. Tindall and David E. Shi for having written the excellent text around which we developed this *Study Guide.* Our hope is that the text and the *Study Guide* will combine to promote in students a clear understanding of the history of the United States. We have a great debt to Steven Forman, our editor at W. W. Norton & Company, who has again used his considerable skill to fashion the final product. He has created a unified revision from the different parts on which we each worked.

C.W.E.
T.S.M.

AMERICA

BRIEF SECOND EDITION

STUDY GUIDE

1

DISCOVERY AND SETTLEMENT

CHAPTER OBJECTIVES

After you complete the reading and study of this chapter you should be able to

1. Describe the cultural and biological exchanges that occurred between Europe and America following the discovery of the New World.
2. Explain the different characteristics of French, Dutch, and English contacts with the New World before the permanent settlements of the seventeenth century.
3. Understand the key features in the settlement and early development of each of the thirteen North American colonies of England, but in particular Virginia, Massachusetts, Maryland, and New York.
4. Understand the chief features of English colonization in North America as a whole and in comparison to the colonization efforts of Spain and France.

CHAPTER OUTLINE

I. Origins of the earliest Americans

II. Development of Indian cultures before Columbus

A. Civilizations in Middle America in contrast with those to the north and south
B. Development of Mayan, Aztec, and Incan cultures in Middle America
C. Major Indian cultures in the area of the United States after about 1000 B.C.
D. Factors aiding the European conquest of the Indians

III. European discovery of the New World
A. Characteristics of "modern" Europe
B. Christopher Columbus and his voyages
C. The cultural and biological diffusion brought by European contact with the New World
D. Professional explorers

IV. The creation of the Spanish Empire
A. Cortés and other conquistadores
B. Patterns of Spanish conquest

V. Impact of Protestant Reformation on Europe

VI. French, Dutch, and English rivalry with the Spanish in North America
A. Verrazano and Cartier
B. Rebellion of the Netherlands and the Dutch privateers
C. English defeat of the Spanish Armada, 1588

VII. English explorations and settlements
A. Early attempts at colonization

B. The Chesapeake Bay region
  1. Virginia from company colony to royal colony
  2. Maryland, the proprietary colony
C. New England
  1. The Pilgrims at Plymouth Colony
  2. Massachusetts Bay Colony and John Winthrop
  3. Roger Williams and the start of Rhode Island
  4. Connecticut, New Hampshire, and Maine

VIII. English Civil War and Restoration
IX. Renewed English settlements
  A. The Carolinas
  B. New York developed from Dutch settlements
  C. New Jersey
  D. William Penn, the Quakers, and Pennsylvania
  E. Delaware a separate colony
  F. Georgia, the last and unique colony
X. General pattern of English settlement

KEY ITEMS OF CHRONOLOGY

Crossing from Siberia to Alaska	about 16,000–14,000 B.C.
Classical cultures of Middle America	A.D. 300–900
Columbus's first voyage to the New World	1492
Voyages of John Cabot	1497–1498
Defeat of Spanish Armada	1588
Settlement of Virginia	1607
Pilgrims settle Plymouth	1620
English Civil War and Restoration	1640–1660
Carolinas settled	1663
Pennsylvania started	1682
Georgia begun	1733

TERMS TO MASTER

Listed below are some important terms or people with which you should be familiar after your study of the chapter. Explain or identify each.

1. Aztecs
2. Christopher Columbus
3. John Cabot
4. Hernando Cortés
5. *encomienda*
6. Reformation
7. Calvinism
8. "lost colonists"
9. joint-stock company
10. proprietary colony
11. Virginia Company
12. George and Cecilius Calvert
13. Pilgrims
14. Mayflower Compact
15. Roger Williams
16. Anne Hutchinson
17. Quakers

VOCABULARY BUILDING

Listed below are some words used in this chapter. Look up each word in your dictionary.

1. nomadic
2. stratified
3. subjugation
4. dead reckoning
5. vestiges
6. marauding
7. scimitar
8. staple
9. enmity
10. proviso
11. charter

12. orthodoxy
13. charismatic
14. audacity

EXERCISES FOR UNDERSTANDING

When you have completed reading the chapter, answer each of the following questions. If you have difficulty, go back to the text and reread that section of the chapter.

Multiple-Choice Questions

Select the letter of the choice which best completes the statement.

1. As part of the "great biological exchange," Europeans brought to the New World
   A. maize
   B. peanuts
   C. olives
   D. tobacco

2. Spanish officers controlled Indian villages under the system called
   A. *hacienda*
   B. democracy
   C. *encomienda*
   D. *Casa de Contracción*

3. Most of the early Spanish settlements and explorations in North America were made in
   A. the East Coast states
   B. the Southwest
   C. South Carolina
   D. along the Mississippi River

4. The defeat of the Spanish Armada gave
   A. the English naval supremacy
   B. Portugal control of the Americas
   C. the French throne to Mary Queen of Scots
   D. independence to the Incas

5. When James I became king of England, the throne fell to the
   A. Stuarts
   B. Elizabethans
   C. Puritans
   D. Tudors

6. The first English colonies were organized by
   A. the English Army
   B. the Anglican church
   C. Parliament
   D. joint-stock companies

7. Which of the following did *not* happen in Virginia in 1619?
   A. the establishment of a representative elected assembly
   B. the arrival of a shipload of young women to be sold as wives
   C. the introduction of the first blacks into the colony
   D. establishment of freedom of religion for all religious groups

8. The English colony that served as a refuge for Catholics was
   A. North Carolina
   B. Maryland
   C. Massachusetts
   D. Pennsylvania

True-False Questions

Indicate whether each statement is true or false.

1. Most authorities agree that the first inhabitants of the New World arrived from Asia, probably crossing from Siberia to Alaska.
2. Europeans infected Indians with syphilis.
3. The French had a monopoly on colonies in the New World throughout the 1500s.
4. The Protestant Reformation in England was more political than religious.
5. The earliest permanent English settlement in America was the Pilgrim colony at Plymouth Rock.
6. The charter of Massachusetts Bay Company was unusual in that it could be brought to America with the settlers.
7. The first staple crop exported from South Carolina was rice.
8. The Dutch were the first Europeans to control the colony that later became New York.

Essay Questions

1. Describe the pre-Columbia civilizations of Indians in the Americas.
2. Make lists of the plants, animals, and diseases brought to the New World and taken from the New World by Europeans. Evaluate the significance of this biological interchange.
3. Describe the development of the Spanish empire in the New World. Be sure to explain how Spain acquired and then governed its colonies.
4. The English colonies were not exactly like one another. Discuss the differences among Massachusetts, Pennsylvania, and South Carolina.
5. Compare Virginia and Massachusetts Bay with regard to the motivations for colonization, land system, religious practice, and general success as colonies. Make a similar comparison for Rhode Island and Pennsylvania.

DOCUMENTS

Document 1. Columbus's Description of the Discovery of America

The passage below is taken from a version of Columbus's journals edited by Bartolomeo de las Casas (see Document 2, below). As you read the passage, imagine the thrill of discovery that would have been experienced by the sailors on board Columbus's ships. For them this was truly a venture into the unknown.

For many years Columbus's landing was judged to have been made on San Salvador (Watling Island). A recent study retracing the voyage suggests that Columbus landed on the island of Samana Cay, more than 60 miles to the southeast of San Salvador. Many scholars will not agree with this new assertion, and the exact location of the island does not change the nature of the reaction shown in this journal. If you wish to examine the new evidence, see the *National Geographic* 170, no. 5 (November 1986): 566–605.

> ... the Admiral requested and admonished them to keep a sharp lookout at the castle of the bow, and to look well for land, and said that he would give to him who first saw land a silk doublet, besides the other rewards which the King and Queen had promised, namely an annual pension of ten thousand maravedis to him who should see it first. Two hours after midnight the land appeared, about two leagues off. They lowered all the sails, leaving only a storm square sail, which is the mainsail without bonnets, and lay to until Friday when they reached a small island of the Lucayos, called *Guanahani* by the natives. They soon saw people naked, and the Admiral went on shore in the armed boat. . . . As soon as they had landed they saw trees of a brilliant green[,] abundance of water[,] and fruits of various kinds. The Admiral called the two captains and the rest who had come on shore. . . . and he called them as witnesses to certify that he in the presence of them all, was taking, as he in fact took[,] possession of said island for the King and Queen his masters, making the declarations that were required as they will be found more fully in the attestations then taken down in writing. Soon after a large crowd of natives congregated there. What follows are the Admiral's own words in his book on the first voyage and discovery of these Indies. "In order to win the friendship and affection of that people, and because I am convinced that their conversion to our Holy Faith would be better promoted through love than

through force; I presented some of them with red caps and some strings of glass beads which they placed around their necks, and with other trifles of insignificant worth that delighted them and by which we have got a wonderful hold on their affections. They afterwards came to the boats of the vessels swimming, bringing us parrots, cotton thread in balls, and spears, and many other things, which they bartered for others we gave them, as glass beads and little bells. . . . I saw but one very young girl, all the rest being very young men, none of them being over thirty years of age; their forms being very well proportioned; their bodies graceful and their features handsome: their hair is as coarse as the hair of a horse's tail and cut short: they wear their hair over their eye brows except a little behind which they wear long, and which they never cut: some of them paint themselves black, and they are of the color of the Canary islanders, neither black nor white, and some paint themselves white, and some red, and some with whatever they find, and some paint their faces, and some the whole body, and some their eyes only, and some their noses only. They do not carry arms and have no knowledge of them, for when I showed them our swords they took them by the edge, and through ignorance, cut themselves. They have no iron; their spears consist of staffs without iron, some of them having a fish's tooth at the end, and others other things. As a body they are of good size, good demeanor, and well formed. . . . They must be good servants and very intelligent, because I see that they repeat very quickly what I told them, and it is my conviction that they would easily become Christians, for they seem not [to] have any sect. . . ."

[From Christopher Columbus, *Journals,* Thursday October 11 and Friday October 12, 1492]

Document 2. Las Casas's Description of the Spanish Conquest of Cuba

Bartolomeo de las Casas was a Spanish cleric who became an early defender of the Indians in the New World. He was one of the first to argue that the Indians were civilized and worthy of the same respect as other humans. What follows is an excerpt from his *History of the Indies,* in which he describes the cruelty inflicted by the Spanish when they overran Cuba.

They [the Spaniards] arrived at the town of Caonao in the evening. Here they found many people, who had prepared a great deal of food consisting of cassava bread and fish, because they had a large river close by and also were near the sea. In a little square were 2,000 Indians, all squatting because they have this custom, all staring, frightened, at the mares. Nearby was a large *bohío,* or large house, in which were more than 500 other Indians, close-packed and fearful, who did not dare come out.

When some of the domestic Indians the Spaniards were taking with them as servants (who were more than 1,000 souls . . .) wished to enter the large house, the Cuban Indians had chickens ready and said to them: "Take these—do not enter here." For they already knew that the Indians who served the Spaniards were not apt to perform any other deeds than those of their masters.

There was a custom among the Spaniards that one person, ap-

pointed by the captain, should be in charge of distributing to each
Spaniard the food and other things the Indians gave. And while the
Captain was thus on his mare and the others mounted on theirs, and
the father himself was observing how the bread and fish were dis-
tributed, a Spaniard, in whom the devil is thought to have clothed
himself, suddenly drew his sword. Then the whole hundred drew
theirs and began to rip open the bellies, to cut and kill those lambs—
men, women, children, and old folk, all of whom were seated, off
guard and frightened, watching the mares and the Spaniards. And
within two credos, not a man of all of them there remains alive.

The Spaniards enter the large house nearby, for this was happen-
ing at its door, and in the same way, with cuts and stabs, begin to
kill as many as they found there, so that a stream of blood was
running, as if a great number of cows had perished. Some of the
Indians who could make haste climbed up the poles and woodwork
of the house to the top, and thus escaped.

The cleric had withdrawn shortly before this massacre to where
another small square of the town was formed, near where they had
lodged him. . . .

The cleric, moved to wrath, opposes and rebukes them harshly to
prevent them, and having some respect for him, they stopped what
they were going to do, so the forty were left alive. The five go to
kill where the others were killing. And as the cleric had been de-
tained in hindering the slaying of the forty carriers, when he went
he found a heap of dead, which the Spaniards had made among the
Indians, which was certainly a horrible sight.

When Narvaez, the captain, saw him he said: "How does Your
Honor like what these our Spaniards have done?"

Seeing so many cut to pieces before him, and very upset at such
a cruel event, the cleric replied: "That I commend you and them
to the devil!" . . . Then the cleric leaves him, and goes elsewhere
through some groves seeking Spaniards to stop them from killing.
For they were passing through the groves looking for someone to
kill, sparing neither boy, child, woman, nor old person. And they did
more, in that certain Spaniards went to the road to the river, which
was nearby. Then all the Indians who had escaped with wounds,
stabs, and cuts—all who could flee to throw themselves into the
river to save themselves—met with the Spaniards who finished
them.

[George Sanderlin (ed. and trans.), *Bartolomé de Las Casas: A
Selection of His Writings* (New York: Alfred A. Knopf, 1971), pp.
63–65]

Questions for Reflection

What questions would you like to ask
about this new land that are not answered
by Columbus's brief comments? Notice how
considerate Columbus was toward the
natives and compare his attitude with that
displayed in the passage from Las Casas.
How accurate is Columbus's description of
the natives? How genuine is the religious

motivation displayed in this passage? How
would you compare this discovery with
the first manned landing on the moon in
1969?

What motivation does Las Casas give for
the horrible slaughter? Does this motivation
explain the incident to your satisfaction?
What kind of reaction does the description

evoke in you? How might it have been understood by readers in the seventeenth century? How do you account for the difference in attitude toward the natives shown in this passage and in the one above on Columbus's discovery?

ANSWERS TO MULTIPLE-CHOICE AND TRUE-FALSE QUESTIONS

Multiple-Choice Questions

1-C, 2-C, 3-B, 4-A, 5-A, 6-D, 7-D, 8-B

True-False Questions

1-T, 2-F, 3-F, 4-T, 5-F, 6-T, 7-T, 8-T

2

COLONIAL WAYS OF LIFE

CHAPTER OBJECTIVES

After you complete the reading and study of this chapter you should be able to

1. Identify population patterns in the colonies and explain their impact on institutions and the development of the colonies.
2. Identify and compare the chief features of the southern, New England, and middle colonies.
3. Explain the land and labor systems developed in the colonies, the reasons for their development, and their long-range influences on the colonies.
4. Describe major features of social life in the colonies in the seventeenth and eighteenth centuries.
5. Explain the effects of the Enlightenment and the Great Awakening upon the colonies.

CHAPTER OUTLINE

I. Migrants to early America

II. The ecology of the English colonies

III. Population patterns in the New World
  A. Population growth
  B. Birth and death rates
    1. Reasons for high birth rate
    2. Causes of lower mortality rate
  C. Social hierarchies

IV. The economy and society of the southern colonies
  A. Agriculture
    1. Tobacco, rice, lumber, naval stores
    2. Headright system
    3. Large-scale production
  B. Labor
    1. Indentured servitude
    2. Slavery
      a. Ethnic diversity
      b. Resistance to slavery
      c. Slave culture
      d. Origins of racial prejudice
  C. The southern gentry
  D. Church of England in the South

V. New England society and economy
  A. The New England town
    1. No headrights or quitrents
    2. Division of land
  B. Commerce and trade
    1. Subsistence agriculture
    2. Fisheries and shipbuilding
    3. Unfavorable balance of trade
    4. Triangular trade
    5. Shortage of hard money
  C. Religion of the Puritans
    1. Moderation in drink and sex
    2. Loyal to Church of England
    3. Organized by congregation
    4. Covenant theory
    5. Unity of church and state

D. Strains within the Puritan consensus
   1. Entrepreneurial spirit
      a. Shortage of land
      b. Disparities of wealth
   2. Individual challenges to authority
   3. Halfway Covenant
   4. Witchcraft hysteria at Salem

VI. The mixed economy and society of the middle colonies
   A. Crops and trade
   B. Land policies
   C. Ethnic diversity
      1. Quakers
      2. Germans
      3. Scotch-Irish

VII. Colonial cities
   A. Disproportionate influence
   B. Class structure
   C. Urban problems

D. The urban web
   1. Transportation
   2. Postal service
   3. Newspapers

VIII. The Enlightenment
   A. Discovery of natural laws
      1. Science of Copernicus and Newton
      2. Ideas of John Locke
   B. Impact of Enlightenment in America
   C. Benjamin Franklin
   D. Education in the colonies

IX. The Great Awakening
   A. Causes
   B. Jonathan Edwards and revivals
   C. George Whitefield
   D. Impact of churches and schools
   E. Long-range effects

KEY ITEMS OF CHRONOLOGY

First blacks arrive in Jamestown	1619
Founding of Harvard College	1636
Halfway Covenant accepted	1662
Newton's theory of gravity	1687
Witchcraft hysteria at Salem	1692
Trial of John Peter Zenger	1735
Great Awakening	1730s–1740s
Jonathan Edwards's "Sinners in the Hands of an Angry God" sermon	1741

TERMS TO MASTER

Listed below are some important terms or people with which you should be familiar after your study of the chapter. Explain or identify each.

1. headright
2. indentured servant
3. "peculiar institution"
4. balance of trade
5. "invisible" charges
6. "triangular trade"
7. covenant theory
8. Halfway Covenant
9. Scotch-Irish
10. John Peter Zenger
11. Deists
12. John Locke
13. Benjamin Franklin
14. Jonathan Edwards
15. George Whitefield

VOCABULARY BUILDING

Listed below are some words or phrases used in this chapter. Look up each word in your dictionary unless the meaning is given.

1. savannas
2. pristine

3. decimate
4. sex ratio—a term used to refer to the relative proportion of males and females in society
5. improvidence
6. idyllic
7. disparity
8. heresy
9. fratricidal
10. patroonship
11. stratification
12. epitomize
13. millennial

EXERCISES FOR UNDERSTANDING

When you have completed reading the chapter, answer each of the following questions. If you have difficulty, go back to the text and reread that section of the chapter.

Multiple-Choice Questions

Select the letter of the choice which best completes the statement.

1. The colonial population, except in the South, grew rapidly because of its
   A. low mortality rate
   B. high birth rate
   C. lower susceptibility to disease
   D. all of the above

2. The most numerous non-English immigrants to the English colonies came from
   A. France
   B. Spain
   C. Africa
   D. Germany

3. The southern colonies were characterized by
   A. large landholdings
   B. staple crops for export
   C. lack of shipping
   D. all of the above

4. In general the Puritans
   A. refused to enjoy sensuous delight in the world
   B. were total abstainers from alcoholic beverages
   C. believed that the things of the world were made by God to be enjoyed by man
   D. wore dark-colored clothes to emphasize their denial of the physical pleasures

5. The unfavorable balance of trade which New England had with the mother country was offset by
   A. printing paper money in the colonies
   B. trading manufactured goods with the southern colonies
   C. selling fish and other goods to the West Indies from which New England realized a profit
   D. taxing English goods when they came into the colonies

6. The Anglican church was strongest in
   A. the middle colonies
   B. the southern colonies
   C. New England
   D. all the colonies equally

7. Two essential elements of the colonial New England economy were
   A. fishing and shipping
   B. slavery and plantations
   C. staple crops for export and ships to carry them
   D. hard money to invest and manufacturing

8. The Great Awakening of the mid-1700s
   A. strengthened the influence of ministers
   B. reunited many churches
   C. led to greater religious intolerance
   D. none of the above

True-False Questions

Indicate whether each statement is true or false.

1. Women were treated with greater consideration in the colonies than they were back in England.
2. The absence of an Anglican bishop in the colonies resulted in greater conformity to rules among the churches.
3. As a result of the Great Awakening many of the religious denominations formed new colleges.
4. The greatest emphasis on education

occurred in the southern colonies, from which most children were sent to England for schooling.

5. Merchants were the primary members of the upper class in colonial towns.

6. By the end of the colonial period Boston was the largest city in the colonies.

7. Benjamin Franklin was the most significant figure in the Great Awakening.

8. By the standards of the Enlightenment, the use of reason was the highest virtue.

Essay Questions

1. What were the major groups that settled in America in the seventeenth and eighteenth centuries, and why did they come to the New World?

2. Describe the ecology that the *first* European settlers encountered, and discuss the long-range effects of the abundance of land and scarcity of labor on American society.

3. Explain the status of women in colonial society.

4. Why did slavery begin in the English colonies and what impact did the presence of Afro-Americans have on the emerging American culture?

5. Compare and contrast colonial agriculture in the southern, middle, and New England colonies.

6. Did the Great Awakening or the Enlightenment have the greater impact on the colonies? Be sure to justify your answer.

DOCUMENTS

Document 1. From the Secret Diary of William Byrd

What follows are selected entries from the diary of William Byrd, a gentleman from Virginia who is representative of the southern landed aristocrat. Byrd's diary was kept in a secret shorthand and discovered only in the twentieth century. It provides insight into the mind of a southern gentleman.

Byrd's diary also lets us see the daily schedule and the thoughts of a colonial gentleman. Byrd committed to his diary some of his most private thoughts and actions. These entries focus especially upon Byrd's relationship with his wife, his treatment of servants, his daily activities, his diet, his description of medical practices, and his observations of nature.

[September 1709] 3. I rose at 5 o'clock and was hindered from reading Hebrew by the company; however, I read some Greek in Josephus. I said my prayers and ate chocolate with Mr. Taylor for breakfast. Then he went away. I read some geometry. We had no court this day. My wife was indisposed again but not to much purpose. I ate roast chicken for dinner. In the afternoon I beat Jenny for throwing water on the couch. I took a walk to Mr. Harrison's who told me he heard the peace was concluded in the last month. After I had been courteously entertained with wine and cake I returned home, where I found all well, thank God. I neglected to say my prayers but had good health, good thoughts, and good humor, thanks be to God Almighty.

5. I rose at 5 o'clock and read some Greek in Josephus and a chapter in Hebrew. I said my prayers and ate milk for breakfast. I danced my dance. My wife was much out of order and had frequent returns of her pains. I read some geometry. I ate roast mutton for dinner. In the afternoon I wrote a letter to England and I read some Greek

in Homer. Then in the evening I took a walk about the plantation
and when I returned I found my wife very bad. I sent for Mrs.
Hamlin and my cousin Harrison about 9 o'clock and I said my
prayers heartily for my wife's happy delivery, and had good health,
good thoughts, and good humor, thanks be to God Almighty. I went
to bed about 10 o'clock and left the women full of expectation with
my wife.

6. About one o'clock this morning my wife was happily delivered
of a son, thanks be to God Almighty. I was awake in a blink and rose
and my cousin Harrison met me on the stairs and told me it was a
boy. We drank some French wine and went to bed again and rose
at 7 o'clock. I read a chapter in Hebrew and then drank chocolate
with the women for breakfast. I returned God humble thanks for
so great a blessing and recommended my young son to His divine
protection.

[October 1709] 6. I rose at 6 o'clock and said my prayers and ate
milk for breakfast. Then I proceeded to Williamsburg, where I
found all well. I went to the capitol where I sent for the wench to
clean my room and when I came I kissed her and felt her, for which
God forgive me. Then I went to see the President, whom I found
indisposed in his ears. I dined with him . . . on beef. Then we went
to his house and played at piquet where Mr. Clayton came to us. We
had much to do to get a bottle of French wine. About 10 o'clock I
went to my lodgings. I had good health but wicked thoughts, God
forgive me.

[February 1710] 26. I rose at 8 o'clock and read nothing because of
my company. I neglected to say my prayers, for which God forgive
me. I ate milk for breakfast. Then we took a walk about the plantation till it was time to go to dinner. I ate fish for dinner. In the
afternoon we saw a good battle between a stallion and Robin about
the mare, but at last the stallion had the advantage and covered the
mare three times. The Captain's bitch killed another lamb for which
she was beat very much. We took another walk about the plantation. My maid Anaka was very well again, thank God, and so was
Moll at the quarters. My wife was out of humor with us for going
to see so filthy a sight as the horse to cover the mare. In the evening
we drank a bottle of wine and were very merry till 9 o'clock. I
neglected to say my prayers but had good health, good thoughts,
and good humor, thanks be to God Almighty.

[March 1710] 31. I rose at 7 o'clock and read some Greek in bed.
I said my prayers and ate milk for breakfast. Then about 8 o'clock
we got a-horseback and rode to Mr. Harrison's and found him very
ill but sensible. . . . In the morning early I returned home and went
to bed. It is remarkable that Mrs. Burwell dreamed this night that
she saw a person that with money scales weighed time and declared
that there was no more than 18 pennies worth of time to come,
which seems to be a dream with some significance either concerning the world or a sick person. In my letters from England I learned
that the Bishop of Worcester was of opinion that in the year 1715
the city of Rome would be burnt to the ground, that before the year
1745 the popish religion would be routed out of the world, that

before the year 1790 the Jews and Gentiles would be converted to the Christianity and then would begin the millenium.

[July 1710] 30. I rose at 5 o'clock and wrote a letter to Major Burwell about his boat which Captain Broadwater's people had brought round and sent Tom with it. I read two chapters in Hebrew and some Greek in Thucydides. I said my prayers and ate boiled milk for breakfast. I danced my dance. I read a sermon in Dr. Tillotson and then took a little [nap]. I ate fish for dinner. In the afternoon my wife and I had a little quarrel which I reconciled with a flourish. Then she read a sermon in Dr. Tillotson to me. . . . I read a little Latin. In the evening we took a walk about the plantation. I neglected to say my prayers but had good health, good thoughts, and good humor, thanks be to God. This month there were many people sick of fever and pain in their heads; perhaps this might be caused by the cold weather which we had this month, which was indeed the coldest weather that ever was known in July in this country. Several of my people have been sick, but none died, thank God.

[February 1712] 20. . . . When I had put myself in order I went with several gentlemen to the Council to wait on the Governor but he was not home. However we saw the Doctor dissect a beaver and take out the castor which is not the stones of the beaver but two glands just above the genitals. Then we returned to the capitol to Council where the Governor laid before us a petition. . . .

27. . . . My overseer brought in a mustrat [*sic*] which I dissected and got out the musk which is in two glands not far from the anus. . . .

[March 1712] 12. . . . About 2 o'clock we went to dinner and I ate some of the beef that was preserved after the new manner and found it very juicy and not very salt. It is the best way of saving meat and will preserve it for several years free from taint and was found out by chance by a poor carpenter who keeps the secret to himself and gets abundance of money. . . .

[Louis B. Wright and Marion Tinlin (eds.), *The Secret Diary of William Byrd of Westover, 1709–1712* (Richmond, Va.: The Dietz Press, 1941), pp. 80, 90–91, 146, 159, 197, 210–211, 488, 492, 499]

Document 2. From the Autobiography of Benjamin Franklin

Benjamin Franklin was the foremost disciple of the Enlightenment in the colonies; moreover he was recognized in the sophisticated intellectual circles of Europe for his scientific experiments and his scientific knowledge. The passages selected here from his *Autobiography* emphasize his philosophical reactions to some of the popular concepts of the Enlightenment. They also reflect some of his ideas about a daily schedule. Compare these to those of Byrd, above.

This library afforded me the means of improvement by constant study, for which I set apart an hour or two each day, and thus repair'd in some degree the loss of the learned education my father once intended for me. Reading was the only amusement I allow'd myself. I spent no time in taverns, games, or frolicks of any kind; and my industry in my business continu'd as indefatigable as it was necessary. I was indebted for my printing-house; I had a young family coming on to be educated, and I had to contend with for business two printers, who were established in the place before me. My circumstances, however, grew daily easier. My original habits of frugality continuing, and my father having, among his instructions to me when a boy, frequently repeated a proverb of Solomon, "Sees thou a man diligent in his calling, he shall stand before kings, he shall not stand before mean men." I from thence considered industry as a means of obtaining wealth and distinction, which encourag'd me, tho' I did not think that I should ever literally *stand before kings,* which, however, has since happened; for I have stood before *five,* and even had the honor of sitting down with one, the King of Denmark, to dinner.

We have an English proverb that says, *"He that would thrive, must ask his wife."* It was lucky for me that I had one as much dispos'd to industry and frugality as myself. She assisted me cheerfully in my business, folding and stitching pamphlets, tending shop, purchasing old linen rags for the papermakers, etc., etc. We kept no idle servants, our table was plain and simple, our furniture of the cheapest. For instance, my breakfast was a long time bread and milk (no tea), and I ate it out of a twopenny earthen porringer, with a pewter spoon. But mark how luxury will enter families, and make a progress, in spite of principle: being call'd one morning to breakfast, I found it in a China bowl, with a spoon of silver! They had been bought for me without my knowledge by my wife, and had cost her the enormous sum of three-and-twenty shillings, for which she had no other excuse or apology to make, but that she thought *her* husband deserv'd a silver spoon and China bowl as well as any of his neighbors. This was the first appearance of plate and China in our house, which afterward, in a course of years, as our wealth increas'd, augmented gradually to several hundred pounds in value.

I had been religiously educated as a Presbyterian; and tho' some of the dogmas of that persuasion, such as *the eternal decrees of God, election, reprobation, etc.,* appeared to me unintelligible, others doubtful, and I early absented myself from the public assemblies of the sect, Sunday being my studying day, I never was without some religious principles. I never doubted, for instance, the existence of the Deity; that he made the world, and govern'd it by his Providence; that the most acceptable service of God was the doing good to man; that our souls are immortal; and that all crime will be punished, and virtue rewarded, either here or hereafter. . . .

Tho' I seldom attended any public worship, I had still an opinion of its propriety, and of its utility when rightly conducted, and I regularly paid my annual subscription for the support of the only Presbyterian minister or meeting we had in Philadelphia. . . .

It was about this time I conceived the bold and arduous project of arriving at moral perfection. I wish'd to live without committing any fault at any time; I would conquer all that either natural inclination, custom, or company might lead me into. . . . But I soon found I had undertaken a task of more difficulty than I had imagined.

The precept of *Order* requiring that *every part of my business should have its allotted time,* one page in my little book contain'd the following scheme of employment for the twenty-four hours of a natural day.

THE MORNING *Question.* What good shall I do this day?	5 6 7	Rise, wash, and address *Powerful Goodness!* Contrive day's business, and take the resolution of
	8	the day; prosecute the present study, and breakfast.
	9 10 11	Work.
NOON	12 1	Read, or overlook my accounts, and dine.
	2 3 4 5	Work.
EVENING. *Question.* What good have I done to-day?	6 7 8 9	Put things in their places. Supper. Music or diversion. Examination of or conversation. Examination of the day.
NIGHT	10 11 12 1 2 3 4	Sleep.

Questions for Reflection

As you read the passage from Byrd's diary, consider the treatment given to his servants. Does he seem relatively arbitrary or cruel in the punishments he metes out? How does his daily schedule compare to Franklin's? What values about wealth are evident in each of the passages? About the importance of learning? What evidence do you have to support your answer? How does each man relate to his wife? How is the Enlightenment reflected in each passage?

ANSWERS TO MULTIPLE-CHOICE AND TRUE-FALSE QUESTIONS

Multiple-Choice Questions

1-D, 2-C, 3-D, 4-C, 5-C, 6-B, 7-A, 8-D

True-False Questions

1-T, 2-F, 3-T, 4-F, 5-T, 6-F, 7-F, 8-T

3

THE IMPERIAL PERSPECTIVE

CHAPTER OBJECTIVES

After you complete the reading and study of this chapter you should be able to

1. Understand the extent and limits of British political and economic control of the colonies.
2. Explain the major institutions of colonial government in the mother-country.
3. Explain the major institutions of colonial government in the colonies.
4. Explain the general relations between the British settlers and the Indians.
5. Describe the nature of French colonization of North America and compare France's colonial policy with Britain's.
6. Explain the general course of the conflict for empire between France and Britain, and indicate why the British won.
7. Explain the consequences of Britain's victory in its Great War for Empire with France.

CHAPTER OUTLINE

I. English administration of the colonies
   A. The mercantile system
      1. Mercantilism
      2. Navigation Acts of 1651, 1660, 1663, and 1673

   3. Enforcement of laws
      a. Lords of Trade
      b. Governors
      c. Massachusetts violations
   B. Dominion of New England
      1. Governor Edmund Andros
      2. Suppression of town meetings
      3. Anglican takeover of Puritan churches
   C. Glorious Revolution
      1. William and Mary to the throne
      2. End of Dominion of New England
      3. Leisler's rebellion in New York
      4. Long-term effects on colonies
   D. More coherent colonial system
      1. Navigation Act of 1696
      2. Board of Trade created
      3. Decline into "wise and salutary neglect"

II. Colonial self-government
   A. Lack of coherent plan
   B. Powers of the governor
      1. Veto power
      2. Power over meetings of assembly
      3. Selection of council members
      4. Creating courts and naming judges
      5. Other authorities
   C. Role of the assembly
      1. Elected by property-owning men
      2. Conflicts with governor
      3. Power to tax and spend
      4. Power to initiate legislation

III. Colonists' neighbors: Indians and French
  A. Fighting with Indians
    1. In Virginia and Connecticut, 1622, 1637, 1644
    2. King Philip's War in New England, 1675–1676
    3. Bacon's Rebellion in Virginia
      a. Involvement of Indians
      b. Other factors in uprising
  B. Competing French influence
    1. Settlement of Québec
    2. Exploration of Great Lakes and Mississippi River
    3. Founding of New Orleans
    4. Limitations and advantages of French colonists
IV. Colonial wars
  A. Four European and intercolonial wars, 1689 to 1763
    1. Causes
    2. Effects on colonies
  B. The final war: French and Indian War, 1754–1763
    1. Start of the war
    2. Albany Congress
    3. War in Europe
    4. Impact of British seapower
    5. Battle of Québec
    6. The Peace of Paris and the results of the war

KEY ITEMS OF CHRONOLOGY

First Navigation Act	1651
Bacon's Rebellion	1672
Glorious Revolution	1689
King William's War	1689–1697
Navigation Acts reenacted (New Colonial System)	1696
Queen Anne's War	1701–1713
Founding of New Orleans	1718
King George's War	1744–1748
Washington's surrender of Fort Necessity and Albany Congress	1754
French and Indian War (Great War for Empire)	1754–1763
Peace of Paris	1763

TERMS TO MASTER

Listed below are some important terms or people with which you should be familiar after your study of the chapter. Identify each as it is significant in this chapter.

1. mercantilism
2. Lords of Trade
3. Dominion of New England
4. Jacob Leisler
5. John Locke
6. Writs of Assistance
7. Board of Trade
8. Nathaniel Bacon
9. Fort Duquesne
10. Albany Congress
11. Acadians

VOCABULARY BUILDING

Listed below are some words used in this chapter. Look in the dictionary for the meaning of each.

1. enumerated
2. prerogatives
3. salutary
4. anomaly
5. prorogue
6. strategic
7. athwart

EXERCISES FOR UNDERSTANDING

When you have completed reading this chapter, answer each of the following questions. If you have difficulty, go back to the text and reread the section of the chapter related to the question.

Multiple-Choice Questions

Select the letter of the response which best completes the statement.

1. Mercantilism involves all of the following *except*
   A. a mother country developing and protecting its own shipping
   B. a belief that the world's wealth equalled the amount of gold and silver available
   C. an expectation that colonies would supply raw materials to the mother country
   D. a mother country developing only those products it could produce cheaply and efficiently

2. In America an effect of England's Glorious Revolution was
   A. the dissolution of the Dominion of New England
   B. a weakening of royal control over the colonies
   C. an end to mercantilism
   D. all of the above.

3. The contract theory of government, which rested on a belief in the natural rights of individuals, was devised by
   A. Edmund Randolph
   B. William and Mary
   C. the English Parliament
   D. John Locke

4. Colonial governors resembled the English crown in that each usually could
   A. veto acts of the legislatures
   B. appoint administrative officials
   C. adjourn the legislatures
   D. name and dismiss judges

5. Bacon's Rebellion in Virginia in 1676 was an example of
   A. the frontier region against the Tidewater area
   B. common men versus aristocrats
   C. political outsiders fighting entrenched power
   D. all of the above

6. French colonial policy in North America primarily focused on
   A. rapidly settling the area around the Great Lakes with people loyal to France
   B. developing fur trading and missionary work rather than colonization
   C. making treaties with the Indians to gain rights to their lands for future French settlements
   D. gaining a route westward across the entire North American continent

7. As a result of the colonial wars after 1676, Boston's population
   A. increased with the arrival of thousands of British troops to help fight the Indians
   B. grew rapidly with refugees from the war zones
   C. remained fairly constant with many poor widows and orphans
   D. declined drastically due to numerous casualties in the fighting

8. One of the chief lessons learned from the long series of wars between Britain and France was
   A. the British navy was not important in warfare with other powers
   B. the American colonists were not loyal to the mother country even in a struggle for survival
   C. the French army was a formidable opponent in the pitched battles of North America
   D. the British could count on Indian allies in their conflicts with the French

True-False Questions

Indicate whether each of the following statements is true or false.

1. The Writs of Assistance were unrestricted search warrants.

2. One important cause of the outbreak of wars between France and England was the decidedly Protestant attitude of William as king of England.

3. After 1725 British policy toward the

colonies became more careful, coordinated, and intense.

4. King Philip's War involved only the Chesapeake colonies.
5. Under its charter New France could accept only French Catholics.
6. A smaller proportion of the population could vote in the colonies than in England.
7. The French and Indian War eliminated the French as a threat to the colonies from the west.
8. The revolts of both Nathaniel Bacon and Jacob Leisler heralded the Revolution because they were uprisings of backcountry farmers against the wealthy Tidewater aristocracy.

Essay Questions

1. Explain how the American colonies could be both aided and hampered by British mercantile policies.
2. Discuss the relative powers of colonial governors and assemblies. Given these relative strengths, which was more powerful? Why?
3. Describe the evolution of British imperial policy from 1651 to 1725.
4. Describe the key events in the French and Indian War, and explain the significant results of the war.
5. Compare and contrast the British and French approaches to colonization.

READING

Francis Parkman was a master historian of the nineteenth century. Noted for the literary quality of his writing, he had the ability to place the reader in the midst of a battle or any other historical scene. He also had a great grasp of the overall significance of events. In the following passages he summarizes his assessment of the French and Indian War.

On the American continent the war was ended, and the British colonists breathed for a space, as they drifted unwittingly towards a deadlier strife. They had learned hard and useful lessons. Their mutual jealousies and disputes, the quarrels of their governors and assemblies, the want of any general military organization, and the absence, in most of them, of military habits, joined to narrow views of their own interest, had unfitted them to the last degree for carrying on offensive war. Nor were the British troops sent for their support remarkable in the beginning for good discipline or efficient command. When hostilities broke out, the army of Great Britain was so small as to be hardly worth the name. A new one had to be created; and thus the inexperienced Shirley and the incompetent Loudon, with the futile Newcastle behind them, had, besides their own incapacity, the disadvantage of raw troops and half-formed officers; while against them stood an enemy who, though weak in numbers, was strong in a centralized military organization, skilful leaders armed with untrammelled and absolute authority, practised soldiers, and a population not only brave, but in good part inured to war.

The nature of the country was another cause that helped to protract the contest. "Geography," says Von Moltke, "is three fourths of military science"; and never was the truth of his words more fully exemplified. Canada was fortified with vast outworks of defence in the savage forests, marshes, and mountains that encompassed her, where the thoroughfares were streams choked with fallen trees and obstructed by cataracts. Never was the problem of moving troops, encumbered with baggage and artillery, a more difficult one. The

question was less how to fight the enemy than how to get at him.
If a few practicable roads had crossed this broad tract of wilderness,
the war would have been shortened and its character changed.

From these and other reasons, the numerical superiority of the
English was to some extent made unavailing. This superiority,
though exaggerated by French writers, was nevertheless immense
if estimated by the number of men called to arms; but only a part
of these could be employed in offensive operations. The rest garri-
soned forts and blockhouses and guarded the far reach of frontier
from Nova Scotia to South Carolina, where a wily enemy, silent and
secret as fate, choosing their own time and place of attack, and
striking unawares at every unguarded spot, compelled thousands of
men, scattered at countless points of defence, to keep unceasing
watch against a few marauders. Full half the levies of the colonies,
and many of the regulars, were used in service of this kind.

In actual encounters the advantage of numbers was often with
the French, through the comparative ease with which they could
concentrate their forces at a given point. Of the ten considerable
seiges or battles of the war, five, besides the great bushfight in which
the Indians defeated Braddock, were victories for France; and in
four of these—Oswego, Fort William Henry, Montmorenci, and
Ste-Foy—the odds were greatly on her side.

Yet in this the most picturesque and dramatic of American wars,
there is nothing more noteworthy than the skill with which the
French and Canadian leaders used their advantages; the indomita-
ble spirit with which, slighted and abandoned as they were, they
grappled with prodigious difficulties, and the courage with which
they were seconded by regulars and militia alike. In spite of occa-
sional lapses, the defence of Canada deserves a tribute of admiration.

The great question was, Should Canada be restored? Should France
be permitted to keep a foothold on the American continent? Ever
since the capitulation of Montreal a swarm of pamphlets had dis-
cussed the momentous subject. Some maintained that the acquisition of Canada was not an original object of the war; that the colony
was of little value and ought to be given back to its old masters; that
Guadeloupe should be kept instead, the sugar trade of that island
being worth far more than the Canadian fur trade; and, lastly, that
the British colonists, if no longer held in check by France, would
spread themselves over the continent, learn to supply all their own
wants, grow independent, and become dangerous. Nor were these
views confined to Englishmen. There were foreign observers who
clearly saw that the adhesion of her colonies to Great Britain would
be jeopardized by the extinction of French power in America. Choi-
seul warned Stanley that they "would not fail to shake off their
dependence the moment Canada should be ceded"; while thirteen
years before, the Swedish traveler Kalm declared that the presence
of the French in America gave the best assurance to Great Britain
that its own colonies would remain in subjection.

The most noteworthy argument on the other side was that of
Franklin, whose words find a strange commentary in the events of
the next few years. He affirmed that the colonies were so jealous
of each other that they could never unite against England. "If they

could not agree to unite against the French and Indians, can it reasonably be supposed that there is any danger of their uniting against their own nation, which it is well known they all love much more than they love one another? I will venture to say union amongst them for such a purpose is not merely improbable, it is impossible"; that is, he prudently adds, without "the most grievous tyranny and oppression," like the bloody rule of "Alva in the Netherlands."

... Thus, in the war just ended two great conditions of success had been supplied: a people instinct with the energies of ordered freedom, and a masterly leadership to inspire and direct them.

All, and more than all, that France had lost England had won. Now, for the first time, she was beyond dispute the greatest of maritime and colonial Powers. Portugal and Holland, her precursors in ocean enterprise, had long ago fallen hopelessly behind. Two great rivals remained, and she had humbled the one and swept the other from her path. Spain, with vast American possessions, was sinking into the decay which is one of the phenomena of modern history; while France, of late a most formidable competitor, had abandoned the contest in despair, England was mistress of the seas, and the world was thrown open to her merchants, explorers, and colonists.

[Francis Parkman, *France and England in North America: Part Seventh, Montcalm and Wolfe* (Boston: Little, Brown and Co., 1896), 2:379–82, 403–404, 410–411]

Questions for Reflection

Note the passages in the selection which you think are of particularly fine literary quality. What gives the passages you have chosen their special quality? Does the literary nature of these passages distract from their ability to provide you with information?

How does Parkman view the consequences of the war? What basis do you have for your judgment?

How does the last paragraph of the selection reflect the imperial perspective which has been the theme of this chapter in the text?

ANSWERS TO MULTIPLE-CHOICE AND TRUE-FALSE QUESTIONS

Multiple-Choice Questions

1-D, 2-A, 3-D, 4-B, 5-D, 6-B, 7-C, 8-B

True-False Questions

1-T, 2-T, 3-F, 4-F, 5-T, 6-F, 7-T, 8-F

4

FROM EMPIRE TO INDEPENDENCE

CHAPTER OBJECTIVES

After you complete the reading and study of this chapter you should be able to

1. Explain how the British victory over France in the Great War for Empire, the new government of George III, and other factors worked together to produce Grenville's program.
2. Account for and assess the importance of colonial reaction to the Grenville program, and especially the stamp tax.
3. Explain the counterplay of British actions and colonial reactions from the repeal of the stamp tax to the Revolution in 1775.
4. Assess British and colonial responsibility for the coming of the Revolution.

CHAPTER OUTLINE

I. Impact of British victory in the Great War for Empire
   A. Growing American nationalism
   B. Problems of managing newly captured lands

II. British politics
   A. The Whigs
   B. Instability

III. Problems in Western lands
   A. Indian uprisings in Ohio region

   B. Proclamation of 1763
      1. Forbade settlers west of Appalachians
      2. Created colony of Quebec

IV. Grenville's program
   A. Revenues to pay British troops
      1. Efficient enforcement of customs
      2. Sugar Act of 1764
      3. Currency Act of 1764
      4. Sugar Act of 1765
      5. Quartering Act of 1765
   B. Colonial reaction
      1. Radical ideas of "Real Whigs"
      2. Tyranny of Grenville's program
      3. Cry of "no taxation without representation"
      4. Theory of "virtual representation"
   C. Stamp Act crisis
      1. Impact on articulate colonists
      2. Mass protests
      3. Nonimportation agreements
      4. Stamp Act Congress, October 1765
      5. Repeal of Stamp Act and passage of Declaratory Act

V. Growing colonial resentment
   A. Townshend Acts
      1. Reigning in New York assembly
      2. "External taxes" and vice-admiralty courts
   B. Colonial reaction to Townshend Acts
      1. Opposition to tax for revenue
      2. Samuel Adams and the Sons of Liberty

3. Boston Massacre
4. Repeal of Townshend duties, except for tax on tea
5. Easing of colonial discontent

VI. Backcountry dissent
   A. Creation of Vermont
   B. Revenge of Paxton Boys in Pennsylvania
   C. Regulator movements in the Carolinas

VII. Growing colonial tensions and protests
   A. Burning of *Gaspée*, 1772
   B. Committees of correspondence formed
   C. Lord North's Tea Act of 1773
      1. Terms of the act
      2. Colonists' refusal to accept it
      3. Boston Tea Party
   D. The Coercive Acts
      1. Closed port of Boston
      2. Allowed trials of government officials to be transferred to England
      3. Colonists to provide lodging for soldiers
      4. Many Massachusetts officials to be appointed

5. Town meetings prohibited
E. Quebec Act
F. First Continental Congress, September 1774
   1. All colonies present except Georgia
   2. Endorsed Suffolk Resolves
   3. Adopted Declaration of American Rights
   4. Adopted Continental Association
   5. Called another congress for May 1775
   6. British reaction

VIII. Colonists take the initiative
   A. Strengthened colonial militias
   B. Battles of Lexington and Concord
   C. Second Continental Congress
   D. Continental Army formed
   E. Battle of Bunker Hill
   F. Olive Branch Petition and Declaration on Taking Up Arms
   G. Continental Congress becomes "government"
   H. Thomas Paine's *Common Sense*
   I. Declaration of Independence

IX. Assessment of the causes of the Revolution

KEY ITEMS OF CHRONOLOGY

Proclamation Line to close settlement beyond the mountains	1763
Stamp Act and Stamp Act Congress	1765
Repeal of Stamp Act and passage of Declaratory Act	1766
Townshend Acts	1767
Boston Massacre	March 1770
Repeal of Townshend duties by Lord North	1770
Tea Act (of Lord North)	1773
Boston Tea Party	1773
Coercive Acts (Intolerable Acts)	1774
First Continental Congress	September 1774
Military confrontation at Lexington	April 19, 1775
Second Continental Congress	May 1775
Publication of Thomas Paine's *Common Sense*	January 1776
Declaration of Independence adopted	July 4, 1776

TERMS TO MASTER

Listed below are some important terms or people with which you should be familiar after your study of the chapter. Identify each term as it is significant in this chapter.

1. George Grenville
2. Whig ideology
3. virtual representation
4. external and internal taxes
5. William Pitt (Earl of Chatham)
6. *Letters of a Pennsylvania Farmer*
7. Samuel Adams
8. Crispus Attucks
9. Paxton Boys
10. Regulators
11. *Gaspée*
12. committees of correspondence
13. Tories
14. Continental Association
15. Battle of Bunker Hill
16. Olive Branch Petition
17. Hessians

VOCABULARY BUILDING

Listed below are some words used in this chapter. Look in the dictionary for the meaning of each.

1. depreciated
2. ideological
3. tyranny
4. effigy
5. impetuous
6. mulatto
7. vigilante
8. consignees
9. wanton
10. gauntlet
11. motley
12. vaunted

EXERCISES FOR UNDERSTANDING

When you have completed reading this chapter, answer each of the following questions. If you have difficulty, go back to the text and reread the section of the chapter related to the question.

Multiple-Choice Questions

Select the letter of the response which best completes the statement.

1. During the Great War for Empire, colonial soldiers
   A. learned frontier fighting tactics from the British soldiers
   B. gained a greater sense of their separate identity as Americans
   C. respected the discipline and moral behavior of the British troops
   D. all of the above

2. The Proclamation of 1763
   A. made Georgia a royal colony for the first time
   B. called for colonial unity against British authority
   C. taxed colonies to pay for the Great War for Empire
   D. prohibited settlements west of the Appalachian mountains

3. The Stamp Act most directly affected
   A. farmers, who would need stamps to take produce to market
   B. lawyers and other articulate groups, who could arouse the population
   C. officeholders under the English government, who would need the stamps to carry on their work
   D. smugglers, who could not continue their activities without buying the stamps

4. The Townshend duties
   A. protected British manufacturing by permitting the colonies to import its products tax free
   B. threatened colonial assemblies by paying the colonial governors from the revenues raised
   C. were easily collected in colonial ports
   D. hurt American manufacturing by taxing all exports

5. After the Boston Massacre in 1770,
   A. colonial protests and violence continuously increased
   B. colonial boycotts of British goods escalated

C. Parliament repealed most Townshend duties
D. Parliament repealed most acts irritating the colonists

6. The first Continental Congress meeting in Philadelphia in 1774 did *not*
   A. grant Parliament's power in purely imperial matters
   B. agree that the Intolerable Acts were null and void
   C. endorse a formal plan of union
   D. recommend a boycott of all British goods

7. Which of the following descriptions most accurately represents the situation in the colonies just prior to the clash of arms at Lexington and Concord?
   A. The British government had determined to quell rebellion and had moved a large number of troops to all the colonies.
   B. The British government was finding increased resistance; royal authorities had lost control to colonial groups in most colonies.
   C. The colonial leaders sought almost any means of reconciliation and found the British unreceptive to any ideas of compromise.
   D. General Gage had firm control of Massachusetts and was seeking to extend his British control into other colonies.

8. The monarchy was attacked and completely rejected by
   A. John Dickinson's *Letters of a Pennsylvania Farmer*
   B. the Whig ideology
   C. Thomas Paine's *Common Sense*
   D. none of the above

True-False Questions

Indicate whether each statement is true or false.

1. George III showed even less interest in controlling the British government than had his two predecessors.
2. For the first time the Sugar Act of 1764 deliberately sought to raise revenue in the colonies, not just regulate colonial trade.
3. In 1765 the colonists obeyed the Stamp Act, even though they disliked and protested it.
4. In repealing the Stamp Act, Parliament forfeited all power to make laws affecting the colonies.
5. Backcountry dissent in the colonies was primarily aimed at the lack of services which the coastal areas were providing for people living on the frontier.
6. John Dickinson was a fiery agitator and revolutionary organizer of protests.
7. The author of the Declaration of Independence was Thomas Jefferson.
8. One important factor leading to the adoption of the Declaration of Independence was the realization of the Americans that they needed to be independent in order to trade with France and other countries.

Essay Questions

1. Outline Grenville's colonial policy and then explain how it clashed with the colonists' Whig ideology.
2. Discuss the distinction between internal and external taxes on the colonies. What was the essence of the colonial grievance against the British in the period 1763–1776?
3. Trace the major stages in the growing sense of colonial unity against the British from 1760 to 1776.
4. Discuss the most serious problems in the colonial West (beyond the Appalachian mountains) in the twenty-five years before 1776.
5. Write in your own words a concise summary of the argument for independence used in the Declaration. Be sure to read in the text George Tindall's explanation of the reasoning used in the Declaration of Independence; then read the document itself in the text's Appendix.

READINGS

As the text indicates near the conclusion of this chapter, there have been numerous explanations for the causes of the American Revolution. Examine the following excerpts from historical interpretations of the Revolution, assessing the quality of reasoning and justification each offers. Note the various weaknesses and strengths of the arguments. Then see if you can develop your own interpretation based on these and other facts you have learned about the Revolution. Some questions at the close of this exercise may assist you further.

Reading 1. Louis Hacker Suggests Economic and Social Causes

As Curtis P. Nettels has so justly insisted, American scholars for more than a generation have been led astray by George Louis Beer's erroneous interpretation of the motives that prompted Pitt in 1763 to demand Canada instead of the sugar islands, Guadeloupe and Martinique, from vanquished France. The Beer argument runs as follows.

Pitt had great visions of empire; this dream and the imperial policies that stemmed from it prepared the way for conflict between colonies and mother country. For a mighty western empire, based as yet on a wilderness, demanded the formulation of a wise program with regard to the Indian problem—hence the shutting off of the lands beyond the crest of the Alleghenies to further settlement and the checks placed on the exploitation of the Indians by colonial traders. It demanded a system of defense—hence the dispatching of a British army to the colonies and provisions for its quartering and maintenance. It demanded a revenue—hence all those methods used by a hard-pressed home government to develop new sources of financing. Thus the chain of circumstances was complete; it had to snap at its weakest link—the raising of funds through tax measures among a liberty-loving and individualistic colonial people which too long had been permitted to go its own way. So Mr. Beer, and after him virtually every American scholar.

The events of 1763–75 have no meaning unless we understand that the character of English imperial policy never really changed: that Pitt and his successors at Whitehall were following exactly the same line that Cromwell had laid down more than a century before. The purpose of their general program was to protect the English capitalist interests which now were being jeopardized as a result of the intensifications of colonial capitalist competition. . . . If in the raising of a colonial revenue lay the heart of the difficulty, how are we to account for the quick repeal of the Stamp Tax and the Townshend Acts and the lowering of the molasses duty? . . . The struggle was not over high-sounding political and constitutional concepts: over the power of taxation or even, in the final analysis, over natural rights. It was over colonial manufacturing, wild lands and furs, sugar, wine, tea, and currency, all of which meant, simply, the survival or collapse of English mercantile capitalism within the imperial-colonial framework of the mercantilist system.

The revenue acts of 1764 and later were used as a screen to conceal the work of compressing the economy of colonial mercantile capitalism within even narrower limits and reducing it to an even more dependent status. . . .

But it was exactly this new Tea Act which clearly revealed the intention of London: that not only was the economic vassalage of the American colonies to be continued but the interest of colonial enterprisers was to be subordinated to every British capitalist group that could gain the ear of Parliament.

[From Louis M. Hacker, *The Triumph of American Capitalism* (New York: Simon and Schuster, 1940), pp. 159–160, 161, 162, 163.]

The English Mercantilist System, in its imperial-colonial relations, following the triumph of English merchant capital in the Puritan Revolution, was based on the economic subservience of the colonies. . . .

Following in the footsteps of the English themselves, colonials looked to public authority to aid in the development of native industries. In the best mercantilist tradition, therefore, colonial statute-books came to be filled with legislation which offered bounties to enterprises, extended public credit to them, exempted them from taxation, gave them easy access to raw materials and in their behalf encouraged the location of new towns. . . .

Thus, at the very time in England when the domestic system was rapidly being converted into the factory system and great advances were being made in the perfection of machinery exactly because the existence of a growing market was demanding more efficient methods of production, in the colonies methods of production remained at a hopelessly backward level because English and colonial capital could not enter manufacturing. . . . The colonial capitalist economy, therefore, was narrowly restricted largely to land speculation, the dealing in furs and the carrying trade. When English mercantilism, for the protection of its home merchant capital, began to narrow these spheres then catastrophe threatened. The American Revolution can be understood only in terms of the necessity for colonial merchant capital to escape from the contracting prison walls of the English Mercantilist System.

. . . Beginning with 1760, imperial England began to tighten the screws with stricter enforcement of the Acts of Trade and Navigation; from thence on, particularly after France had been compelled to sue for peace in 1763, England embarked on a systematic campaign to wipe out the trade between the Northern Colonies and the foreign West Indies. Northern merchant capital, its more important lifeline cut off, was being strangulated; it is not difficult to see why wealthy merchants of Philadelphia, New York, Boston, Newport and Providence should be converted into revolutionists. . . .

Utilizing the tax measures of 1764 and later (presumably designed to raise a revenue for the defense of the colonies) as a screen, Parliament imposed limitation after limitation upon the activities of the merchants.

[From Louis M. Hacker, "The American Revolution: Economic Aspects," *Marxist Quarterly* 1 (1937): 46–67]

Reading 2. Charles Andrews Presents a Political and Constitutional Explanation

The important point to remember is that the plan of governmental control as laid down in England was never in accord with the actual situation in America; that the Privy Council, the Secretary of State, and the Board of Trade seem not to have realized that their system of colonial administration was breaking down at every point. Their minds ran in a fixed groove and they could construe the instances of colonial disobedience and aggression, which they often noted, in no other terms than those of persistent dereliction of duty. Either they did not see or else refused to see the wide divergence that was taking place between colonial administration as they planned it and colonial administration as the colonists were working it out.... They interpreted the attitude of the colonists as something radical and revolutionary, menacing British prosperity, British political integrity, and the British scheme of colonial government.

Primarily, the American Revolution was a political and constitutional movement and only secondarily one that was either financial, commercial, or social. At bottom the fundamental issue was the political independence of the colonies, and in the last analysis the conflict lay between the British Parliament and the colonial assemblies, each of which was probably more sensitive, self-conscious, and self-important than the voting population that it represented. For many years these assemblies had fought the prerogative successfully and would have continued to do so, eventually reducing it to a minimum, as the later self-governing dominions have done; but in the end it was Parliament, whose powers they disputed, that became the great antagonist. . . .

The revolt of the colonies from Great Britain began long before the battles of Moore's Creek Bridge and Lexington; before the time of James Otis and the writs of assistance; before the dispute over the appointment of judges in North Carolina and New York; before the eloquence of Patrick Henry was first heard in the land; and even before the quarrel in Virginia over the Dinwiddie pistole fee. These were but the outward and visible signs of an inward and factual divergence. The separation from the mother country began just as soon as the mercantile system of commercial control, the governmental system of administration, and the whole doctrine of the inferior status of a colonial assembly began to give way before the pressure exerted and the disruptive power exercised by these young and growing colonial communities. New soil had produced new wants, new desires, new points of view, and the colonists were demanding the right to live their own lives in their own way. . . .

. . . The colonies had developed a constitutional organization equally complete with Britain's own and one that in principle was far in advance of the British system, and they were qualified to co-operate with the mother country on terms similar to those of a brotherhood of free nations. . . . But England was unable to see this fact or unwilling to recognize it, and consequently America became the scene of a political unrest, which might have been controlled by compromise, but was turned to revolt by coercion.

[From Charles M. Andrews, "The American Revolution: An Interpretation," *American Historical Review* 31 (January 1926): 228, 230–231]

Reading 3. Oliver Dickerson Denies That the Navigation Acts Caused the Revolution

There was an almost universal acceptance of the desirability of the trade regulations in both England and America as one of the essential foundations of British commercial and industrial prosperity. Besides, the American trade had been developed so long and so much capital was invested in it, so many British subjects made their living out of it, so many localities were so largely dependent upon the continuation of the old commercial relations, and so many millions of pounds had been loaned to American merchants and planters, that a charge that Americans were seeking to break down the complicated legal regulatory system upon which that trade was founded created real alarm. This fear gave the ministerial faction enough popular support for their ill-advised measures to enable them to stay in office and attempt to carry them out. Laws bitterly denounced in America as unconstitutional taxation measures and destructive of British commerce were defended in England as acts designed to restrain the Americans within the commercial system, and thus preserve the commercial relations upon which British prosperity had been built and a vast war debt contracted.

In this way the Navigation Acts became a cause of the Revolution, but not in the sense commonly presented. They were not the source of serious complaint by the Americans, but were used in England to justify and continue the measures after 1764 that were the object of American opposition and ultimately the cause of revolt. . . .

A century of wisely administered trade and navigation laws had developed the greatest and most loyal colonial Empire in the world. Abandonment of that policy destroyed that Empire in less than ten years. . . . The new policy of taxation and exploitation of America in the interests of a political faction in England was a disintegrating force that destroyed loyalty. . . . The heavy taxation, the excessive fees, and the seizures were concentrated in a few trading colonies. These were the centers of the revolutionary movement. The areas where the old trade and navigation laws operated relatively undisturbed by the new taxation program remained loyal.

[From Oliver M. Dickerson, *The Navigation Acts and the American Revolution* (Philadelphia: University of Pennsylvania Press, 1951), pp. 296–297, 299–300]

Reading 4. Lawrence Gipson Blames the Revolution on Changes Brought by the Great War for Empire

In accounting for the radical change in attitude of many leading colonials between the years 1754 and 1774 respecting the nature of the constitution of the empire, surely among the factors that must be weighed was the truly overwhelming victory achieved in the

Great War for the Empire. This victory not only freed colonials for the first time in the history of the English-speaking people in the New World from the dread of the French, their Indian allies, and the Spaniards, but, which is of equal significance, opened up to them the prospect, if given freedom of action, of a vast growth of power and wealth with an amazing westward expansion. Indeed, it is abundantly clear that a continued subordination of the colonies to the government of Great Britain was no longer considered an asset in the eyes of the Americans by 1774, as it had been so judged by them in 1754, but rather an onerous liability. . . . If many Americans thought they had a perfect right to profit personally by trading with the enemy in time of war, how much more deeply must they have resented in time of peace the serious efforts made by the home government to enforce the elaborate restrictions on commercial intercourse? . . .

. . . is it not reasonable to believe that, had Great Britain at the close of the triumphant war left Canada to France and carefully limited her territorial demands in North America to those comparatively modest objectives that she had in mind at its beginning, there would have been no very powerful movement within the foreseeable future for complete colonial autonomy—not to mention American independence? Would not Americans have continued to feel the need as in the past to rely for their safety and welfare upon British sea power and British land power, as well as upon British forces generally? . . .

In conclusion, it may be said that it would be idle to deny that most colonials in the eighteenth century at one time or another felt strongly the desire for freedom of action in a wider variety of ways than was legally permitted before 1754. Indeed, one can readily uncover these strong impulses even in the early part of the seventeenth century. Yet Americans were, by and large, realists, as were the British, and under the functioning of the imperial system from, let us say, 1650 to 1750 great mutual advantages were enjoyed, with a fair division, taking everything into consideration, of the financial burdens necessary to support the system. However, the mounting Anglo-French rivalry in North America from 1750 onward, the outbreak of hostilities in 1754, and the subsequent nine years of fighting destroyed the old equilibrium, leaving the colonials after 1760 in a highly favored position in comparison with the taxpayers of Great Britain. Attempts on the part of the Crown and Parliament to restore by statute the old balance led directly to the American constitutional crisis, out of which came the Revolutionary War and the establishment of American independence. Such, ironically, was the aftermath of the Great War for Empire. . . .

[From Lawrence Henry Gipson, "The American Revolution as an Aftermath of the Great War for the Empire, 1754–1763," *Political Science Quarterly* 65, no. 1 (March 1950): 102–104]

Questions for Analysis

Hacker includes in the section quoted a restatement of the view of George L. Beer as to the cause of the Revolution. Briefly summarize that view and show how Hacker refutes it. In Hacker's view, what is the core cause of the Revolution?

In the second selection from Hacker, he pinpoints the time at which the English chose to tighten the screws on the colonies and explains why. What was that time and reason?

What is the essence of Andrews's argument and how does it differ from Hacker's?

Dickerson's argument is partially economic like Hacker's, but how does he differ from Hacker in the placement of the blame for the Revolution? Are their two arguments essentially the same? Explain. How is Dickerson's argument somewhat like that of Andrews?

The final excerpt, from Gipson, places the blame on the results of the Great War for Empire. Explain Gipson's reasoning. How does his argument relate to the argument of Beer and Hacker mentioned above?

Which of these four (five, if Beer is included) arguments seems the most plausible to you? Is it possible to combine elements of all these arguments in one statement of the causes of the Revolution? If not, which arguments are not compatible with the rest? Based on the points made in these arguments and other information from the textbook, state your own explanation of the causes of the Revolution.

ANSWERS TO MULTIPLE-CHOICE AND TRUE-FALSE QUESTIONS

Multiple-Choice Questions

1-B, 2-D, 3-B, 4-B, 5-C, 6-C, 7-B, 8-C

True-False Questions

1-F, 2-T, 3-F, 4-F, 5-T, 6-F, 7-T, 8-T

5

THE AMERICAN REVOLUTION

CHAPTER OBJECTIVES

After you complete the reading and study of this chapter you should be able to

1. Explain the major military strategies of the war, especially focusing on the turning points.
2. Account for the division of sentiments in the colonial population during the war.
3. Assess the degree to which the Revolution was a social revolution—the impact of the war on slavery, women, religion, and socioeconomic levels.
4. Explain the governmental principles incorporated into the new national and state governments.
5. Describe America's postwar nationalism and show its impact on various aspects of American culture.

CHAPTER OUTLINE

I. The campaigns of 1776
   A. The two armies
   B. British hold New York
   C. Washington scores minor victories in New Jersey

II. Colonial society at war
   A. Divided loyalties
      1. Patriots or Whigs
      2. Tories or Loyalists
   B. Revolution as a civil war
   C. Characteristics of the militia and the Continental Army
   D. Methods of financing and supplying the troops

III. The war expands in 1777
   A. Howe takes Philadelphia in September
   B. Washington winters at Valley Forge
   C. Burgoyne surrenders at Saratoga
   D. French enter the war
      1. Importance of Saratoga
      2. Treaty with Americans
      3. Spain joins French

IV. Stalemate of 1778
   A. Changes in British policy
      1. Peace commission
      2. Clinton replaces Howe in command
      3. On defensive except in South
   B. Renewal of Washington's forces
   C. Indecisive battle around New York City
   D. War in the West
      1. Victories of George Rogers Clark
      2. Destruction of the Iroquois

V. The war in the South
   A. Expected Tory support in South
   B. British take Savannah and Charleston
   C. Cornwallis defeats Gates at Camden
   D. Tarleton and Ferguson defeated at Kings Mountain

1. "Overmountainmen" victorious
2. A turning point of war
E. Greene in command of colonials in South
F. Battle of Guilford Courthouse
G. Yorktown, October 17, 1781
   1. Nature of the Yorktown campaign
   2. Results and their significance

VI. Peace settlement
  A. Peace negotiations
    1. Negotiators
    2. Problems with France and Spain
    3. American initiatives with Britain
  B. Peace of Paris, September 3, 1783

VII. Revolution in American politics
  A. Changes in political thinking
    1. Attitudes become ideology
    2. Radical nature of republican government
  B. Changes in state governments
    1. Written constitutions
    2. Constitutional conventions
  C. The Articles of Confederation
    1. Powers to central government
    2. Role of states under Articles

VIII. Revolution in American society
  A. Impact of Revolution on lower socioeconomic groups

1. Wider suffrage
2. More land for settlement
B. Effects of Revolution on slavery
   1. End of slave trade, except for Georgia
   2. Role of blacks in the war
   3. State efforts toward emancipation
C. Revolution's effects of women
   1. New opportunities during wartime
   2. Limited legal gains for women
D. Impact of Revolution on religion
   1. Growing separation of church and state
   2. Removal of tax support for churches in most states
   3. Development of national church organizations

IX. Sense of nationalism inspired by the Revolution
  A. First generation of native artists and writers
    1. John Trumbull
    2. Charles Willson Peale
  B. Growth in education
    1. Development of state universities
    2. Interest in systems of public schools

KEY ITEMS OF CHRONOLOGY

Battle of Saratoga	October 17, 1777
Battle of Kings Mountain	October 1780
Adoption of Articles of Confederation	March 1781
Battle of Yorktown	October 17, 1781
Peace of Paris	1783

TERMS TO MASTER

Listed below are some important terms or people with which you should be familiar after you complete your study of the chapter. Identify each name or term.

1. *The American Crisis*
2. loyalists
3. Gen. William Howe
4. militia
5. republican ideology
6. Horatio Gates
7. Charles Lord Cornwallis
8. sovereignty
9. Benedict Arnold
10. John Paul Jones
11. John Adams, Benjamin Franklin, John Jay
12. constitutional convention
13. Noah Webster

VOCABULARY BUILDING

Listed below are some words used in this chapter. Look in the dictionary for the meaning of each.

1. fledgling
2. extralegal
3. fratricidal
4. resplendent
5. pillage
6. vanquished
7. attrition
8. redoubts
9. ideology
10. consensus
11. paradox
12. foreboding
13. efflorescence

EXERCISES FOR UNDERSTANDING

When you have completed reading this chapter, answer the following questions. If you have difficulty, go back to the text and reread the section of the chapter related to the question.

Multiple-Choice Questions

Select the letter of the choice which best completes the statement.

1. Called Tories, the loyal supporters of the British during the Revolution
   A. were the largest group of colonists
   B. fled the colonies in large numbers (100,000)
   C. came exclusively from urban and commercial areas
   D. organized effectively and fought aggressively against the rebels

2. George Washington and the army faced severe problems in
   A. maintaining a sizable fighting force
   B. securing guns and powder
   C. obtaining farm produce
   D. all of the above

3. Saratoga was a turning point in the Revolutionary War because

A. it affected the French decision to ally with the colonists
B. during the battle the colonists captured both Cornwallis and Gates
C. as a result the colonial forces captured the vital port of New York City
D. it firmly established Washington as the best colonial military leader

4. In 1782 negotiations to end the war were complicated by
   A. American military setbacks
   B. Jefferson's dominance of diplomatic maneuvers in Europe
   C. relations between Spain and France
   D. the House of Commons's insistence on continuing the war

5. In an innovative step in 1779–1780, the Massachusetts constitution was written by
   A. the Continental Congress
   B. the state assembly
   C. a constitutional convention
   D. a combined session of the town meetings

6. The Articles of Confederation
   A. placed great power in the national congress
   B. failed to establish a system of courts
   C. created a weak president
   D. severely restricted the power of the individual states

7. The Revolution affected education by
   A. encouraging the founding of fourteen new colleges soon after it ended
   B. providing for state universities in the new state constitutions
   C. creating some interest in state systems of education in Virginia and Pennsylvania
   D. all of the above

8. In addition to securing American independence, the American Revolution also
   A. taught Americans to think "continentally"
   B. weakened the major Indian tribes in the West
   C. produced valuable national symbols and heroes
   D. all of the above

True-False Questions

Indicate whether each statement is true or false.

1. If Gen. William Howe had acted quickly in 1776, he could have ended the war by compromising with Franklin and Adams.
2. The only significant American success in 1778 involved George Rogers Clark's forces on the western frontier.
3. Most early fighting in the Revolution occurred in the North, and most later battles were concentrated in the South.
4. Slaves were not permitted to serve in the American armed forces during the Revolution.
5. The Peace of Paris in 1783 gave the new United States control over Florida.
6. The art of the new American nation reflected much interest in heroes of the Revolution.
7. The revolutionary spirit of liberty had great effects on the status of women.
8. During the Revolution all state support for religion ended.

Essay Questions

1. Identify several key events or turning points in the Revolutionary War and explain their importance to the outcome of the war.
2. What were the powers of the government under the Articles of Confederation? How did the colonists' grievances against Britain help shape the new government?
3. How did the "logic of liberty" affect American society in the Revolutionary period?
4. How did diplomatic relations help to win the Revolution and also impede the peace settlement?
5. Discuss the ways in which the Revolution promoted national unity and created a sense of nationalism.

DOCUMENT

Diary of a Revolutionary Army Physician

This document consists of excerpts from the diary of a physician, Lewis Beebe, who was traveling with the Continental Army in New England in an expedition against the British in Canada. Little is known about Beebe. He received a degree from Yale in 1771 and settled in a small Massachusetts town to practice medicine. His wife died in 1775, one year after their marriage. He makes reference to her as his "Consort" in the excerpts below. After the war Beebe was ordained as a Congregational minister and served from 1787 to 1791. His religious beliefs may explain his comments below about the troops' lack of religion and their salty language. From 1791 to his death in 1816 Beebe was a shopkeeper in a small New York town.

As you read the passage, note the miserable conditions endured by the troops and the limited ability of the physician to fight the various camp illnesses. Note also his references to the strong patriotism of the troops. (The spelling of words is as in the original.)

[May 1776] *Sunday 26:* . . . Yesterday & today I have been much unwell, troubled with the quick step, attended with Severe grip-ings. If ever I had a compassionate feeling for my fellow creatures, who were objects in distress, I think it was this day, to see Large barns filled with men in the very heighth of the small pox and not the least thing, to make them Comfortable, was almost Sufficient to excite the pity of Brutes.

[June 1776] *Tuesday 4*[th]*:* one of our Reg[t]. died this morning very suddenly, and was intered in the afternoon, without so much as a Coffin, and with little or no ceremony. Among hundreds of men it was difficult to procure 8 or 10 to bear the corps about 15 rods. Death is a Subject not to be attended to by Soldiers; Hell & Damnation is in allmost every ones mouth from the time they awake till they fall asleep again, the Stupidity of mankind in this situation is beyond all Description. . . .

Wednesday 5th*:* For 10 days past I have been greatly troubled with the dysentery, and for three days it has been very severe, took Physic in the morning. hope for some relief. In the afternoon went across the river to visit Col. Reed who I found to have the disorder very light, the number of sick with the Pekot on this side is about 300, the greater part of which have it by innoculation, and like to do well.

Friday 7. Last evening one died of the small pox, & early this morning one of the Colic, at 10 A.M. one of the Nervous fever, here in the hospital, is to be seen at the same time some dead, some Dying, others at the point of death, some Whistleing, some singing & many Cursing & swearing, this is a strange Composition and its chief intention has not as yet been discovered. . . . Visited many of the sick in the hospital—was moved with a Compassionate feeling for poor Distressed Soldiers, when they are taken sick, are thrown into this dirty, stinking place, and left to take care of themselves. No attendance no provision made, but what must be Loathed & abhorred by all both well & sick.

Monday 10th*:* June this day compleats a year Since the departure of my dear Consort, the memory of whom will ever be sweet to me; O! fleeting time, who dost make no delay, but with rapid force sweeps, all without distinction to one common grave; therefore Let me remember, that the same thing must take place with respect to me, as it did to her—O! that the noise and tumult of war, might not engage my mind so as to forget my own mortallity; may the great things of futurity, the infinite concerns of eternity, have their due weight upon my mind that they might have a place still in my breast. This day died two in Col[o]. Pattersons Reg[t]. with the small pox; No intelligence of importance comes to hand this day; except orders, from the great M[r]. Brigadier Gen[l]. Arnold, for Col[o]. Poor with his Reg[t]. to proceed to Sorrell immediately: Is not this a politick plan, especially since there is not Ten men in the Reg[t]. but what has either now got the small pox; or taken the infection. Some men love to command, however ridiculous their orders may appear. But I am apt to think, we shall remain in this Garrison for the present. It is enough to confuse & distract a rational man to be Surg[n] to a Reg[t]. nothing to be heard from morning to night, but Doct[r]. Doct[r]. Doct[r]. from every side 'till one is deaf, dumb & blind, and almost dead; add to all this, we have nothing to eat; thus poor Soldiers live sometimes better, but never worse.

Monday 17. This morning had Col[o]. Poors orders to repair to Isle aux naux to take care of the sick there; accordingly sailed in a batteau, and arrived there about 3 P.M. was struck with amazement upon my arrival, to see the vast crowds of poor distressed Creatures. Language cannot describe nor imagination paint, the scenes of misery and distress the Soldiery endure. Scarcely a tent upon this Isle but what contains one or more in distress and continually groaning, & calling for relief, but in vain! Requests of this nature are as little regarded, as the singing of Crickets in a Summers evening. The most shocking of all Spectacles was to see a large barn Crowded full of men with this disorder, many of which could not See, Speak, or walk. . . . No mortal will ever believe what these suffered unless they were eye witnesses.

Thursday 27. Buried two of our Reg^t. this day. The hot weather, proves very unfriendly to those who have the small pox. A large Schooner arrived from Isle aux naux, deeply Loaded with Stores. One thing by the way is somewhat remarkable, that a Reg^t. so distressed with sickness as ours is should be so engaged in fatigue and doing duty, that they can by no means find time to attend prayers night & morning or even preaching upon the Sabbath; the Reg^{ts}. are generally Supplied with Chaplains, who are as destitute of employ in their way: as parson who is dismissed from his people, for the most Scandalous of Crimes. At Sorrell I heard one morning & evening prayer, and one Sermon—at Chambly none—at St. Johns none at Isle aux naux, one evening prayer, & one with the sick. At this place none as yet. Indeed it is esteemed very unpopular, and unbecoming a Gentlemen, in the Camps to attend upon any religious exercises, and happy would it be, did not many officers endeavour to inculcate, & establish this principle in the minds of others.

[July 1776] *Thursday 4th:* The army have been here for Several days, and notwithstanding they are under great apprehensions of an attack from the enemy soon—yet they are as Secure & easy as if they were Wholly at peace, and in a Garrison, not to be stormed by any finite power; Not the least preparation for Fortifying the Garrison, which has tumbled to ruin & decay. The Gen^{ls} have their hands full in riding about the camp—prancing their Gay horses The Field officers, set much of their time upon Court marshals. The Capts. & Subs may generally be found at the grog shops. The Soldiers either sleeping, swimming, fishing, or Cursing and Swearing most generally the Latter. . . .

[August] *Wednesday 28th:* the wind being ahead we were not able to cross the lake, visited the hospital found the number of sick to be about 700, viewed the burying place counted upwards of 300 graves, which had been opened in about 5 weeks. the appearance of which was melancholy indeed, to see such desolation made in our army.

[September] *Sunday 6th:* My disorder caused me to rise several times Last night; again at the Revilee beat; at 8 A. M. took a puke of vinum antimoniale; which operated very kindly; was very weak the remainder of the day. I find my experience, and many other ways, that the general principle, upon which our army act, whether they are taken as a body or as individuals, is entirely self. yet doubtless their sinister views, run in very different channels. Some are in persuit of money, some of promotion & honor. But was we free from all; except those who have the cause of Liberty nearest their heart; and who engage, principly with a view of defending, and transmiting, those inestimable prividledges, to posterity; for which our Ancesters Left their native land, and fled to this a howling wilderness, encountering every danger. I say was we free from all, except those who act upon this principle; our army would be reduced to a small number.

Monday 7th: . . . Col°. Poor has lately made his appearance in Scarlet; this, or something not much better, makes him feel his importance, in a very surprising manner. In general he is very sociable and popular; But of an absolute, Despotick turn of mind. As to his principles, respecting religion, it is very difficult to determine, what they are; But in my opinion he has none at all. Our Lieu^t, Col°. McDuffee, is a most excellent arminion &c. Maj^r. Sily, who is rightly named is a very silly man; yet the fool, has learned to swear & damn by rule: to such a degree of perfection, that his equal is scarcely to be found in the Camp. Surprising genius! Our officers & soldiers in general, are remarkably expert in the swearing way, nothing comes more handy, or gives such power and force to their words, as a Blasphemous oath. In general the Reg^t. is composed to Deists, Arminiams, and a few who ridicule the Bible, and everything of a sacred nature. In short they Laugh at death, mock at Hell and damnation; & even challenge the Deity, to remove them out of this world by Thunder and Lightning.

[From "Journal of a Physician on the Expedition against Canada, 1776," *The Pennsylvania Magazine of History and Biography* 59 (1935): 330, 332–339, 343–345, 347, 351–352]

Questions for Reflection

What seems to be the greatest danger faced by the troops? What is Beebe's attitude toward the army officers? How does the religious attitude in the camp compare with what you might have expected from these revolutionary troops? What appears to be the important motivation for the troops? What does this passage add to your knowledge of the Revolutionary War?

ANSWERS TO MULTIPLE-CHOICE AND TRUE-FALSE QUESTIONS

Multiple-Choice Questions

1-B, 2-D, 3-A, 4-C, 5-C, 6-B, 7-D, 8-D

True-False Questions

1-F, 2-T, 3-T, 4-F, 5-F, 6-T, 7-F, 8-F

6

SHAPING A FEDERAL UNION

CHAPTER OBJECTIVES

After you complete the reading and study of this chapter you should be able to

1. Analyze the strengths and weaknesses of the government under the Articles of Confederation.
2. List and explain the key accomplishments of the Confederation government in diplomacy, governmental organization, land policy, and finance.
3. List and explain the major problems which the Confederation government faced in finance and diplomacy.
4. Account for the movement to adopt a new constitution and assess the degree to which a new government was needed.
5. Analyze the principles considered and incorporated in the Constitution.
6. Explain the key historiographical analyses of the constitution-making process, including the contributions of Charles Beard, Forrest McDonald, and Jackson T. Main.
7. Account for the success of the movement to ratify the Constitution.

CHAPTER OUTLINE

I. Government in the Confederation period
   A. Called the "Critical Period"

B. Congress under the Confederation
   1. Great authority
   2. Accomplishments
   3. Nature of congressional administration
C. Confederacy's finances
   1. Robert Morris, secretary of finance
   2. Plans fail to receive unanimous support
   3. Growth of foreign and domestic debt
D. Development of land policies
   1. Clear congressional authority
   2. Areas covered by policies
   3. Land ordinances
      a. Ordinance of 1785
      b. Northwest Ordinance of 1787
      c. Western lands south of the Ohio River
      d. Indian treaties yield lands in West
E. Economic life under the Confederation
   1. Agriculture generally prosperous
   2. New outlets for merchants
   3. Free trade sentiment
   4. Excluded from British West Indies trade
F. Diplomacy
   1. Irritants with British
   2. Problems with Spain
G. Confederation's problems
   1. Protection for industries
   2. Currency shortage

3. Shays's Rebellion
4. Demands for stronger government
  a. Meetings in Mount Vernon and Annapolis
  b. Call for a constitutional convention

II. Adopting the Constitution
  A. Characteristics of the convention
    1. Delegates
    2. Political philosophies
    3. Secrecy
  B. Conflict between Virginia and New Jersey plans
    1. Terms of Virginia plan
    2. Provisions of New Jersey plan
  C. Major issues disputed

1. Need for new constitution
2. Representation in new government
3. North versus South over slavery
D. Major compromises
  1. The Great Compromise
  2. The three-fifths compromise
E. Proposed governmental structure
  1. Separation of powers
  2. Mixed legislature
  3. Office of President
  4. Independent judiciary
  5. Idea of countervailing forces

III. The fight for ratification
  A. Federalists vs. Antifederalists
  B. Economic factors in ratification
  C. Arguments of *The Federalist*
  D. Pattern of ratification

KEY ITEMS OF CHRONOLOGY

Ratification of the Articles of Confederation	1781
Peace with Britain (formal end to Revolution)	1783
Passage of basic land ordinance	1785
Shays's Rebellion	August 1786 to February 1787
Constitutional Convention	May–September 1787
Ninth state (New Hampshire) ratified the Constitution	June 1788
Virginia and New York ratified the Constitution	June–July 1788
New government set to commence	March 1789

TERMS TO MASTER

Listed below are some important terms or people with which you should be familiar after you complete the study of this chapter. Identify each name or term.

1. Critical Period
2. Robert Morris
3. Land Ordinance of 1785
4. Northwest Ordinance
5. Shays's Rebellion
6. checks and balances
7. Virginia and New Jersey plans
8. Nationalists (Federalists) and Antifederalists
9. separation of powers
10. Charles A. Beard
11. James Madison
12. Alexander Hamilton
13. *The Federalist*, No. 10

VOCABULARY BUILDING

Listed below are some words used in this chapter. Look in the dictionary for the meaning of each.

1. hobbled
2. manifesto
3. foreclosure
4. insurgents
5. lexicographer
6. interstate
7. magisterial
8. unicameral
9. levy
10. apportionment
11. impeach
12. countervailing
13. antidote

EXERCISES FOR UNDERSTANDING

When you have completed reading the chapter, answer each of the following questions. If you have difficulty, go back to the text and reread the section of the chapter related to the question.

Multiple-Choice Questions

Select the letter of the response which best completes the statement.

1. The Confederation's greatest success involved
   A. diplomacy with Great Britain
   B. financing the national debt
   C. policies for western lands
   D. regulating the nation's trade and commerce

2. The Northwest Ordinance dealt with the problem of slavery by
   A. prohibiting it from the territory
   B. leaving slavery up to the settlers of western lands
   C. planning for eventual emancipation in 1808
   D. ignoring it entirely

3. A major diplomatic problem with Spain was

   A. disputes about the right of the United States to trade with Spanish territories in South America
   B. the right of the United States to navigate to the mouth of the Mississippi River
   C. the Spanish refusal to retreat from lands west of the Appalachian Mountains
   D. all of the above

4. Shays's Rebellion in Massachussetts
   A. represented a revolt against the lax government of the Articles of Confederation
   B. was largely triggered by a currency shortage among farmers
   C. led to the governor's being captured and held for five days
   D. is correctly represented by *all* of the above

5. The Virginia plan presented to the constitutional convention by Edmund Randolph called for
   A. a two-house congress
   B. three separate branches in the national government
   C. states to be bound by national laws
   D. all of the above

6. The constitutional convention required that the Constitution be ratified by
   A. nine state conventions
   B. a majority of voters in a referendum
   C. three-fourths of the states
   D. all state legislatures

7. In No. 10 of *The Federalist,* James Madison argued that
   A. the Constitution gave the courts too much power
   B. a presidency was unnecessary under the new government
   C. a republic would work especially well in the large, diverse country
   D. tyranny was likely under the strong central government proposed under the Constitution

8. Charles A. Beard argued that the Constitution was written by
   A. power-hungry young politicians who wanted to create offices for themselves

B. men who wanted to give more power to the state governments
C. men who expected to gain increased value for their own securities under the new government
D. a selfless group of men who nonetheless wanted a weaker government because they wanted to decrease the amount of real estate tax they would have to pay

True-False Questions

Indicate whether each statement is true or false.

1. Robert Morris was the most influential person in the Confederation government.
2. American farming and farm income were greatly disrupted by the American Revolution.
3. One of the key weaknesses of the Articles of Confederation was its requirement for unanimous vote of the states to take significant actions.
4. The Peace of Paris allowed Congress to confiscate Tory lands.
5. Mechanics and merchants wanted a stronger central government to provide uniform trade regulations.

6. Thomas Jefferson directed the drafting of the Constitution.
7. The constitutional convention's compromise on the slave trade was tied to a compromise on congressional authority to tax exports.
8. In the debate over ratification, the Antifederalists were well prepared, highly organized, and articulate.

Essay Questions

1. What were the major accomplishments of the government under the Articles of Confederation?
2. What problems under the Articles of Confederation prompted some Americans to call for changes in the structure of government?
3. Discuss the major compromises of the constitutional convention.
4. Explain clearly the powers and duties assigned to either the executive or legislative branch by the Constitution.
5. How have scholars explained the motivations of the Federalists and Antifederalists?
6. Explain the effects of life under British rule and under the Articles of Confederation on the design of the government under the Constitution.
7. Trace the process of ratification of the Constitution.

DOCUMENT

The Federalist, No. 10

As the text explains, *The Federalist* papers, published in New York State, were a means of supporting ratification of the Constitution. The papers written by James Madison, Alexander Hamilton, and John Jay provided an important explanation of the theory and principles incorporated in the new Constitution. Their commentary is so important and enduring that it is still referred to today by attorneys and justices seeking to explain the operation of the Constitution.

One of the most famous of the essays is *The Federalist,* No. 10, written by James Madison, in which he explains how a republic (or representative democracy) will help to avoid the dangers of "faction." This document consists of key excerpts of that paper. As you read the selection, note the careful reasoning Madison used.

Among the numerous advantages promised by a well-constructed union, none deserves to be more accurately developed than its tendency to break and control the violence of faction. . . . Complaints are everywhere heard from our most considerate and virtuous citizens, equally the friends of public and private faith and of public and personal liberty, that our governments are too unstable; that the public good is disregarded in the conflicts of rival parties; and that measures are too often decided, not according to the rules of justice, and the rights of the minor party, but by the superior force of an interested and overbearing majority. . . .

By a faction, I understand a number of citizens, whether amounting to a majority or minority of the whole, who are united and actuated by some common impulse of passion, or of interest, adverse to the rights of other citizens or to the permanent and aggregate interests of the community.

There are two methods of curing the mischiefs of faction: the one, by removing its causes; the other, by controlling its effects.

There are again two methods of removing the causes of faction: the one, by destroying the liberty which is essential to its existence; the other, by giving to every citizen the same opinions, the same passions, and the same interests.

It could never be more truly said than of the first remedy, that it was worse than the disease. Liberty is to faction what air is to fire, an ailment without which it instantly expires. But it could not be less folly to abolish liberty, which is essential to political life, because it nourishes faction, than it would be to wish the annihilation of air, which is essential to animal life, because it imparts to fire its destructive agency.

The second expedient is as impracticable as the first would be unwise. . . . From the protection of different and unequal faculties of acquiring property, the possession of different degrees and kinds of property immediately results; and from the influence of these on the sentiments and views of the respective proprietors, ensues a division of the society into different interests and parties.

The latent causes of faction are thus sown in the nature of man; and we see them everywhere brought into different degrees of activity, according to the different circumstances of civil society. . . . So strong is this propensity of mankind to fall into mutual animosities, that where no substantial occasion presents itself, the most frivolous and fanciful distinctions have been sufficient to kindle their unfriendly passions and excite their most violent conflicts. But the most common and durable source of factions has been the various and unequal distribution of property. . . . The regulation of these various and interfering interests forms the principal task of modern legislation, and involves the spirit of party and faction in the necessary and ordinary operations of the government.

The inference to which we are brought is that the causes of faction cannot be removed, and that relief is only to be sought in the means of controlling its effects.

. . . Either the existence of the same passion or interest in a majority, at the same time, must be prevented; or the majority, having such coexistent passion or interest, must be rendered, by their number and local situation, unable to concert and carry into effect schemes of oppression. . . .

From this view of the subject it may be concluded that a pure democracy, by which I mean a society consisting of a small number of citizens, who assemble and administer the government in person, can admit of no cure for the mischiefs of faction. A common passion or interest will, in almost every case, be felt by a majority of the whole; a communication and concert results from the form of government itself; and there is nothing to check the inducements to sacrifice the weaker party or an obnoxious individual. . . .

A republic, by which I mean a government in which the scheme of representation takes place, opens a different prospect, and promises the cure for which we are seeking. Let us examine the points in which it varies from pure democracy, and we shall comprehend both the nature of the cure and the efficacy which it must derive from the union.

The two great points of difference between a democracy and a republic are: First, the delegation of the government, in the latter, to a small number of citizens elected by the result; secondly, the greater number of citizens, and greater sphere of country, over which the latter may be extended.

The effect of the first difference is, on the one hand, to refine and enlarge the public view, by passing them through the medium of a chosen body of citizens, whose wisdom may best discern the true interest of their country, and whose patriotism and love of justice will be least likely to sacrifice it to temporary or partial considerations. . . . The question resulting is, whether small or extensive republics are most favorable to the election of proper guardians of the public weal; and it is clearly decided in favor of the latter by two obvious considerations.

In the first place, it is to be remarked that, however small the republic may be, the representatives must be raised to a certain number, in order to guard against the cabals of a few; and that, however large it may be, they must be limited to a certain number, in order to guard against the confusion of a multitude. Hence, the number of representatives in the two cases not being in proportion to that of the constituents, and being proportionally greatest in the small republic, it follows that if the proportion of fit characters be not less in the large than in the small republic, the former will present a greater option, and consequently a greater probability of a fit choice.

In the next place, as each representative will be chosen by a greater number of citizens in the large than in the small republic, it will be more difficult for unworthy candidates to practise with success the vicious arts, by which elections are too often carried; and the suffrages of the people, being more free, will be more likely to centre in men who possess the most attractive merit and the most diffusive and established characters.

The other point of difference is, the greater number of citizens and extent of territory which may be brought within the compass of republican than of democratic government; and it is this circumstance principally which renders factious combinations less to be dreaded in the former, than in the latter. The smaller the society, the fewer probably will be the distinct parties and interests composing it; the fewer the distinct parties and interests, the more frequently will a majority be found of the same party; and the smaller the number of individuals composing a majority, and the smaller the compass within which they are placed, the more easily will they concert and execute their plans of oppression. Extend the sphere, and you take in a greater variety of parties and interests; you make it less probable that a majority of the whole will have a common motive to invade the rights of other citizens; or if such a common motive exists, it will be more difficult for all who feel it to discover their own strength, and to act in unison with each other. . . .

Hence, it clearly appears that the same advantage which a republic has over a democracy, in controlling the effects of faction, is enjoyed by a large over a small republic—is enjoyed by the Union over the States composing it. Does the advantage consist in the substitution of representatives, whose enlightened views and virtuous sentiments render them superior to local prejudices, and to schemes of injustice? It will not be denied that the representation of the Union will be most likely to possess these requisite endowments. Does it consist in the great security afforded by a greater variety of parties, against the event of any one party being able to outnumber and oppress the rest? In an equal degree does the increased variety of parties, comprised within the Union, increase this security? Does it, in fine, consist in the greater obstacles opposed to the concert and accomplishment of the secret wishes of an unjust and interested majority? Here, again, the extent of the Union gives it the most palpable advantage.

The influence of factious leaders may kindle a flame within their particular States, but will be unable to spread a general conflagration through the other States. A religious sect may degenerate into a political faction in a part of the confederacy; but the variety of sects dispersed over the entire face of it must secure the national councils against any danger from that source. A rage for paper money, for an abolition of debts, for an equal division of property, or for any other improper or wicked project will be less apt to pervade the whole body of the Union than a particular member of it; in the same proportion as such a malady is more likely to taint a particular county or district than an entire State.

Questions for Reflection

What does Madison mean by the term "faction"? How does he say that the dangers of faction may be avoided? What is the problem with each of these cures for the illness? Why does he reason that the evils of faction cannot be removed?

Since the causes of faction cannot be removed, Madison concludes that the effects of faction must be controlled. How does he propose to exercise that control? How does a republic help to control the effects of faction better than does a democracy?

Is Madison's argument convincing to you?

Does there appear to be any special economic motivation involved in Madison's desire to control faction? Point out where this is seen in the document. Is this reference sufficient to convince you that Charles Beard was right about the economic motivations of the writers of the Constitution?

ANSWERS TO MULTIPLE-CHOICE
AND TRUE-FALSE QUESTIONS

Multiple-Choice Questions

1-C, 2-A, 3-B, 4-B, 5-D, 6-A, 7-C, 8-C

True-False Questions

1-T, 2-F, 3-T, 4-F, 5-T, 6-F, 7-T, 8-F

7

THE FEDERALISTS:
WASHINGTON AND ADAMS

CHAPTER OBJECTIVES

After you complete the reading and study of this chapter you should be able to

1. Explain the challenge which confronted the Washington administration in creating a new government.
2. Name and summarize the three major proposals presented by Alexander Hamilton for establishing the new government on a sound financial basis.
3. Analyze the conflict of philosophy between Hamilton and Jefferson over the constitutionality of the National Bank and explain how that conflict led to the development of two political parties.
4. Account for the diplomatic problems with Britain, France, and Spain which buffeted the new nation, and explain the resolution of each.
5. Explain the differing roles played by Adams, Hamilton, and Washington in Federalist politics and describe their effects on Adams's administration.
6. Explain the significance of the elections of 1796 and 1800.
7. Explain the importance of the Alien and Sedition Acts and the Kentucky and Virginia Resolutions as parts of continuing conflicts between individual

liberty and governmental authority, and states' rights vs. national governmental authority.

CHAPTER OUTLINE

I. Organizing the new government
  A. The President and his cabinet
  B. Bill of Rights added to Constitution
  C. Tariff for revenue enacted

II. Hamilton's vision of America
  A. Personal background
  B. Establishing the public credit
    1. Hamilton's Report on Public Credit
      a. Fund federal debt at face value
      b. Federal assumption of state debts
    2. Reactions to Hamilton's proposals
      a. Concern about speculators
      b. Sectional differences
      c. Compromise solution
  C. Hamilton and a National Bank
    1. Advantages of a bank
    2. Controversy over constitutionality of bank
  D. Hamilton's Report on Manufactures
    1. Advantages of promoting manufacturing

2. Methods to stimulate
    manufacturing
3. Reactions to proposals
E. Assessing Hamilton's achievements

III. Development of political parties
  A. Attitudes toward parties
  B. Hamilton's opponents
      1. James Madison
      2. Jefferson's agrarianism
  C. Jefferson and Hamilton compared

IV. Crises foreign and domestic
  A. Foreign affairs
      1. French Revolution
          a. American policy
          b. Citizen Genêt Affair
          c. Republicans vs. Federalists
      2. Jay's Treaty with Britain
          a. Jay's instructions
          b. Terms accepted by Jay
          c. Reactions to the treaty
  B. Problems with Indians on frontier
  C. Whiskey Rebellion
      1. Basis for the rebellion
      2. Army sent to disperse the
          rebellion
      3. Effects
  D. Treaty with Spain
  E. Development of land policy

1. Conflict over basic principles of
    land policy
2. Partisan divisions over policy
3. Congressional actions 1796 to 1804
F. Washington's Farewell Address
    1. Achievements as President
    2. Principles in address

V. The Adams administration
  A. Election of 1796
      1. Candidates
      2. Hamilton's scheme
      3. Outcome of the election
  B. Adams the man
  C. Troubles with France
      1. Undeclared war
      2. The XYZ Affair
      3. Strengthening of military
      4. Peace settlement
  D. Domestic ramifications of the war
      1. Alien and Sedition Acts
          a. Terms of the laws
          b. Arrests and prosecutions
          c. Kentucky and Virginia
              Resolutions
      2. Taxes to finance war

VI. Election of 1800
  A. Candidates
  B. Outcome of the election
  C. Packing the judiciary

KEY ITEMS OF CHRONOLOGY

Inauguration of Washington	April 1789
Hamilton's Reports	1790–1791
Ratification of Bill of Rights	1791
Creation of Bank of the United States	1791
Citizen Genêt Affair	April–August 1793
Jay's Treaty and Whiskey Rebellion	1794
XYZ Affair	1797
Alien and Sedition Acts	1798
Election of Jefferson	1800

TERMS TO MASTER

*Listed below are some important terms or
events with which you should be familiar
after you complete the study of this chapter.
Identify each name or event.*

1. Bill of Rights
2. Report on a National Bank
3. Report on Manufactures
4. implied powers
5. Citizen Genêt
6. Jay's Treaty

7. Whiskey Rebellion
8. Pinckney's Treaty (Treaty of San Lorenzo)
9. land policy
10. XYZ Affair
11. Alien and Sedition Acts
12. Kentucky and Virginia Resolutions
13. interposition
14. nullification

VOCABULARY BUILDING

Listed below are some words used in this chapter. Look in the dictionary for the meaning of each term not defined here for you.

1. liveried
2. protegé
3. impetuous
4. neomercantilist—*neo* before any term signifies a new form or variation. Neomercantilism refers to Hamilton's late-eighteenth-century version of the government direction and control of the economy that characterized the mercantilism of European states in the seventeenth century.
5. prolific
6. self-aggrandizement
7. pungent
8. infidelity
9. leverage
10. backcountry
11. intrigues
12. baneful
13. corsairs
14. crescendo
15. aliens

EXERCISES FOR UNDERSTANDING

When you have completed reading the chapter, answer each of the following questions. If you have difficulty, go back to the text and reread the section of the chapter relating to the question.

Multiple-Choice Questions

Select the letter of the response which best completes the statement.

1. During its first session, Congress
   A. authorized the creation of the executive departments
   B. enacted a tariff
   C. adopted and sent to the states the Bill of Rights
   D. all of the above

2. Hamilton's financial proposals called for *all but which one* of the following?
   A. a national bank
   B. an excise tax on liquor
   C. a tax on manufactured exports from the United States
   D. the development of a national debt

3. In general, Alexander Hamilton's programs were based on his
   A. own self-interest and the interest of his region
   B. fondness for farmers and settlers on the frontier
   C. strong opposition to capitalism and suspicion of monarchy
   D. nationalist vision and faith in a governing elite

4. The Whiskey Rebellion was a protest by
   A. backcountry grain farmers in Pennsylvania
   B. Hamiltonians against Jeffersonian temperance
   C. importers of rum from the West Indies
   D. tavern owners against a tax on whiskey

5. The rights to navigate the Mississippi River and avoid duties in New Orleans were included in a treaty Thomas Pinckney negotiated with
   A. Britain
   B. France
   C. Spain
   D. None of the above

6. The land policy developed in the United States in its first decades
   A. allowed purchasers to have twenty years to pay for their acreage
   B. continually decreased the minimum size of a plot to be purchased

C. was primarily designed to sell land to large speculators

D. required total cash payment at the time the land was sold

7. The Alien and Sedition Acts
   A. angered Hamilton and the Federalists
   B. were ruled unconstitutional by the Supreme Court
   C. actually affected a small number of people
   D. helped ensure the reelection of John Adams in 1800

8. In 1794, Jay's Treaty with Great Britain
   A. passed the Senate easily
   B. gave Britain permanent right to forts in the Northwest
   C. accepted the British definition of neutral rights
   D. legalized trade with the British West Indies

True-False Questions

Indicate whether each statement is true or false.

1. The style of government under George Washington was formal and almost like a monarchy.
2. After their experiences as part of the British empire, the Founding Fathers rejected mercantilism in favor of laissez-faire.
3. James Madison strongly supported Hamilton's proposals.
4. Jefferson's key ally in Congress was James Madison.

5. Jefferson had significant political ties with George Clinton, Aaron Burr, and others in New York.
6. Citizen Genêt proved a great embarrassment to Hamilton and the Federalists.
7. In the XYZ Affair, the English demanded bribes before negotiating the Pinckney Treaty.
8. The second president was John Adams.

Essay Questions

1. What were the important first steps taken in 1789 to create the new government?
2. Describe Hamilton's vision for the United States and the programs he devised to achieve it.
3. Explain the key issues in domestic and foreign policy that divided the Federalists and the Republicans.
4. Compare the Jay Treaty with Pinckney's Treaty in terms of the issues to be solved and the concessions obtained by the United States.
5. Explain the dual purpose of United States land policy and show how those purposes created a dilemma. How did the provisions of the land policy change up to 1804?
6. How did the Alien and Sedition Acts threaten liberty and how did the Kentucky and Virginia Resolutions defend liberty? Which were correct?
7. Why did the Republicans win the election of 1800 and how was their candidate finally chosen President?

DOCUMENTS

The dispute over the constitutionality of the Bank of the United States (B.U.S.) led to the classical statements of strict and loose construction of the Constitution by Jefferson and Hamilton. Jefferson, who questioned the constitutionality of the B.U.S., was asked by Washington to provide a formal statement regarding the constitutionality of the bill.

After receiving statements from Jefferson and from Attorney-General Edmund Randolph, Washington asked Hamilton to respond to these arguments against his bank bill. Hamilton then wrote the classic defense of loose construction provided in the statement below. As you read the excerpts from each argument, try to determine for yourself which one is sounder.

Document 1. Jefferson Argues Against the Constitutionality of the Bank of the United States

February 15, 1791

I consider the foundation of the Constitution as laid on this ground: That "all powers not delegated to the United States, by the Constitution, nor prohibited by it to the States, are reserved to the States or to the people." To take a single step beyond the boundaries thus specially drawn around the powers of Congress is to take possession of a boundless field of power, no longer susceptible of any definition.

The incorporation of a bank, and the powers assumed by this bill, have not, in my opinion, been delegated to the United States, by the Constitution.

I. They are not among the powers specially enumerated; for these are: 1st. A power to lay taxes for the purpose of paying the debts of the United States; but no debt is paid by this bill, nor any tax laid. . . .

2d. "To borrow money." But this bill neither borrows money nor ensures the borrowing it. . . .

3. To "regulate commerce with foreign nations, and among the States, and with the Indian tribes." To erect a bank, and to regulate commerce, are very different acts. . . .

II. Nor are they within either of the general phrases, which are the two following:

1. To lay taxes to provide for the general welfare of the United States, that is to say, "to lay taxes for *the purpose* of providing for the general welfare." For the laying of taxes is the *power,* and the general welfare the *purpose* for which the power is to be exercised. They are not to lay taxes *ad libitum for any purpose they please; but only to pay the debts or provide for the welfare of the Union.* In like manner, they are not to *do anything they please* to provide for the general welfare, but only to *lay taxes* for that purpose. To consider the latter phrase, not as describing the purpose of the first, but as giving a distinct and independent power to do any act they please, which might be for the good of the Union, would render all the preceding and subsequent enumerations of power completely useless.

It would reduce the whole instrument to a single phrase, that of instituting a Congress with power to do whatever would be for the good of the United States; and, as they would be the sole judges of the good or evil, it would be also a power to do whatever evil they please.

It is an established rule of construction where a phrase will bear either of two meanings, to give it that which will allow some meaning to the other parts of the instrument, and not that which would render all the others useless. . . . It is known that the very power now proposed *as a means* was rejected as *an end* by the Convention which formed the Constitution. A proposition was made to them to authorize Congress to open canals, and an amendatory one to empower them to incorporate. But the whole was rejected, and one of the reasons for rejection urged in debate was that then they would have a power to erect a bank, which would render the great cities, where there were prejudices and jealousies on the subject, adverse to the reception of the Constitution.

2. The second general phrase is, "to make all laws *necessary* and proper for carrying into execution the enumerated powers." But they can all be carried into execution without a bank. A bank therefore is not *necessary*, and consequently not authorized by this phrase.

It has been urged that a bank will give great facility or convenience in the collection of taxes. Suppose this were true; yet the Constitution allows only the means which are *"necessary,"* not those which are merely *"convenient"* for effecting the enumerated powers. If such a latitude of construction be allowed to this phrase as to give any nonenumerated power, it will go to every one, for there is not one which ingenuity may not torture into a *convenience* in some instance *or other, to some one* of so long a list of enumerated powers. . . .

[Paul L. Ford (ed.), *The Writings of Thomas Jefferson* (New York: Putnam, 1904), 5:284–289]

Document 2. Hamilton Argues for the Constitutionality of the Bank

February 23, 1791

The Secretary of the Treasury having perused with attention the papers containing the opinions of the Secretary of State and the Attorney-General, concerning the constitutionality of the bill for establishing a national bank, proceeds, according to the order of the President, to submit the reasons which have induced him to entertain a different opinion.

Through this mode of reasoning respecting the right of employing all the means requisite to the execution of the specified powers of the government, it is to be objected, that none but necessary and proper means are to be employed; and the Secretary of State maintains, that no means are to be considered *necessary* but those without which the grant of the power would be *nugatory*. . . .

It is essential to the being of the national government, that so erroneous a conception of the meaning of the word *necessary* should be exploded.

It is certain, that neither the grammatical nor popular sense of the term requires that construction. According to both, *necessary* often means no more than *needful, requisite, incidental, useful, or conducive to*. . . . And it is the true one in which it is to be understood as used in the Constitution. . . .

To understand the word as the Secretary of State does, would be to depart from its obvious and popular sense, and to give it a restrictive operation, an idea never before entertained. It would be to give it the same force as if the word *absolutely* or *indispensably* had been prefixed to it. . . .

The *degree* in which a measure is necessary can never be a *test* of the legal right to adopt it; that must be a matter of opinion, and can only be a *test* of expediency. . . .

This restrictive interpretation of the word *necessary* is also contrary to this sound maxim of construction; namely, that the powers contained in a constitution of government, especially those which concern the general administration of the affairs of a country, its finances, trade, defence &c., ought to be construed liberally in advancement of the public good. . . . The means by which national exigencies are to be provided for, national inconveniences obviated, national prosperity promoted, are of such infinite variety, extent, and complexity, that there must of necessity be great latitude of discretion in the selection and application of those means. . . .

It leaves, therefore, a criterion of what is constitutional, and of what is not so. This criterion is the *end*, to which the measure relates as a *means*. If the *end* be clearly comprehended within any of the specified powers, and if the measure have an obvious relation to that *end*, and is not forbidden by any particular provision of the Constitution, it may safely be deemed to come within the compass of the national authority. . . .

A hope is entertained that it has, by this time, been made to appear, to the satisfaction of the President, that a bank has a natural relation to the power of collecting taxes—to that of regulating trade—to that of providing for the common defence—and that, as the bill under consideration contemplates the government in the light of a joint proprietor of the stock of the bank, it brings the case within the provision of the clause of the Constitution which immediately respects the property of the United States.

Under a conviction that such a relation subsists, the Secretary of the Treasury, with all deference, conceives, that it will result as a necessary consequence from the position, that all the specified powers of government are sovereign, as to the proper objects; that the incorporation of a bank is a constitutional measure; and that the objections taken to the bill, in this respect, are ill-founded. . . .

[Henry Cabot Lodge (ed.), *The Works of Alexander Hamilton* (New York: Putnam, 1904), 3:445–446]

Questions for Reflection

Is Jefferson right in his assertion that to approve the bank would be to "reduce the whole [Constitution] to a single phrase, that of instituting a Congress with the power to do whatever would be for the good of the United States"? How did he come to that conclusion?

Does Hamilton's argument in favor of using any means to promote a constitutional end grant too broad a power to the government? Does Hamilton's argument remove all checks from the actions of government? Explain.

Which argument is the more convincing to you? Why?

ANSWERS TO MULTIPLE-CHOICE
AND TRUE-FALSE QUESTIONS

Multiple-Choice Questions

1-D, 2-C, 3-D, 4-A, 5-C, 6-B, 7-C, 8-C

True-False Questions

1-T, 2-F, 3-F, 4-T, 5-T, 6-F, 7-F, 8-T

8

REPUBLICANISM:
JEFFERSON AND MADISON

CHAPTER OBJECTIVES

After you complete the reading and study of this chapter you should be able to

1. Assess the impact of Republican control of the government under Jefferson's administration.
2. Understand the growth of the judicial branch under John Marshall and the partisan disputes between Republicans and Federalists over the judiciary.
3. Explain and account for the notable acts of political dissidence in the years 1801–1815.
4. Evaluate the causes of the War of 1812 and draw a conclusion about their relative importance.
5. Explain the impact of the War of 1812 on the United States.

CHAPTER OUTLINE

I. Jefferson in office
  A. The inauguration
    1. New capital
    2. Tone of ceremony
  B. The "Revolution of 1800"

    1. Orderly transfer of power
    2. Jefferson as party leader
  C. Jefferson and the judiciary
    1. Repeal of Judiciary Act of 1801
    2. Importance of *Marbury v. Madison* ruling
  D. Domestic programs
    1. Acceptance of National Bank
    2. Repeal of excise taxes
    3. Sources of revenue
    4. Armed forces cut back
    5. Slave trade outlawed
  E. Conflict with Barbary pirates
  F. The Louisiana Purchase
    1. The negotiations with France
    2. Constitutional issue
  G. Lewis and Clark expedition
  H. Federalist political schemes
    1. The Essex Junto and secession
    2. Burr-Hamilton duel, 1804
  I. Reelection of Jefferson, 1804

II. Divisions within the Republican Party
  A. John Randolph's dissent
  B. Burr Conspiracy
    1. Burr's background and character
    2. Intrigue with James Wilkinson
    3. Trial for treason
      a. Jefferson's use of "executive privilege"
      b. Rigid definition of treason

III. War in Europe
   A. Harassment of shipping by Britain and France
      1. Mutual blockades
      2. Impressment of sailors
   B. The Jefferson Embargo
   C. Election of James Madison, 1808
   D. Drift to war
      1. Nonintercourse Act
      2. Macon's Bill No. 2
      3. Intrigues with Britain and France over trade restrictions
   E. Declaration of war

IV. War of 1812
   A. Causes
      1. Demand for neutral rights
      2. Sectional support for war
      3. Indian uprisings
      4. National honor
   B. Preparations for war
      1. Financial problems
      2. Poor condition of the army
      3. State of the navy
   C. War in the North
      1. Three-pronged drive against Canada
      2. Perry's exploits on Lake Erie
      3. Battle of Thames
   D. War in the South
   E. British plans of attack for 1814
   F. Invasions of Washington and Baltimore
   G. Battle of New Orleans
   H. Treaty of Ghent
   I. The Hartford Convention
      1. Composition
      2. Actions taken
      3. Consequences of meeting
   J. Aftermath of the war
      1. Patriotism and nationalism
      2. Action against pirates of Barbary Coast
      3. Reversal of roles by Republicans and Federalists

KEY ITEMS OF CHRONOLOGY

Marbury v. Madison decision	1803
Louisiana Purchase	1803
Burr-Hamilton duel	1804
Lewis and Clark expedition	1804–1806
Embargo	1807
Slave trade ended	1808
Nonintercourse Act	1809
Macon's Bill No. 2	1810
War declared	1812
Treaty of Ghent	1814
Hartford Convention	December 1814
Battle of New Orleans	January 1815

TERMS TO MASTER

Listed below are some important terms or people with which you should be familiar after you complete the study of this chapter. Identify each name or term.

1. *Marbury v. Madison*
2. Louisiana Purchase
3. Revolution of 1800
4. Lewis and Clark Expedition
5. Essex Junto
6. Burr Conspiracy
7. John Randolph of Roanoke
8. Aaron Burr
9. judicial review
10. executive privilege
11. embargo
12. Nonintercourse Act

13. Macon's Bill No. 2
14. War Hawks
15. Oliver H. Perry
16. William Henry Harrison
17. Fort McHenry
18. Battle of New Orleans

VOCABULARY BUILDING

Listed below are some words used in this chapter. Look in the dictionary for the meaning of each.

1. precedent
2. excises
3. intrude
4. extortion
5. cede
6. scruples
7. mettle
8. capricious
9. intractable
10. impressment
11. anticlimax
12. ineptitude

EXERCISES FOR UNDERSTANDING

When you have completed reading the chapter, answer the following questions. If you have difficulty, go back to the text and reread the section of the chapter related to the question.

Multiple-Choice Questions

Select the letter of the response which best completes the statement.

1. The Supreme Court's decision in *Marbury v. Madison*
   A. was sparked by Adams's "midnight appointment"
   B. established the Court's power to declare laws unconstitutional
   C. had no effect on Marbury's appointment
   D. all of the above

2. The Louisiana Purchase
   A. was delayed by Jefferson until a constitutional amendment could be passed
   B. involved a treaty with Spain
   C. was opposed by the New England Federalists
   D. gave the U.S. claim to land all the way to the Pacific

3. Independence for New England, perhaps joined by New York, was the idea of
   A. the Essex Junto
   B. the Tertium Quid
   C. the War Hawks
   D. Lewis and Clark

4. The trial of Aaron Burr for the still mysterious "Burr Conspiracy" saw
   A. Burr die before a verdict was returned
   B. Burr convicted of treason
   C. President Thomas Jefferson testify in court against Burr
   D. Chief Justice Marshall define treason very strictly

5. Jefferson's Embargo
   A. caused the British to weaken their policies against the United States
   B. was developed because of the strength of the United States Navy which would enforce it
   C. hurt the South more than any other section
   D. was repealed before Madison took office

6. The causes of the War of 1812 probably included
   A. western desire for what became the Louisiana Purchase
   B. fears that the French were assisting the Indians
   C. emotional nationalism
   D. all of the above

7. The Hartford Convention in 1815
   A. was a revival of the Tertium Quid movement
   B. fatally branded the Federalists as disloyal and provincial
   C. called for the immediate secession of New England
   D. sought to limit the power of the Supreme Court

8. The War of 1812 did *not*
   A. stimulate American industry
   B. decrease Republican opposition to federal power
   C. produce important national symbols and heroes
   D. gain western territory for the United States

True-False Questions

Indicate whether each statement is true or false.

1. The "Revolution of 1800" refers to the orderly transfer of power from the Federalists to the Republicans.
2. Jefferson's "wise and frugal government" stressed reducing expenditures for the military.
3. The Lewis and Clark expedition gave the United States a claim to the Oregon territory.
4. Alexander Hamilton killed Aaron Burr in a duel.
5. In the European War that started in 1803, the United States strongly supported the French.
6. The British burned buildings in Washington, D.C., during the War of 1812.
7. Representatives from farming regions of the South and West advocated war in 1812.
8. Coming a day after the peace treaty had been signed, the Battle of New Orleans had absolutely no effect on the outcome of the war.

Essay Questions

1. Discuss the impact of the West on politics during Jefferson's presidency.
2. How did Jefferson try to change the government after his inauguration as president?
3. Trace the coming of the War of 1812 and the dispute historians have had over its causes.
4. What effects did the War of 1812 have on the economy and culture of the United States? Was the war worth the costs?

DOCUMENT

Abigail Adams's Description of Washington in 1800

While momentous events were occurring, the new capital, Washington, was completed at the close of the Adams administration. Abigail Adams, the wife of the president, sent the following description of the city and the White House to her daughter, Mrs. W. S. Smith. The passage reminds us that even amid history-making events, daily life was a subject for reflection.

Washington, 21, November, 1800.

I arrived here on Sunday last, and without meeting with any accident worth noticing, except losing ourselves when we left Baltimore, and going eight or nine miles on the Frederick road, by which means we were obliged to go the other eight through woods, where we wandered two hours without finding a guide, or the path. Fortunately, a straggling black came up with us, and we engaged him as a guide, to extricate us out of our difficulty; but woods are all you see, from Baltimore until you reach *the city*, which is only so in

name. Here and there is a small cot, without a glass window, inter-
spersed amongst the forests, through which you travel miles without seeing any human being. In the city there are buildings enough,
if they were compact and finished, to accommodate Congress and
those attached to it; but as they are, and scattered as they are, I see
no great comfort for them. The river, which runs up to Alexandria,
is in full view of my window, and I see the vessels as they pass and
repass. The house is upon a grand and superb scale, requiring about
thirty servants to attend and keep the apartments in proper order,
and perform the ordinary business of the house and stables; an
establishment very well proportioned to the President's salary. The
lighting the apartments, from the kitchen to parlours and chambers, is a tax indeed; and the fires we are obliged to keep to secure
us from daily agues is another very cheering comfort. To assist us
in this great castle, and render less attendance necessary, bells are
wholly wanting, not one single one being hung through the whole
house, and promises are all you can obtain. This is so great an
inconvenience, that I know not what to do, or how to do. The ladies
from Georgetown and in the city have many of them visited me.
Yesterday I returned fifteen visits,—but such a place as Georgetown
appears,—why, our Milton is beautiful. But no comparisons;—if
they will put me up some bells, and let me have wood enough to
keep fires, I design to be pleased. I could content myself almost
anywhere three months; but, surrounded with forests, can you believe that wood is not to be had, because people cannot be found
to cut and cart it! Briesler entered into a contract with a man to
supply him with wood. A small part, a few cords only, has he been
able to get. Most of that was expended to dry the walls of the house
before we came in, and yesterday the man told him it was impossible for him to procure it to be cut and carted. He has had recourse
to coals; but we cannot get grates made and set. We have, indeed,
come into *a new country.*

You must keep all this to yourself, and, when asked how I like it,
say that I write you the situation is beautiful, which is true. The
house is made habitable, but there is not a single apartment
finished, and all withinside, except the plastering, has been done
since Briesler came. We have not the least fence, yard, or other
convenience, without, and the great unfinished audience-room I
make a drying-room of, to hang up the clothes in. The principal
stairs are not up, and will not be this winter. Six chambers are made
comfortable; two are occupied by the President and Mr. Shaw; two
lower rooms, one for a common parlour, and one for a levee-room.
Up stairs there is the oval room, which is designed for the drawing-
room, and has the crimson furniture in it. It is a very handsome
room now; but, when completed, it will be beautiful. If the twelve
years, in which this place has been considered as the future seat of
government, had been improved, as they would have been if in
New England, very many of the present inconveniences would
have been removed. It is a beautiful spot, capable of every improvement, and, the more I view it, the more I am delighted with it.

Questions for Reflection

How does the scene described here compare with the Washington you have seen or heard of? What passages give you an impression of the grand, almost monarchical, style the president maintained?

Why was wood difficult to obtain in the new city? Would the house described here be more or less suitable for Thomas Jefferson than for the Adams family?

ANSWERS TO MULTIPLE-CHOICE AND TRUE-FALSE QUESTIONS

Multiple-Choice Questions

1-A, 2-C, 3-A, 4-D, 5-D, 6-C, 7-B, 8-C

True-False Questions

1-T, 2-T, 3-T, 4-F, 5-F, 6-T, 7-T, 8-F

9

NATIONALISM AND SECTIONALISM

CHAPTER OBJECTIVES

After you complete the reading and study of this chapter you should be able to

1. Explain the emergence of nationalism after the War of 1812 in the economy, the government, diplomacy, Supreme Court decisions, and politics.
2. Explain the outbursts of sectionalism in the era 1816–1828.
3. Explain the demise of the first political party system and analyze the shifting patterns of party principles in this era.
4. Explain the significant Supreme Court decisions of this time.
5. Account for the political rise of Andrew Jackson.

CHAPTER OUTLINE

I. Development of nationalism
   A. Stages in growth of nationalism
   B. War of 1812 and nationalism

II. Economic nationalism
   A. National Bank
      1. Results of expiration of National Bank in 1811
      2. New Bank of the United States chartered
      3. Debate over Second National Bank
   B. Protective tariff of 1816
   C. Internal improvements
      1. The National Road
      2. Calhoun's proposal
      3. Madison's veto of bill
      4. State and private responsibility

III. "Era of Good Feeling"
   A. James Monroe
      1. Election of 1816
      2. Cabinet and administration
   B. Accuracy of "Era of Good Feeling"
   C. Election of 1820 and end of party system
   D. Rapprochement with Britain
      1. Rush-Bagot Agreement, 1817
      2. Convention of 1818
   E. Acquisition of Florida
      1. Weakened Spanish control
      2. Andrew Jackson in charge
      3. Settlement with Spain

IV. Signs of growing political disharmony
   A. Panic of 1819
      1. Collapse of cotton
      2. Excessive credit and speculation
      3. Irresponsible B.U.S.
   B. The Missouri Compromise
      1. Slave-state/free-state balance
      2. Debate over Missouri's statehood
      3. Terms of the compromise

V. Supreme Court and judicial nationalism
   A. Assertion of judicial review

1. *Marbury v. Madison* (1803)
2. *Fletcher v. Peck* (1810)
B. Protection of contract rights in *Dartmouth College v. Woodward* (1819)
C. Curb on state power in *McCulloch v. Maryland* (1819)
D. National supremacy in commerce, *Gibbons v. Ogden* (1824)

VI. Nationalist diplomacy
   A. Negotiating Russia out of Oregon
   B. The Monroe Doctrine
      1. Latin American liberation wars
      2. British efforts in Latin America
      3. Assertion of Monroe Doctrine
      4. Effects of doctrine

VII. One-party politics
   A. Election of 1824
      1. Candidates and issues
      2. Result
      3. Charges of "Corrupt Bargain"
   B. Presidency of John Quincy Adams
      1. Strong nationalism
      2. Blueprint for development
      3. Mistakes and frustrations
      4. Tariff of 1828
   C. Election of 1828
      1. Opposition to Andrew Jackson
      2. Jackson's appeal
      3. Extension of suffrage in states
      4. Jackson's background
      5. Outcome of election

KEY ITEMS OF CHRONOLOGY

Second National Bank (B.U.S.) chartered	1816
Protective tariff	1816
Monroe's administrations	1817–1825
Rush-Bagot Agreement	1817
Convention with Britain	1818
Acquisition of Florida	1819
Financial panic	1819
Dartmouth College v. Woodward	1819
McCulloch v. Maryland	1819
Missouri Compromise	1820
Monroe Doctrine	1823
Gibbons v. Ogden	1824
John Quincy Adams's administrations	1825–1829
Election of Andrew Jackson	1828

TERMS TO MASTER

Listed below are some important terms or people with which you should be familiar after you complete the study of this chapter. Identify each name or term.

1. "Era of Good Feeling"
2. John C. Calhoun
3. James Monroe
4. internal improvements
5. Henry Clay
6. Tallmadge Amendment
7. judicial review
8. *Dartmouth College v. Woodward*
9. *McCulloch v. Maryland*
10. *Gibbons v. Ogden*
11. Monroe Doctrine
12. "corrupt bargain"
13. *South Carolina Exposition and Protest*
14. Rachel Jackson

VOCABULARY BUILDING

Listed below are some words used in this chapter. Look in the dictionary for the meaning of each.

1. maxim
2. rancorous
3. stratification
4. rapprochement
5. repugnance
6. deprivation
7. unilateral
8. swoop
9. scurrilousness

EXERCISES FOR UNDERSTANDING

When you have completed reading the chapter, answer each of the following questions. If you have difficulty, go back to the text and reread the section of the chapter related to the question.

Multiple-Choice Questions

Select the letter of the response which best completes the statement.

1. "The Republicans out-Federalized Federalism" means that the Republicans in the late 1810s
   A. changed their party's name
   B. supported a national bank and a protective tariff
   C. conducted dishonest and deceitful campaigns
   D. none of the above

2. John C. Calhoun in the 1810s was
   A. more nationalistic than he later was
   B. a stronger advocate of states' rights than he was in the 1830s
   C. the same as later—his positions did not change
   D. as always, in complete agreement with Daniel Webster

3. After the War of 1812, an unresolved problem in United States relations with Great Britain involved
   A. naval power on the Great Lakes
   B. the border between the United States and Canada
   C. trade with British colonies
   D. all of the above

4. The Missouri Compromise of 1820
   A. outlawed the foreign slave trade and declared slavery an evil
   B. banned slavery from all of the Louisiana Purchase territory
   C. ended the slave-state/free-state balance in the U.S. Senate
   D. admitted Missouri as a slave state

5. John Quincy Adams's presidency was distinctive for
   A. his frustration and failure
   B. his keen political skill in dealing with Congress
   C. his lack of vision and program for the nation
   D. all of the above

6. The decision in *McCulloch v. Maryland*
   A. protected the right of private contracts
   B. restricted state control of interstate commerce
   C. was based on a strict Constitution
   D. denied the right of a state to tax the National Bank

7. The Monroe Doctrine
   A. was issued jointly with Great Britain
   B. brought a storm of protest from other nations
   C. gave the United States control over internal affairs in Latin America
   D. promised that the United States would not interfere with existing European colonies

8. The presidential candidates in the 1828 campaign
   A. concentrated almost exclusively on the issues of internal improvements and the National Bank
   B. thoroughly debated the theories of nationalism
   C. focused discussions entirely on the tariff and foreign affairs
   D. engaged in personal attacks

True-False Questions

Indicate whether each statement is true or false.

1. Beginning in the 1810s, Congress systematically supported internal improvements.
2. James Madison was president during what was called the "era of good feeling."
3. The policies of the Bank of the United States under Langdon Cheves were a primary cause of the Panic of 1819.
4. Andrew Jackson played a major role in the acquisition of Florida.
5. John Marshall's decision in *Gibbons v. Ogden* established state supremacy in matters involving transportation.
6. The "corrupt bargain" of 1824 allegedly was a deal between the speaker of the House of Representatives and Andrew Jackson.
7. The political party shifts of 1816–1820 resulted in a Federalist party which opposed a National Bank and loose construction of the Constitution.
8. John C. Calhoun's *South Carolina Exposition and Protest,* which claimed that a state could nullify an act of Congress, was prompted by the Missouri Compromise.

Essay Questions

1. From 1814 through 1828 differences increased among the sections of the nation. On what issues did the various sections differ, and why?
2. How did the Supreme Court contribute to the growing nationalism of the early nineteenth century? Cite specific cases as examples.
3. Explain the causes of the "era of good feeling" and the reasons for its decline.
4. Explain the significance of the Missouri Compromise.
5. What personal and political factors led to the election of Andrew Jackson in 1828?

DOCUMENT

McCulloch v. The State of Maryland et al. (4 Wheaton 316)

Among the important reflections of nationalism in this era were the decisions of the United States Supreme Court under Chief Justice John Marshall. One of the strongest of these assertions of nationalism was the case of *McCulloch v. Maryland* (1819), in which the Maryland statute taxing the branch of the Bank of the United States in that state was declared unconstitutional. This opinion further clearly upheld the constitutionality of the bank, a matter of some dispute earlier between Hamilton and Jefferson. As you read the excerpts below from the opinion of the Court, compare them with Hamilton's opinion of the bank (see Chapter 7).

> Is it true, that this is the sense in which the word "necessary" is always used? Does it always import an absolute physical necessity, so strong, that one thing, to which another may be termed necessary, cannot exist without the other? We think it does not. . . . To employ the means necessary to an end, is generally understood as employing any means calculated to produce the end, and not as being confined to those single means, without which the end would be entirely unattainable. Such is the character of human language, that no word conveys to the mind, in all situations, one single definite idea; and nothing is more common than to use words in a figurative sense. . . . It is essential to just construction, that many

words which import something excessive, should be understood in a more mitigated sense—in that sense which common usage justifies. The word "necessary" is of this description. It has not a fixed character peculiar to itself. It admits of all degrees of comparison; and is often connected with other words, which increase or diminish the impression the mind receives of the urgency it imports. A thing may be necessary, very necessary, absolutely or indispensably necessary. To no mind would the same idea be conveyed, by these several phrases. . . . This word, then, like others, is used in various senses; and, in its construction, the subject, the context, the intention of the person using them, are all to be taken into view.

Let this be done in the case under consideration. The subject is the execution of those great powers on which the welfare of a nation essentially depends. It must have been the intention of those who gave these powers, to insure, as far as human prudence could insure, their beneficial execution. This could not be done by confining the choice of means to such narrow limits as not to leave it in the power of congress to adopt any which might be appropriate, and which were conducive to the end. This provision is made in a constitution intended to endure for ages to come, and consequently, to be adapted to the various crises of human affairs. To have prescribed the means by which government should, in all future time, execute its powers, would have been to change, entirely, the character of the instrument, and give it the properties of a legal code. It would have been an unwise attempt to provide, by immutable rules, for exigencies which, if foreseen at all, must have been seen dimly, and which can be best provided for as they occur.

Take, for example, the power "to establish post-offices and post-roads." This power is executed by the single act of making the establishment. But, from this has been inferred the power and duty of carrying the mail along the post-road, from one post-office to another. And, from this implied power, has again been inferred the right to punish those who steal letters from the post-office, or rob the mail. It may be said, with some plausibility, that the right to carry the mail, and to punish those who rob it, is not indispensably necessary to the establishment of a post-office and post-road. This right is, indeed, essential to the beneficial exercise of the power, but not indispensably necessary to its existence. So, of the punishment of the crimes of stealing or falsifying a record or process of a court of the United States, or of perjury in such court.

But the argument which most conclusively demonstrates the error of the construction contended for by the counsel for the State of Maryland, is founded on the intention of the convention, as manifested in the whole clause. To waste time and argument in proving that, without it, congress might carry its powers into execution, would be not much less idle than to hold a lighted taper to the sun.

That the power to tax involves the power to destroy; that the power to destroy may defeat and render useless the power to create; that there is a plain repugnance, in conferring on one government a power to control the constitutional measures of another, which other, with respect to those very measures, is declared to be supreme over that which exerts the control, are propositions not to be denied. But all inconsistencies are to be reconciled by the magic of the word confidence. Taxation, it is said, does not necessarily and unavoidably destroy. To carry it to the excess of destruction would be an abuse, to presume which would banish that confidence which is essential to all government.

But is this a case of confidence? Would the people of any one State trust those of another, with a power to control the most insignificant operations of their state government? We know they would not. Why, then, should we suppose that the people of any one State would be willing to trust those of another with a power to control the operations of a government to which they have confided their most important and most valuable interests? In the legislature of the Union alone, are all represented. The legislature of the Union alone, therefore, can be trusted by the people with the power of controlling measures which concern all, in the confidence that it will not be abused.

If the States may tax one instrument, employed by the government in the execution of its powers, they may tax any and every other instrument. They may tax the mail; they may tax the mint; they may tax patent rights; they may tax the papers of the customhouse; they may tax judicial process; they may tax all the means employed by the government, to an excess which would defeat all the ends of government. This was not intended by the American people. They did not design to make their government dependent on the States.

This is not all. If the controlling power of the States be established; if their supremacy as to taxation be acknowledged; what is to restrain their exercising this control in any shape they may please to give it? Their sovereignty is not confined to taxation. That is not the only mode in which it might be displayed. The question, in truth, a question of supremacy; and if the right of the States to tax the means employed by the general government be conceded, the declaration that the constitution, and the laws made in pursuance thereof, shall be the supreme law of the land, is empty and unmeaning declamation.

Questions for Reflection

Explain what Marshall meant when he said that to have included in the Constitution "the means by which government should, in all future time, execute its powers, would have been to change entirely, the character of the [Constitution], and give it the properties of a legal code." What does this decision tell us about the relative success of Hamilton's and Jefferson's views of the Constitution? What is meant by "the power to tax is the power to destroy"? Explain the ways in which this decision asserts the supremacy of the national government. How did that attitude reflect the general trends of the era after 1815?

ANSWERS TO MULTIPLE-CHOICE
AND TRUE-FALSE QUESTIONS

Multiple-Choice Questions

1-B, 2-A, 3-C, 4-D, 5-A, 6-D, 7-D, 8-D

True-False Questions

1-F, 2-F, 3-F, 4-T, 5-F, 6-F, 7-T, 8-F

10

THE JACKSONIAN IMPULSE

CHAPTER OBJECTIVES

After you complete the reading and study of this chapter you should be able to

1. Explain the political controversy between Jackson and Calhoun.
2. Understand and explain the nullification controversy with South Carolina.
3. Understand and explain the bank war and its economic consequences.
4. Assess Jackson's Indian policy.
5. Analyze and explain the emergence of the second political party system.
6. Assess the significance of Jacksonian democracy.

CHAPTER OUTLINE

I. The start of the Jackson presidency
  A. Inauguration
  B. Appointments by rotation in office
  C. Rivalry between Calhoun and Van Buren
    1. The Peggy Eaton Affair
    2. Internal improvements
      a. Maysville Road bill
      b. Jackson's veto

II. Nullification issue and crisis
  A. Situation in Calhoun's South Carolina

B. Calhoun's theory of nullification
  1. Abandons nationalism
  2. *South Carolina Exposition and Protest*
C. The Webster-Hayne debate
  1. Initial issue of western lands
  2. States' rights vs. nationalism
D. Jefferson Day dinner
  1. Jackson: "Our Union—it must be preserved!"
  2. Calhoun: "The Union, next to our Liberty most dear!"
E. Jackson's break with Calhoun
  1. Calhoun's 1818 letter proposing disciplining General Jackson
  2. Cabinet shake-up
  3. Jackson–Van Buren ticket
F. Nullification Crisis
  1. Tariff of 1832
  2. South Carolina's nullification
  3. Jackson's firm response
  4. Clay's compromise

III. Jackson's Indian policy
  A. Jackson's attitude
  B. Indian Removal Act and treaties
  C. Cherokees' "trail of tears"
    1. Georgia's legal actions toward Indians
    2. Supreme Court rulings
    3. Jackson's reaction
    4. Cherokee removal

IV. The bank controversy
   A. Opponents of the B.U.S.
   B. Effort to recharter
      1. Biddle's plan
      2. Jackson's veto
   C. Election of 1832
      1. Innovations
         a. Anti-Masonic party
         b. National conventions
      2. Results of election
   D. Jackson's renewed war on B.U.S.
      1. Removal of deposits
      2. Use of "pet banks"
      3. Economic reaction to removal
         a. B.U.S.'s tightening of credit
         b. Speculative binge
         c. Increase in land sales
         d. State indebtedness
      4. Bursting the bubble
         a. Distribution Act
         b. Specie Circular
         c. International complications

V. The new party system and Van Buren
   A. The Whig Party
      1. Sources of coalition
      2. Whig philosophy
   B. The election of 1836
      1. Candidates
      2. Results
   C. Van Buren administration
      1. Van Buren's background
      2. The panic of 1837
         a. Causes and effects
         b. Government reaction
      3. Independent treasury
         a. Basis for proposal
         b. Passage in 1840
   D. The election of 1840
      1. Candidates
      2. Defeat of Van Buren

VI. Assessing the Jackson years
   A. Growth of political parties
   B. Conflicting interpretations of Jackson
   C. Return to Jeffersonian vision

KEY ITEMS OF CHRONOLOGY

Calhoun's *Exposition and Protest*	1828
Jackson's administrations	1829–1837
Veto of the Maysville Road Bill	1830
Webster-Hayne Debate	1830
Indian Removal Act	1830
Veto of bank recharter	1832
Worcester v. Georgia	1832
Force Bill and Compromise Tariff	1833
Cherokee Treaty and "trail of tears"	1835–1838
Distribution Act and Specie Circular	1836
Van Buren's administration	1837–1841
Independent Treasury passed	1840

TERMS TO MASTER

Listed below are some important terms or people with which you should be familiar after you complete the study of this chapter. Identify each name or term.

1. Peggy Eaton
2. John C. Calhoun
3. "Spoils System"
4. Maysville Road Bill
5. Webster-Hayne Debate
6. *Worcester v. Georgia*
7. "trail of tears"
8. Nullification Proclamation
9. Force Bill
10. Nicholas Biddle
11. Anti-Masonic party
12. "pet banks"
13. Distribution Act
14. Whigs

15. Independent Treasury
16. "Log Cabin and Hard Cider Campaign"

VOCABULARY BUILDING

Listed below are some words used in this chapter. Look in the dictionary for the meaning of each.

1. succulent
2. precedent
3. malaise
4. secession
5. mastiff
6. adroitly
7. enigmatic
8. rift
9. tacit
10. mandate
11. fiscal
12. bonanza
13. temperance
14. precarious

EXERCISES FOR UNDERSTANDING

When you have completed reading the chapter, answer each of the following questions. If you have difficulty, go back to the text and reread the section of the chapter related to the question.

Multiple-Choice Questions

Select the letter of the response which best completes the statement.

1. In dealing with internal improvements, Andrew Jackson
   A. opposed all federal financing of roads, bridges, and railroads
   B. wanted federal aid only to local projects
   C. supported federal funds only for interstate programs
   D. approved all expenditures passed by Congress

2. John C. Calhoun's theory of nullification provided
   A. encouragement for secession from the Union
   B. that the United States Supreme Court could overrule a state's nullification
   C. for nullification only by a specially elected state convention
   D. a satisfactory compromise between his views and the position of Jackson

3. The South Carolina Ordinance of 1832
   A. forced Calhoun to resign as vice-president
   B. nullified the Missouri Compromise
   C. was rejected in a referendum by the people
   D. none of the above

4. Jackson's action in regard to the Indians was to
   A. oppose their removal to the West
   B. refuse to enforce a Supreme Court decision in the Indians' favor
   C. defend Indian rights to disputed lands in Georgia
   D. send troops to slaughter the Indians

5. Jackson helped to bring an early end to the Bank of the United States by
   A. suing the bank in federal court
   B. beginning to deposit government funds in state banks rather than the Bank of the United States
   C. getting Congress to pass an act killing the bank
   D. persuading the English to withdraw their funds from the bank

6. Daniel Webster and Henry Clay were important members of the
   A. Anti-Masonic Party
   B. Whig Party
   C. Democratic Party
   D. Republican Party

7. To keep the government financially sound after the panic of 1837, Van Buren proposed
   A. reviving the Bank of the United States
   B. government aid to state banks
   C. an Independent Treasury
   D. a higher tariff and an increase in the money supply

8. During the Jackson years, politics changed with the
   A. tripling of the proportion of white males who voted
   B. acceptance of political parties
   C. emergence of national nominating conventions
   D. all of the above

True-False Questions

Indicate whether each statement is true or false.

1. President Andrew Jackson fired most political appointees in the government and replaced them with his political supporters.
2. The issue of public lands in the West triggered the Webster-Hayne debate.
3. Andrew Jackson's statement—"The Union, next to our Liberty most dear!"—furthered alienated him from John C. Calhoun.
4. In *Worcester v. Georgia,* the Supreme Court ruled that Georgia law did not apply to the Cherokee nation.
5. In 1832 Congress defeated an attempt to recharter the Bank of the United States.

6. The Distribution Act of 1836 made the states share in paying off the enormous national debt.
7. James K. Polk was chosen to run for vice-president when Martin Van Buren was chosen to run as president.
8. The "log cabin and hard cider" slogan of 1840 referred to William Henry Harrison's poor background.

Essay Questions

1. Assess the character and philosophy of Andrew Jackson as president.
2. Describe the positions in the argument over states' rights and the Union and show how the tariff issue affected the debate.
3. The Bank of the United States was very controversial. Explain what its supporters liked about the bank and what its opponents disliked about it.
4. How did national politics change between 1828 and 1840? Be sure to mention specific developments.
5. Compare the Whig philosophy and program to those of the Democrats.
6. Briefly describe the different interpretations of Jackson's significance.

READINGS

Historians have disagreed strongly about the significance of Andrew Jackson and the social changes that accompanied his rise to power. The several selections presented here provide a brief view of these contrasting interpretations. The first selection, from Arthur Schlesinger, although written in 1945, presents clearly the progressive interpretation of class conflict. A contrary view of a decade later comes from Bray Hammond, who saw Jackson's destruction of the bank as an effort to assist and liberate a rising class of entrepreneurs. The final selection, from Lee Benson, gives a taste of the quantitative studies which in recent years have attempted to locate more precisely at local levels the different types of people who supported Jacksonian democracy or its countermovement, the Whig Party. Read each of the selections carefully, looking for agreement and disagreement among them and thinking of questions which are left unanswered in the very brief passages presented here.

Reading 1. Arthur Schlesinger Describes Conflict Between the Haves and Have-nots.

The Bank War compelled people to speculate once again about the conflict of classes. "There are but two parties," exclaimed Thomas Hart Benton, giving the period its keynote; "there never has been but two parties . . . founded in the radical question, whether PEO-PLE, or PROPERTY, shall govern? Democracy implies a government of the rich. . . . and in these words are contained the sum of party distinction."

The paper banking system was considered to play a leading role in this everlasting struggle. Men living by the issue and circulation of paper money produced nothing; they added nothing to the national income; yet, they flourished and grew wealthy. Their prosperity, it was argued, must be stolen from the proceeds of productive labor—in other words, from the honest but defenseless "humble members of society." . . .

. . . Taney described the big Bank as "the centre, and the citadel of the moneyed power." . . . To a lesser degree all banks acted as strongholds of conservatism. They provided the funds and often the initiative for combat. Their lawyers, lobbyists and newspapers were eternally active. . . .

The hard-money policy attacked both the techniques of plunder and the general strategy of warfare. By doing away with paper money, it proposed to restrict the steady transfer of wealth from the farmer and laborer to the business community. By limiting banks to commercial credit and denying them control over the currency, it proposed to lessen their influence and power. By reducing the proportion of paper money, it proposed to moderate the business cycle, and order the economy to the advantage of the worker rather than the speculator. . . .

By origin and interest, it was a policy which appealed mainly to the submerged classes of the East and to the farmers of the South rather than to the frontier. Historians have too long been misled by the tableau of Jackson, the wild backwoodsman, erupting into the White House. In fact, the hard-money doctrine, which was not at all a frontier doctrine, was the controlling policy of the administration from the winter of 1833 on; and for some time it had been the secret goal of a small group. . . . From the removal of the deposits to the end of Van Buren's presidency in 1840 this clique of radical Democrats sought to carry out the policy in its full implications.

The Jacksonians believed that there was a deep-rooted conflict in society between the "producing" and "non-producing" classes—the farmers and laborers, on the one hand, and the business community on the other. The business community was considered to hold big cards in this conflict through its network of banks and corporations, its control of education and the press, above all, its power over the state: it was therefore able to strip the working classes of the fruits of their labor. . . .

If they wished to preserve their liberty, the producing classes would have to unite against the movement "to make the rich richer and the potent more powerful." Constitutional prescriptions and political promises afforded no sure protection. . . .

The specific problem was to control the power of the capitalistic groups, mainly Eastern, for the benefit of the noncapitalist groups, farmers and laboring men, East, West and South. The basic Jacksonian ideas came naturally enough from the East, which best understood the nature of business power and reacted most sharply against it. The legend that Jacksonian democracy was the explosion of the frontier, lifting into the government some violent men filled with rustic prejudices against big business, does not explain the facts, which were somewhat more complex. Jacksonian democracy was rather a second American phase of that enduring struggle between the business community and the rest of society which is the guarantee of freedom in a liberal capitalist state.

Like any social philosophy, Jacksonian democracy drew on several intellectual traditions. Basically, it was a revival of Jeffersonianism, but the Jeffersonian inheritance was strengthened by the infusion of fresh influences; notably the antimonopolistic tradition . . . and the pro-labor tradition. . . .

[From Arthur M. Schlesinger, Jr., *The Age of Jackson* (Boston: Little, Brown and Company, 1945), pp. 125–126, 306–308]

Reading 2. Bray Hammond Sees Destruction of the Bank as Helping the Entrepreneurial Classes

Socially, the Jacksonian revolution signified that a nation of democrats was tired of being governed, however well, by the gentlemen from Virginia and Massachusetts. . . . Economically, the revolution signified that a nation of potential money-makers could not abide traditionary, conservative limitations on business enterprise, particularly by capitalists in Philadelphia. The Jacksonian revolution was a consequence of the Industrial Revolution and of a farm-born people's realization that now anyone in America could get rich and through his own efforts, if he had a fair chance. A conception of earned wealth arose which rendered the self-made man as superior morally to the hereditary well-to-do as the agrarian had been. . . . The humbly born and rugged individualists who were gaining fortunes by their own toil and sweat, or wits, were still simple Americans, Jeffersonian, anti-monopolistic, anti-governmental, but fraught with the spirit of enterprise and fired with a sense of what soon would be called manifest destiny. They envied the social and economic advantages of the established urban capitalists, mercantile and financial; and they fought these aristocrats with far more zeal and ingenuity than the agrarians ever had. They resented the federal Bank's interference with expansion of the monetary supply. . . . They democratized business under a great show of agrarian idealism and made the age of Jackson a festival of *laisser faire*. . . .

In their attack on the Bank of the United States, the Jacksonians still employed the vocabulary of their agrarian backgrounds. . . . the Jacksonians' destruction of the Bank of the United States was in no sense a blow at capitalism or property or the "money power." It was a blow at an older set of capitalists by a newer, more numerous set. It was incident to the democratization of business, the diffusion of enterprise among the mass of people, and the transfer of economic primacy from an old and conservative merchant class to a newer, more aggressive, and more numerous body of business men and speculators of all sorts.

The Jacksonians were unconventional and skillful in politics. In their assault on the Bank they united five important elements, which, incongruities notwithstanding, comprised an effective combination. These were Wall Street's jealousy of Chestnut Street, the business man's dislike of the federal Bank's restraint upon bank credit, the politician's resentment at the Bank's interference with states' rights, popular identification of the Bank with the aristocracy of business, and the direction of agrarian antipathy away from banks in general to the federal Bank in particular. Destruction of the Bank ended federal regulation of bank credit and shifted the money center of the country from Chestnut Street to Wall Street. It left the poor agrarian as poor as he had been before and left the money power possessed of more money and more power than ever.

[From Bray Hammond, *Banks and Politics in America from the Revolution to the Civil War* (Princeton, N.J.: Princeton University Press, 1957), pp. 326–328]

Reading 3. Lee Benson's Quantitative Study of New York State

During the decade 1834 to 1844, the two major parties in New York displayed striking similarities and profound differences. This chapter will analyze the social composition of their leadership. . . .

If parties were characterized solely by the leaders they keep, it would be difficult to distinguish between the Democrats and Whigs. A composite account of their social and economic backgrounds reveals striking similarities. Perhaps their most significant difference is that several Democratic leaders claimed Dutch or German ancestry, while the Whigs invariably claimed British ancestry (mostly by way of New England). And Democratic leaders tended to be more affluent than their Whig counterparts, or to have more affluent relatives who supported their political careers. Unless fine criteria are used, however, both parties can be said to have recruited their leaders from *the same social and economic strata.* That generalization seems warranted when we sketch the socioeconomic attributes of the half-dozen men who led each party.

To say that the major parties recruited their top leaders from essentially the same social strata only partially answers the question of who led the Democrats and Whigs. . . .

. . . upon which groups did the top party leaders depend for financial, intellectual and moral assistance and stimulus? Did men of wealth strongly tend to give their resources, talents, and prestige to the Whigs rather than to the Democrats? Did a large proportion of the business community—however defined—adhere to the Whig faith?

After Jackson's Bank veto message in 1832, and particularly after 1837, when Martin Van Buren awoke to the political possibilities of Locofocoism . . . Democratic rhetoric was designed to sound something like class war. One Whig response to that rhetoric was to portray Democrats as "desperate and revolutionary enemies of Law and Order." . . . But class war rhetoric need not reflect reality. In fact, it has frequently been used to conceal rather than to reveal the socioeconomic status and the political objectives of those who use it. . . .

. . . More precisely, who from 1834 to 1844 took the campaign claptrap literally? Had not partisan rhetoric come to be regarded as another form of American folklore, an oratorical indulgence to be enjoyed at regular intervals and ignored once the election was over and the country again "saved"? . . .

The relative stability of New York voting patterns from 1832 to 1844 . . . suggests that later historians have been more vulnerable to partisan claims than were contemporaries who experienced them directly. Populistic rhetoric had become so standard a feature of election campaigns that voters may well have developed immunity to it. . . . In short, political rhetoric is not a reliable source for inferences about the social structure of American political leadership.

But an 1845 *Tribune* editorial made specific claims, which are subject to verification. "The Whigs are by no means all wealthy, nor are the wealthy all Whigs. A large proportion of the Capitalists, Landlords, Bankers, etc., belong to the other party. For instance, of the manors of this State, we observe that far more than half the leased lands are owned by those who belong to what is called the Democratic party.—Most of the Banks of our City were chartered by that party, and a good many are still controlled by its members and officered from its ranks. The present Collector of Customs at this Port stepped out of a Bank Presidency into the Collectorship. *There are many members of the so-called 'Democratic' party in this city who are worth from $100,000 each to $1,000,000 or over* [italics added]."

The design of this study does not permit the research necessary to test all the claims made in the editorial quoted above. But testing one of them does provide a basis for assessing the *Tribune*'s claims about party divisions among economic elite groups in New York.

1. RATIFICATION MEETING OFFICERS WHO WERE "WEALTHY CITIZENS." In January 1845, the sixth edition of a fascinating social document was published; the lengthy title suggests its contents: *Wealth and Biography of the Wealthy Citizens of New York City, Comprising An Alphabetical Arrangement of Persons Estimated To Be Worth $100,000, And Upwards—With The Sums Appended To Each Name*. . . . If the *Tribune*'s claims are verifiable, the men listed on that roll-call should not have displayed heavily disproportionate preference for the Whig Party. And for our purposes, the publication date could not have been better timed. If the much-advertised Democratic conversion to Locofocoism in 1837 to 1838 had really driven or frightened the "rich men" away, the purge should have been complete by 1844, when the sixth edition was prepared.

In order to carry out this test, some sampling procedure must be devised for an analysis of the register of approximately one thousand *Wealthy Citizens*. Since our aim here is to get at the social structure of party leadership, not the sources of mass support, it is desirable, to find an objective basis for classifying as "middle-grade party leaders" a limited number of "Wealthy Citizens." I believe that the independent criteria used to draw up two separate lists satisfy that requirement.

In New York City, during the 1844 campaign, both the Democrats and Whigs held their customary great public meetings to "ratify" the nominees of their national conventions. Designed to heal intraparty wounds and to rally the faithful against the enemy, these meetings followed standard formats. Much the same considerations, we may assume, governed both parties in their choice of the president and many vice-presidents who nominally controlled them. Since the ratification meetings formed an important part of the campaign, in all likelihood politically active men, who can accurately be classified as middle-grade party leaders, were selected for these positions. Although the *Wealthy Citizens* register cannot be considered a comprehensive collective biography, we can learn from it how many of the men who made the honor list at Democratic and Whig ratification meetings also made its pages.

Analysis of the register essentially supports the *Tribune*'s claim about party divisions among the "rich men" of New York City. Of the 54 Democrats honored by their party, the president and 13 vice-presidents, or 26 per cent, were "Wealthy Citizens." Of the 35 Whigs honored by their party, 12 vice-presidents, or 34 per cent, belonged to the same class. Not large enough to be significant in any case, the percentage difference disappears when *the same size sample is used*. Neither party was alphabetical. Men's party status as well as their prestige in the community apparently determined their rank order position. Thus, of the first 10 names on each list, 60 per cent were "Wealthy Citizens." When we restrict analysis to the 35 highest ranking Democrats (the total number in the Whig sample), the proportion of Democratic rich men rises to 34 per cent. On this level of leadership, therefore, the Democrats and the Whigs had drawn upon rich men in the same proportion. Using another criterion to select a sample of rich, middle-grade party leaders, we get the same results.

Aside from supporting the *Tribune*'s claims, our analysis of party divisions among New York's wealthy citizens is also consonant with our findings about the top Democratic and Whig leaders. I do not claim to have "proved" that the men who led and controlled both major parties in New York belonged to the same socioeconomic strata. I do claim, however, that the above data make that hypothesis appear potentially verifiable. If subsequent research does verify it, and if the same situation is found to have obtained elsewhere during the 1840's, American historians will be confronted by this interesting and difficult question: what, if anything, differentiated men who belonged to the same socioeconomic strata but who led parties that advocated different and directly conflicting theories of liberalism? For, as I shall now try to show, contrary to the concept of Jacksonian Democracy, party battles in New York cannot be viewed primarily as battles between "liberals" and "conservatives."

[From Lee Benson, *The Concept of Jacksonian Democracy: New York as a Test Case* (Princeton, N.J.: Princeton University Press, 1961), pp. 64–66, 68]

Questions for Reflection

Describe the two groups, or classes, that Schlesinger says were pitted against each other in the Jacksonian era. How do those groups differ from the two clashing groups described by Hammond?

What does Schlesinger mean by the "hard money doctrine"? How was "hard money" supposed to help one group and hurt another? Explain the five groups which comprised the combination against the Bank of the United States. (Chestnut Street refers to the Philadelphia headquarters of the Bank of the United States; Wall Street refers to New York and the community of state-chartered banks which were hostile to the Bank of the United States.)

What is Lee Benson's first key assertion about the similarities and differences of Democrats and Whigs in New York State? Why is Benson wise not to be content simply with a comparison of top leaders of the two parties?

(Locofocoism refers to the urban radical element of the Democratic Party in New York State.) Why does Benson say that "class war rhetoric need not reflect reality"? What caution should we learn from his other statement, "political rhetoric is not a reliable source for inferences about the social structure of American political leadership"?

Benson uses a special method to verify the assertion of the *Tribune* about Whigs and Democrats. Explain his method for verifying the claim. Is his method sound?

Notice how carefully his final assertion here is worded. What does Benson claim to have proved? If his proof is accepted, what implications does Benson's work have for the assertions by Schlesinger and Hammond? Overall, what does this section tell you about the scholarship on the Jacksonian period?

ANSWERS TO MULTIPLE-CHOICE AND TRUE-FALSE QUESTIONS

Multiple-Choice Questions

1-C, 2-C, 3-D, 4-B, 5-B, 6-B, 7-C, 8-D

True-False Questions

1-F, 2-T, 3-F, 4-T, 5-F, 6-F, 7-F, 8-F

11

THE DYNAMICS OF GROWTH

CHAPTER OBJECTIVES

After you complete the reading and study of this chapter you should be able to

1. Explain changes in agriculture from 1800 to 1860 and describe their social and economic impact.
2. List and describe improvements in transportation from 1800 to 1860.
3. Analyze the significant advances in technology from 1800 to 1860 and their impact on society.
4. Account for the emergence of the factory as a method of production and assess its social impact.
5. Explain how the growth of manufacturing affected urbanization, and vice versa.
6. Describe the nature of immigration prior to 1860 and the reaction of previously settled Americans to this new immigration.
7. Analyze the early development of labor unions and account for their failure to gain widespread acceptance.
8. Describe and explain the distribution of wealth in the United States in "the era of the common man."

CHAPTER OUTLINE

I. National agriculture
  A. The importance of southern cotton
    1. Invention of the cotton gin
    2. Revolutionary impact of the cotton gin
      a. Effects on slavery
      b. Spurs westward migration
      c. Increases cotton exports
  B. The westward movement
    1. Appalachians to the Pacific
    2. New lands laws
    3. Improvements in iron plow

II. Improvements in transportation
  A. New roads and turnpikes
  B. River transportation
    1. Flatboats
    2. Steamboats
    3. Canals
  C. Railroads
    1. Advantages
    2. Negative effects
  D. Ocean travel
    1. Packet service
    2. Clipper ships
    3. Steamboats

III. Growth of industry
  A. Early textile manufacturing
    1. Persistence of handicrafts
    2. Britain's lead in industry

3. Early American mills
    a. In New England
    b. The Waltham mill
4. Impact of War of 1812
B. Technological advances
  1. Steam engines
  2. Other inventions
C. The Lowell system
  1. Chief features
    a. Large capital investment
    b. Unified management
    c. Minimum skills of workers
  2. Republican characteristics
  3. "Lowell girls"
  4. Transformations in system
D. Family system
E. Industry and growth of cities
  1. Atlantic seaports
  2. Inland river cities

IV. Immigration
A. Continuing need for labor
B. Major ethnic groups
  1. Irish
  2. Germans

3. British
4. Scandinavians
5. Chinese
C. Nativist reaction
  1. Causes
  2. Examples of nativist activity
  3. Nativist organizations
D. Importance of ethnic labor

V. Labor organizations
A. Early urban unions
B. Importance of *Commonwealth v. Hunt* decision (1842)
C. Labor in politics
  1. Working men's parties
  2. "Locofocos" in New York
  3. Impact of parties
D. Workers' cooperatives
E. Revival of unions

VI. Jacksonian inequality
A. Limited reality of "rags to riches"
B. Distribution of wealth
C. Increasing social rigidity

KEY ITEMS OF CHRONOLOGY

Fulton's steamboat sails up Hudson River	1807
First factory founded at Waltham, Mass.	1813
Opening of the Erie Canal	1825
John Deere invents steel plow	1837
Commonwealth v. Hunt	1842
Establishment of the Know-Nothing Party	1854

TERMS TO MASTER

Listed below are some important terms or people with which you should be familiar after you complete the study of this chapter. Identify each name or term.

1. cotton gin
2. Preemption Act of 1830
3. turnpikes
4. steamboats
5. Erie Canal
6. transatlantic packet service
7. Samuel Slater
8. Waltham plan
9. "Lowell girls"
10. nativism
11. Know-Nothing Party
12. *Commonwealth v. Hunt*
13. producers' and consumers' cooperatives
14. John Jacob Astor

VOCABULARY BUILDING

Listed below are some words used in this chapter. Look in the dictionary for the meaning of each.

1. proliferation
2. tempo
3. assuage
4. paternalistic
5. luminaries
6. idyllic
7. haughty
8. chronic
9. infinitesimal
10. nativism
11. fraternal
12. heterogeneous
13. egalitarianism
14. irony

EXERCISES FOR UNDERSTANDING

When you have completed reading the chapter, answer each of the following questions. If you have difficulty, go back to the text and reread the section of the chapter related to the question.

Multiple-Choice Questions

Select the letter of the response which best completes the statement.

1. The cotton gin started a revolution that included
   A. eliminating the need for black slaves
   B. ending cotton exports
   C. migration into the Old Southwest
   D. all of the above

2. Developments in transportation usually occurred in the following order:
   A. railroads, flatboats, canals, and turnpikes
   B. turnpikes, steamboats, canals, and railroads
   C. turnpikes, canals, flatboats, and steamboats
   D. canals, turnpikes, railroads, and steamboats

3. Internal improvements received financial support from
   A. private investors only because government help was unconstitutional
   B. state and local governments only after the veto of the Maysville Road Bill
   C. state governments only
   D. various combinations of government at all levels and private business

4. The first industry to which the factory system was applied in the United States was
   A. steel
   B. food processing
   C. textiles
   D. machine tools

5. One reason factories appeared first in New England was that
   A. the region had failed to succeed in other commercial activities
   B. the states supported early manufacturing with subsidies
   C. its slaves had little cotton to pick and could work in factories
   D. the profits from its trade provided the needed capital to invest

6. Most Irish workers who came to the United States before the Civil War took jobs
   A. as farmhands and storekeepers
   B. as domestic servants and unskilled workers
   C. as machinists and shopkeepers
   D. in the priesthood

7. Prejudice against immigrants in the 1830s and 1840s focused on
   A. German Jews
   B. Catholics
   C. Chinese
   D. Italians

8. In the decades before the Civil War,
   A. American society was becoming more egalitarian
   B. many workers experienced rags-to-riches success
   C. a distinct working class appeared
   D. all of the above

True-False Questions

Indicate whether each statement is true or false.

1. Squatters gained some rights to their land under the Preemption Act of 1830.

2. The Erie Canal, in effect, joined the Great Lakes to Boston.
3. Railroad track first exceeded canals in mileage by 1830.
4. Railroads aided the expansion of manufacturing more than farming.
5. In the early 1800s Americans imported most inventions from Europe.
6. The Waltham Plan for factories stressed employing entire families as workers.
7. The Know-Nothing party was primarily dedicated to restricting immigration and reducing the power of immigrants who were already in this country.
8. In *Commonwealth v. Hunt,* the Supreme Court ruled all labor unions illegal.

Essay Questions

1. Why did cotton farming expand in the nineteenth century, and what effects did the increased production have on the Old South, the Old Southwest, and New England?
2. What were the key elements in the transportation revolution, and how did they help create a national economy?
3. Describe the features of the Lowell system.
4. Discuss the emergence of cities in the antebellum period.
5. Discuss the impact of immigration on the American economy and politics.
6. What did Tocqueville mean by his assertion, "In America most of the rich men were formerly poor"?

DOCUMENT

Immigration into the United States from 1820 to 1860, Listed by Country and Continent

The chart on the next page shows immigration to the United States by country and continent of origin. Study the chart carefully to discern patterns and to make judgments about why immigration patterns changed.

Questions for Reflection

Based on the chart on the next page, explain how each of the following changes occurred:

1. The significant increase in immigration in 1832. From which countries did most of it come?
2. The great decrease in immigration in 1838
3. The significant increase in 1842. From which countries did it come?
4. The major decrease in immigration in 1843
5. The drop in immigration after 1854
6. The increase in Asian immigration in 1854. Is it significant that this increase occurred at the same time overall immigration was decreasing? Explain.

In what years did the heaviest immigration from Ireland occur? From Germany?

Why was immigration from Scandinavia so light compared to some other European countries?

In what year between 1820 and 1860 did the greatest overall immigration occur? In what year did the least immigration occur?

Did the immigration from any one country or area continue to increase steadily from 1820 through 1860? If so, which one? If not, why not?

What country or area, other than Europe as a whole, sent the most immigrants in the 1820s? in the 1830s? in the 1840s? in the 1850s?

What other trends do you see in the chart? What other information would you like to have in order to analyze the trends?

Year	All countries	All Europe	Britain	Ireland	Scand-inavia	Other N.W. Eur.	Germany	Italy	Asia	South and Central America	Africa
1860	153,640	141,209	29,737	48,637	840	5,278	54,491	1,019	5,476	6,343	126
1859	121,282	110,949	26,163	35,216	1,590	3,727	41,784	932	3,461	5,466	11
1858	123,126	111,354	28,956	26,873	2,662	4,580	45,310	1,240	5,133	5,821	17
1857	251,306	216,224	58,479	54,361	2,747	6,879	91,781	1,007	5,945	6,811	25
1856	200,436	186,083	44,658	54,349	1,330	12,403	71,028	1,365	4,747	9,058	6
1855	200,877	187,729	47,572	49,627	1,349	14,571	71,918	1,052	5,540	9,260	14
1854	427,833	405,542	58,647	101,606	4,222	23,070	215,009	1,263	13,100	8,533	—
1853	368,645	361,576	37,576	162,649	3,396	14,205	141,946	555	47	6,030	8
1852	371,603	362,484	40,699	159,548	4,106	11,278	145,918	351	4	7,695	—
1851	379,466	369,510	51,487	221,253	2,438	20,905	72,482	447	2	9,703	3
1850	369,980	308,323	51,085	164,004	1,589	11,470	78,896	431	7	15,768	—
1849	297,024	286,501	55,132	159,398	3,481	7,634	60,235	209	11	8,904	3
1848	226,527	218,025	35,159	112,934	1,113	9,877	58,465	241	8	7,989	10
1847	234,968	229,117	23,302	105,536	1,320	24,336	74,281	164	12	5,231	—
1846	154,416	146,315	22,180	51,752	2,030	12,303	57,561	151	11	5,525	1
1845	114,371	109,301	19,210	44,821	982	9,466	34,355	137	6	5,035	4
1844	78,615	74,745	14,353	33,490	1,336	4,343	20,731	141	6	3,740	14
1843	52,496	49,013	8,430	19,670	1,777	4,364	14,441	117	11	2,854	6
1842	104,565	99,945	22,005	51,342	588	5,361	20,370	100	8	3,944	3
1841	80,289	76,216	16,188	37,772	226	6,077	15,291	179	3	3,429	14
1840	84,066	80,126	2,613	39,430	207	7,978	29,704	37	1	3,815	6
1839	68,069	64,148	10,271	23,963	380	7,891	21,028	84			
1838	38,914	34,070	5,420	12,645	112	3,839	11,683	86			
1837	79,340	71,039	12,218	28,508	399	5,769	23,740	36			
1836	76,242	70,465	13,106	30,578	473	5,189	20,707	115			
1835	45,374	41,987	8,970	20,927	68	3,369	8,311	60			
1834	65,365	57,510	10,490	24,474	66	4,468	17,686	105			
1833	58,640	29,111	4,916	8,648	189	5,355	6,988	1,699			
1832	60,482	34,193	5,331	12,436	334	5,695	10,194	3			
1831	22,633	13,039	2,475	5,772	36	2,277	2,413	28			
1830	23,322	7,217	1,153	2,721	19	1,305	1,906	9			
1829	22,520	12,523	3,179	7,415	30	1,065	597	23			
1828	27,382	24,729	5,352	12,488	60	4,700	1,851	34			
1827	18,875	16,719	4,186	9,766	28	1,829	432	35			
1826	10,837	9,751	2,319	5,408	26	968	511	57			
1825	10,199	8,543	2,095	4,888	18	719	450	75			
1824	7,912	4,965	1,264	2,345	20	671	230	45			
1823	6,354	4,016	1,100	1,908	7	528	183	33			
1822	6,911	4,418	1,221	2,267	28	522	148	35			
1821	9,127	5,936	3,210	1,518	24	521	383	63			
1820	8,385	7,691	2,410	3,614	23	452	968	30			

The pattern for the remaining years is stable.

[*Historical Statistics of the United States* (Washington, D.C.: 1961), pp. 56–59]

ANSWERS TO MULTIPLE-CHOICE
AND TRUE-FALSE QUESTIONS

Multiple-Choice Questions

1-C, 2-B, 3-D, 4-C, 5-D, 6-B, 7-B, 8-C

True-False Questions

1-T, 2-F, 3-F, 4-F, 5-T, 6-F, 7-T, 8-F

12

AN AMERICAN RENAISSANCE: ROMANTICISM AND REFORM

CHAPTER OBJECTIVES

After you complete the reading and study of this chapter you should be able to

1. Describe the religious denominations developed after the Enlightenment.
2. Account for the Second Great Awakening and trace its impact on society.
3. Explain the nature of transcendentalism and describe its impact on the intellectual life of the United States.
4. List the major literary figures of the antebellum period and describe their contributions.
5. Describe the stirrings for improvement in education.
6. Explain the impetus for reform and show its manifestations in temperance, prisons, asylums, and women's rights.
7. Account for the movement for utopian communities and describe significant examples.

CHAPTER OUTLINE

I. The Enlightenment's impact on nineteenth-century America

A. Concept of America's mission
B. Three new rational religions
   1. Deism
      a. The Master Clockmaker
      b. Jefferson and Franklin
   2. Unitarianism
      a. Centered in Boston
      b. Role of William Ellery Channing
   3. Universalism
      a. Appeal to more humble people
      b. Stresses salvation of all

II. The Second Great Awakening
A. The frontier phase of revivalism
   1. Rise of the camp meeting
   2. Role of the Baptists
   3. Impact of the Methodists' circuit riders
B. The "Burned-Over District" in New York
   1. Importance of Charles G. Finney
   2. Nature of Oberlin College
   3. Mormons
      a. Founded by Joseph Smith, Jr.
      b. Led by Brigham Young
      c. Church's characteristics

III. Romanticism in America
A. Transcendentalism as expression of romanticism
   1. Origin and nature of transcendentalism

2. Transcendental Club
B. Role of Ralph Waldo Emerson
  1. Writer and speaker
  2. Optimistic, self-reliant
C. Importance of Henry David Thoreau
  1. A different drummer
  2. Walden Pond experiment
  3. "Civil Disobedience"
D. Impact of transcendentalism

IV. The flowering of American literature
A. Emily Dickinson
B. Nathaniel Hawthorne
C. Edgar Allan Poe
D. Herman Melville
E. Walt Whitman
F. The popular press
  1. Technological advances
  2. Sensational New York papers
  3. Horace Greeley's New York
    Tribune

V. Education
A. Level of literacy
B. Early public schools
  1. Need for literate electorate
  2. Education for social reform
  3. Horace Mann's efforts
  4. Lagging of South
C. Higher education
  1. Post-revolution surge
  2. Conflicts over funding and curricula

3. For women
VI. Reform movements
A. Roots of reform
B. Varieties of reform
C. Temperance
  1. Rate of alcohol consumption
  2. Arguments for temperance
  3. Formation of American
    Temperance Union (1833)
  4. State and local efforts
D. Prison reform
  1. Idea of penitentiary
  2. Auburn Penitentiary in New York
E. Asylums for insane
  1. Growth of public facilities
  2. Dorothea Dix
F. Crusade for women's rights
  1. Women's roles and status in
    antebellum era
  2. Seneca Falls Convention (1848)
  3. Declaration of Sentiments
  4. Obstacles to movement
  5. Successes of movement
  6. Women in professions
  7. Margaret Fuller
G. Utopian communities
  1. Proliferation in nineteenth century
  2. Importance of the Shakers
  3. Nature of the Oneida community
  4. The secular New Harmony
  5. The significance of Brook Farm
  6. Impact of utopian efforts

KEY ITEMS OF CHRONOLOGY

Second Great Awakening begins	1800
First free public secondary school opened	1821
American Unitarian Association formed	1826
Mormon church founded	1830
American Temperance Union founded	1833
Seneca Falls conference on women's rights	1848
Oneida Community started	1848
The Scarlet Letter	1850
Moby Dick	1851
Walden	1854
Leaves of Grass	1855

TERMS TO MASTER

Listed below are some important terms or people with which you should be familiar after you complete the study of this chapter. Identify each name or term.

1. deism
2. Unitarianism
3. Universalism
4. Charles Grandison Finney
5. Mormons
6. Brigham Young
7. romanticism
8. transcendentalism
9. Ralph Waldo Emerson
10. Henry David Thoreau
11. "Civil Disobedience"
12. Nathaniel Hawthorne
13. Walt Whitman
14. Horace Greeley
15. Horace Mann
16. Oberlin College
17. Sylvester Graham
18. Dorothea Lynde Dix
19. "cult of domesticity"
20. Lucretia Mott
21. Elizabeth Cady Stanton
22. Margaret Fuller
23. Shakers
24. John Humphrey Noyes
25. phalanxes

VOCABULARY BUILDING

Listed below are some words used in this chapter. Look in the dictionary for the meaning of each.

1. perfectionism
2. remnants
3. inherent
4. depravity
5. degeneration
6. primacy
7. secularism
8. redemption
9. disdain
10. cataleptic
11. exemplar
12. polygamy
13. unrequited
14. allegory
15. obsessive

EXERCISES FOR UNDERSTANDING

When you have completed reading the chapter, answer each of the following questions. If you have difficulty, go back to the text and reread the section of the chapter related to the question.

Multiple-Choice Questions

Select the letter of the response which best completes the statement.

1. Unitarianism
   A. placed emphasis on reason and conscience rather than creeds
   B. drew its conceptions from romanticism
   C. emphasized the sinfulness of man
   D. was centered in Philadelphia

2. The Mormons were founded by
   A. Charles G. Finney
   B. Joseph Smith, Jr.
   C. Brigham Young
   D. James McGready

3. American Romanticism
   A. closely resembled the Enlightenment
   B. showed little interest in the Middle Ages
   C. emphasized the common man's virtue
   D. all of the above

4. A central figure in the American literary world of the mid-1800s was
   A. Washington Irving
   B. Emily Dickinson
   C. Herman Melville
   D. Edgar Allan Poe

5. Proponents argued public schools would
   A. create an informed electorate
   B. reduce crime and poverty
   C. give all children an equal chance
   D. all of the above

6. The yearly per capita (including women and children) production of alcoholic spirits (not including beer, wine, and cider) in 1810 was
   A. 1 pint
   B. 1 quart
   C. 1 gallon
   D. 3 gallons
7. Prison reformers wanted prisons to
   A. punish prisoners severely
   B. rehabilitate prisoners
   C. remove criminals permanently from society
   D. make a substantial profit
8. The organized movement for women's rights had its origins in
   A. the Second Great Awakening
   B. the lyceum movement
   C. transcendentalism
   D. a split in the antislavery movement

True-False Questions

Indicate whether each statement is true or false.

1. Charles G. Finney was the leading revivalist in the Second Great Awakening.
2. The camp meeting was a crucial event for Unitarians.
3. The leading transcendentalist was Ralph Waldo Emerson.

4. Emily Dickinson was a popular poet in New England in the 1850s.
5. Horace Greeley wrote *The Leatherstocking Tales.*
6. In the nineteenth century Americans had the highest literacy rate in the Western world.
7. When Oberlin College opened in 1833, it admitted both women and blacks.
8. The most successful utopian communities were those based on sexual liberation.

Essay Questions

1. Explain how Unitarianism and Universalism were rooted in both the Enlightenment and Puritanism, and compare the two religions.
2. What caused the Second Great Awakening and what changes did it bring to organized society?
3. Briefly describe the leading literary figures of the American Renaissance. What, if anything, did they have in common?
4. Describe the growth of the popular press in the early nineteenth century.
5. Explain the discrimination encountered by women in education and other areas in the early nineteenth century. Discuss the major efforts they made to overcome discrimination.
6. What were the major efforts at utopian communities, and why did so many emerge between 1820 and 1860?

DOCUMENT

The Women's Declaration of Sentiments

When the first women's rights convention met in Seneca Falls, New York, in 1848, it adopted the following declaration, based on the phrasing of the Declaration of Independence. The document was an attempt to summarize the major grievances of women at the time. As you read it, notice the parallels with the Declaration of Independence. (Compare the two by looking at the latter in the Appendix to your textbook.) Notice also the grievances described by the convention.

When, in the course of human events, it becomes necessary for one portion of the family of man to assume among the people of the earth a position different from that which they have hitherto occupied, but one to which the laws of nature and of nature's God entitle them, a decent respect to the opinions of mankind requires that they should declare the causes that impel them to such a course.

We hold these truths to be self-evident that all men and women are created equal; that they are endowed by their Creator with certain inalienable rights. . . . [The wording which is omitted here is almost verbatim from the Declaration of Independence.]

Such has been the patient sufferance of the women under this government, and such is now the necessity which constrains them to demand the equal station to which they are entitled.

The history of mankind is a history of repeated injuries and usurpations on the part of man toward woman, having in direct object the establishment of an absolute tyranny over her. To prove this, let facts be submitted to a candid world.

He has never permitted her to exercise her inalienable right to the elective franchise.

He has compelled her to submit to laws, in the formation of which she had no voice.

He has withheld from her rights which are given to the most ignorant and degraded men—both natives and foreigners.

Having deprived her of this first right of a citizen, the elective franchise, thereby leaving her without representation in the halls of legislation, he has oppressed her on all sides.

He has made her, if married, in the eye of the law, civilly dead.

He has taken from her all right in property, even to the wages she earns.

He has made her, morally, an irresponsible being, as she can commit many crimes with impunity, provided they be done in the presence of her husband. In the covenant of marriage, she is compelled to promise obedience to her husband, he becoming, to all intents and purposes, her master—the law giving him power to deprive her of her liberty, and to administer chastisement.

He has so framed the laws of divorce, as to what shall be the proper causes, and in case of separation, to whom the guardianship of the children shall be given, as to be wholly regardless of the happiness of women—the law, in all cases, going upon a false supposition of the supremacy of man, and giving all power into his hands.

After depriving her of all rights as a married woman, if single, and the owner of property, he has taxed her to support a government which recognizes her only when her property can be made profitable to it.

He has monopolized nearly all the profitable employments, and from those she is permitted to follow, she receives but a scanty remuneration. He closes against her all the avenues to wealth and distinction which he considers most honorable to himself. As a teacher of theology, medicine, or law, she is not known.

He has denied her the facilities for obtaining a thorough education, all colleges being closed against her.

He allows her in Church, as well as State, but a subordinate position, claiming Apostolic authority for her exclusion from the ministry, and, with some exceptions, from any public participation in the affairs of the Church.

He has created a false public sentiment by giving to the world a different code of morals for men and women, by which moral delinquencies which exclude women from society, are not only tolerated, but deemed of little account in man.

He has usurped the prerogative of Jehovah himself, claiming it as his right to assign for her a sphere of action, when that belongs to her conscience and to her God.

He has endeavored, in every way that he could, to destroy her confidence in her own powers, to lessen her self-respect, and to make her willing to lead a dependent and abject life.

Now, in view of the entire disfranchisement of one-half the people of this country, their social and religious degradation—in view of the unjust laws above mentioned, and because women do feel themselves aggrieved, oppressed, and fraudulently deprived of their most sacred rights, we insist that they have immediate admission to all the rights and privileges which belong to them as citizens of the United States.

Questions for Reflection

Why do you think those attending the convention chose to express their sentiments in a document so closely parallel to the Declaration of Independence?

As you study the list of accusations, do you see any which overlap? (Consider, for example, "never permitted her to exercise . . . the elective franchise" and "compelled her to submit to laws, in the formation of which she had no voice.") Was this a good technique to use?

Which grievances presented in the document remain grievances today?

ANSWERS TO MULTIPLE-CHOICE AND TRUE-FALSE QUESTIONS

Multiple-Choice Questions

1-A, 2-B, 3-C, 4-A, 5-D, 6-D, 7-B, 8-D

True-False Questions

1-T, 2-F, 3-T, 4-F, 5-F, 6-T, 7-T, 8-F

13

MANIFEST DESTINY

CHAPTER OBJECTIVES

After you complete the reading and study of this chapter you should be able to

1. Account for Tyler's difficulties with Congress and explain the accomplishments of his administration.
2. Explain the issues settled in the Webster-Ashburton Treaty and account for its compromises.
3. Describe the westward surge and trace the impact of settlement in Oregon, California, and Utah.
4. Explain how the annexation of Texas developed.
5. Account for the acquisition of a clear claim to Oregon.
6. Analyze the responsibility for starting the Mexican War.
7. Describe the results of the Mexican War.

CHAPTER OUTLINE

I. Harrison's brief beginning

II. The Tyler years
   A. His position on issues
   B. Domestic affairs
   C. Foreign affairs
      1. Problems with Britain needing solution
      2. Webster-Ashburton Treaty (1842)

III. Westward expansion
   A. The idea of "manifest destiny"
   B. Movement to Santa Fe
   C. Move to Oregon Country
      1. Joint occupation with Britain
      2. Mass migration of Americans by 1843
      3. Difficulties of the journey
   D. Eyeing California
      1. Ship trading with the area
      2. Sutter's colony
      3. Frémont's activities
      4. Efforts to acquire California

IV. Annexing Texas
   A. American settlements
      1. Role of Stephen F. Austin
      2. Mexico prohibits immigration
   B. Independence for Texas
      1. American demands
      2. Santa Anna's actions
      3. Independence declared
   C. War for Texas independence
      1. Battle of the Alamo
      2. Role of Sam Houston
      3. Santa Anna's trade
   D. The Republic of Texas
      1. Role of Sam Houston
      2. Efforts for annexation
         a. Jackson's delayed recognition
         b. Recognition by France and Britain
         c. Calhoun's treaty rejected

V. The election of 1844
  A. Desire to keep Texas issue out of the campaign
  B. Democrats nominate Polk
  C. Clay's hedging gives votes to the Liberty party
  D. Polk's victory

VI. Polk's presidency
  A. Polk's background
  B. Polk's program
    1. Lower tariff
    2. Independent Treasury
    3. Settle Oregon dispute
    4. Acquire California
  C. Annexation of Texas by Tyler
  D. Acquisition of Oregon
    1. 54° 40' or fight
    2. British hesitancy for war
    3. Compromise treaty

VII. Mexican War
  A. Negotiations with Mexico
  B. Provocation of an attack
  C. The request for war
  D. Opposition to the war
  E. Preparation for war
    1. Troops compared
    2. Comparisons of other factors
    3. Selection of a commander
  F. Taylor's conquest of northern Mexico
  G. Annexation of California
    1. Frémont's efforts
    2. Republic of California
  H. Taylor's battles
    1. Victory at Monterey
    2. Polk's assumptions and suspicions
    3. Santa Anna's return to power
    4. Battle of Buena Vista
  I. Scott's move to Mexico City
    1. Amphibious attack on Vera Cruz
    2. Troop reinforcements
    3. Attack on Mexico City
  J. Treaty of Guadalupe Hidalgo
  K. The war's legacies

KEY ITEMS OF CHRONOLOGY

Texas declared its independence from Mexico	1836
Harrison's administration	March 4–April 4, 1841
Tyler's administration	April 4, 1841–1845
Webster-Ashburton Treaty	1842
Texas formally annexed	December 1845
Polk's administration	1845–1849
Oregon Treaty	1846
Mexican War	1846–1848
Settlement of Salt Lake by the Mormons	1847

TERMS TO MASTER

Listed below are some important terms or people with which you should be familiar after you complete the study of this chapter. Identify each name or term.

1. John Tyler
2. Webster-Ashburton Treaty
3. "manifest destiny"
4. John Charles Frémont
5. Stephen F. Austin
6. Battle of the Alamo
7. Sam Houston
8. Santa Anna
9. Liberty party
10. "Fifty-four forty or fight"
11. Zachary Taylor
12. Stephen W. Kearny
13. Winfield Scott
14. Treaty of Guadalupe Hidalgo

VOCABULARY BUILDING

Listed below are some words used in this chapter. Look in the dictionary for the meaning of each term not defined here for you.

1. peevish
2. impressment
3. motley
4. tutelage
5. foil
6. hedge
7. unilateral
8. goad
9. capitulate
10. *hacienda*—Spanish word for house

EXERCISES FOR UNDERSTANDING

When you have completed reading the chapter, answer each of the following questions. If you have difficulty, go back to the text and reread the section of the chapter related to the question.

Multiple-Choice Questions

Select the letter of the response which best completes the statement.

1. Clay's program for the United States in the early 1840s did not include
   A. repeal of the Independent Treasury
   B. establishment of a third National Bank
   C. distribution of government funds to the states
   D. reductions in the tariff

2. Early traders between Independence and Santa Fe discovered
   A. that Mexico tightly controlled its northern territory
   B. the technique of traveling in caravans for protection
   C. that wagons could not go across the mountains and the plains
   D. the many admirable qualities of the Mexican people

3. The leading explorer and publicist of the Far West was
   A. John A. Sutter
   B. Christopher "Kit" Carson
   C. Stephen F. Austin
   D. John Charles Frémont

4. In the 1844 presidential election, James K. Polk
   A. was the first candidate to win the presidency with a minority of the popular vote
   B. carried New York because the Liberty party drew votes from Henry Clay
   C. advocated expansionism
   D. all of the above

5. Opponents of the war with Mexico included
   A. New England abolitionists
   B. a majority in the U.S. Congress
   C. residents of the Mississippi valley
   D. all of the above

6. According to the Treaty of Guadalupe Hidalgo, the United States
   A. forfeited all claims above the 54° 40' line
   B. received $15 million from Mexico
   C. gained California and New Mexico
   D. prohibited slavery in Texas

7. The Mexican War created a presidential contender in
   A. Zachary Taylor
   B. Winfield Scott
   C. neither of the above
   D. both of the above

8. Important "firsts" achieved by the United States in the Mexican War included
   A. the first successful offensive war
   B. the first foreign war fought by Americans
   C. the first combat experience of later Civil War generals
   D. all of the above

True-False Questions

Indicate whether each statement is true or false.

1. John Tyler was the first vice-president to succeed to the presidency on the death of a president.
2. The slave trade was a major issue separating the U.S. and Britain in the 1840s.
3. At the time of the Texas rebellion, ten times more Americans than Mexicans lived in Texas.
4. James K. Polk achieved few of his objectives as president.
5. The controversy over the Oregon territory was finally settled only by a brief war with Britain.
6. Zachary Taylor commanded the forces that seized California.
7. President Polk engineered Santa Anna's return to power in Mexico, from which position he was better able to fight the United States.
8. The United States sought no territory in the Mexican War but instead wanted to defend the principles of democracy and liberty.

Essay Questions

1. What attracted migrants to different areas of the Far West?
2. Why is James K. Polk often considered a successful president? Do you agree?
3. Explain the origins and results of the Mexican War.
4. Compare and contrast the resolution of American disputes in the Southwest with Mexico and in the Northwest with Great Britain.

DOCUMENTS

Document 1. Polk's Request for War with Mexico

In May 1846 President Polk sent to Congress the following message recounting the problems with Mexico and asking for war based on what he described as Mexico's aggressive action. As you read the excerpts of the message below, look for evidence that Mexico is guilty of aggression. See also if you can find any indication that Polk is not giving the full facts of the situation.

Washington, May 11, 1846

To the Senate and House of Representatives:
    The existing state of the relations between the United States and Mexico renders it proper that I should bring the subject to the consideration of Congress. In my message at the commencement of your present session the state of these relations, the causes which led to the suspension of diplomatic intercourse between the two countries in March, 1845, and the long-continued and unredressed wrongs and injuries committed by the Mexican Government on citizens of the United States in their persons and property were briefly set forth.

    The strong desire to establish peace with Mexico on liberal and honorable terms, and the readiness of this Government to regulate and adjust our boundary and other causes of difference with that power on such fair and equitable principles as would lead to perma-nent relations of the most friendly nature, induced me in September last to seek the reopening of diplomatic relations between the two countries. Every measure adopted on our part had for its object the furtherance of these desired results. In communicating to Congress a succinct statement of the injuries which we had suffered from Mexico, and which have been accumulating during a period of more than twenty years, every expression that could tend to inflame the people of Mexico or defeat or delay a pacific result was carefully avoided. An envoy of the United States repaired to Mexico with full powers to adjust every existing difference. But though present on the Mexican soil by agreement between the two Governments, invested with full powers, and bearing evidence of the most friendly dispositions, his mission has been unavailing. The Mexican Government not only refused to receive him or listen to his propositions, but after a long-continued series of menaces have at last invaded our territory and shed the blood of our fellow-citizens on our own soil.

It now becomes my duty to state more in detail the origin, progress, and failure of that mission. . . .

Mr. Slidell arrived at Vera Cruz on the 30th of November, and was courteously received by the authorities of that city. But the Government of General Herrera was then tottering to its fall. The revolutionary party had seized upon the Texas question to effect or hasten its overthrow. Its determination to restore friendly relations with the United States, and to receive our minister to negotiate for the settlement of this question, was violently assailed, and was made the great theme of denunciation against it. The Government of General Herrera, there is good reason to believe, was sincerely desirous to receive our minister; but it yielded to the storm raised by its enemies, and on the 21st of December refused to accredit Mr. Slidell upon the most frivolous pretexts. . . .

General Herrera yielded the Government to General Paredes without a struggle, and on the 30th of December resigned the Presidency. This revolution was accomplished solely by the army, the people having taken little part in the contest; and thus the supreme power in Mexico passed into the hands of a military leader.

Determined to leave no effort untried to effect an amicable adjustment with Mexico, I directed Mr. Slidell to present his credentials to the Government of General Paredes and ask to be officially received by him. There would have been less ground for taking this step had General Paredes come into power by a regular constitutional succession. In that event his administration would have been considered but a mere constitutional continuance of the Government of General Herrera, and the refusal of the latter to receive our minister would have been deemed conclusive unless an intimation had been given by General Paredes of his desire to reverse the decision of his predecessor. But the Government of General Paredes owes its existence to a military revolution, by which the subsisting constitutional authorities had been subverted. The form of government was entirely changed, as well as all the high functionaries by whom it was administered.

Under this circumstance, Mr. Slidell, in obedience to my direction, addressed a note to the Mexican minister of foreign relations, under date of the 1st of March last, asking to be received by that

Government in the diplomatic character to which he had been appointed. This minister in his reply, under date of the 12th of March, reiterated the arguments of his predecessor, and in terms that may be considered as giving just grounds of offense to the Government and people of the United States denied the application of Mr. Slidell. Nothing therefore remained for our envoy but to demand his passports and return to his own country.

Thus the Government of Mexico, though solemnly pledged by official acts in October last to receive and accredit an American envoy, violated their plighted faith and refused the offer of a peaceful adjustment of our difficulties. Not only was the offer rejected, but the indignity of its rejection was enhanced by the manifest breach of faith in refusing to admit the envoy who came because they had bound themselves to receive him. . . .

In my message at the commencement of the present session I informed you that upon the earnest appeal both of the Congress and convention of Texas I had ordered an efficient military force to take a position "between the Nueces and the Del Norte." This had become necessary to meet a threatened invasion of Texas by the Mexican forces, for which extensive military preparations had been made. The invasion was then threatened solely because Texas had determined, in accordance with a solemn resolution of the Congress of the United States, to annex herself to our Union, and under these circumstances it was plainly our duty to extend our protection over her citizens and soil.

The Congress of Texas, by its act of December 19, 1836, had declared the Rio del Norte to be the boundary of that Republic. Its jurisdiction had been extended and exercised beyond the Nueces. The country between that river and the Del Norte had been represented in the Congress and in the convention of Texas, had thus taken part in the act of annexation itself, and is now included within one of our Congressional districts. Our own Congress had moreover, with great unanimity, by the act approved December 31, 1845, recognized the country beyond the Nueces as a part of our territory by including it within our own revenue system, and a revenue officer to reside within that district has been appointed by and with the advice and consent of the Senate. It became, therefore, of urgent necessity to provide for the defense of that portion of our country. . . .

The movement of the troops to the Del Norte was made by the commanding general under positive instructions to abstain from all aggressive acts toward Mexico or Mexican citizens and to regard the relations between that Republic and the United States as peaceful unless she should declare war or commit acts of hostility indicative of a state of war. He was specially directed to protect private property and respect personal rights. . . .

The Army moved from Corpus Christi on the 11th of March, and on the 28th of that month arrived on the left bank of the Del Norte opposite to Matamoras, where it encamped on a commanding position, which has since been strengthened by the erection of field-works. . . .

The Mexican forces at Matamoras assumed a belligerent attitude, and on the 12th of April General Ampudia, then in command, notified General Taylor to break up his camp within twenty-four hours and to retire beyond the Nueces River, and in the event of his failure to comply with these demands announced that arms, and arms alone, must decide the question. But no open act of hostility was committed until the 24th of April. . . .

The grievous wrongs perpetrated by Mexico upon our citizens throughout a long period of years remain unredressed, and solemn treaties pledging her public faith for this redress have been disregarded. A government either unable or unwilling to enforce the execution of such treaties fails to perform one of its plainest duties.

Upon the pretext that Texas, a nation as independent as herself, thought proper to unite its destinies with our own, she has affected to believe that we have severed her rightful territory, and in official proclamations and manifestoes has repeatedly threatened to make war upon us for the purpose of reconquering Texas. In the meantime we have tried every effort at reconciliation. The cup of forbearance had been exhausted even before the recent information from the frontier of the Del Norte. But now, after reiterated menaces, Mexico has passed the boundary of the United States, has invaded our territory and shed American blood upon the American soil. She has proclaimed that hostilities have commenced, and that the two nations are now at war.

As war exists, and notwithstanding all our efforts to avoid it, exists by the act of Mexico herself, we are called upon by every consideration of duty and patriotism to vindicate with decision the honor, the rights, and the interests of our country.

JAMES K. POLK

Document 2. Rep. Abraham Lincoln Disagrees with President Polk

Polk's statement on the start of the war continued to be a matter of dispute between defenders of the war and its opponents. A young congressman from Illinois who opposed the war challenged the president's version of events. Excerpted below are passages from a speech by Abraham Lincoln on January 12, 1848.

Note that this material comes from the *Congressional Globe*, which paraphrased the statements of congressmen instead of directly quoting them. Thus the frequent use of "he" in the passage refers to Lincoln himself. Read Lincoln's remarks carefully and compare them with the passage from Polk, above.

First, as to the declaration that the Rio Grande was the western boundary of Louisiana, as purchased by France. All knew that purchase was in 1803; and the President himself told us that by the treaty of 1819 we sold the land east of the Rio Grande—to the Sabine, he believed—to Spain. He wanted to make but a single remark upon this point. How the line that divided your land and mine still remains the dividing line after I have sold my land to you, was to him past all comprehension. And how a man, with the honest purpose of telling "the truth, and nothing but the truth," could have ever thought of introducing such a piece of "proof," was equally incomprehensible.

The next point was, the declaration that the Republic of Texas always claimed the Rio Grande as her western boundary. That was not true in point of fact. She did not "always" claim it. She did claim it, but not always. The constitution by which she was admitted into the Union—which, being her last act as a Republic, might be said to be her "last will and testament," "revoking all others"—made no such claim. But suppose it were true that she had always claimed it, had not Mexico always claimed that it was not so? If Texas had always claimed that the Rio Grande was her western boundary, had not Mexico always claimed directly the reverse? So that it was nothing but claim against claim, and there was nothing proved until you got behind the claims, and saw which stood upon the best foundation. And what he here said in reference to these claims of his was equally applicable to all the President said about Texas, under her republican constitution, having always claimed to the Rio Grande; and her laying out her congressional districts, towns, counties, &c., all stood on the same ground. You might just as well say I could get a valid title to your land by writing a deed and signing it, as to say that Texas could get the land of another by, at home, including within her boundary, upon paper, a certain piece of territory, when it was itself where she dare not go. The thing was preposterous!

Next came the declaration that Santa Anna, by his treaty with the Republic of Texas, recognized the Rio Grande as the western boundary of Texas. . . . The fact was, it was nothing more or less than an article of agreement, and it was so called on its own face, entered into by Santa Anna, by which to get his liberty. He stipulated that he would not himself take up arms, nor encourage the Mexican people to do so, during the existing war, leaving it expressly understood that there was no termination of the war. Nobody supposed it was a treaty, because it was well known, as it has many times been stated, that Santa Anna, being a prisoner of war at the time, could not have made a treaty, if he had tried to do so. But he never intended to make—he never made—any such thing. There was no mark, no characteristic about it of a treaty at all.

He next came to notice the declaration of the President, that Texas before annexation, and the United States since annexation, had exercised jurisdiction over the country between the two rivers—the Nueces and the Rio Grande. . . . He did not understand that exercising jurisdiction over territory between two rivers necessarily implied the exercise of jurisdiction over the whole territory between them. . . . He knew, then, from actual experience, that it was *possible* [a laugh] to exercise jurisdiction over a piece of land between two rivers without owning the *whole country* between them. And when you come to examine this declaration, this was just the amount of it.

Questions for Reflection

What does Polk say was the reason he sent an envoy to Mexico? How was Slidell treated by the Mexican government? By the time Slidell was sent to Mexico, the United States had determined to annex Texas. Could that action have had any effect upon the Mexican government's reaction to Slidell? Why or why not?

Why do you think that both Herrera and Paredes refused to receive Slidell? What demands does it appear to you they might have made as a condition for receiving Slidell?

What is the basis for Polk's claim that the Rio Del Norte (Rio Grande) river is the boundary of Texas and Mexico? Is that a valid reason for making the claim?

Why would Mexico have ordered its troops to take action against the troops of the United States? Who was in the right here?

How do Lincoln's arguments counter those of President Polk? When Santa Anna was captured by the Texans in the War for Texas Independence, he made the agreement to which Lincoln refers. Does it seem logical that he would have made a different kind of agreement while a captive than when released? Could he be bound by the earlier treaty?

On the basis of the excerpts here, who is right, Polk or Lincoln? What additional information would you need in order to make a more accurate judgment?

ANSWERS TO MULTIPLE-CHOICE AND TRUE-FALSE QUESTIONS

Multiple-Choice Questions

1-D, 2-B, 3-D, 4-D, 5-A, 6-C, 7-D, 8-D

True-False Questions

1-T, 2-T, 3-T, 4-T, 5-F, 6-F, 7-F, 8-F

14

THE OLD SOUTH:
AN AMERICAN TRAGEDY

CHAPTER OBJECTIVES

*After you complete the reading and study
of this chapter you should be able to*

1. Describe the conditions that helped
   shape the antebellum South.
2. Separate reality from myth in
   descriptions of the antebellum South.
3. Analyze and explain the economic
   development of the antebellum South.
4. Describe and account for the different
   levels of white, black, and multiracial
   society in the antebellum South.
5. Trace the development of the antislavery
   movement in the nation up to the early
   1840s.
6. Explain the major reactions to
   antislavery agitation.
7. Explain some of the significant defenses
   of slavery developed in the South.

CHAPTER OUTLINE

I. Myth and reality in the Old South
   A. Southern mythology
   B. The southern condition
      1. Causal effects of the environment
      2. Human decisions and actions which
         contribute a sense of sectional
         distinction
         a. A biracial population
         b. Highly native population
         c. Architecture, work ethic,
            penchant for the military,
            country-gentleman ideal
         d. Preponderance of farming
   C. Myth of the cotton kingdom
      1. Agricultural diversity
         a. Corn
         b. Livestock
      2. Exhaustion of the soil
   D. Manufacturing and trade
      1. Causes for southern lag
      2. The false image of the planter
      3. Profitability of slavery
      4. South's link to the demand for
         cotton

II. White society in the South
    A. The plantation defined
    B. The planter
       1. Ownership of slaves
       2. Style of life
       3. Overseers
    C. The middle class
       1. Largest group of whites
       2. Land ownership
       3. General style of life

D. Poor whites
  1. General characteristics
  2. Effects of infections and dietary deficiencies

III. Black society in the South
  A. Free blacks
    1. Methods of obtaining freedom
    2. Occupations for free blacks
  B. Slave trade
    1. Statistics of population and value
    2. Prices of slaves
    3. End of foreign slave trade
    4. Trade with Southwest
  C. Plantation slave life
    1. Classes among plantation slaves
    2. Provision of the necessities of life
    3. Work schedules
    4. Punishment
    5. Slave rebellions
    6. Dependency and antagonism
  D. Forging the slave community
  E. Slave religion and folklore
  F. The slave family
    1. Legal status
    2. Importance of the nuclear family
    3. Sexual exploitation of slaves

IV. Antislavery movements
  A. Establishment and work of the American Colonization Society (1817)
  B. The movement toward abolition
    1. David Walker's demand for insurrection
    2. William Lloyd Garrison's call for immediate emancipation
    3. Nat Turner's insurrection
  C. The American Anti-Slavery Society

D. The antislavery movement split
  1. Garrison and the radical wing refuse compromise
  2. Others only want to purge American society of slavery
  3. Showdown in 1840
  4. Garrisonians win the right of women to participate
  5. New Yorkers break away
E. Black antislavery advocates
  1. Conflicts over right of blacks to participate in antislavery activities
  2. Former slaves who became public speakers
    a. Sojourner Truth
    b. Frederick Douglass
F. The Underground Railroad
G. Discrimination against blacks in the North

V. Reactions to antislavery agitation
  A. Suppression of abolitionist efforts in the South
  B. The "gag rule" in Congress
  C. Development of the Liberty party (1840)
  D. Freedom of thought limited in the South
  E. Defenses of slavery
    1. Virginia plan
    2. Biblical arguments
    3. Inferiority of blacks argument
    4. Practical considerations
    5. Slavery better than northern wage slavery
    6. George Fitzhugh
    7. A positive good

KEY ITEMS OF CHRONOLOGY

American Colonization Society founded   1817
William Lloyd Garrison published first issue
    of the *Liberator*   1831
American Anti-Slavery Society created   1833
Liberty party founded   1840

TERMS TO MASTER

Listed below are some important terms or people with which you should be familiar after you complete the study of this chapter. Identify each name or term.

1. Old South
2. mythology
3. staple crops
4. planters
5. yeoman farmers
6. lazy diseases
7. Nat Turner
8. American Colonization Society
9. William Lloyd Garrison
10. Frederick Douglass
11. underground railroad
12. "gag rule"
13. American Anti-Slavery Society
14. George Fitzhugh

VOCABULARY BUILDING

Listed below are some words used in this chapter. Look in the dictionary for the meaning of each.

1. pernicious
2. imperious
3. paucity
4. lethargy
5. malinger
6. balm
7. infinitesimal
8. insurrection
9. expatriation
10. expediency
11. intrinsic
12. organic

EXERCISES FOR UNDERSTANDING

When you have completed reading the chapter, answer each of the following questions. If you have difficulty, go back to the text and reread the section of the chapter related to the question.

Multiple-Choice Questions

Select the letter of the response which best completes the statement.

1. The most important factor in making the South distinctive was
   A. slavery
   B. warmer weather suitable for growing cotton
   C. the lack of immigrants
   D. a belief that the South was distinctive

2. Though usually associated with just cotton, the southern economy also produced
   A. more than one half the nation's corn
   B. nearly all the textiles in the United States
   C. 50 percent of the country's iron
   D. all of the above

3. In a white population of more than 8 million in 1860, the total number of planters (holding more than twenty slaves each) was
   A. about 46,000
   B. about 384,000
   C. about 25 percent of the white population
   D. about 2,300

4. The closing of the African slave trade in 1808 caused
   A. a decline in the westward expansion of cotton growing
   B. a rise in the price of slaves
   C. the slave population to stop growing
   D. an end to slavery

5. To protect themselves, slaves most frequently
   A. violently rebelled
   B. formed unions to negotiate with their masters
   C. malingered or committed sabotage
   D. ran away from their owners

6. The split in the American Anti-Slavery Society in 1840 was over the issue of
   A. the colonization of freed blacks in Africa
   B. the right of blacks to speak in racially mixed gatherings
   C. the right of women to participate in the antislavery society

D. the role of blacks and women in the antislavery movement
7. An important black abolitionist was
  A. Frederick Douglass
  B. Sarah Grimké
  C. George Fitzhugh
  D. all of the above
8. The defenders of slavery
  A. admitted that blacks and whites were equal
  B. ignored the teachings of the Bible
  C. never argued that slavery was practical or profitable
  D. said it was better than northern industrial work

True-False Questions

Indicate whether each statement is true or false.

1. Cotton became the South's most important staple crop only after 1812.
2. Black slaves did work in industry in the South.
3. Scholars now believe that slavery was profitable for slaveowners.

4. Planters (who each owned at least 20 slaves) owned more than half the South's slaves.
5. Most southern whites owned at least one or two slaves.
6. Many slaves became actively involved in revolts against slavery.
7. William Lloyd Garrison advocated colonization as a solution to the evil of slavery.
8. Sojourner Truth was a black abolitionist.

Essay Questions

1. Discuss one way in which the real South differed from the mythical South.
2. Describe the diversity of agriculture in the South.
3. Why did the South lack industrial development before the Civil War?
4. Describe the ways in which slaves showed their resistance to the slave system.
5. Describe the development of the antislavery movement.
6. What arguments did southerners use to defend the institution of slavery?

DOCUMENTS

Document 1. Moses Grandy, Fugitive Slave, Describes Life under Slavery

As the text notes, recent scholarship has given serious attention to narratives and life stories written by former slaves and to later interviews with former slaves. The excerpts below come from a narrative written in 1844 by a slave who had recently escaped from the South.

> ... We had to work, even in long summer days, till twelve o'clock, before we tasted a morsel, men, women, and children all being served alike. At noon the cart appeared with our breakfast. It was in large trays, and was set on the ground. There was bread, of which a piece was cut off for each person; then there was small hominy boiled, that is, Indian-corn, ground in the hand-mill, and besides this two herrings for each of the men and women, and one for each of the children. Our drink was the water in the ditches, whatever might be its state; if the ditches were dry, water was brought to us by the boys. The salt fish made us always thirsty, but no other drink than water was ever allowed. However thirsty a slave may be, he is not allowed to leave his employment for a moment to get water; he can only have it when the hands in working have reached the

ditch, at the end of the rows. The overseer stood with his watch in his hand, to give us just an hour; when he said, "Rise," we had to rise and go to work again. The women who had children laid them down by the hedge-row, and gave them straws and other trifles to play with; here they were in danger from snakes; I have seen a large snake found coiled round the neck and face of a child, when its mother went to suckle it at dinner-time. The hands work in a line by the side of each other; the overseer puts the swiftest hands in the fore row, and all must keep up with them. One black man is kept on purpose to whip the others in the field; if he does not flog with sufficient severity, he is flogged himself; he whips severely, to keep the whip from his own back. . . .

The treatment of slaves is mildest near the border, where the free and slave states join: it becomes more severe, the farther we go from the free states. It is more severe in the west and south than where I lived. The sale of slaves most frequently takes place from the milder to the severer parts: there is great traffic in slaves in that direction, which is carried on by the speculators. On the frontier between the slave and free States there is a guard; no colored person can go over a ferry without a pass. By these regulations, and the great numbers of patrols, escape is made next to impossible.

Formerly slaves were allowed to have religious meetings of their own; but after the insurrection which I spoke of before, they were forbidden to meet even for worship. Often they are flogged if they are found singing or praying at home. They may go to the places of worship used by the whites; but they like their own meetings better. My wife's brother Isaac was a colored preacher. A number of slaves went privately into a wood to hold meetings; when they were found out, they were flogged, and each was forced to tell who else was there. Three were shot, two of whom were killed, and the other was badly wounded. For preaching to them, Isaac was flogged, and his back pickled; when it was nearly well, he was flogged and pickled again, and so on for some months; then his back was suffered to get well, and he was sold. A little while before this, his wife was sold away with an infant at her breast; and out of six children, four had been sold away by one at a time. On the way with his buyers he dropped down dead; his heart was broken.

Having thus narrated what has happened to myself, my relatives and near friends, I will add a few matters about slaves and colored people in general.

Slaves are under fear in every word they speak. If, in their master's kitchen, they let slip an expression of discontent, or a wish for freedom, it is often reported to the master or mistress by the children of the family who may be playing about: severe flogging is often the consequence.

I have already said that it is forbidden by law to teach colored persons to read or write. A few well-disposed white young persons, of the families to which the slaves belonged, have ventured to teach them, but they dare not let it be known they have done so. . . .

The only time when a man can visit his wife, when they are on different estates, is Saturday evening and Sunday. If they be very near to each other, he may sometimes see her on Wednesday evening. He must always return to his work by sunrise; if he fail to do so, he is flogged. When he has got together all the little things he can for his wife and children, and has walked many miles to see them, he may find that they have all been sold away, some in one direction, and some in another. He gives up all hope of seeing them again, but he dare not utter a word of complaint.

It often happens that, when a slave wishes to visit his wife on another plantation, his own master is busy or from home, and therefore he cannot get a pass. He ventures without it. If there be any little spite against his wife or himself, he may be asked for it when he arrives, and, not having it, he may be beaten with thirty-nine stripes, and sent away. On his return, he may be seized by the patrol, and flogged again for the same reason; and he will not wonder if he is again seized and beaten for the third time.

If a negro has given offence to the patrol, even by so innocent a matter as dressing tidily to go to a place of worship, he will be seized by one of them, and another will tear up his pass; while one is flogging him, the others will look another way; so when he or his master makes complaint of his having been beaten without cause, and he points out the person who did it, the others will swear they saw no one beat him. His oath, being that of a black man, would stand for nothing; but he may not even be sworn; and, in such a case, his tormentors are safe, for they were the only whites present.

In all the slave states there are men who make a trade of whipping negroes; they ride about inquiring for jobs of persons who keep no overseer; if there is a negro to be whipped, whether man or woman, this man is employed when he calls, and does it immediately; his fee is half a dollar. Widows and other females, having negroes, get them whipped in this way. Many mistresses will insist on the slave who has been flogged begging pardon for her fault on her knees, and thanking her for the correction. . . .

The very severe punishments to which slaves are subjected, for trifling offences, or none at all, their continued liability to all kinds of ill usage, without a chance of redress, and the agonizing feelings they endure at being separated from the dearest connections, drive many of them to desperation, and they abscond. They hide themselves in the woods, where they remain for months, and, in some cases, for years. When caught, they are flogged with extreme severity, their backs are pickled, and the flogging repeated as before described: after months of this torture, the back is allowed to heal, and the slave is sold away. Especially is this done when the slave has attempted to reach a free state.

In violent thunder-storms, when the whites have got between feather-beds to be safe from the lightning, I have often seen negroes, the aged as well as others, go out, and, lifting up their hands, thank God that judgment was coming at last. So cruelly are many of them used, that judgment, they think, would be a happy release from their horrible slavery. . . .

Document 2. George Fitzhugh Argues the Positive Values of Slavery

A highly different picture of slavery is presented by George Fitzhugh in the excerpts below. This material is taken from his book *Cannibals All!* which was one of several defenses of slavery written by this self-educated planter from Virginia. Fitzhugh was one of those propagandists who viewed slavery as a positive good and warned that the slave system was superior to the system of "wage slavery" practiced in the North. In the excerpt below he warns of the sinister motives of the abolitionists.

The negro slaves of the South are the happiest, and, in some sense, the freest people in the world. The children and the aged and infirm work not at all, and yet have all the comforts and necessaries of life provided for them. They enjoy liberty, because they are oppressed neither by care nor labor. The women do little hard work, and are protected from the despotism of their husbands by their masters. The negro men and stout boys work, on the average, in good weather, not more than nine hours a day. The balance of their time is spent in perfect abandon. Besides, they have their Sabbaths and holidays. White men, with so much of license and liberty, would die of ennui; but negroes luxuriate in corporeal and mental repose. With their faces upturned to the sun, they can sleep at any hour; and quiet sleep is the greatest of human enjoyments. "Blessed be the man who invented sleep." 'Tis happiness in itself—and results from contentment with the present, and confident assurance of the future. We do not know whether free laborers ever sleep. They are fools to do so; for, whilst they sleep, the wily and watchful capitalist is devising means to ensnare and exploitate them. The free laborer must work or starve. He is more of a slave than the negro, because he works longer and harder for less allowance than the slave, and has no holiday, because the cares of life with him begin when its labors end. He has no liberty, and not a single right. We know, 'tis often said, air and water are common property, which all have equal right to participate and enjoy; but this is utterly false. The appropriation of the lands carries with it the appropriation of all on or above the lands, *usque ad coelum, aut ad inferos.* A man cannot breathe the air, without a place to breathe it from, and all places are appropriated. All water is private property "to the middle of the stream," except the ocean, and that is not fit to drink.

Free laborers have not a thousandth part of the rights and liberties of negro slaves. Indeed, they have not a single right or a single liberty, unless it be the right or liberty to die. But the reader may think that he and other capitalists and employers are freer than negro slaves. Your capital would soon vanish, if you dared indulge in the liberty and abandon of negroes. You hold your wealth and position by the tenure of constant watchfulness, care and circumspection. You never labor; but you are never free.

. . . Free society, asserts the right of a few to the earth—slavery, maintains that it belongs, in different degrees, to all.

A common charge preferred against slavery is, that it induces idleness with the masters. The trouble, care and labor, of providing for wife, children and slaves, and of properly governing and administering the whole affairs of the farm, is usually borne on small estates by the master. On larger ones, he is aided by an overseer or manager. If they do their duty, their time is fully occupied. If they do not, the estate goes to ruin. The mistress, on Southern farms, is usually more busily, usefully and benevolently occupied than any one on the farm. She unites in her person the offices of wife, mother, mistress, housekeeper, and sister of charity. And she fulfills all these offices admirably well. The rich men, in free society, may, if they please, lounge about town, visit clubs, attend the theatre, and have no other trouble than that of collecting rents, interest and dividends of stock. In a well-constituted slave society, there should be no idlers. But we cannot divine how the capitalists in free society are to be put to work. The master labors for the slave, they exchange industrial value. But the capitalist, living on his income, gives nothing to his subjects. He lives by mere exploitation.

It is objected that slavery permits or induces immorality and ignorance. This is a mistake. The intercourse of the house-servants with the white family, assimilates, in some degree, their state of information, and their moral conduct, to that of the whites. The house-servants, by their intercourse with the field hands, impart their knowledge to them. The master enforces decent morality in all. Negroes are never ignorant of the truths of Christianity, all speak intelligible English, and are posted up in the ordinary occurrences of the times. The reports to the British Parliament show, that the agricultural and mining poor of England scarce know the existence of God, do not speak intelligible English, and are generally depraved and ignorant. They learn nothing by intercourse with their superiors, as negroes do. They abuse wives and children, because they have no masters to control them, and the men are often dissipated and idle, leaving all the labor to be done by the women and children—for the want of this same control.

Slavery, by separating the mass of the ignorant from each other, and bringing them in contact and daily intercourse with the well-informed, becomes an admirable educational system—no doubt a necessary one. By subjecting them to the constant control and supervision of their superiors, interested in enforcing morality, it becomes the best and most efficient police system; so efficient, that the ancient Romans had scarcely any criminal code whatever.

We warn the North, that every one of the leading Abolitionists is agitating the negro slavery question merely as a means to attain ulterior ends, and those ends nearer home. They would not spend so much time and money for the mere sake of the negro or his master, about whom they care little. But they know that men once fairly committed to negro slavery agitation—once committed to the sweeping principle "that man being a moral agent, accountable to God for his actions, should not have those actions controlled and directed by the will of another," are, in effect, committed to Socialism and Communism, . . . to no private property, no church, no law, no government,—to free love, free lands, free women and free churches.

Socialism, not Abolition, is the real object of Black Republicanism. . . . the agitators of the North look upon free society as a mere transition state to be a better, but untried, form of society.

Questions for Reflection

How long did the slaves work, according to Grandy? How nourishing and appetizing were their lunches? How were young children cared for? How did whites react to their religious interests? How was marriage treated among slaves? What mood pervades this whole selection from Grandy? Does any of the material from Grandy appear to be biased or self-serving? Would he have reason to report other than the truth?

How do you account for the vastly different picture of slavery presented by Fitzhugh? Would he have reason to perpetrate inaccuracies? Is it likely that he believed the image of slavery that he presented?

What general impression does Fitzhugh have of the activities of slaves? Why does he think that wage earners are less free than slaves? Is he correct? How does he view the life of the masters? Explain how he argues that slavery promoted high moral standards and learning as opposed to what was found among factory workers. What fear does he try to raise about abolitionists?

The two images of slavery are vastly different. From reading these two views, what do you learn? Which is probably the more accurate portrayal of slave life? Why?

ANSWERS TO MULTIPLE-CHOICE AND TRUE-FALSE QUESTIONS

Multiple-Choice Questions

1-D, 2-A, 3-A, 4-B, 5-C, 6-D, 7-A, 8-D

True-False Questions

1-T, 2-T, 3-T, 4-T, 5-F, 6-F, 7-F, 8-T

15

THE CRISIS OF UNION

CHAPTER OBJECTIVES

*After you complete the reading and study
of this chapter you should be able to*

1. Explain the controversies which grew
   over the issue of slavery in the western
   lands acquired from Mexico.
2. List and explain the terms of the
   Compromise of 1850 and show to what
   extent those terms were fulfilled through
   1861.
3. Account for the decline of the Whig
   Party and the rise of the Republican
   Party, noting the consequences of the
   change.
4. Explain the controversy over the
   Kansas-Nebraska Act and the resolution
   of that controversy.
5. Explain the meaning and importance of
   the *Dred Scott* decision.
6. Show how the election of 1860
   demonstrated the breakup of political
   cohesion in the United States.

CHAPTER OUTLINE

I. Quarrels arising from the conquest of
   Mexican territory in the Southwest
   A. "The Wilmot Proviso"
   B. Calhoun's resolutions in reaction to the
      Proviso

C. Other proposals to deal with slavery in
   the territories
   1. Extension of the Missouri
      Compromise line
   2. Popular, or squatter, sovereignty
   D. Controversy over admission of Oregon
      as a free state

II. Presidential election of 1848
   A. Democratic candidate and platform
   B. Whig candidate and issues for the
      election
   C. Development of the Free Soil Party
   D. Election results

III. The push for California statehood
   A. California gold rush
   B. Zachary Taylor as president
   C. Taylor calls for admission of
      California as a free state

IV. The development of the Compromise of
   1850
   A. Clay's compromise package of eight
      resolutions
   B. Calhoun's response
   C. Webster's plea for union
   D. Seward's response for the abolitionists
   E. The Foote Committee proposes an
      "Omnibus Bill"
   F. Taylor's death
   G. Fillmore supports the Clay
      compromise
   H. The Douglas strategy of six (later five)
      separate bills
   I. Terms of the Compromise

V. Reaction to the Compromise
  A. Southern states assemble at the
     Nashville Convention
  B. The Fugitive Slave Act
     1. Terms of the law
     2. Northern reaction to the law
  C. The effect of *Uncle Tom's Cabin*

VI. The election of 1852
  A. Democratic nominee
  B. Free-Soiler candidate
  C. Whig candidate
  D. Results of the election

VII. Manifest Destiny on the world scene
  A. Efforts to expand southward
     1. Early efforts to capture Cuba
     2. The Ostend Manifesto
  B. Achievements of American
     diplomacy in the Pacific
     1. Opening of China to Americans
     2. Perry's expedition to Japan
  C. The Gadsden Purchase of 1853

VIII. The Kansas-Nebraska Act
  A. Ideas for a transcontinental railroad
  B. Douglas's Nebraska bill leads to
     repeal of the Missouri Compromise
  C. Antislavery opposition to the
     proposal
  D. Support from Pierce and the South

IX. Northern reactions to the extension of
    slavery
  A. Mob reaction in Boston
  B. Formation of the Republican Party

X. The "battle" for Kansas
  A. Efforts to promote settlement of
     Kansas by free-soilers and proslavery
     forces
  B. The proslavery government
  C. The countergovernment in Topeka
  D. Violence in Lawrence and
     Pottawatomie
  E. The Sumner-Butler-Brooks clash in
     Congress

XI. The election of 1856
  A. The American and Whig parties
     combine their nomination
  B. The Republican choice
  C. The Democratic nominee
  D. The campaign and election
  E. Nature of the Buchanan presidency

XII. The *Dred Scott* decision
  A. Nature of the case
  B. Analysis of the Court's decision

XIII. Movements for Kansas statehood
  A. Legislature vs. convention
  B. The Lecompton Constitution
  C. Buchanan's support for Lecompton
  D. Defeat of the proposal
  E. Postponement of Kansas statehood

XIV. Financial panic of 1857
  A. Causes and nature of the economic
     reversal
  B. Sectional reactions to the economic
     problems

XV. The Lincoln-Douglas senatorial contest
    in Illinois
  A. The candidates and their situation
  B. The Freeport Doctrine
  C. Douglas's efforts to bait Lincoln
  D. Results of the election

XVI. John Brown's raid
  A. The raid at Harpers Ferry
  B. The effects of Brown's raid and
     martyrdom
     1. North
     2. South

XVII. The election of 1860
  A. The Democratic convention
     nominates Douglas
  B. The rump Democrats nominate
     Breckinridge
  C. The Republican convention's
     nominee and platform
  D. The Constitutional Union Party
     formed to support preservation of
     the Union
  E. Nature of the campaign
  F. Outcome of the election

XVIII. Secession begins
  A. Secession of states of the Deep South
  B. Buchanan's reactions to secession
  C. Problems of federal property in
     the seceded South
  D. Last efforts to compromise

KEY ITEMS OF CHRONOLOGY

The Wilmot Proviso introduced	1846
Gold discovered in California	1848
Death of Zachary Taylor	July 1850
Compromise of 1850	1850
Uncle Tom's Cabin	1852
Ostend Manifesto	1854
Kansas-Nebraska Act	1854
Creation of the Republican Party	1854
Dred Scott v. Sandford case	1857
Financial panic	1857
Lincoln-Douglas debates	1858
John Brown's raid at Harpers Ferry	1859
Secession of South Carolina	December 20, 1860
Lincoln's inauguration	March 4, 1861

TERMS TO MASTER

Listed below are some important terms or people with which you should be familiar after you complete the study of this chapter. Identify each name or term.

1. Wilmot Proviso
2. popular sovereignty
3. Free-Soil Party
4. "conscience" Whigs and "cotton" Whigs
5. Compromise of 1850
6. Stephen A. Douglas
7. fire eaters
8. Fugitive Slave Act of 1850
9. Ostend Manifesto
10. Gadsden Purchase
11. "bleeding" Kansas
12. Pottawatomie Massacre
13. Charles Sumner
14. Kansas-Nebraska Act
15. *Dred Scott v. Sandford*
16. Lecompton Constitution
17. Freeport Doctrine
18. Harpers Ferry, Virginia

VOCABULARY BUILDING

Listed below are some words used in this chapter. Look in the dictionary for the meaning of each.

1. expedite
2. proviso
3. sporadic
4. formidable
5. infernal
6. tout
7. ruffians
8. censure
9. recrimination
10. whipsawed
11. junta
12. sinewy
13. tier
14. lament
15. secession

EXERCISES FOR UNDERSTANDING

When you have completed reading the chapter, answer each of the following questions. If you have difficulty, go back to the text and reread the section of the chapter related to the question.

Multiple-Choice Questions

Select the letter of the response which best completes the statement.

1. Lewis Cass's idea of popular sovereignty called for
   A. a national referendum on controversial issues such as the tariff, slavery, and the national bank
   B. the citizens of a territory to decide the fate of slavery in the territory
   C. electing presidents by popular vote without an electoral college
   D. giving blacks, including slaves, the right to vote in national elections

2. The new Free-Soil Party did not include
   A. cotton Whigs
   B. Barnburner Democrats from New York
   C. Wilmot Democrats
   D. Liberty Party members

3. The Compromise of 1850
   A. was one bill devised by Henry Clay
   B. was eight different proposals by Stephen A. Douglas
   C. admitted California as a free state
   D. included a provision to end the capture of fugitive slaves in the North

4. The Kansas-Nebraska Act
   A. provided for popular sovereignty
   B. in effect repealed the Missouri Compromise ban on slavery north of 36° 30′
   C. was a creation of Stephen A. Douglas
   D. is accurately described by all of the above

5. The violence in "bleeding" Kansas involved clashes between
   A. white settlers and Indians
   B. blacks and whites
   C. proslavery and antislavery groups
   D. residents of Nebraska who invaded Kansas

6. The *Dred Scott* decision of the United States Supreme Court involved
   A. a slave who had been taken to live in Kansas
   B. a slave suing for his freedom because his master had taken him into free territory
   C. a former slave who sued for his wife's freedom on the grounds that she had been married to a free black
   D. a slave who had been freed by his master challenged the Fugitive Slave Act of 1850

7. In response to Lincoln's questions, Stephen A. Douglas's Freeport Doctrine
   A. attacked popular sovereignty in the territories
   B. argued that slavery could exist only where local police supported it
   C. endorsed slavery in Kansas and Nebraska but not in Illinois
   D. claimed the *Dred Scott* decision should be overturned by a constitutional amendment

8. When the first states seceded from the Union, the president of the United States was
   A. Andrew Jackson
   B. Franklin Pierce
   C. James Buchanan
   D. Abraham Lincoln

True-False Questions

Indicate whether each statement is true or false.

1. The Wilmot Proviso was an attempt to protect slavery in the territory acquired through the Mexican War.

2. A parliamentary maneuver by Stephen A. Douglas made the Compromise of 1850 succeed.

3. The Fugitive Slave Act actually worked to strengthen antislavery forces in the North.

4. The Ostend Manifesto was an offer to buy Cuba from Spain.

5. The Kansas-Nebraska Act grew out of an effort to develop a transcontinental railroad.

6. John Brown resorted to violence to protect slavery in Kansas.

7. As a result of the controversy over the Lecompton Constitution, Kansas entered the Union as a slave state, even though no slaves lived there.

8. Preston Brooks of South Carolina caned
   Charles Sumner of Massachusetts because
   Sumner had tried to discredit Brooks's
   uncle, Sen. A. P. Butler.

Essay Questions

1. Why was the question of slavery in the
   territories so controversial in the 1840s?
   How did the Compromise of 1850
   temporarily settle the issue?
2. Why did diplomatic efforts of the United
   States in the 1850s often fail to turn

attention away from the sectional
differences and slavery? Which
diplomatic successes did not bring
sectional repercussions?
3. How did the Kansas-Nebraska Act
   attempt to solve the rivalry between the
   sections? Was it successful?
4. Argue the position for or against the
   notion that the Civil War was inevitable.
5. Explain the issues and describe the clash
   of forces in "bleeding" Kansas.
6. Describe the differences between
   Abraham Lincoln and Stephen A.
   Douglas in 1858 and 1860.

DOCUMENT

Dred Scott v. Sandford (19 Howard 393)

One of the momentous decisions of the
Supreme Court and one which worsened
sectional tensions before the Civil War, was
Dred Scott v. Sandford (1857). The opinion
of the Court, written by Chief Justice Taney,
stated simply that blacks had no right to
appear as citizens before a United States
court because they were not citizens of the

United States. The opinion reveals something
of the mentality of southern whites in the
era before the Civil War. Read the excerpts
below for the sentiment in the ruling as well
as the reasoning by which Taney, speaking
for the Court, disallowed black citizenship
and overruled an act of Congress.

This is certainly a very serious question, and one that now for the
first time has been brought for decision before this court. But it is
brought here by those who have a right to bring it, and it is our duty
to meet it and decide it.

The question is simply this: Can a negro, whose ancestors were
imported into this country, and sold as slaves, become a member of
the political community formed and brought into existence by the
constitution of the United States, and as such become entitled to all
the rights, and privileges, and immunities, guaranteed by that instrument to the citizen? One of which rights is the privilege of suing
in a court of the United States in the cases specified in the constitution.

It will be observed, that the plea applies to that class of persons
only whose ancestors were negroes of the African race, and imported into this country, and sold and held as slaves. The only
matter in issue before the court, therefore, is, whether the descendants of such slaves, when they shall be emancipated, or who are
born of parents who had become free before their birth, are citizens
of a State, in the sense in which the word citizen is used in the
constitution of the United States.

The situation of this population was altogether unlike that of the
Indian race. . . . Indian governments were regarded and treated as

foreign governments, as much so as if an ocean had separated the red man from the white; and their freedom has constantly been acknowledged, from the time of the first emigration to the English colonies to the present day, by the different governments which succeeded each other.

The words "people of the United States" and "citizens" are synonymous terms, and mean the same thing. They both describe the political body who, according to our republican institutions, form the sovereignty, and who hold the power and conduct the government through their representatives. They are what we familiarly call the "sovereign people," and every citizen is one of this people, and a constituent member of this sovereignty. The question before us is, whether the class of persons described in the plea in abatement compose a portion of this people, and are constituent members of this sovereignty? We think they are not, and that they are not included, and were not intended to be included, under the word "citizen" in the constitution, and can therefore claim none of the rights and privileges which that instrument provides for and secures to citizens of the United States.

It is not the province of the court to decide upon the justice or injustice, the policy or impolicy, of these laws. The decision of that question belonged to the political or law-making power; to those who formed the sovereignty and framed the constitution. The duty of the court is, to interpret the instrument they have framed. . . .

. . . we must not confound the rights of citizenship which a State may confer within its own limits, and the rights of citizenship as a member of the Union. It does not by any means follow, because he has all the rights and privileges of a citizen of a state, that he must be a citizen of the United States.

It is true, every person, and every class and description of persons, who were at the time of the adoption of the constitution recognized as citizens in the several states, became also citizens of this new political body; but none other; it was formed by them, and for them and their posterity, but for no one else. . . .

It becomes necessary, therefore, to determine who were citizens of the several States when the constitution was adopted. . . .

In the opinion of the court, the legislation and histories of the times, and the language used in the declaration of independence, show, that neither the class of persons who had been imported as slaves, nor their descendants, whether they had become free or not, were then acknowledged as a part of the people, nor intended to be included in the general words used in that memorable instrument.

They had for more than a century before been regarded as beings of an inferior order, and altogether unfit to associate with the white race, either in social or political relations; and so far inferior, that they had no rights which the white man was bound to respect; and that the negro might justly and lawfully be reduced to slavery for his benefit. He was bought and sold, and treated as an ordinary article of merchandise and traffic, whenever a profit could be made by it. This opinion was at that time fixed and universal in the civilized portion of the white race. . . .

We give both of these laws in the words used by the respective legislative bodies, because the language in which they are framed, as well as the provisions contained in them, show, too plainly to be misunderstood, the degraded condition of this unhappy race. They were still in force when the revolution began, and are a faithful index to the state of feeling towards the class of persons of whom they speak. . . . They show that a perpetual and impassible barrier was intended to be erected between the white race and the one which they had reduced to slavery, and governed as subjects with absolute and despotic power . . . that intermarriages between white persons and negroes or mulattoes were regarded as unnatural and immoral, and punished as crimes, not only in the parties, but in the person who joined them in marriage. And no distinction in this respect was made between the free negro or mulatto and the slave, but this stigma, of the deepest degradation, was fixed upon the whole race.

. . . But it is too clear for dispute, that the enslaved African race were not intended to be included, and formed no part of the people who framed and adopted this declaration; for if the language, as understood in that day, would embrace them, the conduct of the distinguished men who framed the declaration of independence would have been utterly and flagrantly inconsistent with the principles they asserted; and instead of the sympathy of mankind, to which they so confidently appealed, they would have deserved and received universal rebuke and reprobation.

And upon a full and careful consideration of the subject, the court is of opinion, that, upon the facts stated in the plea in abatement, Dred Scott was not a citizen of Missouri within the meaning of the constitution of the United States, and not entitled as such to sue in its courts; and, consequently, that the circuit court had no jurisdiction of the case, and that the judgment on the plea in abatement is erroneous.

In the case before us, we have already decided that the circuit court erred in deciding that it had jurisdiction upon the facts admitted by the pleadings. And it appears that, in the further progress of the case, it acted upon the erroneous principle it had decided on the pleadings, and gave judgment for the defendant, where, upon the facts admitted in the exception, it had no jurisdiction.

The plaintiff was a negro slave, belonging to Dr. Emerson, who was a surgeon in the army of the United States. In the year 1834, he took the plaintiff from the State of Missouri to the military post at Rock Island, in the State of Illinois, and held him there as a slave until the month of April or May, 1836. At the time last mentioned, said Dr. Emerson removed the plaintiff from said military post at Rock Island to the military post at Fort Snelling, situate on the west bank of the Mississippi river, in the territory known as upper Louisiana . . . situate north of the latitude of thirty-six degrees thirty minutes north, and north of the State of Missouri. . . .

In considering this part of the controversy, two questions arise: 1. Was he, together with his family, free in Missouri by reason of the stay in the territory of the United States herein before mentioned?

And 2. If they were not, is Scott himself free by reason of his removal to Rock Island, in the State of Illinois, as stated in the above admissions?

. . . Thus the rights of property are united with the rights of person, and placed on the same ground by the fifth amendment to the constitution, which provides that no person shall be deprived of life, liberty, and property, without due process of law. And an act of congress which deprives a citizen of the United States of his liberty or property, merely because he came himself or brought his property into a particular territory of the United States, and who had committed no offense against the laws, could hardly be dignified with the name of due process of law.

. . . And if the constitution recognizes the right of property of the master in a slave, and makes no distinction between that description of property and other property owned by a citizen, no tribunal, acting under the authority of the United States, whether it be legislative, executive, or judicial, has a right to draw such a distinction, or deny to it the benefit of the provisions and guarantees which have been provided for the protection of private property against the encroachments of the government.

Upon these considerations, it is the opinion of the court that the act of congress which prohibited a citizen from holding and owning property of this kind in the territory of the United States north of the line therein mentioned, is not warranted by the constitution, and is therefore void; and that neither Dred Scott himself, nor any of his family, were made free by being carried into this territory. . . .

Questions for Reflection

Summarize Taney's argument as to why blacks had no legal standing in the United States. Did he make any distinction between descendants of slaves and other blacks? What were the implications of this decision for slaveowners in the United States? Explain how this decision affected sectional tensions in the 1850s.

ANSWERS TO MULTIPLE-CHOICE AND TRUE-FALSE QUESTIONS

Multiple-Choice Questions

1-B, 2-A, 3-C, 4-D, 5-C, 6-B, 7-B, 8-C

True-False Questions

1-F, 2-T, 3-T, 4-F, 5-T, 6-F, 7-F, 8-T

16

THE WAR OF THE UNION

CHAPTER OBJECTIVES

After you complete the reading and study of this chapter you should be able to

1. Explain how the outbreak of fighting occurred.
2. Analyze the advantages which each side had in the war.
3. Describe the problems associated with raising an army for both the North and the South.
4. Trace the major strategic and military developments of the Civil War.
5. Explain the political problems of the governments in both the North and the South.
6. Account for the emancipation of the slaves and describe its impact.
7. Describe Confederate diplomatic aspirations.
8. Explain how each side financed the war and the economic effects of the war on the North.

CHAPTER OUTLINE

I. War's outcome not inevitable

II. The start of the war
   A. Lincoln's inauguration
   B. The first conflict
      1. Resupply of Fort Sumter
      2. The South's response
      3. Surrender of Fort Sumter
      4. Lincoln's call for militia
      5. Blockade of southern ports
   C. Secession of upper South
      1. Virginia, Arkansas, Tennessee, and North Carolina
      2. Creation of West Virginia
   D. Fate of other slave states
      1. Suspension of *habeas corpus* in Maryland
      2. Divisions in Kentucky
      3. The battle in Missouri
   E. Personal agonies caused by war
   F. Battle of Bull Run
      1. Caused by naive optimism
      2. Northern retreat

III. A modern war
   A. Scope of involvement
   B. Mechanical, impersonal aspects of fighting
   C. Effects of science and industry
   D. Impact of war on women
   E. Use of a military draft

IV. Early course of the war
   A. Union's three-pronged strategy
      1. Defend Washington and pressure Richmond
      2. Blockade South
      3. Divide Confederacy

B. Confederate strategy
  1. Stalemate with Union
  2. Foreign support
  3. Negotiated settlement
C. Naval actions
  1. Ironclads
  2. Union seizures along southern coasts
D. Activity in West
  1. Grant and unconditional surrender in Tennessee
  2. Battle of Shiloh
E. McClellan's campaign in East
  1. McClellan's character
  2. Advance on Richmond
  3. Lee's attack on McClellan
  4. Halleck replaces McClellan
F. Second Battle of Bull Run
G. Lee's invasion to Antietam
H. Battle of Fredericksburg
I. Results of fighting by end of 1862

V. Emancipation and blacks
  A. War's effects on emancipation
  B. Lincoln's considerations
  C. The proclamation
  D. Reactions to emancipation
  E. Blacks in the military
  F. Thirteenth Amendment

VI. Wartime government
  A. Power in Union shifts to North
    1. Protective tariff
    2. Transcontinental railroad
    3. Homestead act
    4. Other legislation

B. Financing the war
  1. Union's revenues
    a. Taxes
    b. Greenbacks
    c. Bonds
  2. Confederate problems
    a. Failure of tariffs and taxes
    b. Paper money and inflation
C. Confederate diplomacy
  1. Attempts at recognition
  2. Supplies
D. Wartime politics
  1. Union
    a. Pressure of the Radicals
    b. Divided Democrats
    c. Suspension of *habeas corpus*
    d. Election of 1862
    e. Election of 1864
  2. Confederate
    a. Discontent in South
    b. Problems of states' rights

VII. The faltering Confederacy in 1863
  A. Hooker leads the Union
  B. Battle of Chancellorsville
  C. Grant and Vicksburg
  D. Lee and Gettysburg
  E. Chattanooga

VIII. Defeat of the Confederacy
  A. Grant, Sherman, and war of attrition
  B. Wilderness campaign
  C. Sherman through the South
  D. Surrender at Appomattox

IX. Why the North won and the South lost

KEY ITEMS OF CHRONOLOGY

Lincoln's inauguration	March 4, 1861
The guns fire on Fort Sumter	4:30 A.M., April 12, 1861
Emancipation Proclamation (Preliminary, September 1862)	January 1, 1863
Victories at Vicksburg and Gettysburg	July 4, 1863
Surrender at Appomattox	April 9, 1865 (Palm Sunday)

TERMS TO MASTER

Listed below are some important terms or people with which you should be familiar after you complete the study of this chapter. Identify each name or term.

1. Battle of Bull Run
2. *Merrimac* and *Monitor*
3. Battle of Shiloh
4. George B. McClellan
5. Ulysses S. Grant
6. Emancipation Proclamation
7. contrabands
8. "greenbacks"
9. Copperheads
10. Battle of Vicksburg
11. Battle of Gettysburg
12. Robert E. Lee
13. William T. Sherman
14. Battle of Chattanooga
15. Appomattox Court House

VOCABULARY BUILDING

Listed below are some words used in this chapter. Look in the dictionary for the meaning of each.

1. epochal
2. epitomize
3. decimate
4. conscription
5. amphibious
6. unpretentious
7. torrential

EXERCISES FOR UNDERSTANDING

When you have completed reading the chapter, answer correctly each of the following questions. If you have difficulty, go back to the text and reread the section of the chapter related to the question.

Multiple-Choice Questions

Select the letter of the response which best completes the statement.

1. The first shots of the Civil War were fired at
   A. Fort Sumter
   B. Bull Run
   C. Gettysburg
   D. none of the above

2. The Union forces consisted of
   A. volunteers of state militia units
   B. draftees
   C. the Union Army
   D. all of the above

3. In the months after the first Battle of Manassas, most fighting occurred
   A. in Virginia
   B. in sea battles between the navies
   C. along the rivers in and near Tennessee
   D. in Maryland and southern Pennsylvania

4. The Emancipation Proclamation
   A. finally ended slavery
   B. freed slaves in rebellious territory
   C. compensated slaveowners in the border states
   D. began colonization efforts of freed slaves

5. The North financed the war by all the following except
   A. excise taxes and bands
   B. higher tariffs
   C. printing more money
   D. property taxes

6. The Confederate diplomacy was based on their
   A. impressive control of the sea
   B. expectation that European nations would need their cotton
   C. assumption that Europe would want to support revolutionary ideals
   D. expectation that the Monroe Doctrine would force Europe to recognize them

7. On July 4, 1863, Union forces won at
   A. Vicksburg
   B. Gettysburg
   C. both Vicksburg and Gettysburg
   D. Chancellorsville

8. The Civil War ended when
   A. Union forces captured Jefferson Davis
   B. Lee surrendered at Appomattox
   C. Grant captured Richmond
   D. Sherman finished his march in Atlanta

True-False Questions

Indicate whether each statement is true or false.

1. All states with slaves joined the Confederacy.

2. The Confederacy used a military draft before the Union did.

3. The most costly early battle in the war was at Shiloh.

4. The Union forces won the second Battle of Bull Run.

5. Blacks provided about 10 percent of Union Army forces.

6. Union victories at Mobile and Atlanta in 1864 helped Lincoln win reelection.

7. The Union forces won a great victory in 1863 near Chattanooga.

8. Sherman's march through the South was primarily designed to arouse slaves to join the Union Army.

Essay Questions

1. Compare the advantages of the South and the North in the Civil War.

2. How did each side in the Civil War assemble its armies?

3. Why did President Lincoln issue the Emancipation Proclamation? What were its effects?

4. Explain what you consider to be the crucial factor in the North's victory.

5. Describe the course of the war from Lee's defeat at Gettysburg to his surrender.

DOCUMENTS

The Civil War has generated more work for American historians than probably any other event in United States history. One reason for the fascination with the war is that it pitted Americans against each other. The documents that follow are the formal accounts of Gen. Robert E. Lee and Maj.-Gen. George Meade describing their armies participation in the Battle of Gettysburg (July 1–3, 1863), a turning point in the war. Lee's report was a preliminary account written before all the reports had come to him from field commanders. The last few paragraphs are from his more detailed report submitted in January 1864. The Meade account is the formal account written after he had received reports from his unit commanders. You may wish to review in the text George Tindall's description of the battle, and to examine the map of the battle, prior to reading these reports.

Document 1. Robert E. Lee's Account of the Battle of Gettysburg

HEADQUARTERS, ARMY OF NORTHERN VIRGINIA
July 31, 1863

GENERAL: I have the honor to submit the following outline of the recent operations of this army, for the information of the Department:

The position occupied by the enemy opposite Fredericksburg being one in which he could not be attacked to advantage, it was determined to draw him from it. The execution of this purpose embraced the relief of the Shenandoah Valley from the troops that had occupied the lower part of it during the winter and spring, and, if practicable, the transfer of the scene of hostilities north of the Potomac. It was thought that the corresponding movements on the part of the enemy to which those contemplated by us would probably give rise, might offer a fair opportunity to strike a blow at the army then commanded by General Hooker, and that in any event that army would be compelled to leave Virginia, and, possibly, to draw to its support troops designed to operate against other parts of the country. In this way it was supposed that the enemy's plan of campaign for the summer would be broken up, and part of the season of active operations be consumed in the formation of new combinations, and the preparations that they would require. . . . Actuated by these and other important considerations that may hereafter be presented, the movement began on June 3. . . .

Preparations were . . . made to advance upon Harrisburg; but, on the night of the 28th, information was received from a scout that the Federal Army, having crossed the Potomac, was advancing northward, and that the head of the column had reached the South Mountain. As our communications with the Potomac were thus menaced, it was resolved to prevent his farther progress in that direction by concentrating our army on the east side of the mountains. Accordingly, Longstreet and Hill were directed to proceed from Chambersburg to Gettysburg, to which point General Ewell was also instructed to march from Carlisle.

The leading division of Hill met the enemy in advance of Gettysburg on the morning of July 1. Driving back these troops to within a short distance of the town, he there encountered a larger force, with which two of his divisions became engaged. Ewell, coming up with two of his divisions by the Heidlersburg road, joined in the engagement. The enemy was driven through Gettysburg with heavy loss, including about 5,000 prisoners and several pieces of artillery. He retired to a high range of hills south and east of the town. The attack was not pressed that afternoon, the enemy's force being unknown, and it being considered advisable to await the arrival of the rest of our troops. Orders were sent back to hasten their march, and, in the meantime, every effort was made to ascertain the numbers and position of the enemy, and find the most favorable point of attack. It had not been intended to fight a general battle at such a distance from our base, unless attacked by the enemy, but, finding ourselves unexpectedly confronted by the Federal Army, it became a matter of difficulty to withdraw through the mountains with our large trains. At the same time, the country was unfavorable for collecting supplies while in the presence of the enemy's main body, as he was enabled to restrain our foraging parties by occupying the passes of the mountains with regular and local troops. A battle thus became, in a measure, unavoidable. Encouraged by the successful issue of the engagement of the first day, and in view of the valuable results that would ensue from the defeat of the army of General Meade, it was thought advisable to renew the attack. . . .

The preparations for attack were not completed until the afternoon of the 2d. The enemy held a high and commanding ridge, along which he had massed a large amount of artillery. . . . In front of General Longstreet the enemy held a position from which, if he could be driven, it was thought our artillery could be used to advantage in assailing the more elevated ground beyond, and thus enable us to reach the crest of the ridge. That officer was directed to endeavor to carry this position, while General Ewell attacked directly the high ground on the enemy's right, which had already been partially fortified. After a severe struggle, Longstreet succeeded in getting possession of and holding the desired ground. Ewell also carried some of the strong positions which he assailed, and the result was such as to lead to the belief that he would ultimately be able to dislodge the enemy. The battle ceased at dark.

These partial successes determined me to continue the assault next day. Pickett, with three of his brigades, joined Longstreet the following morning, and our batteries were moved forward to the positions gained by him the day before. The general plan of attack was unchanged, excepting that one division and two brigades of Hill's corps were ordered to support Longstreet.

The enemy, in the meantime, had strengthened his lines with earthworks. The morning was occupied in necessary preparations, and the battle recommenced in the afternoon of 3d, and raged with great violence until sunset. Our troops succeeded in entering the advanced works of the enemy, and getting possession of some of his batteries, but our artillery having nearly expended its ammunition, the attacking columns became exposed to the heavy fire of the numerous batteries near the summit of the ridge, and, after a most determined and gallant struggle were compelled to relinquish their advantage, and fall back to their original positions with severe loss.

The conduct of the troops was all that I could desire or expect, and they deserve success so far as it can be deserved by heroic valor and fortitude. More may have been required of them than they were able to perform, but my admiration of their noble qualities and confidence in their ability to cope successfully with the enemy has suffered no abatement from the issue of this protracted and sanguinary conflict.

Owing to the strength of the enemy's position, and the reduction of our ammunition, a renewal of the engagement could not be hazarded, and the difficulty of procuring supplies rendered it impossible to continue longer where we were. Such of the wounded as were in condition to be removed, and part of the arms collected on the field, were ordered to Williamsport.

The army remained at Gettysburg during the 4th, and at night began to retire by the road to Fairfield, carrying with it about 4,000 prisoners. Nearly 2,000 had previously been paroled, but the enemy's numerous wounded that had fallen into our hands after the first and second days' engagements were left behind.

The highest praise is due to both officers and men for their conduct during the campaign. The privations and hardships of the march and camp were cheerfully encountered, and borne with a fortitude unsurpassed by our ancestors in their struggle for independence, while their courage in battle entitles them to rank with the soldiers of any army and of any time. Their forbearance and discipline, under strong provocation to retaliate for the cruelty of the enemy to our own citizens, is not their least claim to the respect and admiration of their countrymen and of the world.

I forward returns of our loss in killed, wounded, and missing. Many of the latter were killed or wounded in the several assaults at Gettysburg, and necessarily left in the hands of the enemy. I cannot speak of these brave men as their merits and exploits deserve. Some of them are appropriately mentioned in the accompanying reports, and the memory of all will be gratefully and affectionately cherished by the people in whose defense they fell.

There were captured at Gettysburg nearly 7,000 prisoners, of whom about 1,500 were paroled, and the remainder brought to Virginia. Seven pieces of artillery were also secured.

Respectfully submitted.

R. E. Lee,
General.

[From *The War of the Rebellion: A Compilation of the Official Records of the Union and Confederate Armies,* Series I (Washington, D.C.: U.S. Government Printing Office, 1889), 27 (Part I): 114–119]

Document 2. Maj.-Gen. George Meade's Account of the Battle of Gettysburg

HEADQUARTERS, ARMY OF THE POTOMAC
October 1, 1863

GENERAL: I have the honor to submit herewith a report of the operations of this army during the month of July last, including the details of the battle of Gettysburg, delayed by the failure to receive until now the reports of several corps and division commanders, who were severely wounded in the battle.

On June 28, I received the orders of the President of the United States placing me in command of the Army of the Potomac. The situation of affairs at that time was briefly as follows:

The Confederate army, commanded by General R. E. Lee, estimated at over 100,000 strong, of all arms, had crossed the Potomac River and advanced up the Cumberland Valley. Reliable intelligence, placed his advance (Ewell's corps) on the Susquehanna, at Harrisburg and Columbia. . . . My own army, of which the most recent return showed an aggregate of a little over 100,000, was situated in and around Frederick, Md., extending from Harper's Ferry to the mouth of the Monocacy, and from Middletown to Frederick.

June 28 was spent in ascertaining the position and strength of the different corps of the army, but principally in bringing up the cavalry, which had been covering the rear of the army in its passage over the Potomac. . . .

On the 30th . . . General Buford having reported from Gettysburg the appearance of the enemy on the Cashtown road in some force, General Reynolds was directed to occupy Gettysburg.

On reaching that place on July 1, General Reynolds found Buford's cavalry warmly engaged with the enemy. . . . Major-General Reynolds immediately moved around the town of Gettysburg, and advanced on the Cashtown road, and without a moment's hesitation deployed his advanced division and attacked the enemy. . . .

Up to this time the battle had been with the forces of the enemy debouching from the mountains on the Cashtown road, known to be Hill's corps. In the early part of the action, success was on our side, Wadsworth's division, of the First Corps, having driven the enemy back some distance, capturing numerous prisoners, among them General Archer, of the Confederate army. The arrival of reenforcements for the enemy on the Cashtown road, and the junction of Ewell's corps, coming on the York and Harrisburg roads, which occurred between 1 and 2 P.M., enabled the enemy to bring vastly superior forces against both the First and Eleventh Corps, outflanking our line of battle, and pressing it so severely that about 4 P.M. Major-General Howard deemed it prudent to withdraw these two corps to the Cemetery Ridge, on the south side of the town, which operation was successfully accomplished; not, however, without considerable loss in prisoners, arising from the confusion incident to portions of both corps passing through the town, and the men getting confused in the streets.

About the time of this withdrawal, Major-General Hancock arrived, whom I had dispatched to represent me on the field, on hearing of the death of General Reynolds. In conjunction with Major-General Howard, General Hancock proceeded to post the troops on the Cemetery Ridge, and to repel an attack that the enemy made on our right flank. This attack was not, however, very vigorous, and the enemy, seeing the strength of the position occupied, seemed to be satisfied with the success he had accomplished, desisting from any further attack this day.

About 7 P.M. . . . [b]eing satisfied from the reports received from the field that it was the intention of the enemy to support with his whole army the attack already made, and the reports from Major-Generals Hancock and Howard on the character of the position being favorable, I determined to give battle at this point; and, early in the evening of the 1st, issued orders to all the corps to concentrate at Gettysburg, directing all trains to be sent to the rear, at Westminster.

At 10 P.M. of the 1st, I broke up my headquarters, which until then had been at Taneytown, and proceeded to the field, arriving there at 1 A.M. of the 2d. So soon as it was light, I proceeded to inspect the position occupied, and to make arrangements for posting the several corps as they should reach the ground.

By 7 A.M. the Second and Fifth Corps, with the rest of the Third, had reached the ground, and were posted as follows: The Eleventh Corps retained its position on the Cemetery Ridge, just opposite the town; the First Corps was posted on the right of the Eleventh, on an elevated knoll connecting with a ridge extending to the south and east, on which the Twelfth Corps was placed, the right of the

Twelfth Corps resting on a small stream at a point where it crossed the Baltimore pike, and which formed, on the right flank of the Twelfth, something of an obstacle. The Cemetery Ridge extended in a westerly and southerly direction, gradually diminishing in elevation until it came to a very prominent ridge called Round Top, running east and west. The Second and Third Corps were directed to occupy the continuation of the Cemetery Ridge on the left of the Eleventh Corps. The Fifth Corps, pending the arrival of the Sixth, was held in reserve.

While these dispositions were being made, the enemy was massing his troops on an exterior ridge, distant from the line occupied by us from 1 mile to 1½ miles.

During the heavy assault upon our extreme left, portions of the Twelfth Corps were sent as re-enforcements. During their absence, the line on the extreme right was held by a very much reduced force. This was taken advantage of by the enemy, who, during the absence of Geary's division of the Twelfth Corps, advanced and occupied a part of his line.

With this exception, the quiet of the lines remained undisturbed till 1 P.M. on the 3d, when the enemy opened from over one hundred and twenty-five guns, playing upon our center and left. This cannonade continued for over two hours, when our guns, in obedience to my orders, failing to make any reply, the enemy ceased firing, and soon his masses of infantry became visible, forming for an assault on our left and left center. The assault was made with great firmness, directed principally against the point occupied by the Second Corps, and was repelled with equal firmness by the troops of that corps. . . . This terminated the battle, the enemy retiring to his lines, leaving the field strewn with his dead and wounded, and numerous prisoners in our hands.

On the morning of the 4th, reconnaissances developed that the enemy had drawn back his left flank, but maintained his position in front of our left, apparently assuming a new line parallel to the mountains.

On the morning of the 5th, it was ascertained the enemy was in full retreat by the Fairfield and Cashtown roads. . . .

July 5 and 6 were employed in succoring the wounded and burying the dead. . . . I determined to follow the enemy a flank movement, and, accordingly, leaving McIntosh's brigade of cavalry and Neill's brigade of infantry to continue harassing the enemy, put the army in motion for Middletown, Md.

The result of the campaign may be briefly stated in the defeat of the enemy at Gettysburg, his compulsory evacuation of Pennsylvania and Maryland, and withdrawal from the upper valley of the Shenandoah, and in the capture of 3 guns, 41 standards, and 13,621 prisoners; 24,978 small-arms were collected on the battle-field.

Our own losses were very severe, amounting, as will be seen by the accompanying return, to 2,834 killed, 13,709 . . . wounded, and 6,643 missing; in all, 23,286. . . .

It is impossible in a report of this nature to enumerate all the instances of gallantry and good conduct which distinguished such a hard-fought field as Gettysburg. . . . I will only add my tribute to the heroic bravery of the whole army, officers and men, which, under the blessing of Divine Providence, enabled a crowning victory to be obtained, which I feel confident the country will never cease to bear in grateful remembrance.

Very respectfully, your obedient servant,

Geo. G. Meade,
Major-General, Commanding.

Brig. Gen. Lorenzo Thomas,
Adjutant-General, U.S. Army, Washington, D.C.

[From *The War of the Rebellion: A Compilation of the Official Records of the Union and Confederate Armies,* Series I (Washington, D.C.: U.S. Government Printing Office, 1889), 27 (Part I): 305, 307–309, 324–325]

Questions for Reflection

Compare the circumstances that led to the battle from the two perspectives offered here. Why do you think Meade would have given more attention to the details of the troop maneuvers than to the reasons for engaging the enemy? How did both commanders assess the outcome of the battle? How would you describe the tone of these two accounts of the great Battle of Gettysburg?

ANSWERS TO MULTIPLE-CHOICE AND TRUE-FALSE QUESTIONS

Multiple-Choice Questions

1-A, 2-D, 3-C, 4-B, 5-D, 6-B, 7-C, 8-B

True-False Questions

1-F, 2-T, 3-T, 4-F, 5-T, 6-T, 7-T, 8-F

17

RECONSTRUCTION: NORTH AND SOUTH

CHAPTER OBJECTIVES

After you complete the reading and study of this chapter you should be able to

1. Describe the impact of the Civil War on both the South and the North and on the status of freed blacks.
2. Explain the circumstances that led to Radical Reconstruction.
3. Describe the nature and extent of Radical Reconstruction.
4. Explain the process that returned control of the South to the conservatives.
5. Evaluate the contributions and failures of the Grant administration.
6. Explain the outcome of the election of 1876 and the effects of that election and the special arrangements made to conclude it.
7. Evaluate the overall impact of Reconstruction.

CHAPTER OUTLINE

I. Development of a plan of Reconstruction
   A. Military governors in Tennessee, Arkansas, and Louisiana
   B. Lincoln's plan of Reconstruction
      1. Provisions
      2. Implementation in Tennessee, Arkansas, and Louisiana
      3. Congressional reaction
      4. Counterclaims of Lincoln and Congress
      5. Wade-Davis Bill
      6. Lincoln's response to the Wade-Davis Bill
      7. Creation of Freedmen's Bureau
      8. Lincoln's final statement on Reconstruction

II. The assassination of Lincoln

III. Andrew Johnson and Reconstruction
   A. Johnson's background
   B. Radicals' perception of him
   C. Johnson's plan for Reconstruction

IV. Southern state reorganization
   A. Actions taken
   B. Congressional reaction to southern states
   C. Provisions and impact of black codes

V. The Radicals
   A. Joint Committee on Reconstruction
   B. Radical motivation
   C. Constitutional theories of status of southern states

VI. Johnson and Congress in battle
  A. Veto of Freedmen's Bureau extension
  B. Effect of Johnson's Washington's Birthday speech
  C. Congress overrides veto of the Civil Rights Act
  D. The Fourteenth Amendment
  E. Race riots in the South
  F. The congressional elections

VII. Congressional Reconstruction triumphant in 1867
  A. Command of the Army Act
  B. Tenure of Office Act
  C. Military Reconstruction Act

VIII. Constitutional issues and the Supreme Court

IX. The impeachment and trial of Johnson
  A. Failure of early efforts to impeach him
  B. Violation of Tenure of Office Act
  C. The articles of impeachment
  D. The Senate trial
  E. Ramifications of the impeachment

X. Radical rule in the South
  A. Readmission of southern states
  B. Duration of Radical control
  C. Role of the Union League prior to Reconstruction
  D. Blacks in southern politics
    1. Characteristics of black control
    2. Extent of black control
  E. Carpetbaggers and scalawags
  F. Nature of new state constitutions

XI. Achievements of the Radical governments

XII. The development of white terror techniques
  A. Objections to black participation in government
  B. The Ku Klux Klan
  C. Enforcement Acts to protect black voters

XIII. The return of conservative control
  A. Reasons for abandonment of the Radical programs
  B. Duration of Radical control

XIV. The Grant years
  A. The election of 1868
    1. Reasons for support of Grant
    2. The Grant ticket and platform
    3. Democratic programs and candidates
    4. Results
  B. The character of Grant's leadership
  C. Social revolution during Civil War
    1. Reduction in South's power
    2. Allegiance to business
  D. Proposal to pay the government debt
  E. Scandals
    1. Jay Gould's effort to corner the gold market
    2. The Crédit-Mobilier exposure
    3. Secretary of War and the Indian Bureau
    4. Other scandals
    5. Grant's personal role in the scandals
  F. Reform and the election of 1872
    1. Liberal Republicans nominate Greeley in 1872
    2. Grant's advantages
  G. Economic panic
    1. Causes for the depression
    2. Severity of the depression
  H. Democratic control of the House in 1874
  I. Reissue of greenbacks
  J. Resumption of specie payments approved in 1875

XV. Election of 1876
  A. Elimination of Grant and Blaine
  B. Republicans nominate Hayes
  C. Democrats nominate Tilden
  D. Views of the parties
  E. Results of the popular vote
  F. The Electoral Commission
  G. Wormley House bargain
    1. Promises of each side
    2. Promises filled and unfilled
  H. The end of Reconstruction
    1. A betrayal of the blacks?
    2. An enduring legacy

KEY ITEMS OF CHRONOLOGY

Lincoln's plan for Reconstruction announced	1863
Thirteenth Amendment ratified	1865
Creation of Freedmen's Bureau	1865
Assassination of Lincoln	April 14, 1865
Johnson's plan for Reconstruction announced	May 29, 1865
Veto of Freedmen's Bureau Extension Bill	February 1866
Congress overrode Johnson's veto of Civil Rights Bill	April 1866
Ku Klux Klan organized in the South	1866
Military Reconstruction Act	March 2, 1867
Johnson replaced Stanton with Grant as secretary of war	August 1867
House voted to impeach Johnson	February 1868
Trial of Johnson in Senate	March 5 to May 26, 1868
Fourteenth Amendment ratified	1868
All southern states except Mississippi, Texas, and Virginia readmitted to Congress	June 1868
Texas v. White decision of Supreme Court	1869
Grant administrations	1869–1877
Mississippi, Texas, and Virginia readmitted	1870
Fifteenth Amendment ratified	1870
Resumption Act	1875

TERMS TO MASTER

Listed below are some important terms or people with which you should be familiar after you complete the study of this chapter. Identify each name or term.

1. Freedmen's Bureau
2. Wade-Davis Bill
3. "iron clad oath"
4. black codes
5. Radicals
6. Fourteenth Amendment
7. Military Reconstruction
8. Command of the Army Act
9. Tenure of Office Act
10. carpetbaggers and scalawags
11. Ku Klux Klan
12. Liberal Republicans
13. Jay Gould
14. Crédit-Mobilier
15. Samuel J. Tilden
16. Compromise of 1877

VOCABULARY BUILDING

Listed below are some words used in this chapter. Look in the dictionary for the meaning of each.

1. usurp
2. pernicious
3. intransigence
4. repressive
5. inversion
6. foment
7. boor
8. appellate
9. impeachment
10. rescind
11. jaundiced
12. despotism
13. cesspool
14. buccaneering

EXERCISES FOR UNDERSTANDING

When you have completed reading the chapter, answer each of the following questions. If you have difficulty, go back to the text and reread the section of the chapter related to the question.

Multiple-Choice Questions

Select the letter of the response which best completes the statement.

1. Southerners received the right to form new state governments as soon as 10 percent of a state's 1860 voters had sworn allegiance to the United States, according to the Reconstruction plans proposed by
   A. Lincoln
   B. Andrew Johnson
   C. Sen. Benjamin Wade and Rep. Henry Winter Davis
   D. the Radical Republicans
2. The Reconstruction policies of the Radical Republicans were probably motivated by
   A. a humanitarian concern for the former slaves
   B. hopes for Republican power in the South
   C. bitterness over having to fight the costly war
   D. all of the above
3. The Fourteenth Amendment to the Constitution
   A. outlawed slavery
   B. guaranteed citizens the equal protection of the laws
   C. specifically gave the former slaves the right to vote
   D. ended Reconstruction in the South
4. Johnson was impeached for
   A. embezzling federal funds
   B. refusing to obey the Tenure of Office Act
   C. refusing to turn documents over to Congress for their investigation
   D. all of the above
5. In the southern Reconstruction governments, blacks frequently
   A. served as state governors

B. controlled the legislatures
   C. dominated delegations to the national Congress
   D. none of the above
6. The Radical southern governments during Reconstruction
   A. were unusually honest and moral
   B. operated frugally and did not go into debt
   C. refused to aid private corporations such as railroads
   D. gave unusual attention to education and poor relief
7. U. S. Grant was guilty of
   A. refusing to turn documents over to Congress for its investigation
   B. trying to block the implementation of Reconstruction laws
   C. choosing his appointees unwisely
   D. taking funds from the federal treasury
8. The Compromise of 1877 included provisions for
   A. the impeachment of Grant for corruption
   B. an end to Radical Reconstruction in the South
   C. a southerner as Speaker of the House
   D. all of the above

True-False Questions

Indicate whether each statement is true or false.

1. The problem of Reconstruction began in 1865 with the conclusion of the war.
2. The black codes were laws enacted by southern legislatures that were controlled by the former slaves.
3. Congress generally accepted the "forfeited rights theory" in explaining secession.
4. The Military Reconstruction Act did not provide for a radical reconstruction of the South.
5. Scalawags were white, southern-born Republicans.
6. Andrew Johnson was never elected president.
7. The Crédit-Mobilier was involved in trading greenbacks to France for gold.
8. Grant as president sought to encourage

inflation through the issuing of more greenbacks by the federal government.

Essay Questions

1. Discuss the impact of the Civil War on the South, the North, and the slaves.
2. Compare and contrast the Reconstruction plans of Presidents Lincoln and Johnson.
3. Assess the Radical southern governments and their accomplishments.
4. Radical Reconstruction was not imposed until two years after the end of the Civil War and caused bitter opposition from the whites in the South. Would it have been better accepted if it had been imposed in May 1865 instead of March 1867? Explain why or why not.
5. Why was Andrew Johnson impeached? What was the outcome?
6. What were the major provisions of the Fourteenth Amendment?
7. Explain the provisions of the Compromise of 1877 and its effects on the South.

READINGS

Reading 1. Claude Bowers Sees Venal Radicals Torturing the South

Like other significant periods in American history, the Reconstruction era has gone through cycles of interpretation. Some of the earliest scholarly work on the period was carried out by William A. Dunning and his students, who believed that the Radicals sought to impose their rule on the South for selfish motives of personal gain. Later revisionists have considerably altered that view. The passage below comes from a popular account of Reconstruction written in 1929. It presents the negative image of Radical motives and accomplishments.

If Hilaire Belloc is right in his opinion that "readable history is melodrama," the true story of the twelve tragic years that followed the death of Lincoln should be entertaining. They were years of revolutionary turmoil, with the elemental passions predominant, and with broken bones and bloody noses among the fighting factionalists. The prevailing note was one of tragedy, though, as we shall see, there was an abundance of comedy, and not a little of farce. Never have American public men in responsible positions, directing the destiny of the Nation, been so brutal, hypocritical, and corrupt. The Constitution was treated as a doormat on which politicians and army officers wiped their feet after wading in the muck. Never has the Supreme Court been treated with such ineffable contempt, and never has that tribunal so often cringed before the clamor of the mob.

So appalling is the picture of these revolutionary years that even historians have preferred to overlook many essential things. Thus, Andrew Johnson, who fought the bravest battle for constitutional liberty and for the preservation of our institutions ever waged by an Executive, until recently was left in the pillory to which unscrupulous gamblers for power consigned him, because the unvarnished truth that vindicates him makes so many statues in public squares and parks seem a bit grotesque. That Johnson was maligned by his enemies because he was seeking honestly to carry out the conciliatory and wise policy of Lincoln is now generally understood, but even now few realize how intensely Lincoln was hated by the Radicals at the time of his death.

A complete understanding of this period calls for a reappraisal of many public men. Some statesmen we have been taught to reverence will appear in these pages in sorry rôles. Others, who played conspicuous parts, but have been denied the historical recognition due them, are introduced and shown in action. Thus the able leaders of the minority in Congress are given fuller treatment than has been fashionable, since they represented more Americans, North and South, than the leaders of the Radical majority, and were nearer right on the issues of reconstruction. Thus, too, the brilliant and colorful leaders and spokesmen of the South are given their proper place in the dramatic struggle for the preservation of Southern civilization and the redemption of their people. I have sought to re-create the black and bloody drama of these years, to show the leaders of the fighting factions at close range, to picture the moving masses, both whites and blacks, in North and South, surging crazily under the influence of the poisonous propaganda on which they were fed.

That the Southern people literally were put to the torture is vaguely understood, but even historians have shrunk from the unhappy task of showing us the torture chambers. It is impossible to grasp the real significance of the revolutionary proceedings of the rugged conspirators working out the policies of Thaddeus Stevens without making many journeys among the Southern people, and seeing with our own eyes the indignities to which they were subjected. Through many unpublished contemporary family letters and diaries, I have tried to show the psychological effect upon them of the despotic policies of which they were the victims. Brutal men, inspired by personal ambition or party motives, assumed the pose of philanthropists and patriots, and thus deceived and misguided vast numbers of well-meaning people in the North.

[From Claude G. Bowers, *The Tragic Era: The Revolution after Lincoln* (New York: Blue Ribbon Books, 1929), pp. v–vi]

Reading 2. William A. Dunning Explains the Failure of Reconstruction

William A. Dunning, a historian at Columbia University around the turn of the century, wrote a synthesis of Reconstruction from a southern point of view and directed a school of scholars who investigated developments in states in the South from a similar viewpoint. In these excerpts Dunning, while explaining the failure of Reconstruction, reveals his attitude about the corruption and inadequacy of Reconstruction governments and his reservations about race. What insights do you find in his views?

The leading motive of the reconstruction had been, at the inception of the process, to insure to the freedmen an effective protection of their civil rights,—of life, liberty, and property. In the course of the process, the chief stress came to be laid on the endowment of the blacks with full political rights,—with the electoral franchise and eligibility to office. And by the time the process was complete, a very important, if not the most important part had been played by the desire and the purpose to secure to the Republican party the permanent control of several Southern states in which hitherto such a political organization had been unknown. This last motive had a plausible and widely accepted justification in the view that the rights of the negro and the "results of the war" in general would be secure only if the national government should remain indefinitely in Republican hands, and that therefore the strengthening of the party was a primary dictate of patriotism.

Through the operation of these various motives successive and simultaneous, the completion of the reconstruction showed the following situation: (1) the negroes were in the enjoyment of the equal political rights with the whites; (2) the Republican party was in vigorous life in all the Southern states, and in firm control of many of them; and (3) the negroes exercised an influence in political affairs out of all relation to their intelligence or property, and, since so many of the whites were defranchised, excessive even in proportion to their numbers. At the present day, in the same states, the negroes enjoy practically no political rights; the Republican party is but the shadow of a name; and the influence of the negroes in political affairs is nil. This contrast suggests what has been involved in the undoing of reconstruction.

Before the last state was restored to the Union the process was well under way through which the resumption of control by the whites was to be effected. The tendency in this direction was greatly promoted by conditions within the Republican party itself. Two years of supremacy in those states which had been restored in 1868 had revealed unmistakable evidences of moral and political weakness in the governments. The personnel of the party was declining in character through the return to the North of the more substantial of the carpet-baggers, who found Southern conditions, both social and industrial, far from what they had anticipated, and through the very frequent instances in which the "scalawags" ran to open disgrace. Along with this deterioration in the white element of the party, the negroes who rose to prominence and leadership were very frequently of a type which acquired and practiced the tricks and knavery rather than the useful arts of politics, and the vicious courses of these negroes strongly confirmed the prejudices of the whites. But at the same time that the incapacity of the party in power to administer any government was becoming demonstrable the problems with which it was required to cope were made by its adversaries such as would have taxed the capacity of the most efficient statesmen the world could produce. . . . No attention was paid to the claim that the manifest inefficiency and viciousness of the Republican governments afforded a partial, if not wholly adequate explanation of their overthrow. Not even the relative quiet and order that followed the triumph of the whites in these states were recognized as justifying the new regime.

[From William A. Dunning, "The Undoing of Reconstruction," in *The Atlantic Monthly*, October 1901, pp. 437–438]

Reading 3. Eric Foner Contends That Reconstruction Did Not Go Far Enough

Historical scholarship on the Reconstruction era continues to grow at a remarkable rate. In the following excerpt Eric Foner summarizes some of the most recent scholarship and suggests a new way to view Reconstruction.

Despite the excellence of recent writing and the continual expansion of our knowledge of the period, historians of Reconstruction today face a unique dilemma. An old interpretation has been overthrown, but a coherent new synthesis has yet to take its place. The revisionists of the 1960s effectively established a series of negative points: the Reconstruction governments were not as bad as had been portrayed, black supremacy was a myth, the Radicals were not cynical manipulators of the freedmen. Yet no convincing overall portrait of the quality of political and social life emerged from their writings.

. . . a new portrait of Reconstruction ought to begin by viewing it not as a specific time period, bounded by the years 1865 and 1877, but as an episode in a prolonged historical process—American society's adjustment to the consequences of the Civil War and emancipation.

. . . the focal point of Reconstruction was the social revolution known as emancipation. Plantation slavery was simultaneously a system of labor, a form of racial domination, and the foundation upon which arose a distinctive ruling class within the South. Its demise threw open the most fundamental questions of economy, society, and politics. A new system of labor, social, racial, and political relations had to be created to replace slavery.

Few modern scholars believe the Reconstruction governments established in the South in 1867 and 1868 fulfilled the aspirations of their humble constituents. While their achievements in such realms as education, civil rights, and the economic rebuilding of the South are now widely appreciated, historians today believe they failed to affect either the economic plight of the emancipated slave or the ongoing transformation of independent white farmers into cotton tenants. Yet their opponents did perceive the Reconstruction governments in precisely this way—as representatives of a revolution that had put the bottom rail, both racial and economic, on top. This perception helps explain the ferocity of the attacks leveled against them and the pervasiveness of violence in the postemancipation South.

The spectacle of black men voting and holding office was anathema to large numbers of Southern whites. Even more disturbing, at least in the view of those who still controlled the plantation regions of the South, was the emergence of local officials, black and white, who sympathized with the plight of the black laborer. . . . During presidential Reconstruction, and after "Redemption," with planters and their allies in control of politics, the law emerged as a means of stabilizing and promoting the plantation system. If Radical Reconstruction failed to redistribute the land of the South, the ouster of the planter class from control of politics at least ensured that the sanctions of the criminal law would not be employed to discipline the black labor force.

An understanding of this fundamental conflict over the relation between government and society helps explain the pervasive complaints concerning corruption and "extravagance" during Radical Reconstruction. Corruption there was aplenty; tax rates did rise sharply. More significant than the rate of taxation, however, was the change in its incidence. For the first time, planters and white farmers had to pay a significant portion of their income to the government, while propertyless blacks often escaped scot-free. Several states, moreover, enacted heavy taxes on uncultivated land to discourage land speculation and force land onto the market, benefiting, it was hoped, the freedmen.

As time passed, complaints about the "extravagance" and corruption of Southern governments found a sympathetic audience among influential Northerners. The Democratic charge that universal suffrage in the South was responsible for high taxes and governmental extravagance coincided with a rising conviction among the urban middle classes of the North that city government had to be taken out of the hands of the immigrant poor and returned to the "best men"—the educated, professional, financially independent citizens unable to exert much political influence at a time of mass parties and machine politics. Increasingly the "respectable" middle classes began to retreat from the very notion of universal suffrage. The poor were no longer perceived as honest producers, the backbone of the social order; now they became the "dangerous classes," the "mob." As the historian Francis Parkman put it, too much power rested with "masses of imported ignorance and hereditary ineptitude." To Parkman the Irish of the Northern cities and the blacks of the South were equally incapable of utilizing the ballot: "Witness the municipal corruptions of New York, and the monstrosities of negro rule in South Carolina." Such attitudes helped to justify Northern inaction as, one by one, the Reconstruction regimes of the South were overthrown by political violence.

In the end, then, neither the abolition of slavery nor Reconstruction succeeded in resolving the debate over the meaning of freedom in American life. Twenty years before the American Civil War, writing about the prospect of abolition in France's colonies, Alexis de Tocqueville had written, "If the Negroes have the right to become free, the [planters] have the incontestable right not to be ruined by the Negroes' freedom." And in the United States, as in nearly every plantation society that experienced the end of slavery, a rigid social and political dichotomy between former master and former slave, an ideology of racism, and a dependent labor force with limited economic opportunities all survived abolition. Unless one means by freedom the simple fact of not being a slave, emancipation thrust blacks into a kind of no-man's land, a partial freedom that made a mockery of the American ideal of equal citizenship.

Yet by the same token the ultimate outcome underscores the uniqueness of Reconstruction itself. Alone among the societies that abolished slavery in the nineteenth century, the United States, for a moment, offered the freedmen a measure of political control over their own destinies. However brief its sway, Reconstruction allowed scope for a remarkable political and social mobilization of the black community. It opened doors of opportunity that could never be completely closed. Reconstruction transformed the lives of Southern blacks in ways unmeasurable by statistics and unreachable by law. It raised their expectations and aspirations, redefined their status in relation to the larger society, and allowed space for the creation of institutions that enabled them to survive the repression that followed. And it established constitutional principles of civil and political equality that, while flagrantly violated after Redemption, planted the seeds of future struggle.

[From Eric Foner, "The New View of Reconstruction," in *American Heritage* 34, no. 6 (October-November 1983): 13–15]

Questions for Reflection

What evidence is there in the first two readings to show that Dunning found Reconstruction less despicable a development than Bowers did? What good does Dunning seem to imply came from Reconstruction? Select some of the words and phrases which Bowers used to give an emotional tone to his account. Is Dunning more convincing to the reader? What appear to be Dunning's views on race?

What does Dunning mean by "The failure of Radicalism is thus a part of the wider failure of bourgeois liberalism to solve the problems of the new age which was dawning"?

According to Eric Foner, how did Reconstruction lead to the ouster of the planter class from control of politics and why was that important? How did attitudes toward blacks in Reconstruction interact with attitudes toward immigrants and other oppressed groups in the North? Why does Foner think that Reconstruction did not succeed in giving blacks freedom?

All three passages find a failure in Reconstruction from one perspective or another. How do you think the problems of Reconstruction of the South could have been better solved?

ANSWERS TO MULTIPLE-CHOICE AND TRUE-FALSE QUESTIONS

Multiple-Choice Questions

1-A, 2-D, 3-B, 4-B, 5-D, 6-D, 7-C, 8-B

True-False Questions

1-F, 2-F, 3-T, 4-T, 5-T, 6-T, 7-F, 8-F

18

NEW FRONTIERS: SOUTH AND WEST

CHAPTER OBJECTIVES

After you complete the reading and study of this chapter you should be able to

1. Explain the concept of the New South, its development, and how it affected the South after the Civil War.
2. Account for the rise of the Bourbons to power in the South and explain their impact on the region.
3. Explain the causes and process of disfranchisement of blacks in the South.
4. Compare the views of Washington and Du Bois on the place of blacks in American life.
5. Describe the Indian wars and explain the new Indian policy of 1887.
6. Describe the rise and decline of the cattle industry.
7. Describe the problems of farming on the western frontier.
8. Explain the importance of Turner's theory of the significance of the frontier in American history.

CHAPTER OUTLINE

I. The New South
  A. Concept of the New South
    1. Henry Grady's background
    2. His vision

    3. Other prophets of the New South creed
    4. Industrial fairs: Atlanta International Cotton Exposition of 1881
  B. Economic growth
    1. Growth of cotton textile manufacturing
    2. Development of the tobacco industry
      a. Duke family
      b. Techniques used by Buck Duke for growth
      c. Creation and breakup of the American Tobacco Company
    3. Coal production
    4. Lumbering
    5. Beginnings of petroleum and hydroelectric power
  C. Agriculture in the New South
    1. Limited diversity in agriculture
    2. Features of sharecropping and tenancy
    3. Impact of the crop lien system
  D. Role of the Bourbon Redeemers
    1. Nature of the Bourbons
    2. Bourbon economic policies
      a. Laissez-faire
      b. Retrenchment in government spending
      c. Assistance of private philanthropy
      d. Convict lease system
      e. Repudiation of Confederate debts in some states

    f. Positive contributions of the
      Bourbons
    g. Varied development of color
      lines in social relations
E. Disfranchisement of blacks
  1. Impetus for elimination of the
    black vote
    a. Fears of retrogression
    b. Impact of Populists
  2. Techniques used to exclude blacks
    a. Mississippi
    b. Louisiana
  3. Spread of segregation
    a. Segregation in railway cars
    b. Impact of Civil Rights Cases,
      1883
    c. Impact of *Plessy v. Ferguson,*
      1896
  4. Spread of violence against blacks
F. Clash of Booker T. Washington and
  W. E. B. Du Bois
G. Role of myth in the New South
  1. Curious linkage of Old and New
    South
  2. Benefits of linking the New South
    with the Old
  3. The ultimate achievement of the
    New South prophets

II. The New West
  A. Nature of the West after the war
  B. Environment beyond 98° West
    longitude
  C. Developments that altered the Great
    American Desert
  D. The mining frontier
    1. Pattern of mining development
    2. Locations of major mineral
      discoveries
    3. Development of new states

E. Displacement of the Indians
  1. Conflicts that arose during the Civil
    War
  2. Establishment of Indian Peace
    Commission, 1867
    a. Policy of large reservations
    b. Agreements with the Indians in
      1867 and 1868
  3. Continued resistance of Indians
    a. Massacre at Little Big Horn
    b. Conquest of Sioux and others
    c. Significance of Chief Joseph and
      Nez Perce
  4. Impact of annihilation of buffalo
    herds
  5. Stirrings for reform in Indian policy
    a. Eastern view of Indian slaughter
    b. Role of Helen Hunt Jackson
  6. Dawes Severalty Act, 1887
    a. Concept of new policy
    b. Provisions of Dawes and
      subsequent acts
    c. Impact of new policy
F. The cattle industry in the West
  1. Development of the open range
  2. Long drives after the Civil War
    a. Joseph McCoy
    b. Features of the cowtown
  3. Codes of the open range
G. The farming frontier
  1. Land policy after the Civil War
  2. Changed institutions in the West
  3. Efforts for reclamation of arid lands
  4. An assessment of land distribution
  5. Aspects of farming and life on the
    Great Plains
  6. New farming implements
    a. Bonanza farms
    b. Small farms
H. Turner's frontier thesis
  1. Turner's claims for the frontier
  2. Other views

KEY ITEMS OF CHRONOLOGY

Homestead Act	1862
First of the long drives	1866
Indian Peace Commission settlements	1867–1868
Civil Rights Cases	1883
Dawes Severalty Act	1887

Mississippi Constitution incorporates disfranchisement of blacks	1890
Census shows frontier closed	1890
Turner frontier thesis presented	1893
B. T. Washington's "Atlanta Compromise" speech	1895
Plessy v. Ferguson	1896
Disfranchisement of blacks essentially completed in southern states	1910

TERMS TO MASTER

Listed below are some important terms or people with which you should be familiar after you complete the study of this chapter. Explain the significance of each name or term.

1. Henry W. Grady
2. James Buchanan Duke
3. sharecropping
4. crop lien system
5. Bourbons
6. Peabody Fund for Education
7. Convict lease system
8. Mississippi Plan for disfranchisement
9. grandfather clauses
10. segregation
11. *Plessy v. Ferguson*
12. Booker T. Washington
13. W. E. B. Du Bois
14. Great American Desert
15. Indian Peace Commission
16. George A. Custer
17. Chief Joseph
18. *A Century of Dishonor*
19. Dawes Severalty Act
20. "dry farming"
21. Frederick Jackson Turner

VOCABULARY BUILDING

Listed below are some words used in this chapter. Look up each word in your dictionary.

1. lien
2. epithet
3. austerity
4. scrimping
5. paragons
6. disfranchise
7. bestiality
8. octoroon
9. salved
10. inexorable
11. spoliation
12. bushwhackers
13. sedentary
14. sodbusters

EXERCISES FOR UNDERSTANDING

When you have completed reading the chapter, answer each of the following questions. If you have difficulty, go back and reread the section of the chapter related to the question.

Multiple-Choice Questions

Select the letter of the response which best completes the statement.

1. James B. Duke's greatest contribution to the South's progress was in
   A. development of the cigarette industry
   B. promotion of education
   C. inventions for textile manufacturing
   D. stimulating competition among industries in the South

2. The most significant impact of the crop lien system in the South was that it
   A. made possible cash payments for goods
   B. provided a source of labor in the post-Reconstruction South

C. made possible low-interest-rate loans for blacks

D. encouraged the South to raise only one crop, cotton

3. Mississippi's techniques for disfranchising blacks included all of the following *except* a
    A. residency requirement
    B. poll tax
    C. grandfather clause
    D. literacy test

4. "In all things that are purely social we can be as separate as the five fingers, yet one as the hand in all things essential to mutual progress," said
    A. Henry Grady
    B. W. E. B. Du Bois
    C. the Supreme Court in *Plessy v. Ferguson*
    D. Booker T. Washington

5. The idea of the West as the Great American Desert was overcome by
    A. the rush for gold and silver
    B. the transcontinental railroad
    C. the rise of cattle ranching
    D. all of the above

6. In the Battle of Little Big Horn, Gen. George A. Custer fought
    A. gold and silver miners in Colorado
    B. Indians in the Montana territory
    C. "Calamity Jane" and "Wild Bill Hickok" in South Dakota
    D. Indians in the Southwest

7. Helen Hunt Jackson's *A Century of Dishonor* aroused concern about the
    A. plight of Indians
    B. need for law and order in western mining towns
    C. disfranchisement of southern blacks
    D. corruption in the Grant administration

8. The institutions of the West were shaped most by
    A. government land policies
    B. climate
    C. barbed wire
    D. cattle

True-False Questions

Indicate whether each statement is true or false.

1. Henry Grady's view of the New South emphasized the development of industry.
2. The Peabody and Slater Funds provided subsidies to southern industrial development.
3. In the 1870s Bourbons quickly ended all black influence in southern politics.
4. The *Plessy v. Ferguson* decision included a ruling that states could not interfere with the rights of blacks.
5. A leading critic of Booker T. Washington was W. E. B. Du Bois.
6. General George Custer was defeated at the battle of Little Big Horn.
7. The decline of buffalo herds played a significant role in ending Indian resistance in the West.
8. Between 1851 and 1871 the federal government granted railroads about 200 million acres in the West.

Essay Questions

1. Describe the economic growth in the South after Reconstruction.
2. Describe three techniques used to disfranchise blacks in the South.
3. Explain how the sharecropping and tenant systems worked in southern agriculture.
4. Contrast the visions of Booker T. Washington and W. E. B. Du Bois for freed blacks.
5. What impact did the boom and bust in cattle ranching have on the settlement of the West?
6. Did the federal government's Indian policy have more or less effect on the development of the West than its land policy?
7. How did black social and political life change in the South during the 1890s?

DOCUMENTS

Document 1. Booker T. Washington Proposes the "Atlanta Compromise"

Invited to appear before a national audience at the Atlanta Exposition in 1895, Booker T. Washington carefully honed a speech asserting the importance of the black contribution to America and the South, but avoiding the offending of white sensibilities. The speech was widely acclaimed among whites and blacks alike.

One-third of the population of the South is of the Negro race. No enterprise seeking the material, civil, or moral welfare of this section can disregard this element of our population and reach the highest success. . . .

Ignorant and inexperienced, it is not strange that in the first years of our new life we began at the top instead of at the bottom; that a seat in Congress or the state legislature was more sought than real estate or industrial skill; that the political convention or stump speaking had more attractions than starting a dairy farm or truck garden.

A ship lost at sea for many days suddenly sighted a friendly vessel. From the mast of the unfortunate vessel was seen a signal, "Water, water; we die of thirst!" The answer from the friendly vessel at once came back, "Cast down your bucket where you are." A second time the signal, "Water, water; send us water!" ran up from the distressed vessel, and was answered, "Cast down your bucket where you are." The captain of the distressed vessel, at last heeding the injunction, cast down his bucket, and it came up full of fresh, sparkling water from the mouth of the Amazon River. To those of my race who depend on bettering their condition in a foreign land or who underestimate the importance of cultivating friendly relations with the Southern white man, who is their next-door neighbour, I would say: "Cast down your bucket where you are"—cast it down in making friends in every manly way of the people of all races by whom we are surrounded.

Cast it down in agriculture, mechanics, in commerce, in domestic service, and in the professions. And in this connection it is well to bear in mind that whatever other sins the South may be called to bear, when it comes to business, pure and simple, it is in the South that the Negro is given a man's chance in the commercial world, and in nothing is this Exposition more eloquent than in emphasizing this chance. Our greatest danger is that in the great leap from slavery to freedom we may overlook the fact that the masses of us are to live by the productions of our hands, and fail to keep in mind that we shall prosper in proportion as we learn to dignify and glorify common labour and put brains and skill into the common occupation of life; shall prosper in proportion as we learn to draw the line between the superficial and the substantial, the ornamental gewgaws of life and the useful. No race can prosper till it learns that there is as much dignity in tilling a field as in writing a poem. It is at the bottom of life we must begin, and not at the top. Nor should we permit our grievances to overshadow our opportunities.

To those of the white race who look to the incoming of those of foreign birth and strange tongue and habits for the prosperity of the

South, were I permitted I would repeat what I say to my own race, "Cast down your bucket where you are." Cast it down among the eight millions of Negroes whose habits you know, whose fidelity and love you have tested in days when to have proved treacherous meant the ruin of your firesides. Cast down your bucket among these people who have, without strikes and labour wars, tilled your fields, cleared your forests, builded your railroads and cities, and brought forth treasures from the bowels of the earth, and helped make possible this magnificent representation of the progress of the South. Casting down your bucket among my people, helping and encouraging them as you are doing on these grounds, and to education of head, hand, and heart, you will find that they will buy your surplus land, make blossom the waste places in your fields, and run your factories. While doing this, you can be sure in the future, as in the past, that you and your families will be surrounded by the most patient, faithful, law-abiding, and unresentful people that the world has seen. As we have proved our loyalty to you in the past, in nursing your children, watching by the sick-bed of your mothers and fathers, and often following them with tear-dimmed eyes to their graves, so in the future, in our humble way, we shall stand by you with a devotion that no foreigner can approach, ready to lay down our lives, if need be, in defence of yours, interlacing our industrial, commercial, civil, and religious life with yours in a way that shall make the interests of both races one. In all things that are purely social we can be as separate as the fingers, yet one as the hand in all things essential to mutual progress.

There is no defence or security for any of us except in the highest intelligence and development of all. If anywhere there are efforts tending to curtail the fullest growth of the Negro, let these efforts be turned into stimulating, encouraging, and making him the most useful and intelligent citizen. Effort or means so invested will pay a thousand per cent interest. These efforts will be twice blessed—"blessing him that gives and him that takes."

The wisest among my race understand that the agitation of questions of social equality is the extremest folly, and that progress in the enjoyment of all the privileges that will come to us must be the result of severe and constant struggle rather than of artificial forcing. No race that has anything to contribute to the markets of the world is long in any degree ostracized. It is important and right that all privileges of the law be ours, but it is vastly more important that we be prepared for the exercises of these privileges. The opportunity to earn a dollar in a factory just now is worth infinitely more than the opportunity to spend a dollar in an opera-house.

[Booker T. Washington, *Up from Slavery* (New York: Doubleday, Page & Co., 1902), pp. 218–224]

Document 2. W. E. B. Du Bois Disagrees with Washington

Educated at Fisk and Harvard Universities, W. E. B. Du Bois became the leader of blacks who disagreed with Washington's prescriptions. The passage below reflects Du Bois's disagreements with Washington.

Mr. Washington represents in Negro thought the old attitude of adjustment and submission; but adjustment at such a peculiar time as to make his programme unique. This is an age of unusual economic development, and Mr. Washington's programme naturally takes an economic cast, becoming a gospel of Work and Money to such an extent as apparently almost completely to overshadow the higher aims of life. Moreover, this is an age when the more advanced races are coming in closer contact with the less developed races, and the race-feeling is therefore intensified; and Mr. Washington's programme practically accepts the alleged inferiority of the Negro races. Again, in our own land, the reaction from the sentiment of war time has given impetus to race-prejudice against Negroes, and Mr. Washington withdraws many of the high demands of Negroes as men and American citizens. In other periods of intensified prejudice all the Negro's tendency to self-assertion has been called forth; at this period a policy of submission is advocated. In the history of nearly all other races and peoples the doctrine preached at such crises has been that manly self-respect is worth more than lands and houses, and that a people who voluntarily surrender such respect, or cease striving for it, are not worth civilizing.

In answer to this, it has been claimed that the Negro can survive only through submission. Mr. Washington distinctly asks that black people give up, at least for the present, three things—

First, political power,

Second, insistence on civil rights,

Third, higher education of Negro youth,—and concentrate all their energies on industrial education, the accumulation of wealth, and the conciliation of the South. This policy has been courageously and insistently advocated for over fifteen years, and has been triumphant for perhaps ten years. As a result of this tender of the palm-branch, what has been the return? In these years there have occurred:

1. The disfranchisement of the Negro.

2. The legal creation of a distinct status of civil inferiority for the Negro.

3. The steady withdrawal of aid from institutions for the higher training of the Negro.

These movements are not, to be sure, direct results of Mr. Washington's teachings; but this propaganda has, without a shadow of doubt, helped their speedier accomplishment. The question then comes: Is it possible, and probable, that nine millions of men can make effective progress in economic lines if they are deprived of political rights, made a servile caste, and allowed only the most meagre chance for developing their exceptional men? If history and reason give any distinct answer to these questions, it is an emphatic *No.* And Mr. Washington thus faces the triple paradox of his career:

1. He is striving nobly to make Negro artisans, businessmen and property-owners; but it is utterly impossible, under modern competitive methods, for workingmen and property-owners to defend their rights and exist without the right of suffrage.

2. He insists on thrift and self-respect, but at the same time counsels a silent submission to civic inferiority such as is bound to sap the manhood of any race in the long run.

3. He advocates common-school and industrial training, and depreciates institutions of higher learning; but neither the Negro common-schools, nor Tuskegee itself, could remain open a day were it not for teachers trained in Negro colleges, or trained by their graduates.

This triple paradox in Mr. Washington's position is the object of criticism by two classes of colored Americans. One class is spiritually descended from Toussaint the Savior, through Gabriel, Vesey, and Turner, and they represent the attitude of revolt and revenge; they hate the white South blindly and distrust the white race generally, and so far as they agree on definite action, think that the Negro's only hope lies in emigration beyond the borders of the United States. And yet, by the irony of fate, nothing has more effectually made this programme seem hopeless than the recent course of the United States toward weaker and darker peoples in the West Indies, Hawaii, and the Philippines,—for where in the world may we go and be safe from lying and brute force?

The other class of Negroes who cannot agree with Mr. Washington has hitherto said little aloud. They deprecate the sight of scattered counsels, or internal disagreement; and especially they dislike making their just criticism of a useful and earnest man an excuse for a general discharge of venom from small-minded opponents. . . . Such men feel in conscience bound to ask of this nation three things:

1. The right to vote.
2. Civic equality.
3. The education of youth according to ability.

They acknowledge Mr. Washington's invaluable service in counselling patience and courtesy in such demands; they do not ask that ignorant black men vote when ignorant whites are debarred, or that any reasonable restrictions in the suffrage should not be applied; they know that the low social level of the mass of the race is responsible for much discrimination against it, but they also know, and the nation knows, that relentless color-prejudice is more often a cause than a result of the Negro's degradation; they seek the abatement of this relic of barbarism, and not its systematic encouragement and pampering by all agencies of social power from the Associated Press to the Church of Christ. They advocate, with Mr. Washington, a broad system of Negro common schools supplemented by thorough industrial training; but they are surprised that a man of Mr. Washington's insight cannot see that no such educational system ever has rested or can rest on any other basis than that of the well-equipped college and university, and they insist that there is a demand for a few such institutions throughout the South to train the best of the Negro youth as teachers, professional men, and leaders.

This group of men honor Mr. Washington for his attitude of conciliation toward the white South; they accept the "Atlanta Compromise" in its broadest interpretation; they recognize, with him, many signs of promise, many men of high purpose and fair judgment, in this section; they know that no easy task has been laid upon a region already tottering under heavy burdens. But, nevertheless, they insist that the way to truth and right lies in straightforward honesty, not in indiscriminate flattery; in praising those of the South who do well and criticising uncompromisingly those who do ill; in taking advantage of the opportunities at hand and urging their fellows to do the same, but at the same time in remembering that only a firm adherence to their higher ideals and aspirations will ever keep those ideals within the realm of possibility. They do not expect that the free right to vote, to enjoy civic rights, and to be educated, will come in a moment; they do not expect to see the bias and prejudices of years disappear at the blast of a trumpet; but they are absolutely certain that the way for a people to gain their reasonable rights is not by voluntarily throwing them away and insisting that they do not want them; that the way for a people to gain respect is not by continually belittling and ridiculing themselves; that, on the contrary, Negroes must insist continually, in season and out of season, that voting is necessary to modern manhood, that color discrimination is barbarism, and that black boys need education as well as white boys.

[W. E. B. Du Bois, "Of Mr. Booker T. Washington and Others," in *Souls of Black Folk* (Chicago: A. C. McClurg, 1903), pp. 50–55]

Questions for Reflection

What evidence do you see in Washington's speech that he was trying not to offend his predominantly white audience? Do you see evidence that Washington feared that blacks might be replaced by another group? What groups? How justified was his fear?

Does Du Bois seem to acknowledge the tightrope which Washington had to walk in developing his compromise position?

Are Du Bois's criticisms of Washington's position valid? Which of these men had a better concept of what blacks needed to do? Why?

ANSWERS TO MULTIPLE-CHOICE AND TRUE-FALSE QUESTIONS

Multiple-Choice Questions

1-A, 2-D, 3-C, 4-D, 5-D, 6-B, 7-A, 8-B

True-False Questions

1-T, 2-F, 3-F, 4-F, 5-T, 6-T, 7-T, 8-T

19

BIG BUSINESS AND ORGANIZED LABOR

CHAPTER OBJECTIVES

After you complete the reading and study of this chapter you should be able to:

1. Describe the economic impact of the Civil War.
2. Explain the important factors in the growth of the economy in the late nineteenth century.
3. Describe the role of the major entrepreneurs like Rockefeller, Carnegie, and Morgan.
4. Account for the limited growth of unions in this period, and the success of the Knights of Labor and the American Federation of Labor.
5. Describe the major labor confrontations in the period.
6. Account for the limited appeal of socialism for American labor.

CHAPTER OUTLINE

I. The post–Civil War economy
  A. Economic changes in the 1869–1899 period
  B. Railroad building
    1. The transcontinental plan for the Central Pacific and the Union Pacific
    2. Financing the railroads
      a. Crédit-Mobilier fraud

      b. Jay Gould's work
      c. Cornelius Vanderbilt
    3. Railroads controlled by seven major groups
  C. New products and inventions
    1. Number of patents
    2. Improvements and inventions
    3. Development of the telephone
    4. Edison's work with electricity
  D. Entrepreneurs of the era
    1. Rockefeller and the oil industry
      a. Background
      b. Concentration on refining and transportation
      c. Development of the trust
      d. Evolution of the holding company
    2. Andrew Carnegie and the Gospel of Wealth
      a. Background
      b. Concentration on steel
      c. Philosophy for big business
      d. Other proponents of the Gospel of Wealth
    3. J. P. Morgan and investment banking
      a. Background
      b. Concentration on railroad financing
      c. Control of organizations
      d. Consolidation of the steel industry
  E. Impact of growth on the distribution of wealth

II. Developments in labor
  A. Circumstances for workers
    1. Wages and hours
    2. Living and working conditions
    3. Control by impersonal forces
  B. Obstacles to unions
  C. Molly Maguires
  D. Railroad strike of 1877
    1. Causes
    2. Scope and violence
    3. Effects
  E. Efforts at union building
    1. National Labor Union
    2. Knights of Labor
      a. Early development
      b. Emphasis on the union
      c. Role of Terence Powderly
      d. Victories of the Knights
      e. Haymarket Affair
      f. Lasting influence of the Knights
         of Labor

    3. Development of the American
       Federation of Labor
      a. Development of craft unions
      b. Role of Samuel Gompers
      c. Growth of the union
  F. Violence in the 1890s
    1. Homestead Strike, 1892
    2. Pullman Strike, 1894
      a. Causes
      b. Role of the government
      c. Impact on Eugene V. Debs
  G. Socialism and American labor
    1. Daniel De Leon and Eugene Debs
    2. Social Democratic party
      a. Early work
      b. Height of influence
  H. Rise of the IWW
    1. Sources of strength
    2. Revolutionary goals
    3. Causes for decline

KEY ITEMS OF CHRONOLOGY

National Labor Union formed	1866
Completion of the first transcontinental railroad	1869
Standard Oil of Ohio incorporated	1870
Telephone patented	1876
Incandescent light bulb invented	1879
Terence Powderly became president of the Knights of Labor	1879
First electric current supplied to 85 customers in New York City	1882
Creation of the Standard Oil Trust	1882
Haymarket Affair	1886
Founding of the American Federation of Labor	1886
Pullman Strike	1894
U.S. Steel Corporation formed	1901
IWW founded	1905

TERMS TO MASTER

Listed below are some important terms or people with which you should be familiar after you complete the study of this chapter. Explain the significance of each name or term.

1. Union Pacific
2. transcontinental railroads
3. Crédit-Mobilier
4. Cornelius Vanderbilt
5. Alexander Graham Bell
6. Thomas Alva Edison
7. George Westinghouse

8. John D. Rockefeller
9. Gospel of Wealth
10. Horatio Alger
11. J. Pierpont Morgan
12. United States Steel Company
13. holding company
14. Molly Maguires
15. industrial and craft unions
16. Knights of Labor
17. American Federation of Labor
18. Haymarket Affair
19. Samuel Gompers
20. Pullman Strike
21. Eugene V. Debs
22. Wobblies

VOCABULARY BUILDING

Listed below are some words used in this chapter. Look up each word in your dictionary.

1. cornucopia
2. baron
3. patent
4. prototype
5. trust
6. precarious
7. impromptu
8. jurisdictional
9. idyllic
10. injunction
11. doctrinaire
12. nomadic
13. socialism

EXERCISES FOR UNDERSTANDING

When you have completed reading the chapter, answer each of the following questions. If you have difficulty, go back and reread the section of the chapter related to the question.

Multiple-Choice Questions

Select the letter of the response which best completes the statement.

1. The first transcontinental railroad was built by
   A. the federal government
   B. private companies granted a monopoly by the government
   C. private companies with no federal assistance
   D. private companies with government subsidies

2. The profiteering of railroad companies included
   A. bribes to congressmen
   B. construction companies that overcharged for building railroads and made a profit
   C. shoddy workmanship in building the railroad lines
   D. all of the above

3. Rockefeller's success depended in large part on
   A. vertical integration
   B. his ownership of most Pennsylvania oilfields
   C. corruption of government officials
   D. many favorable loans from bankers

4. Andrew Carnegie's Gospel of Wealth called on the rich to
   A. support overseas missionaries
   B. get richer
   C. provide for the public good
   D. help others gain wealth by turning their businesses over to the workers

5. The social costs of industrialization included
   A. closer relationships between workers and factory owners
   B. numerous job-related injuries and deaths
   C. rising wages for workers
   D. healthier working conditions for most workers

6. The Knights of Labor
   A. organized only skilled workers
   B. shunned politics and strikes
   C. was damaged by the Haymarket Affair
   D. all of the above

7. American workers tended to reject unions because
   A. they believed they would only be workers for a short time until they could own their own farms or move up otherwise
   B. they were so strongly committed to a system of equality and uniform wages for all
   C. they did not like the association with immigrants in unions
   D. they thought all unions were corrupt
8. The leader of the socialist movement in the United States was
   A. Samuel Gompers
   B. Terence V. Powderly
   C. Henry Clay Frick
   D. Eugene V. Debs

True-False Questions

Indicate whether each statement is true or false.

1. The first big business with large-scale bureaucracies was in the steel industry.
2. In gaining his immense personal fortune, Jay Gould exploited and ruined many businesses.
3. George Westinghouse developed air brakes for railroads and alternating electric current.

4. Horatio Alger's novels portrayed the lives of robber barons in the late nineteenth century.
5. In 1900 the average worker in manufacturing worked only about 45 hours per week.
6. The first major interstate strike was led by the Molly Maguires in the coal industry.
7. The American Federation of Labor was an organization of national craft unions.
8. The most conservative labor organization was the Industrial Workers of the World.

Essay Questions

1. List and explain the factors that promoted the growth of industry in the United States in the late nineteenth century.
2. What was the relationship among inventors, entrepreneurs, and great wealth in the late–nineteenth-century United States? Give several examples.
3. Compare and contrast the business practices of J. P. Morgan and Jay Gould.
4. Describe some of the benefits and drawbacks of industrialization for workers. What was their response to it?
5. Explain the appeal of socialism and other forms of radicalism to some American workers.

DOCUMENTS

Document 1. Andrew Carnegie Provides Rules for Disposing of Wealth

As the textbook indicates, Andrew Carnegie developed the concept of the Gospel of Wealth in an essay originally entitled "Wealth." Excerpted below are sections dealing with the best method for a person to use in disposing of his fortune.

It will be understood that *fortunes* are here spoken of, not moderate sums saved by many years of effort, the returns from which are required for the comfortable maintenance and education of families. This is not *wealth*, but only *competence*, which it should be the aim of all to acquire.

There are but three modes in which surplus wealth can be disposed of. It can be left to the families of the decedents; or it can be bequeathed for public purposes; or, finally, it can be administered during their lives by its possessors. Under the first and second modes

most of the wealth of the world that has reached the few has hitherto been applied. Let us in turn consider each of these modes. The
first is the most injudicious. In monarchical countries, the estates
and the greatest portion of the wealth are left to the first son, that
the vanity of the parent may be gratified by the thought that his
name and title are to descend to succeeding generations unim-
paired. The condition of this class in Europe to-day teaches the
futility of such hopes or ambitions. The successors have become
impoverished through their follies or from the fall in the value of
land. . . . Under republican institutions the division of property
among the children is much fairer, but the question which forces
itself upon thoughtful men in all lands is: Why should men leave
great fortunes to their children? If this is done from affection, is it
not misguided affection? Observation teaches that, generally speaking, it is not well for the children that they should be so burdened.
Neither is it well for the State. Beyond providing for the wife and
daughters moderate sources of income, and very moderate allow-
ances indeed, if any, for the sons, men may well hesitate, for it is no
longer questionable that great sums bequeathed oftener work more
for the injury than for the good of the recipients. Wise men will soon
conclude that, for the best interests of the members of their families
and of the State, such bequests are an improper use of their means.

It is not suggested that men who have failed to educate their
sons to earn a livelihood cast them adrift in poverty. If any man
has seen fit to rear his sons with a view to their living idle lives, or,
what is highly commendable, has instilled in them the sentiment
that they are in a position to labor for public ends without reference to pecuniary considerations, then, of course, the duty of the
parent is to see that such are provided for *in moderation.* There
are instances of millionaires' sons unspoiled by wealth, who, being
rich, still perform great services in the community. Such are the
very salt of the earth, as valuable as, unfortunately, they are rare;
still it is not the exception, but the rule, that men must regard,
and, looking at the usual result of enormous sums conferred upon
legatees, the thoughtful man must shortly say, "I would as soon
leave to my son a curse as the almighty dollar," and admit to himself that it is not the welfare of the children, but family pride,
which inspires these enormous legacies.

As to the second mode, that of leaving wealth at death for public
uses, it may be said that this is only a means for the disposal of
wealth, provided a man is content to wait until he is dead before he
becomes of much good in the world. Knowledge of the results of
legacies bequeathed is not calculated to inspire the brightest hopes
of much posthumous good being accomplished. The cases are not
few in which the real object sought by the testator is not attained,
nor are they few in which his real wishes are thwarted. In many
cases the bequests are so used as to become only monuments of his
folly. It is well to remember that it requires the exercise of no less
ability than that which acquired the wealth to use it so as to be really
beneficial to the community. Besides this, it may fairly be said that
no man is to be extolled for doing what he cannot help doing, nor
is he to be thanked by the community to which he only leaves
wealth at death. Men who leave vast sums in this way may fairly be

thought men who would not have left it at all, had they been able to take it with them. The memories of such cannot be held in grateful remembrance, for there is no grace in their gifts. It is not to be wondered at that such bequests seem so generally to lack the blessing.

The growing disposition to tax more and more heavily large estates left at death is a cheering indication of the growth of a salutary change in public opinion. The State of Pennsylvania now takes—subject to some exceptions—one-tenth of the property left by its citizens. . . . Of all forms of taxation, this seems the wisest. Men who continue hoarding great sums all their lives, the proper use of which for public ends would work good to the community, should be made to feel that the community, in the form of the State, cannot thus be deprived of its proper share. By taxing estates heavily at death the State marks its condemnation of the selfish millionaire's unworthy life.

It is desirable that nations should go much further in this direction. Indeed, it is difficult to set bounds to the share of a rich man's estate which should go at his death to the public through the agency of the State, and by all means such taxes should be graduated, beginning at nothing upon moderate sums to dependents, and increasing rapidly as the amounts swell, until of the millionaire's hoard, as of Shylock's, at least

> The other half
> Comes to the privy coffer of the state.

This policy would work powerfully to induce the rich man to attend to the administration of wealth during his life, which is the end that society should always have in view, as being that by far the most fruitful for the people. Nor need it be feared that this policy would sap the root of enterprise and render men less anxious to accumulate, for to the class whose ambition it is to leave great fortunes and be talked about after their death, it will attract even more attention, and, indeed, be a somewhat nobler ambition to have enormous sums paid over to the state from their fortunes.

There remains, then, only one mode of using great fortunes; but in this we have the true antidote for the temporary unequal distribution of wealth, the reconciliation of the rich and the poor—a reign of harmony—another ideal, differing, indeed, from that of the Communist in requiring only the further evolution of existing conditions, not the total overthrow of our civilization. It is founded upon the present most intense individualism, and the race is prepared to put it in practice by degrees whenever it pleases. . . .

This, then, is held to be the duty of the man of Wealth: First, to set an example of modest, unostentatious living, shunning display or extravagance; to provide moderately for the legitimate wants of those dependent upon him; and after doing so to consider all surplus revenues which come to him simply as trust funds, which he is called upon to administer, and strictly bound as a matter of duty to administer in the manner which, in his judgment, is best calculated to produce the most beneficial results for the community—the man of wealth thus becoming the mere agent and trustee for his poorer brethen, bringing to their service his superior wisdom, experience, and ability to administer, doing for them better than they would or could do for themselves.

. . . It were better for mankind that the millions of the rich were thrown into the sea than so spent as to encourage the slothful, the drunken, the unworthy. Of every thousand dollars spent in so called charity to-day, it is probable that $950 is unwisely spent, so spent, indeed, as to produce the very evils which it proposes to mitigate or cure. A well-known writer of philosophic books admitted the other day that he had given a quarter of a dollar to a man who approached him as he was coming to visit the house of his friend. He knew nothing of the habits of this beggar, knew not the use that would be made of this money, although he had every reason to suspect that it would be spent improperly. This man professed to be a disciple of Herbert Spencer; yet the quarter-dollar given that night will probably work more injury than all the money which its thoughtless donor will ever be able to give in true charity will do good. He only gratified his own feelings, saved himself from annoyance—and this was probably one of the most selfish and very worst actions of his life, for in all respects he is most worthy.

In bestowing charity, the main consideration should be to help those who will help themselves; to provide part of the means by which those who desire to improve may do so; to give those who desire to rise the aids by which they may rise; to assist, but rarely or never to do all. Neither the individual nor the race is improved by alms-giving. Those worthy of assistance, except in rare cases, seldom require assistance. The really valuable men of the race never do, except in cases of accident or sudden change. Every one has, of course, cases of individuals brought to his own knowledge where temporary assistance can do genuine good, and these he will not overlook. But the amount which can be wisely given by the individual for individuals is necessarily limited by his lack of knowledge of the circumstances connected with each. He is the only true reformer who is as careful and as anxious not to aid the unworthy as he is to aid the worthy, and, perhaps, even more so, for in alms-giving more injury is probably done by rewarding vice than by relieving virtue.

[Andrew Carnegie, "Wealth," *North American Review* 148, no. 391 (June 1889): 657–663]

Document 2. Russell Conwell Encourages Christians to Obtain Wealth

In the sermon "Acres of Diamonds," which Russell Conwell delivered more than 6,000 times, he advised Christians to use their talent and energy to obtain wealth.

. . . I say you ought to be rich; you have no right to be poor. . . . You ought to be rich. But persons with certain religious prejudice will ask, "How can you spend your time advising the rising generation to give their time to getting money—dollars and cents—the commercial spirit?"

Yet I must say that you ought to spend time getting rich. You and I know there are some things more valuable than money; of course, we do. Ah, yes! By a heart made unspeakably sad by a grave on which the autumn leaves now fall, I know there are some things higher and grander and sublimer than money. Well does the man know, who has suffered, that there are some things sweeter and holier and more sacred than gold. Nevertheless, the man of common sense also knows that there is not one of those things that is not greatly enhanced by the use of money. Money is power. . . . Money is power; money has powers; and for a man to say, "I do not want money," is to say, "I do not wish to do any good to my fellowmen." It is absurd thus to talk. It is absurd to disconnect them. This is a wonderfully great life, and you ought to spend your time getting money, because of the power there is in money. And yet this religious prejudice is so great that some people think it is a great honor to be one of God's poor. . . . We ought to get rich if we can by honorable and Christian methods, and these are the only methods that sweep us quickly toward the goal of riches.

I remember, not many years ago a young theological student who came into my office and said to me that he thought it was his duty to come in and "labor with me." I asked what had happened, and he said: "I feel it is my duty to come in and speak to you, sir, and say that the Holy Scriptures declare that money is the root of all evil." I asked him where he found that saying, and he said he found it in the Bible. . . . So he took the Bible and read it: "The *love* of money is the root of all evil." . . . Oh, that is it. It is the worship of the means instead of the end, though you cannot reach the end without the means. When a man makes an idol of the money instead of the purposes for which it may be used, when he squeezes the dollar until the eagle squeals, then it is made the root of all evil. Think, if you only had the money, what you could do for your wife, your child, and for your home and your city.

[Agnes Rush Burr, *Russell H. Conwell, Founder of the Institutional Church in America: The Work and the Man* (Philadelphia: The John C. Winston Co., 1905), pp. 324–326]

Questions for Reflection

Has Carnegie listed all the methods for the disposal of fortunes? Would most wealthy people today agree with his notions of how to treat members of the family? How do you react to his notion of using the inheritance tax? Does it appear to you that most very wealthy people today follow his dictates for modest living? Is Carnegie right about the harm of almsgiving? What appear to be the sources for Carnegie's ideas? Are his concepts valid today or were they appropriate only for the nineteenth century, if that?

How does Russell Conwell's sermon reflect attitudes similar to Carnegie's? Is Conwell providing an appropriate reflection of the ethic of modern Christianity? How would Conwell's ideas have been received by the wealthy people of his era? Why? Based on a reading of this portion of Conwell's sermon, how would you define the "Gospel of Wealth"?

ANSWERS TO MULTIPLE-CHOICE
AND TRUE-FALSE QUESTIONS

Multiple-Choice Questions

1-D, 2-D, 3-A, 4-C, 5-B, 6-C, 7-A, 8-D

True-False Questions

1-F, 2-T, 3-T, 4-F, 5-F, 6-F, 7-T, 8-F

20

THE EMERGENCE OF
MODERN AMERICA

CHAPTER OBJECTIVES

*After you complete the reading and study
of this chapter you should be able to*

1. Discuss the important intellectual trends
   in the period 1877–1890.
2. Describe city growth in the
   late-nineteenth century.
3. Account for the new immigration and
   the reaction which it engendered.
4. Trace major developments in higher
   education after the Civil War.
5. Explain the concepts of Social Darwinism
   and Reform Darwinism.
6. Describe the local color, realist, and
   naturalist movements in literature.
7. Explain the social gospel and describe its
   manifestations.

CHAPTER OUTLINE

I. Urbanization
   A. Urbanization reflected in westward
      migration
   B. Factors important to urban prowess
   C. Characteristics of the new urban scene
   D. Vertical and horizontal growth of cities
      1. Development of elevators
   2. Introduction of cast-iron and
      steel-frame construction
   3. Development of electric streetcars
   E. City problems
      1. Tenements
      2. Health
      3. City services
   F. Role of city boss
   G. Lure of the city

II. The new immigration
   A. Reasons for emigration to America
   B. Nature of the new immigrants
   C. The nativist response
      1. Reasons for objection to new
         immigrants
      2. Rise of American Protective
         Association
   D. Efforts at immigration restriction

III. Growth of education
   A. Indication of the spread of schooling
   B. Developments in higher education
      1. Growth of colleges
      2. Growth of the elective system
      3. Expansion of opportunities for
         women
      4. Development of graduate schools
   C. The rise of professionalism
      1. Nature of the movement
      2. Fields developed

IV. Theories of social change
  A. Darwinism
    1. Darwin's ideas and their implications
    2. Social Darwinism
      a. Herbert Spencer's contributions
      b. William Graham Sumner's contributions
    3. Lester Frank Ward and Reform Darwinism
  B. Developments in other fields of learning
    1. Developments in history
    2. Pragmatism
      a. Ideas of William James
      b. John Dewey and instrumentalism

V. Realism in American literature
  A. The local colorists
    1. Sarah Orne Jewett
    2. George Washington Cable
    3. Joel Chandler Harris
  B. Mark Twain
  C. William Dean Howells
  D. Henry James
  E. Literary naturalism
    1. Frank Norris
    2. Stephen Crane

  3. Jack London
  4. Theodore Dreiser

VI. Social critics
  A. Henry George and the single tax
  B. Henry Demarest Lloyd and cooperation
  C. Thorstein Veblen and conspicuous consumption
  D. Edward Bellamy and the utopian novel

VII. The religious response: social gospel
  A. Abandonment of inner-city churches
  B. Development of the institutional church
    1. YMCA and the Salvation Army
    2. Other facilities
  C. Washington Gladden
  D. Catholic responses to modernity

VIII. Early efforts at urban reform
  A. The settlement house movement
  B. Women's rights
    1. Growth of the female labor force
    2. Women's suffrage
      a. Conflicts in the movement
      b. Gains in the states
    3. Other women's efforts
  C. The status of laissez-faire at the end of the century

KEY ITEMS OF CHRONOLOGY

Founding of the Johns Hopkins University	1876
Henry George's *Progress and Poverty*	1879
Publication of *Dynamic Sociology*	1883
Publication of *Huckleberry Finn*	1883
First electric elevator	1889
Electric streetcar systems in cities	1890s
Publication of *Maggie: A Girl of the Streets*	1893
Veblen's *The Theory of the Leisure Class*	1899

TERMS TO MASTER

Listed below are some important terms or people with which you should be familiar after you complete the study of this chapter. Explain the significance of each name or term.

1. Frederick Law Olmstead
2. "streetcar suburbs"
3. the "new" immigration
4. American Protective Association
5. The Johns Hopkins University
6. professionalism
7. Social Darwinism

8. William Graham Sumner
9. Lester Frank Ward
10. "scientific" history
11. pragmatism
12. John Dewey
13. local color movement
14. Henry James
15. naturalism
16. Henry George
17. Edward Bellamy
18. social gospel
19. settlement houses
20. Susan B. Anthony

VOCABULARY BUILDING

Listed below are some words used in this chapter. Look up each in your dictionary.

1. tenement
2. sinister
3. beguile
4. nativism
5. accreditation
6. inviolable
7. ameliorate
8. milieu
9. folkways
10. pecuniary

EXERCISES FOR UNDERSTANDING

When you have completed the reading of the chapter, answer each of the following questions. If you have difficulty, go back and reread the section of the chapter related to the question.

Multiple-Choice Questions

Select the letter of the response which best completes the statement.

1. The most urbanized population in the United States by 1900 was
   A. along the East Coast
   B. on the Pacific Coast
   C. in the South
   D. in the Midwest

2. Urban political machines did *not*
   A. help immigrants cope with city life
   B. operate honestly
   C. provide needed city services
   D. aid the poor and needy

3. Most immigrants probably came to the United States because of
   A. famine and poverty in Europe
   B. religious and ethnic persecution in their home countries
   C. wars in Europe
   D. the chance for jobs and land in America

4. The *most* important trend in higher education after the Civil War was
   A. coeducation
   B. the development of a varied curriculum
   C. the rise of graduate schools
   D. the creation of land-grant colleges

5. Lester Frank Ward stressed
   A. the power of folkways in determining social conditions
   B. the potential of human intelligence in planning change
   C. the importance of heredity in human progress
   D. the similarity of social evolution and biological evolution

6. Henry George believed that all social ills could be solved by
   A. an income tax
   B. socialization of all private property
   C. a tax on unearned wealth coming from land ownership
   D. a tax on the number of windows in a house

7. The social gospel of Washington Gladden encouraged
   A. assistance to middle-class Christians
   B. a focus on personal sins and saving souls
   C. community services and helping the poor
   D. the laissez-faire business philosophy

8. A leader in the settlement house movement was
   A. Thorstein Veblen
   B. William Dean Howells
   C. Jane Addams
   D. Susan B. Anthony

True-False Questions

Indicate whether each statement is true or false.

1. After the Civil War, more people moved to the frontier than to cities.
2. The great immigration into the United States in the late nineteenth century was part of the movement from the country to the city.
3. From 1870 to 1890, the American college student population tripled.
4. Social Darwinism supported government regulation of business.
5. The idea of "scientific" history was based on the belief that events could be reproduced exactly as they had occurred.
6. *The Theory of the Leisure Class* was written by Henry Demarest Lloyd.
7. Women's suffrage was achieved first in the urban states of the Northwest.
8. Railroads in the late-nineteenth century were effectively regulated by state laws strongly enforced by judges.

Essay Questions

1. What factors fueled the growth of cities in the late 1800s?
2. How did native-born Americans respond to the influx of the "new" immigrants?
3. Compare and contrast the policies of social Darwinism and reform Darwinism regarding such public issues as public education and regulation of business.
4. Describe the Social Gospel movement and assess its impact.
5. What characterized the local color, realist, and naturalist schools of literature in America?

DOCUMENT

Circumstances of Typical Illinois Working Families

In 1884 the Illinois Bureau of Labor Statistics conducted a survey of typical laboring families. The survey included over 2,000 families, of whom 167 were selected for detailed accounts. Excerpted here are the accounts of eight families diverse in occupation, income, and circumstances.

> In order to present a closer view of the manner of living, the surroundings, habits, tastes and daily diet of the Illinois workingman of to-day, under various circumstances and conditions, and to afford a more definite impression as to the details of his environment than can be obtained from the mere contemplation of columns of figures, we transcribe, for a limited number of representative families, their entire record, as procured by our agents, together with the notes of observation, made at the time of the visit. . . .
>
> This minute catalogue of the details governing the life of each family portrays more vividly than any mere array of figures can the common current of daily life among the people. The extremes of condition and the average types are alike presented, and it may be seen, not only what manner of life ordinarily prevails with a given income, but also how some families, by thrift, temperance and prudence, save money and increase their store, upon earnings which other families find insufficient for their support. . . .

No. 1   Baker   Scandinavian

Earnings—Of father $375
                  Of daughter, aged eighteen   150
                  Of son, aged fifteen   48
                  Total $573

Condition—Family numbers 7—father, mother and five children, three girls and two boys. The girls aged eight, eleven and eighteen; boys, six and fifteen. The children attend school regularly. The house they occupy contains four rooms, and they pay $9 per month rent. The house is in an unhealthy and dirty locality, furnished very poorly, and kept in poor condition. The children, when out of school, pick fuel from the railroad tracks and accompanying lumber yards. The family are very ignorant, and live as the generality of the Swede race. Life insurance and trades unions are ignored.

Food—Breakfast—Coffee, bread, syrup.
          Dinner—Lunches, always.
          Supper—Meat, soup and bread.

Cost of Living—
          Rent $108
          Fuel   12
          Meat and groceries   200
          Clothing, boots and shoes, and dry goods   150
          Books, papers, etc.   3
          Sundries [miscellaneous items]   50
          Total $523

No. 23   Cigar Maker   French

Earnings—Of father $790

Condition—Family numbers 4—parents and two children, girl aged seven years and boy five. Live in house containing 6 rooms and pay for same rent at the rate of $10 per month. Both children attend school. Father carries some life insurance and belongs to trades union, and claims his wages this year are increased thereby about $200 over his wages of previous years, enabling them to live more comfortably, dress the children better, and eat more substantial and healthy food. Children healthy, bright and intelligent, and attend Sunday school. House is well furnished and has a small library. Live well and seem to be well satisfied, although their expenses equal their earnings.

Food—Breakfast—Coffee, bread, butter, milk, sugar and potatoes.
          Dinner—Tea, bread, butter, ham and eggs, poultry and dessert.
          Supper—Coffee, bread, butter, cheese, potatoes.

Cost of Living—

Rent	$120
Fuel	35
Meat	100
Groceries	300
Clothing	75
Boots and shoes	15
Dry goods	20
Books, papers, etc.	8
Life insurance	17
Trades union	11
Sickness	80
Sundries	9
Total	$790

No. 65   Plumber   Scotch-American

Earnings—Of father $1,050

Condition—Family numbers 3—parents and one girl seven years old, who attends school. Occupy 3 rooms, for which they pay $13 per month rent; situation not very pleasant, but healthy; have had very little sickness. Rooms comfortably furnished. Family dress plainly, are below the average in intelligence, do not attend church or better class of public entertainments. The head of the family has employment fifty weeks during the year, and earns more than the average of wage-workers, which would indicate sobriety and industry, notwithstanding much of his leisure time is spent in beer-gardens and like places of amusement.

Food—Breakfast—Bread, butter, meat, potatoes, eggs, fruit.
        Dinner—Lunch.
        Supper—About the same as breakfast.

Cost of Living—

Rent	$156
Fuel	36
Meat	100
Groceries	200
Clothing	60
Boots and shoes	27
Dry goods	15
Books, papers, etc.	7
Sickness	10
Sundries	150
Total	$761

No. 77   Street-Car Conductor   American

Earnings—Of father $691

Condition—Family numbers 4—parents and two boys, aged two and four years. Father works 38 weeks in the year and 12 hours per day, and receives for his services an average of $2.60 per day.

Occupies house containing 4 comfortable rooms. Husband belongs to trades union, but does not carry any life insurance. Father does not have steady employment the entire year, and has very unpleasant hours to work. Goes to work at 5 o'clock A.M., works about six hours, then lays off until 4 P.M., from which time he works until 11 P.M.

Food—Breakfast—Bread, steak, and coffee.
        Dinner—Bread, vegetables, meat and fish.
        Supper—Same as breakfast.

Cost of Living—
Rent	$120
Fuel	60
Meat and groceries	280
Clothing, boots and shoes and dry goods	150
Books, papers, etc.	15
Trades union	5
Sickness	20
Sundries	40
Total	$690

No. 100   Upholsterer   Bohemian

Earnings—Of father $420

Condition—Family numbers 8—husband, wife and six children, four girls and two boys, the former aged, respectively, one month, one and a half, three and nine years, the latter five and seven. One of the children attends school; the rest of them, that are old enough, pick up coal, and go to the fruit warehouses and collect decayed fruit and other spoiled food. The family eat poor and spoiled meats, and live miserably, but seem to grow fat on it, and have but very little sickness. House contains three rooms, into which the eight persons are huddled. They pay $6 per month for the house. Family is dirty and ignorant in the extreme. The stench from the rooms is as bad as that from the stock yards.

Food—Breakfast—Coffee and bread.
        Dinner—Soup and potatoes.
        Supper—Coffee and bread.

Cost of Living—
Rent	$72
Fuel	8
Meat and groceries	240
Clothing, boots and shoes	80
Dry goods	10
Sickness	10
Total	$420

No. 129   **Coal Miner**   **Irish**

Earnings—Of father $368
          Of son, 17 years of age   368
          Of son, 14 years of age   172
              Total $908

Condition—Family numbers 9—parents and seven children, five boys and two girls, their ages ranging from two to seventeen years. Three of these attend school, and the two oldest boys work in the mines. Family occupy a house containing 3 rooms, with an addition of a shanty, for which they pay $5 per month rent. Father is an industrious and hard-working man, but only had thirty weeks work during the year. He is a leader among his class, is a great reader, belongs to temperance society, life insurance society, and trades union. Family healthy, and members of a church. They work half an acre of land, and raise vegetables enough for family use. They are making payments on a lot, sewing machine and back debts.

Food—Breakfast—Bread, butter, meat and coffee.
       Dinner—Bread, butter, cheese or meat and tea.
       Supper—Meat, potatoes, vegetables, bread, butter, pie and
          tea.

Cost of Living—
      Rent $60
      Fuel   15
      Meat   120
      Groceries   360
      Clothing   170
      Boots, shoes and dry goods   63
      Books, papers, etc.   8
      Life insurance   30
      Trades union   5
      Sickness   4
      Sundries   63
         Total $898

No. 142   **Laborer**   **American**

Earnings—Of father $324

Condition—Family numbers 5—parents and three children, all boys, aged two, five and nine years respectively. Family occupy a house containing 3 rooms, situated in a very unhealthy locality, miserable surroundings, in the vicinity of a slough. Have a few chairs, bedstead, two poor stoves, but no carpets. Family poorly dressed; father works in saw mill; one cent per hour is retained by his employers on condition that he loses it if he leaves their service before the season closes. Father claims to have lost this 11 cts per day for the year 1881, as he had three of his fingers cut off, and could not work the season out.

Food—Breakfast—Bread, butter and coffee.
Dinner—Bread, meat and coffee.
Supper—Bread, butter, coffee and potatoes.

Cost of Living—

Rent	$48
Fuel	22
Meat and groceries	220
Clothing, boots, shoes and dry goods	30
Sickness	35
Total	$355

No. 165   Superintendent, Glass Works   American

Earnings—

Of father	$1,010
Of son, 17 years old	612
Of son, 15 years old	180
Total	$1,802

Condition—Family numbers 8—parents and six children, three boys, aged eight, sixteen and eighteen years, and three girls, aged one, five and eleven years. Two of the children attend school. Family occupy a comfortable house, containing 7 rooms, for which they pay a rental of $25 per month. Floors are all carpeted. Have piano and sewing machine. Family intelligent, and attend church regularly. They manage to save but little of their earnings. Father receives $125 per month, but only worked thirty-six weeks of the past year. He carries no life insurance.

Food—Breakfast—Bread, meat, coffee, and potatoes.
Dinner—Meats, vegetables, coffee and fruits.
Supper—Meat, potatoes, tea and fruits.

Cost of Living—

Rent	$300
Fuel	40
Meat	200
Groceries	300
Clothing	125
Boots and shoes	75
Dry goods	100
Books, papers, etc.	20
Sickness	100
Sundries	150
Total	$1,410

[From *Third Biennial Report of the Bureau of Labor Statistics of Illinois* (Springfield, Ill.: State Printer and Binder, 1884), pp. 357–358, 361, 365, 379, 383, 391, 401, 405, 413]

Questions for Reflection

Analyze carefully the different amounts spent by each family on the major catagories. What factors seem to affect family income? Which categories seem to increase most as families become more affluent? After examining this information, how much would you estimate to be the minimum amount required for a family to live comfortably?

The comments about family lifestyles were made by investigators who visited the families. What evidence can you cite to show the basic assumptions or attitudes about family life which were likely held by these investigators?

From all this information, what conclusions can you draw about family life among the working class in Illinois in the 1880s?

ANSWERS TO MULTIPLE-CHOICE AND TRUE-FALSE QUESTIONS

Multiple-Choice Questions

1-B, 2-B, 3-D, 4-C, 5-B, 6-C, 7-C, 8-C

True-False Questions

1-F, 2-T, 3-T, 4-F, 5-T, 6-F, 7-F, 8-F

21

GILDED AGE POLITICS
AND AGRARIAN REVOLT

CHAPTER OBJECTIVES

After you complete the reading and study of this chapter you should be able to

1. Describe the major features of politics in the late-nineteenth century.
2. Describe the political alignments and issues in the "third political system."
3. Explain the major issues in the presidential elections of 1888, 1892, and 1896.
4. Account for the rise of the farmers' protest movement of the 1890s.
5. Explain the impact of populism on the American scene.

CHAPTER OUTLINE

I. Nature of Gilded Age politics
   A. National political parties
      1. Evasion of issues
      2. Some disagreement on tariff
      3. Even division between parties in popular vote (1868–1912)
      4. No strong president
      5. Importance of patronage
   B. The voters
      1. High voter participation

   2. Belief in reality of issues
   3. Intense cultural conflicts
   C. Ethnic and religious divisions
      1. Republicans
      2. Democrats
      3. Issues
         a. Nativism
         b. Prohibition

II. The Hayes administration
   A. Hayes's background
   B. Divided Republicans
      1. Stalwarts and Conkling
      2. Half-Breeds and Blaine
   C. Support for civil service reform
   D. Hayes's limited version of government

III. The election of 1880
   A. Republican nomination
      1. The Grant candidacy
      2. Garfield's nomination as a dark horse
   B. Democratic nomination of Winfield Scott Hancock
   C. Closest election results of the century

IV. The Garfield-Arthur administration
   A. Garfield's background and his assassination
   B. Arthur's background
   C. His strong actions as president
      1. Support of Pendleton Civil Service Act, 1883

164

2. Support for tariff reduction
   a. Effects of treasury surplus
   b. Nature of the Mongrel Tariff of 1883
D. Scurrilous campaign of 1884
   1. Reasons Arthur was not a candidate
   2. Republican nomination of Blaine and Logan
      a. Blaine's background
      b. Effect of Mulligan letters
      c. Emergence of "Mugwumps"
   3. Democratic nomination of Cleveland
      a. Cleveland's political background
      b. His illegitimate child
      c. Concept of "Rum, Romanism, and Rebellion"
   4. Election results

V. Cleveland's presidency
A. Cleveland's view of the role of government
B. His actions on civil service
C. His stand against veterans' pensions
D. The Interstate Commerce Act
E. His stand for tariff reform
F. Election of 1888
   1. Cleveland renominated
   2. Republican nomination of Benjamin Harrison
   3. Campaign focuses on the tariff
   4. Personal attacks
   5. Results

VI. Republican reform under Harrison
A. Treatment of veterans
B. Republican control of Congress, 1889–1891
   1. Passage of Sherman Antitrust Act, 1890
   2. Sherman Silver Purchase Act, 1890
   3. Effect of McKinley Tariff, 1890
C. Democratic congressional victories of 1890
   1. Ostensible reaction to heavy spending of Republicans
   2. Impact on the election of prohibition and social issues

VII. Problems of farmers
A. Worsening economic and social conditions
   1. Causes for declining agricultural prices

   a. Overproduction
   b. Worldwide competition
   2. The railroads as villains
   3. Effects of the tariff on farmers
   4. Problems of currency deflation
   5. Problems of geography and climate
   6. Isolation of farmers
B. Development of Patrons of Husbandry
   1. Development of the Grange
   2. Effects of Granger political activity
C. Rise of the Greenback Party
D. Emergence of Farmers' Alliances
   1. Cooperative ideal
   2. Economic program
   3. Entry into politics
   4. Mary Elizabeth Lease and Jerry Simpson
E. The Populist Party
   1. Development of the party
   2. Platform stands
   3. Presidential nominees
   4. Victory of Cleveland in 1892

VIII. Depression of 1893
A. Nature of the depression
B. Reactions to the depression
C. Results of the 1894 elections

IX. Focus on silver
A. The gold drain
B. Agitation for free silver
C. Effect on nominations of 1896
   1. Republican actions
   2. Democratic candidate
   3. Populist position
D. Campaign of 1896 and its results
E. The postelection shift to gold

KEY ITEMS OF CHRONOLOGY

Patrons of Husbandry founded	1867
Hayes administration	1877–1881
Munn v. Illinois	1877
Garfield administration	March–September 1881
Arthur administration	September 1881–1885
Pendleton Civil Service Act	1883
Mongrel Tariff Act	1883
Cleveland administrations	1885–1889; 1893–1897
Interstate Commerce Act	1887
Benjamin Harrison administration	1889–1893
Sherman Anti-Trust Act	1890
Sherman Silver Purchase Act	1890
McKinley Tariff Act	1890
Populist Party founded	1892
Economic depression	1893
McKinley administrations	1897–1901

TERMS TO MASTER

Listed below are some important terms or people with which you should be familiar after you complete the study of this chapter. Explain the significance of each name or term.

1. Stalwarts and Half-Breeds
2. Bland-Allison Act
3. Pendleton Civil Service Act (1883)
4. "Mongrel Tariff" of 1883
5. James G. Blaine
6. Mugwumps
7. *Wabash Railroad v. Illinois*
8. Sherman Anti-Trust Act
9. Sherman Silver Purchase Act
10. McKinley Tariff
11. "free and unlimited coinage of silver"
12. Patrons of Husbandry
13. Farmers' Alliances
14. Populist Party
15. Jacob S. Coxey
16. William Jennings Bryan

VOCABULARY BUILDING

Listed below are some words used in this chapter. Look up each word in your dictionary.

1. jaundiced
2. bipartisan
3. static
4. disfranchisement
5. electorate
6. besmirched
7. sartorial
8. sop
9. scurrilous
10. consummate
11. commodity
12. fester

EXERCISES FOR UNDERSTANDING

When you have completed reading the chapter, answer each of the following questions. If you have difficulty, go back and reread the section of the chapter related to the question.

Multiple-Choice Questions

Select the letter of the response which best completes the statement.

1. The political parties from 1870 to 1896 generally
   A. disagreed about the issue of civil service reform
   B. pursued a policy of evasion on all issues
   C. most closely agreed with each other on the issue of the tariff
   D. disagreed most strongly over the regulation of business

2. The Republican party generally consisted of
   A. southern whites, political insiders, and immigrants
   B. Catholics, reformers, and prohibitionists
   C. nativists, Catholics, and blacks
   D. moral reformers, Protestants, and political insiders

3. The Pendleton Civil Service Act provided that
   A. most government jobs would be filled on merit
   B. presidents could increase the jobs covered by civil service
   C. Congress had to approve all civil service appointees
   D. presidents could not appoint any political friends to office

4. As president, Cleveland did *not*
   A. try to add pensions for Confederate veterans
   B. restore to the public domain exploited public lands in the West
   C. work to reduce the tariff
   D. create an agency to regulate railroads and other interstate commerce

5. The Sherman Silver Purchase Act of 1890
   A. reduced the government's purchases of silver
   B. led to the inflation desired by farmers
   C. worried eastern business and financial groups
   D. did all of the above

6. The basic problem of farmers in the late-nineteenth century was
   A. high rates charged by railroads
   B. overproduction of agricultural products
   C. inflation
   D. high prices for manufactured goods caused by high tariffs

7. The Populist Party demanded
   A. government ownership of railroads
   B. coinage of silver
   C. an income tax
   D. all of the above

8. The Democratic candidate for president in 1896 was
   A. William Jennings Bryan
   B. James G. Blaine
   C. Grover Cleveland
   D. William McKinley

True-False Questions

Indicate whether each statement is true or false.

1. The Republican Party clearly dominated American politics in the Gilded Age.
2. Party loyalty and voter turnout in the Gilded Age were primarily motivated by intense cultural conflicts among ethnic groups.
3. President Arthur supported *both* civil service reform and tariff reform.
4. "Rum, Romanism, and Rebellion" referred to the Republican Party in the 1888 election.
5. The key issue in the 1888 election was the tariff.
6. Republicans suffered severe losses in the 1890 elections.
7. In the 1870s the Grangers primarily sought inflation of the currency.
8. "You shall not crucify mankind upon a cross of gold," said Grover Cleveland.

Essay Questions

1. Describe the difference between the Democratic Party and the Republican Party in the late-nineteenth century. Pay special attention to their stands on the issues and the nature of their supporters.

2. Of the presidents between 1876 and 1896, which would you say was the most successful? Explain your response.

3. Explain why the coinage of silver was an important issue in the late-nineteenth century.

4. What issues divided the Republicans in the 1870s and 1880s?

5. What caused the farmers' problems in the Gilded Age? Explain.

6. Describe the programs advocated by the Populist Party in the 1890s. How would you judge their success?

DOCUMENT

The Omaha Platform of the Populist Party

The platform adopted by the Populist Party in 1892 shows what the Populists thought was wrong with America and how they proposed to remedy these ills.

National People's Party Platform

Assembled upon the 116th anniversary of the Declaration of Independence, the People's Party of America, in their first national convention, invoking upon their action the blessing of Almighty God, put forth in the name and on behalf of the people of this country, the following preamble and declaration of principles:

Preamble

The conditions which surround us best justify our co-operation; we meet in the midst of a nation brought to the verge of moral, political, and material ruin. Corruption dominates the ballot-box, the Legislatures, the Congress, and touches even the ermine of the bench. The people are demoralized; most of the States have been compelled to isolate the voters at the polling places to prevent universal intimidation and bribery. The newspapers are largely subsidized or muzzled, public opinion silenced, business prostrated, homes covered with mortgages, labor impoverished, and the land concentrating in the hands of capitalists. The urban workmen are denied the right to organize for self-protection, imported pauperized labor beats down their wages, a hireling standing army, unrecognized by our laws, is established to shoot them down, and they are rapidly degenerating into European conditions. The fruits of the toil of millions are boldly stolen to build up colossal fortunes for a few, unprecedented in the history of mankind; and the possessors of those, in turn, despite the Republic and endanger liberty. From the same prolific womb of governmental injustice we breed the two great classes—tramps and millionaires.

The national power to create money is appropriated to enrich bondholders; a vast public debt payable in legal tender currency has been funded into gold-bearing bonds, thereby adding millions to the burdens of the people.

Silver, which has been accepted as coin since the dawn of history, has been demonetized to add to the purchasing power of gold by decreasing the value of all forms of property as well as human labor, and the supply of currency is purposely abridged to fatten usurers, bankrupt enterprise, and enslave industry. A vast conspiracy against mankind has been organized on two continents, and it is rapidly taking possession of the world. If not met and overthrown at once it forebodes terrible social convulsions, the destruction of civilization, or the establishment of an absolute despotism.

We have witnessed for more than a quarter of a century the struggles of the two great political parties for power and plunder, while grievous wrongs have been inflicted upon the suffering people. We charge that the controlling influences dominating both these parties have permitted the existing dreadful conditions to develop without serious effort to prevent or restrain them. Neither do they now promise us any substantial reform. They have agreed together to ignore, in the coming campaign, every issue but one. They propose to drown the outcries of a plundered people with the uproar of a sham battle over the tariff, so that capitalists, corporations, national banks, rings, trusts, watered stock, the demonetization of silver and the oppressions of the usurers may all be lost sight of. They propose to sacrifice our homes, lives, and children on the altar of mammon; to destroy the multitude in order to secure corruption funds from the millionaires.

Assembled on the anniversary of the birthday of the nation, and filled with the spirit of the grand general and chief who established our independence, we seek to restore the government of the Republic to the hands of "the plain people," with which class it originated. We assert our purposes to be identical with the purposes of the National Constitution; to form a more perfect union and establish justice, insure domestic tranquility, provide for the common defence, promote the general welfare, and secure the blessings of liberty for ourselves and our posterity.

We declare that this Republic can only endure as a free government while built upon the love of the whole people for each other and for the nation; that it cannot be pinned together by bayonets; that the civil war is over, and that every passion and resentment which grew out of it must die with it, and that we must be in fact, as we are in name, one united brotherhood of free men.

Our country finds itself confronted by conditions for which there is no precedent in the history of the world; our annual agricultural productions amount to billions of dollars in value, which must, within a few weeks or months, be exchanged for billions of dollars' worth of commodities consumed in their production; the existing currency supply is wholly inadequate to make this exchange; the results are falling prices, the formation of combines and rings, the impoverishment of the producing class. We pledge ourselves that if given power we will labor to correct these evils by wise and reasonable legislation, in accordance with the terms of our platform.

We believe that the power of government—in other words, of the people—should be expanded (as in the case of the postal service) as rapidly and as far as the good sense of an intelligent people and the teachings of experience shall justify, to the end that oppression, injustice, and poverty shall eventually cease in the land.

While our sympathies as a party of reform are naturally upon the side of every proposition which will tend to make men intelligent, virtuous, and temperate, we nevertheless regard these questions, important as they are, as secondary to the great issues now pressing for solution, and upon which not only our individual prosperity but the very existence of free institutions depend; and we ask all men to first help us to determine whether we are to have a republic to administer before we differ as to the conditions upon which it is to be administered, believing that the forces of reform this day organized will never cease to move forward until every wrong is remedied and equal rights and equal privileges securely established for all the men and women of this country.

Platform

We declare, therefore—

First.—That the union of the labor forces of the United States this day consummated shall be permanent and perpetual; may its spirit enter into all hearts for the salvation of the Republic and the uplifting of mankind.

Second.—Wealth belongs to him who creates it, and every dollar taken from industry without an equivalent is robbery. "If any will not work, neither shall he eat." The interests of rural and civic labor are the same; their enemies are identical.

Third.—We believe that the time has come when the railroad corporations will either own the people or the people must own the railroads, and should the government enter upon the work of owning and managing all railroads, we should favor an amendment to the Constitution by which all persons engaged in the government service shall be placed under a civil-service regulation of the most rigid character, so as to prevent the increase of the power of the national administration by the use of such additional government employes.

Finance.—We demand a national currency safe, sound, and flexible, issued by the general government only, a full legal tender for all debts, public and private, and that without the use of banking corporations, a just, equitable, and efficient means of distribution direct to the people, at a tax not to exceed 2 per cent per annum, to be provided as set forth in the sub-treasury plan of the Farmers' Alliance, or a better system; also by payments in discharge of its obligations for public improvements.

1. We demand free and unlimited coinage of silver and gold at the present legal ratio of 16 to 1.

2. We demand that the amount of circulating medium be speedily increased to not less than $50 per capita.

3. We demand a graduated income tax.

4. We believe that the money of the country should be kept as much as possible in the hands of the people, and hence we demand that all State and national revenues shall be limited to the necessary expenses of the government, economically and honestly administered.

5. We demand that postal savings banks be established by the government for the safe deposit of the earnings of the people and to facilitate exchange.

Transportation.—Transportation being a means of exchange and a public necessity, the government should own and operate the railroads in the interest of the people. The telegraph, telephone, like the post-office system, being a necessity for the transmission of news, should be owned and operated by the government in the interest of the people.

Land.—The land, including all the natural sources of wealth, is the heritage of the people, and should not be monopolized for speculative purposes, and alien ownership of land should be prohibited. All land now held by railroads and other corporations in excess of their actual needs, and all lands now owned by aliens should be reclaimed by the government and held for actual settlers only.

Expression of Sentiments

Your Committee on Platform and Resolutions beg leave unanimously to report the following:

Whereas, Other questions have been presented for our consideration, we hereby submit the following, not as a part of the Platform of the People's Party, but as resolutions expressive of the sentiment of the Convention.

1. *Resolved,* That we demand a free ballot and a fair count in all elections, and pledge ourselves to secure it to every legal voter without Federal intervention, through the adoption by the States of the unperverted Australian or secret ballot system.

2. *Resolved,* That the revenue derived from a graduated income tax should be applied to the reduction of the burden of taxation now levied upon the domestic industries of this country.

3. *Resolved,* That we pledge our support to fair and liberal pensions to ex-Union soldiers and sailors.

4. *Resolved,* That we condemn the fallacy of protecting American labor under the present system, which opens our ports to the pauper and criminal classes of the world and crowds out our wage-earners; and we denounce the present ineffective laws against contract labor, and demand the further restriction of undesirable emigration.

5. *Resolved,* That we cordially sympathize with the efforts of organized workingmen to shorten the hours of labor, and demand a rigid enforcement of the existing eight-hour law on Government work, and ask that a penalty clause be added to the said law.

6. *Resolved,* That we regard the maintenance of a large standing army of mercenaries, known as the Pinkerton system, as a menace to our liberties, and we demand its abolition; and we condemn the recent invasion of the Territory of Wyoming by the hired assassins of plutocracy, assisted by Federal officers.

7. *Resolved,* That we commend to the favorable consideration of the people and the reform press the legislative system known as the initiative and referendum.

8. *Resolved,* That we favor a constitutional provision limiting the office of President and Vice-President to one term, and providing for the election of Senators of the United States by a direct vote of the people.

9. *Resolved,* That we oppose any subsidy or national aid to any private corporation for any purpose.

10. *Resolved,* That this convention sympathizes with the Knights of Labor and their righteous contest with the tyrannical combine of clothing manufacturers of Rochester, and declare it to be the duty of all who hate tyranny and oppression to refuse to purchase the goods made by the said manufacturers, or to patronize any merchants who sell such goods.

[*The World Almanac,* 1893 (New York: Publisher, 1893), pp. 83–85, reprinted in *A Populist Reader,* edited by George B. Tindall (New York: Harper and Row, 1966), pp. 90–96]

Questions for Reflection

What ideas expressed in the preamble do you recognize from your study of this period? (For example, the "hireling standing army" refers to the Pinkerton detectives often used in cases of industrial violence.)

Which planks of the platform and expressions of sentiments were later enacted in one form or another?

ANSWERS TO MULTIPLE-CHOICE AND TRUE-FALSE QUESTIONS

Multiple-Choice Questions

1-B, 2-D, 3-B, 4-A, 5-C, 6-B, 7-D, 8-A

True-False Questions

1-F, 2-T, 3-T, 4-F, 5-T, 6-T, 7-F, 8-F

22

THE COURSE OF EMPIRE

CHAPTER OBJECTIVES

After you complete the reading and study of this chapter you should be able to

1. Explain why the United States entered upon a policy of imperialism.
2. Account for the outbreak of the Spanish-American War.
3. Explain the course of United States relations with Latin America during the late-nineteenth century and its impact on later relations with Latin America.
4. Contrast the arguments in 1899 for and against imperialism.
5. Explain the development of America's policy for dealing with its imperial possessions.
6. Account for the acquisition of the Panama Canal.
7. Assess the foreign policies of Theodore Roosevelt and William Howard Taft.

CHAPTER OUTLINE

I. Stirrings of imperialism
   A. Isolationism prior to the Civil War
   B. Seward's diplomacy
      1. Napoleon III's Mexican adventure (1867)
      2. Purchase of Alaska (1867)
      3. Annexation of Midway Islands (1867)
   C. Fish's settlements of claims with Britain (1871)
   D. Expansionist visions in the Pacific
      1. Early whaling and missionary interests
      2. Acquisition of Samoa
      3. Relations with Hawaii
         a. Early American settlements
         b. Reciprocal trade agreement of 1875
         c. Constitutional government
         d. Dole revolution and desire for annexation (1893)
         e. Hawaii proclaimed a republic (1894)

II. Motivation for imperialism
   A. Economic motivations
   B. Mahan's concept of sea power
   C. Social Darwinian justifications
      1. Concept of Social Darwinism
      2. Racial corollaries
   D. Religious justification

III. Development of the Spanish-American War
   A. Effects of American investments and tariffs
   B. Guerrilla warfare by revolutionaries
   C. Weyler's reconcentration policy
   D. Role of the press in the war
      1. Contest between Hearst's *Journal* and Pulitzer's *World*

2. Examples of yellow journalism
E. Cleveland's efforts for compromise
F. Spanish response to McKinley's stance
G. Arousal of public opinion
   1. de Lôme letter (February 9, 1898)
   2. Sinking of the *Maine* (February 15, 1898)
H. The final moves to war
I. Motives for war

IV. Fighting the "splendid little war"
  A. Role of war correspondents
  B. Naval victory at Manila Bay
  C. Cuban blockade
    1. Problems of the army
    2. The Rough Riders
    3. Siege of Santiago
  D. Puerto Rican campaign
  E. Terms of the armistice

V. Developing and debating imperialism
  A. Negotiations for the Treaty of Paris (December 10)
    1. Cuban debt question
    2. Annexation of the Philippines
  B. Motives for annexation
  C. Terms of the treaty
  D. Other territorial acquisitions
  E. Debate over the treaty
    1. Anti-imperialist arguments
    2. Bryan's support
    3. Ratification (February 1899)
  F. Filipino insurrection
  G. Emergence of the Anti-Imperialist League (October 1899)

VI. Organizing the new acquisitions
  A. The Philippines under Taft
  B. Civil government for Puerto Rico
  C. The Insular Cases
    1. The questions at issue
    2. Lack of incorporation for overseas possessions
  D. Problems in Cuba
    1. Leonard Wood as military governor
    2. Efforts to control yellow fever
    3. Cuban constitution
    4. Platt Amendment
    5. Insurrection of 1906
  E. Imperial rivalries and the Open-Door Policy in the Far East
    1. The scramble for spheres of influence in China
    2. The Open-Door Policy

    a. British initiatives
    b. Unilateral action
    c. Policies of the Open-Door Note
    d. Reactions of other nations
   3. The Boxer Rebellion
   4. Success of Hay's policy

VII. Rise of Theodore Roosevelt
  A. Election of 1900
    1. Democrats and imperialism
    2. Republican nominees
    3. Outcome of election
  B. McKinley's assassination
  C. TR's background and character
    1. Strenuous life
    2. Life in the West
    3. New York politics

VIII. TR's foreign policies
  A. The Panama Canal
    1. Negotiations with British and French
    2. Difficulties with Colombia
    3. Revolution in Panama
    4. Treaty with Panama
    5. Opening of Canal
  B. The Roosevelt Corollary
    1. Problems of debt collection
    2. Principles in new policy
  C. TR's role in the Russo-Japanese War
  D. American relations with Japan
    1. Agreements on Korea, China, and Philippines
    2. Racism
    3. Gentlemen's Agreement of 1907
  E. The United States and Europe
    1. Conference at Algeciras
    2. Tour of the "Great White Fleet"

KEY ITEMS OF CHRONOLOGY

Purchase of Alaska	1867
Mahan's *The Influence of Seapower upon History*	1890
de Lôme letter revealed	February 9, 1898
Maine sunk	February 15, 1898
War formally declared between Spain and the United States	April 1898
Hawaii annexed	July 1898
Armistice	August 1898
Treaty of Paris	December 1898
Anti-Imperialist League formed	1899
Open-Door Notes	1899
Assassination of McKinley	1901
Panama Canal acquired	1903
Roosevelt Corollary announced	1904
Gentlemen's Agreement with Japan	1907

TERMS TO MASTER

Listed below are some important terms or people with which you should be familiar after you complete the study of this chapter. Explain the significance of each name or term.

1. William H. Seward
2. Alfred Thayer Mahan
3. John Fiske
4. Josiah Strong
5. yellow journalism
6. de Lôme letter
7. Teller Amendment
8. Platt Amendment
9. Open-Door Policy
10. Boxer Rebellion
11. Panama Canal
12. Roosevelt Corollary
13. Portsmouth conference
14. Gentlemen's Agreement
15. "Great White fleet"

VOCABULARY BUILDING

Listed below are some words used in this chapter. Look up each word in your dictionary.

1. annexation
2. isthmian
3. sanction
4. chagrin
5. unilateral
6. reminiscent
7. euphoria
8. anarchist
9. taxidermist
10. pristine

EXERCISES FOR UNDERSTANDING

When you have completed reading the chapter, answer each of the following questions. If you have difficulty, go back and reread the section of the chapter related to the question.

Multiple-Choice Questions

Select the letter of the response which best completes the statement.

1. The "new imperialism" of the 1890s especially stressed
   A. access to new markets
   B. converting heathens to Christianity
   C. annexing territory to the United States
   D. military conquests of other nations

2. The ideas of Charles Darwin were used by some, including John Fiske, to
   A. justify imperialism by all nations
   B. support Anglo-Saxon dominance
   C. criticize colonialism
   D. advocate revolution by oppressed peoples

3. According to the text, a key factor propelling the United States into the Spanish-American War was
   A. the desire of businessmen to control trade and manufacturing in Cuba
   B. the hope of missionaries to convert the Cuban people
   C. McKinley's desire to gain political support from his acquisitions
   D. the frenzy of public opinion for war

4. The Teller Amendment called for
   A. war against Spain and the Philippines
   B. annexation of Hawaii and Cuba
   C. unlimited immigration to the United States
   D. none of the above

5. Anti-imperialist arguments after the Spanish-American War included all of the following *except*
   A. the white man's burden
   B. traditional American isolationism
   C. the incompatibility of "bananas and self-government"
   D. the cost of defending the Philippines

6. The Platt Amendment
   A. gave women the right to vote in national elections
   B. annexed Puerto Rico
   C. limited the independence of the new Cuban government
   D. gave the president expanded power in foreign affairs

7. The proposal that each nation should have equal access to trade with China was known as the
   A. Gentlemen's Agreement
   B. Open-Door Policy
   C. Teller Amendment
   D. white man's burden

8. The Roosevelt Corollary
   A. extended the Open-Door Policy to Cuba
   B. applied the Monroe Doctrine to Hawaii
   C. repudiated the Teller and Platt Amendments
   D. did none of the above

True-False Questions

Indicate whether each statement is true or false.

1. In the 1880s the major field of United States overseas activity was the Pacific Ocean.
2. Henry Cabot Lodge wrote *The Influence of Sea Power Upon History.*
3. The United States sided with the rebel Valeriano Weyler in the Cuban revolution.
4. The de Lôme letter explained why the *Maine* had been sunk.
5. The toughest question in American foreign policy in the 1890s involved the Philippines.
6. By 1920 both Puerto Rico and the Philippines had gained complete independence from the United States.
7. In the Russo-Japanese War the United States fought with the Japanese.
8. Theodore Roosevelt won a Nobel Prize for his work at the Portsmouth and Algeciras conferences.

Essay Questions

1. Describe three arguments Americans used to justify their imperialism in the late-nineteenth century.
2. What were the various factors that caused the Spanish-American War?
3. Discuss the arguments for and against acquisition of the Philippines.

4. Explain the Open-Door Policy and its effects.

5. How did United States policy in Latin America change between 1890 and 1912?
6. Trace developments leading to the acquisition of the Panama Canal.

DOCUMENT

McKinley's "War" Message to Congress

McKinley's message of April 11, 1898, attempted to summarize American relations with Cuba. Read it carefully to gain an understanding of his perception of events.

Obedient to that precept of the Constitution which commands the President to give from time to time to the Congress information of the state of the Union and to recommend to their consideration such measures as he shall judge necessary and expedient, it becomes my duty now to address your body with regard to the grave crisis that has arisen in the relations of the United States to Spain by reason of the warfare that for more than three years has raged in the neighboring island of Cuba. . . .

Since the present revolution began, in February, 1895, this country has seen the fertile domain at our threshold ravaged by fire and sword in the course of a struggle unequaled in the history of the island and rarely paralleled as to the numbers of the combatants and the bitterness of the contest by any revolution of modern times where a dependent people striving to be free have been opposed by the power of the sovereign state. . . .

Our trade has suffered, the capital invested by our citizens in Cuba has been largely lost, and the temper and forbearance of our people have been so sorely tried as to beget a perilous unrest among our own citizens. . . .

The agricultural population to the estimated number of 300,000 or more was herded within the towns and their immediate vicinage, deprived of the means of support, rendered destitute of shelter, left poorly clad, and exposed to the most unsanitary conditions. As the scarcity of food increased with the devastation of the depopulated areas of production, destitution and want became misery and starvation. Month by month the death rate increased in an alarming ratio. By March, 1897, according to conservative estimates from official Spanish sources, the mortality among the reconcentrados from starvation and diseases thereto incident exceeded 50 per cent of their total number. . . .

The war in Cuba is of such a nature that short of subjugation or extermination, a final military victory for either side seems impracticable. The alternative lies in the physical exhaustion of the one or the other party, or perhaps of both. . . . The prospect of such a protraction and conclusion of the present strife is a contingency hardly to be contemplated with equanimity by the civilized world, and least of all by the United States, affected and injured as we are, deeply and intimately, by its very existence. . . .

The forcible intervention of the United States as a neutral to stop the war, according to the large dictates of humanity and following many historical precedents where neighboring States have interfered to check the hopeless sacrifices of life by internecine conflicts beyond their borders, is justifiable on rational grounds. It involves, however, hostile constraint upon both the parties to the contest as well to enforce a truce as to guide the eventual settlement.

. . . The present condition of affairs in Cuba is a constant menace to our peace and entails upon this Government an enormous expense. With such a conflict waged for years in an island so near us and with which our people have such trade and business relations; when the lives and liberty of our citizens are in constant danger and their property destroyed and themselves ruined; where our trading vessels are liable to seizure and are seized at our very door by war ships of a foreign nation, the expeditions of filibustering that we are powerless to prevent altogether, and the irritating questions and entanglements thus arising—all these and others that I need not mention, with the resulting strained relations, are a constant menace to our peace and compel us to keep on a semi-war footing with a nation with which we are at peace.

These elements of danger and disorder already pointed out have been strikingly illustrated by a tragic event which has deeply and justly moved the American people. I have already transmitted to Congress the report of the naval court of inquiry on the destruction of the battle ship *Maine* in the harbor of Havana during the night of the 15th of February. The destruction of that noble vessel has filled the national heart with inexpressible horror. Two hundred and fifty-eight brave sailors and marines and two officers of our Navy, reposing in the fancied security of a friendly harbor, have been hurled to death, grief and want brought to their homes and sorrow to the nation.

The naval court of inquiry, which, it is needless to say, commands the unqualified confidence of the Government, was unanimous in its conclusion that the destruction of the *Maine* was caused by an exterior explosion—that of a submarine mine. It did not assume to place the responsibility. That remains to be fixed.

In any event the destruction of the *Maine,* by whatever exterior cause, is a patent and impressive proof of a state of things in Cuba that is intolerable. That condition is thus shown to be such that the Spanish Government can not assure safety and security to a vessel of the American Navy in the harbor of Havana on a mission of peace, and rightfully there.

In view of these facts and of these considerations I ask the Congress to authorize and empower the President to take measures to secure a full and final termination of hostilities between the Government of Spain and the people of Cuba, and to secure in the island the establishment of a stable government, capable of maintaining order and observing its international obligations, insuring peace and tranquillity and the security of its citizens as well as our own, and to use the military and naval forces of the United States as may be necessary for these purposes. . . .

The issue is now with the Congress. It is a solemn responsibility. I have exhausted every effort to relieve the intolerable condition of affairs which is at our doors. . . .

Yesterday, and since the preparation of the foregoing message, official information was received by me that the latest decree of the Queen Regent of Spain directs General Blanco, in order to prepare and facilitate peace, to proclaim a suspension of hostilities, the duration and details of which have not yet been communicated to me.

This fact with every other pertinent consideration will, I am sure, have your just and careful attention in the solemn deliberations upon which you are about to enter. If this measure attains a successful result, then our aspirations as a Christian, peace-loving people will be realized. If it fails, it will be only another justification for our contemplated action.

[James D. Richardson (ed.), *A Compilation of the Messages and Papers of the Presidents, 1789–1897* (Washington, D.C.: U.S. Government Printing Office, 1899), 10: 139–150]

Questions for Reflection

Does McKinley anywhere in the message ask Congress to declare war on Spain? How could a declaration of war be justified in light of his request? How accurate was McKinley's description of developments between Cuba and the United States? Can you see any reason why Congress might have been skeptical of McKinley's claim that Spain had offered to cease hostilities in Cuba? Does this document suggest that the United States was justified in becoming involved in the Cuban matter and ultimately in the Spanish-American War?

ANSWERS TO MULTIPLE-CHOICE AND TRUE-FALSE QUESTIONS

Multiple-Choice Questions

1-A, 2-B, 3-D, 4-D, 5-A, 6-C, 7-B, 8-D

True-False Questions

1-T, 2-F, 3-F, 4-F, 5-F, 6-F, 7-F, 8-T

23

PROGRESSIVISM:
ROOSEVELT, TAFT, AND WILSON

CHAPTER OBJECTIVES

After you complete the reading and study of this chapter you should be able to

1. Explain the nature and the goals of the progressive movement.
2. Compare the progressive movement with the populist movement.
3. Describe Roosevelt's brand of progressivism.
4. Account for Taft's mixed record as a progressive.
5. Describe Wilson's efforts for progressive reform.
6. Assess the impact of progressivism on American politics, society, and economy.

CHAPTER OUTLINE

I. The nature of progressivism
   A. General features
      1. Aimed against the abuses of the Gilded Age bosses
      2. More businesslike and efficient than populism
      3. A paradox of regulation of business by businessmen
      4. A diverse movement
   B. Antecedents
      1. Populism
      2. Mugwumps
      3. Socialist critiques of living and working conditions
      4. Role of the muckrakers
         a. Henry Demarest Lloyd and Jacob Riis
         b. Brought popular support for reform
         c. Stronger on diagnosis than remedy
   C. The themes of progressivism
      1. Efforts to democratize government
         a. Direct primaries
         b. Initiative, referendum, recall, and other local actions
         c. Direct election of senators
      2. A focus on efficiency and good government
         a. Role of Frederick W. Taylor and scientific management
         b. Commission and city-manager forms of city government
         c. Use of specialists in government and business
      3. Regulation of giant corporations
         a. Acceptance and regulation of big business
         b. Problem of regulating the regulators

4. Impulse toward social justice
   a. Use of private charities and state power
   b. Outlawing child labor
   c. Restricting night work and dangerous occupations
   d. Erratic course of the Supreme Court
   e. Stricter building codes and factory inspection acts
   f. Pressure for prohibition

II. Roosevelt's progressivism
  A. Need for his cautious role
  B. Focus on trust regulation
    1. Opposition to sheer trustbusting
    2. Northern Securities case (1904) used to promote the issue
  C. Coal strike of 1902
    1. Basis for the UMW strike
    2. Recalcitrant attitude of management
    3. Roosevelt's efforts to force arbitration
    4. Effects of the incident
  D. Congressional action
    1. Department of Commerce and Labor
    2. Elkins Act
  E. Other antitrust suits

III. TR's second term
  A. Election of 1904
    1. Republican nomination
    2. Democratic positions and candidate
    3. Campaign and results
  B. Roosevelt's legislative leadership
    1. Hepburn Act
    2. Roosevelt's support of regulation of food and drugs
     a. Role of muckrakers: Upton Sinclair and others
     b. Legislation achieved
  C. Efforts for conservation
    1. Earlier movements for conservation
    2. Roosevelt's actions

IV. Taft's administration
  A. Selection of a successor in 1908
    1. TR's choice
    2. Democrats and Bryan
    3. Election results
  B. Taft's background and character

  C. Campaign for tariff reform
    1. Problems in the Senate
    2. Taft's clash with the Progressive Republicans
  D. Ballinger-Pinchot controversy
  E. Roosevelt's response upon his return to the United States
    1. Initial silence
    2. Development of the New Nationalism
    3. TR enters the race
  F. Taft's achievements
    1. In conservation
    2. Mann-Elkins Act
    3. Antitrust actions
    4. Constitutional amendments

V. The election of 1912
  A. The Republican nomination of 1912
  B. Creation of the Progressive Party
  C. Wilson's rise to power
    1. His background
    2. His actions in New Jersey
    3. His nomination
  D. Focus of the campaign on the New Nationalism and the New Freedom
  E. Wilson's election
  F. Significance of the election of 1912
    1. High-water mark for progressivism
    2. Brought Democrats back into office
    3. Brought southerners into control

VI. Wilsonian reform
  A. Wilson's style
  B. Tariff reform
    1. Personal appearance before Congress
    2. Tariff changes in the Underwood-Simmons Act
    3. Income tax provisions
  C. The Federal Reserve Act
    1. Compromises required
    2. Description of the Federal Reserve System
  D. Efforts for new antitrust laws
    1. Wilson's approach in 1912
    2. Federal Trade Commission Act (September 1914)
    3. Clayton Antitrust Act (October 1914)
     a. Practices outlawed
     b. Provisions for labor and farm organizations

4. Disappointments with
   administration of the new laws
E. The shortcomings of Wilson's
   progressivism
F. Wilson's return to reform
   1. Plight of the Progressive Party
   2. Appointment of Brandeis to the
      Supreme Court
   3. Support for land banks and
      long-term farm loans

4. Farm demonstration agents and
   agricultural education
5. Labor reform legislation
VII. The paradoxes of progressivism
   A. Disfranchisement of southern blacks
   B. Manipulation of democratic reforms
   C. Decision-making by faceless
      bureaucratic experts
   D. Decline of voter participation
   E. From optimism to war

KEY ITEMS OF CHRONOLOGY

Roosevelt administration	1901–1909
Anthracite coal strike	1902
Northern Securities Case	1904
Elkins Act	1904
Hepburn Act	1906
Pure Food and Drug Act	1906
Mann-Elkins Act	1910
The Principles of Scientific Management published	1911
Wilson administrations	1913–1921
Sixteenth Amendment (income tax) ratified	1913
Seventeenth Amendment (direct Senate election) ratified	1913
Underwood-Simmons Tariff Act	1913
Federal Reserve Act	1913
Federal Trade Commission Act	1914
Clayton Antitrust Act	1914
Adamson Act	1916

TERMS TO MASTER

Listed below are some important terms or people with which you should be familiar after you complete the study of this chapter. Explain the significance of each name or term.

1. muckrakers
2. initiative and referendum
3. Frederick W. Taylor
4. Northern Securities case
5. anthracite coal strike
6. Robert M. La Follette
7. Elkins Act
8. Hepburn Act
9. Upton Sinclair's *The Jungle*
10. Ballinger-Pinchot controversy
11. New Nationalism
12. New Freedom
13. Federal Reserve System
14. Federal Trade Commission
15. Clayton Antitrust Act

VOCABULARY BUILDING

Listed below are some words used in this chapter. Look up each word in your dictionary.

1. antecedent
2. foster
3. salient
4. dissolution

5. intrastate
6. dubious
7. arbitration
8. irrevocably

EXERCISES FOR UNDERSTANDING

When you have completed reading the chapter, answer each of the following questions. If you have difficulty, go back and reread the section of the chapter related to the question.

Multiple-Choice Questions

Select the letter of the response which best completes the statement.

1. Antecedents contributing to the rise of progressivism included all of the following *except*
   A. Mugwump reformers
   B. populism
   C. isolationism
   D. socialism

2. Social justice reforms included
   A. laws restricting child labor
   B. the Sherman Antitrust Act
   C. the initiative and the referendum
   D. the Seventeenth Amendment to the Constitution

3. In dealing with trusts, President Roosevelt
   A. tried to restore small businesses
   B. wanted efficient regulation
   C. was a powerful trust-buster
   D. advocated government ownership of large industry

4. Under President Roosevelt, Gifford Pinchot directed programs related to the
   A. breaking up of trusts
   B. conservation of natural resources
   C. protection of consumers of foods and drugs
   D. regulation of the major railroads

5. In the Ballinger-Pinchot controversy, President Taft
   A. stayed out and let the courts settle it
   B. followed the policy established by Roosevelt
   C. fired Ballinger for insubordination
   D. did none of the above

6. The phrase "Hamiltonian means to achieve Jeffersonian ends" summarizes the 1912 views of
   A. Woodrow Wilson
   B. William Howard Taft
   C. Theodore Roosevelt
   D. Eugene V. Debs

7. The Clayton Antitrust Act attempted to regulate trusts by
   A. defining actions of unfair competition
   B. placing control in a small group of regulators
   C. taking control of trusts from the courts
   D. repealing the Sherman Antitrust Act

8. About 1916, Wilson renewed his support for progressive reforms because
   A. he needed to build a coalition for reelection
   B. World War I gave the president unlimited powers to act
   C. he was about to leave office and wanted to create an enduring legacy
   D. all of the above are true

True-False Questions

Indicate whether each statement is true or false.

1. Muckraker Henry Demarest Lloyd exposed the evils of the Standard Oil Company.
2. The easiest problem for progressives to solve was the regulation of business.
3. In the anthracite coal strike of 1902 President Roosevelt used troops to keep the mines open.
4. Taft brought more antitrust suits in four years than TR did in eight years.
5. Robert La Follette ran for president on the Progressive Party ticket in 1912.
6. Before entering politics Woodrow Wilson worked as president of a large industrial corporation.
7. The Underwood-Simmons Tariff of 1913 sought to restore competition by lowering import duties.
8. Wilson preferred the Federal Trade Commission Act to the Clayton Antitrust Act.

Essay Questions

1. Explain the major themes of progressivism.
2 Explain the significance of the election of 1912.
3. Compare and contrast the policies of Presidents Roosevelt and Wilson regarding big business.
4. In what ways was President Taft a progressive?
5. Was Theodore Roosevelt or Wilson the more successful progressive president? Explain your answer.
6. What were the limitations of progressivism? What lasting contributions did it make?

DOCUMENT

Wilson's First Inaugural Address, March 4, 1913

Woodrow Wilson's first inaugural address is an eloquent expression of the New Freedom philosophy he espoused during the 1912 campaign. Reprinted here in its entirety, the address also set the legislative agenda for Wilson's first term.

My Fellow Citizens:

There has been a change of government. It began two years ago, when the House of Representatives became Democratic by a decisive majority. It has now been completed. The Senate about to assemble will also be Democratic. The offices of President and Vice-President have been put into the hands of Democrats. What does the change mean? That is the question that is uppermost in our minds to-day. That is the question I am going to try to answer, in order, if I may, to interpret the occasion.

It means much more than the mere success of a party. The success of a party means little except when the Nation is using that party for a large and definite purpose. No one can mistake the purpose for which the Nation now seeks to use the Democratic Party. It seeks to use it to interpret a change in its own plans and point of view. Some old things with which we had grown familiar, and which had begun to creep into the very habit of our thought and of our lives, have altered their aspect as we have latterly looked critically upon them, with fresh, awakened eyes; have dropped their disguises and shown themselves alien and sinister. Some new things, as we look frankly upon them, willing to comprehend their real character, have come to assume the aspect of things long believed in and familiar, stuff of our own convictions. We have been refreshed by a new insight into our own life.

We see that in many things that life is very great. It is incomparably great in its material aspects, in its body of wealth, in the diversity and sweep of its energy, in the industries which have been conceived and built up by the genius of individual men and the limitless enterprise of groups of men. It is great, also, very great, in its moral force.

Nowhere else in the world have noble men and women exhibited in more striking forms the beauty and the energy of sympathy and helpfulness and counsel in their efforts to rectify wrong, alleviate suffering, and set the weak in the way of strength and hope. We have built up, moreover, a great system of government, which has stood through a long age as in many respects a model for those who seek to set liberty upon foundations that will endure against fortuitous change, against storm and accident. Our life contains every great thing, and contains it in rich abundance.

But the evil has come with the good, and much fine gold has been corroded. With riches has come inexcusable waste. We have squandered a great part of what we might have used, and have not stopped to conserve the exceeding bounty of nature, without which our genius for enterprise would have been worthless and impotent, scorning to be careful, shamefully prodigal as well as admirably efficient. We have been proud of our industrial achievements, but we have not hitherto stopped thoughtfully enough to count the human cost, the cost of lives snuffed out, of energies overtaxed and broken, the fearful physical and spiritual cost to the men and women and children upon whom the dead weight and burden of it all has fallen pitilessly the years through. The groans and agony of it all had not yet reached our ears, the solemn, moving undertone of our life, coming up out of the mines and factories and out of every home where the struggle had its initimate and familiar seat. With the great Government went many deep secret things which we too long delayed to look into and scrutinize with candid, fearless eyes. The great Government we loved has too often been made use of for private and selfish purposes, and those who used it had forgotten the people.

At last a vision has been vouchsafed us of our life as a whole. We see the bad with the good, the debased and decadent with the sound and vital. With this vision we approach new affairs. Our duty is to cleanse, to reconsider, to restore, to correct the evil without impairing the good, to purify and humanize every process of our common life without weakening or sentimentalizing it. There has been something crude and heartless and unfeeling in our haste to succeed and be great. Our thought has been "Let every man look out for himself, let every generation look out for itself," while we reared giant machinery which made it impossible that any but those who stood at the levers of control should have a chance to look out for themselves. We had not forgotten our morals. We remembered well enough that we had set up a policy which was meant to serve the humblest as well as the most powerful, with an eye single to the standards of justice and fair play, and remembered it with pride. But we were very heedless and in a hurry to be great.

We have come now to the sober second thought. The scales of heedlessness have fallen from our eyes. We have made up our minds to square every process of our national life again with the standards we so proudly set up at the beginning and have always carried at our hearts. Our work is a work of restoration.

We have itemized with some degree of particularity the things that ought to be altered and here are some of the chief items: A tariff which cuts us off from our proper part in the commerce of the world, violates the just principles of taxation, and makes the Government a facile instrument in the hands of private interests; a banking and currency system based upon the necessity of the Government to sell its bonds fifty years ago and perfectly adapted to concentrating cash and restricting credits; an industrial system which, take it on all its sides, financial as well as administrative, holds capital in leading strings, restricts the liberties and limits the opportunities of labor, and exploits without renewing or conserving the natural resources of the country; a body of agricultural activities never yet given the efficiency of great business undertakings or served as it should be through the instrumentality of science taken directly to the farm, or afforded the facilities of credit best suited to its practical needs; water-courses undeveloped, waste places unreclaimed, forests untended, fast disappearing without plan or prospect of renewal, unregarded waste heaps at every mine. We have studied as perhaps no other nation has the most effective means of production, but we have not studied cost or economy as we should either as organizers of industry, as statesmen, or as individuals.

Nor have we studied and perfected the means by which government may be put at the service of humanity, in safeguarding the health of the Nation, the health of its men and its women and its children, as well as their rights in the struggle for existence. This is no sentimental duty. The firm basis of government is justice, not pity. These are matters of justice. There can be no equality or opportunity, the first essential of justice in the body politic, if men and women and children be not shielded in their lives, their very vitality, from the consequences of great industrial and social processes which they can not alter, control, or singly cope with. Society must see to it that it does not itself crush or weaken or damage its own constituent parts. The first duty of law is to keep sound the society it serves. Sanitary laws, pure food laws, and laws determining conditions of labor which individuals are powerless to determine for themselves are intimate parts of the very business of justice and legal or efficiency.

These are some of the things we ought to do, and not leave the others undone, the old-fashioned, never-to-be-neglected, fundamental safeguarding of property and of individual right. This is the high enterprise of the new day: To lift everything that concerns our life as a Nation to the light that shines from the hearthfire of every man's conscience and vision of the right. It is inconceivable that we should do this as partisans; it is inconceivable we should do it in ignorance of the facts as they are or in blind haste. We shall restore, not destroy. We shall deal with our economic system as it is and as it may be modified, not as it might be if we had a clean sheet of paper to write upon; and step by step we shall make it what it should be, in the spirit of those who question their own wisdom and seek counsel and knowledge, not shallow self-satisfaction or the excitement of excursions whither they can not tell. Justice, and only justice, shall always be our motto.

And yet it will be no cool process of mere science. The Nation has been deeply stirred, stirred by a solemn passion, stirred by the knowledge of wrong, of ideals lost, of government too often debauched and made an instrument of evil. The feelings with which we face this new age of right and opportunity sweep across our heartstrings like some air out of God's own presence, where justice and mercy are reconciled and the judge and the brother are one. We know our task to be no mere task of politics but a task which shall search us through and through, whether we be able to understand our time and the need of our people, whether we be indeed their spokesmen and interpreters, whether we have the pure heart to comprehend and the rectified will to choose our high course of action.

This is not a day of triumph; it is a day of dedication. Here muster, not the forces of party, but the forces of humanity. Men's hearts wait upon us; men's lives hang in the balance; men's hopes call upon us to say what we will do. Who shall live up to the great trust? Who dares fail to try? I summon all honest men, all patriotic, all forward-looking men, to my side. God helping me, I will not fail them, if they will but counsel and sustain me!

[U.S., 63rd Congress, Special Session, *Senate Doc. 3*]

Questions for Reflection

Why does Wilson begin his address by commenting on the significance of parties? What is Wilson's assessment of American society—its achievements and its failures?

How successful was Wilson in implementing his legislative goals? Was he effective in changing "the things that ought to be altered"?

ANSWERS TO MULTIPLE-CHOICE AND TRUE-FALSE QUESTIONS

Multiple-Choice Questions

1-C, 2-A, 3-B, 4-B, 5-D, 6-C, 7-A, 8-A

True-False Questions

1-T, 2-F, 3-F, 4-T, 5-F, 6-F, 7-T, 8-T

24

WILSON AND THE GREAT WAR

CHAPTER OBJECTIVES

After you complete the reading and study of this chapter you should be able to

1. Describe Wilson's idealistic diplomacy and show the clash of ideals and reality in Mexico.
2. Explain early United States reaction to the World War.
3. Account for the entry of the United States into World War I.
4. Explain the status of civil liberties during World War I and during the Red Scare afterward.
5. Explain the process and product of peacemaking after World War I.
6. Account for the failure of the United States to ratify the peace treaty after World War I.
7. Describe the problems of reconversion from World War I to civilian life.

CHAPTER OUTLINE

I. Wilson and foreign affairs
  A. Inexperience and idealism
  B. Intervention in Mexico
    1. Overthrow of Diaz
    2. Nonrecognition of the Huerta government

    3. Invasion at Vera Cruz
    4. Carranza's government
    5. The pursuit of Pancho Villa
  C. Problems in the Caribbean

II. World War I and the early American response
  A. Outbreak of the war
  B. Initial American response
    1. Declaration of neutrality
    2. Attitudes of hyphenated Americans
    3. Views of other American groups
    4. Effect of propaganda on Americans
  C. Extension of economic credit to the Allies
  D. Problems of neutrality
    1. Conflicts over neutral rights at sea
    2. British declaration of the North Sea war zone and other restrictions
    3. German use of submarines
    4. Sinking of the *Lusitania*
      a. American protests
      b. Bryan's resignation
      c. *Arabic* pledge
  E. Debate over preparedness
    1. Demands for stronger army and navy
    2. Antiwar advocates
    3. National Defense Act of 1916
    4. Move for a stronger navy
    5. Efforts to obtain revenue for preparedness

III. Election of 1916
  A. Republicans nominated

B. Democratic program
C. Issues of the campaign
D. Results of the election

IV. Steps toward war
  A. Wilson's effort to mediate
  B. Wilson's assertion of terms of peace
  C. German decision for unrestricted submarine warfare
  D. Diplomatic break with Germany
  E. The Zimmerman telegram
  F. The Russian Revolution

V. United States's entry into the war
  A. The sinking of American vessels
  B. Wilson's call for war
  C. An assessment of reasons for United States's entry into the war
  D. Limited expectations from the U.S.
  E. Financial assistance to the Allies
  F. First contingents of troops

VI. Mobilizing a nation
  A. Raising the armed forces
  B. Regulation of the economy
  C. The bureaucracy of mobilization
    1. War Industries Board
    2. Committee on Public Information
    3. Other significant agencies
  D. Civil liberties in the war
    1. Popular disdain for all things German
    2. Espionage and Sedition Acts
      a. Terms of the acts
      b. Prosecutions
      c. Impact of the Acts
      d. *Schenck v. United States*

VII. The American role in war
  A. Little action through 1917
  B. American offensives in 1918
  C. The Fourteen Points
    1. Origins
    2. Content

3. Purposes
4. Responses
D. Terms of the armistice
E. Intervention in Russia

VIII. The fight for the peace
  A. Wilson's role
    1. Decision to attend the conference
    2. Effects of congressional elections of 1918
    3. Wilson's reception in Europe
    4. Structure of the conference
  B. Emphasis on the League of Nations
    1. Article X of the Covenant
    2. Machinery of the League
  C. Early warning from Lodge
  D. Amendments made to respond to critics at home
  E. Compromises on national self-determination
  F. The agreement for reparations
  G. Obtaining the German signature

IX. Wilson's loss at home
  A. Support for the peace
  B. Lodge's reaction
  C. Opponents of the treaty
  D. Wilson's speaking tour
  E. Wilson's stroke
  F. Failure of the Senate votes
  G. Formal ending of the war

X. Conversion to peace
  A. Lack of leadership and planning
  B. Postwar boom and slump
  C. Labor unrest
  D. Race riots
  E. The Red Scare
    1. Fear of radicals
    2. Bombs in the mail
    3. Deportation of aliens
    4. Evaporation of the Red Scare
    5. Legacy of the Red Scare

KEY ITEMS OF CHRONOLOGY

Huerta in power in Mexico	February 1913
Invasion of Vera Cruz	April 1914
Outbreak of World War I	August 1914
Lusitania sunk	May 1915
Arabic pledge from Germany	September 1915

Germany resumed unrestricted submarine warfare	February 1917
United States declared war	April 1917
Creation of War Industries Board	July 1917
Armistice	November 1918
Paris Peace Conference	January-May 1919
Senate votes on treaty	November 1919 and March 1920
Red Scare	1919–1920

TERMS TO MASTER

Listed below are some important terms or people with which you should be familiar after you complete the study of this chapter. Explain the significance of each name or term.

1. Victoriano Huerta
2. hyphenated Americans
3. Central Powers
4. *Lusitania*
5. *Arabic* pledge
6. Revenue Act of 1916
7. Zimmerman telegram
8. War Industries Board
9. Committee on Public Information
10. Espionage and Sedition Acts
11. *Schenck v. United States*
12. Fourteen Points
13. Big Four
14. Henry Cabot Lodge
15. reparations
16. Irreconcilables
17. Boston Police Strike
18. A. Mitchell Palmer
19. Red Scare

VOCABULARY BUILDING

Listed below are some words used in this chapter. Look up each word in your dictionary.

1. obliquely
2. enmity
3. autocracy
4. attrition
5. magnanimous
6. ruse
7. bellicosity
8. envoy
9. conscription
10. peevish

EXERCISES FOR UNDERSTANDING

When you have completed the reading of the chapter, answer each of the following questions. If you have difficulty, go back and reread the section of the chapter related to the question.

Multiple-Choice Questions

Select the letter of the response which best completes the statement.

1. When World War I began in Europe,
   A. most Americans supported Germany
   B. Irish-Americans and German-Americans instinctively opposed the Central Powers
   C. many high U.S. officials were pro-British
   D. none of the above was true

2. After the sinking of the *Lusitania,* William Jennings Bryan
   A. urged Wilson to declare war
   B. resigned in protest over American demands on Germany
   C. called for arming all passenger ships
   D. campaigned for strengthening the military preparation for war

3. The Revenue Act of 1916 placed most of the financial burden of preparedness on
   A. the farmers
   B. munitions manufacturers

C. banks that lent money to foreign nations
D. wealthy persons
4. The Zimmerman telegram
   A. asked Theodore Roosevelt to raise an army battalion to go to war
   B. revealed Germany's policy of unrestricted submarine warfare
   C. warned Germany not to sink unarmed passenger ships
   D. suggested a wartime alliance between Mexico and Germany
5. The wartime Espionage and Sedition Acts
   A. were upheld by the Supreme Court
   B. led to the persecution of more than 1,500 people
   C. hit hard at socialists and radicals
   D. did all the above
6. The U.S. sent troops into Russia in 1918 to
   A. support the Bolshevik revolution
   B. maintain the fighting against Germany in the East
   C. protect Allied supplies in Russia
   D. ensure Russian participation in postwar negotiations
7. For Wilson the most important part of the peace negotiations involved
   A. the League of Nations
   B. Germany's admission of "war guilt"
   C. war debts and reparations
   D. the principle of self-determination
8. Postwar demobilization problems included all of the following *except*
   A. an economic depression in 1919
   B. general labor unrest with numerous strikes
   C. more than 20 race riots
   D. an abrupt end to many wartime government agencies

True-False Questions

Indicate whether each statement is true or false.

1. Under President Wilson, United States military forces never intervened in Mexico.
2. The United States did not enter World War I when it began in Europe.
3. "He kept us out of war" was the 1916 Republican campaign cry against Wilson.
4. The War Industries Board was the most important agency mobilizing the nation for war.
5. The Committee on Public Information enforced censorship of newspapers and magazines.
6. With the Fourteen Points, Wilson sought to keep Russia in the war and to create disunity among the Central Powers.
7. Sen. Henry Cabot Lodge was a supporter of the Versailles Treaty.
8. The Red Scare was directed against racist and conservative groups like the KKK.

Essay Questions

1. Was Wilson's policy toward Mexico characteristic of his diplomacy? Explain.
2. Trace the major developments in American policy on intervention from the start of World War I in 1914 to the United States entry into the War in 1917.
3. Describe the Red Scare that followed World War I. Were restrictions on civil liberties justified in this case? Why or why not?
4. Describe how the United States mobilized men, arms, and money for World War I.
5. What factors led to the defeat of Wilson's plans for the postwar peace? Assess Wilson's success as a leader in foreign policy.
6. Assess the American contribution to the Allied victory in World War I.

DOCUMENT

The Fourteen Points: Wilson's Address to Congress, January 8, 1918

In his famous address to Congress of January 8, 1918, Wilson explained the war aims of the United States. His Fourteen Points formed the basis for peace negotiations.

Gentlemen of the Congress:

. . . It will be our wish and purpose that the processes of peace, when they are begun, shall be absolutely open and that they shall involve and permit henceforth no secret understandings of any kind. The day of conquest and aggrandizement is gone by; so is also the day of secret covenants entered into in the interest of particular governments and likely at some unlooked-for moment to upset the peace of the world. It is this happy fact, now clear to the view of every public man whose thoughts do not still linger in an age that is dead and gone, which makes it possible for every nation whose purposes are consistent with justice and the peace of the world to avow now or at any other time the objects it has in view.

We entered this war because violations of right had occurred which touched us to the quick and made the life of our own people impossible unless they were corrected and the world secured once for all against their recurrence. What we demand in this war, therefore, is nothing peculiar to ourselves. It is that the world be made fit and safe to live in; and particularly that it be made safe for every peace-loving nation which, like our own, wishes to live its own life, determine its own institutions, be assured of justice and fair dealing by the other peoples of the world as against force and selfish aggression. All the peoples of the world are in effect partners in this interest, and for our own part we see very clearly that unless justice be done to others it will not be done to us. The program of the world's peace, therefore, is our program; and that program, the only possible program, as we see it, is this:

I. Open covenants of peace, openly arrived at, after which there shall be no private international understandings of any kind but diplomacy shall proceed always frankly and in the public view.

II. Absolute freedom of navigation upon the seas, outside territorial waters, alike in peace and in war, except as the seas may be closed in whole or in part by international action for the enforcement of international covenants.

III. The removal, so far as possible, of all economic barriers and the establishment of an equality of trade conditions among all the nations consenting to the peace and associating themselves for its maintenance.

IV. Adequate guarantees given and taken that national armaments will be reduced to the lowest point consistent with domestic safety.

V. A free, open-minded, and absolutely impartial adjustment of all colonial claims, based upon a strict observance of the principle that in determining all such questions of sovereignty the interests of the populations concerned must have equal weight with the equitable claims of the government whose title is to be determined.

VI. The evacuation of all Russian territory and such a settlement of all questions affecting Russia as will secure the best and freest coöperation of the other nations of the world in obtaining for her an unhampered and unembarrassed opportunity for the independent determination of her own political development and national policy and assure her of a sincere welcome into the society of free nations under institutions of her own choosing; and, more than a welcome, assistance also of every kind that she may need and may herself desire. The treatment accorded Russia by her sister nations in the months to come will be the acid test of their good will, of their comprehension of her needs as distinguished from their own interests, and of their intelligent and unselfish sympathy.

VII. Belgium, the whole world will agree, must be evacuated and restored, without any attempt to limit the sovereignty which she enjoys in common with all other free nations. No other single act will serve as this will serve to restore confidence among the nations in the laws which they have themselves set and determined for the government of their relations with one another. Without this healing act the whole structure and validity of international law is forever impaired.

VIII. All French territory should be freed and the invaded portions restored, and the wrong done to France by Prussia in 1871 in the matter of Alsace-Lorraine, which has unsettled the peace of the world for nearly fifty years, should be righted, in order that peace may once more be made secure in the interest of all.

IX. A readjustment of the frontiers of Italy should be effected along clearly recognizable lines of nationality.

X. The peoples of Austria-Hungary, whose place among the nations we wish to see safeguarded and assured, should be accorded the freest opportunity of autonomous development.

XI. Rumania, Serbia, and Montenegro should be evacuated; occupied territories restored; Serbia accorded free and secure access to the sea; and the relations of the several Balkan states to one another determined by friendly counsel along historically established lines of allegiance and nationality; and international guarantees of the political and economic independence and territorial integrity of the several Balkan states should be entered into.

XII. The Turkish portions of the present Ottoman Empire should be assured a secure sovereignty, but the other nationalities which are now under Turkish rule should be assured an undoubted security of life and an absolutely unmolested opportunity of autonomous development, and the Dardanelles should be permanently opened as a free passage to the ships and commerce of all nations under international guarantees.

XIII. An independent Polish state should be erected which should include the territories inhabited by indisputably Polish populations, which should be assured a free and secure access to the sea, and whose political and economic independence and territorial integrity should be guaranteed by international covenant.

XIV. A general association of nations must be formed under specific covenants for the purpose of affording mutual guarantees of political independence and territorial integrity to great and small states alike.

In regard to these essential rectifications of wrong and assertions of right we feel ourselves to be intimate partners of all the governments and peoples associated together against the Imperialists. We cannot be separated in interest or divided in purpose. We stand together until the end.

For such arrangements and covenants we are willing to fight and to continue to fight until they are achieved; but only because we wish the right to prevail and desire a just and stable peace such as can be secured only by removing the chief provocations to war, which this program does not remove. We have no jealousy of German greatness, and there is nothing in this program that impairs it. We grudge her no achievement or distinction of learning or of pacific enterprise such as have made her record very bright and very enviable. We do not wish to injure her or to block in any way her legitimate influence or power. We do not wish to fight her either with arms or with hostile arrangements of trade if she is willing to associate herself with us and the other peace-loving nations of the world in covenants of justice and law and fair dealing. We wish her only to accept a place of equality among the peoples of the world,—the new world in which we now live,—instead of a place of mastery.

Neither do we presume to suggest to her any alteration or modification of her institutions. But it is necessary, we must frankly say, and necessary as a preliminary to any intelligent dealings with her on our part, that we should know whom her spokesmen speak for when they speak to us, whether for the Reichstag majority or for the military party and the men whose creed is imperial domination.

We have spoken now, surely, in terms too concrete to admit of any further doubt or question. An evident principle runs through the whole program I have outlined. It is the principle of justice to all peoples and nationalities, and their right to live on equal terms of liberty and safety with one another, whether they be strong or weak. Unless this principle be made its foundation no part of the structure of international justice can stand. The people of the United States could act upon no other principle; and to the vindication of this principle they are ready to devote their lives, their honor, and everything that they possess. The moral climax of this the culminating and final war for human liberty has come, and they are ready to put their own strength, their own highest purpose, their own integrity and devotion to the test.

[From *A Compilation of the Messages and Papers of the Presidents,* Supplement, 1917–1921 (New York: Bureau of National Literature, Inc., 1921), 2: 8421*ff*]

Questions for Reflection

Were Wilson's Fourteen Points a practical program for peace? Explain. Describe the controversy sparked by Point XIV. How would you assess Wilson's role in this controversy? Is the "principle of justice to all peoples and nationalities" a useful basis for foreign policy? Why or why not?

ANSWERS TO MULTIPLE-CHOICE
AND TRUE-FALSE QUESTIONS

Multiple-Choice Questions

1-C, 2-B, 3-D, 4-D, 5-D, 6-C, 7-A, 8-A

True-False Questions

1-F, 2-T, 3-F, 4-T, 5-F, 6-T, 7-F, 8-F

25

SOCIETY AND CULTURE
BETWEEN THE WARS

CHAPTER OBJECTIVES

After you complete the reading and study of this chapter you should be able to

1. Describe and account for the mood of the 1920s.
2. Describe the nativist reaction in the twenties and the revival of the Ku Klux Klan, along with the consequences of these developments.
3. Trace the emergence of fundamentalism and its effects.
4. Account for the experiment in prohibition and its persistence in the face of widespread evasion of the law.
5. Describe and compare the political and social position of women and blacks in the twenties.
6. Explain the scientific basis of the moral relativism of the decade.
7. Describe the literary flowering of the 1920s and 1930s and the contributions of major American novelists and poets of the era.

CHAPTER OUTLINE

I. Reaction in the 1920s
   A. Changing moods
      1. Disillusionment
      2. Defiance against change
   B. Nativism
      1. Sacco and Vanzetti case
      2. Efforts to restrict immigration
      3. Revival of the Ku Klux Klan
   C. Fundamentalism
      1. Emergence of fundamentalism
      2. William Jennings Bryan
      3. Scopes trial
   D. Prohibition
      1. An expression of reforming zeal
      2. Organization for the cause
      3. Crusade for a constitutional amendment
      4. Effectiveness of prohibition
      5. Its link with organized crime
      6. Al Capone

II. Social tensions
   A. A time of cultural conflict
      1. Urban disdain for rural small-town values
      2. Rural fears of cities
   B. The new morality
      1. Emphasis on youth
      2. Obsession with sex

3. Impact of Freud
4. Aspects of persistence into the
   thirties
C. The women's movement
1. The work for women's suffrage
   a. Alice Paul and new tactics
   b. Contributions of Carrie
      Chapman Catt
   c. Passage and ratification of the
      amendment
   d. Effects of women's suffrage
2. Push for an Equal Rights
   Amendment
3. Women in the workforce
D. The "New Negro"
1. The "Great Migration" north
   a. Demographics
   b. Impact of the move
2. The Harlem Renaissance
3. Marcus Garvey and Negro
   Nationalism
4. Development of the NAACP
   a. Emergence of the organization
   b. Role of Du Bois
   c. Strategy
   d. The campaign against lynching
   e. Scottsboro case

III. The culture of modernism
A. Loss of faith in progress
B. Einstein and the Theory of Relativity
C. Toward the Principle of Uncertainty
1. The relationship of mass and
   energy
2. Planck's quantum theory
3. Heisenberg's Principle of
   Uncertainty
D. Impact of relativity and uncertainty

1. Denial of absolute values
2. Assertion of relativism in cultures
E. Modernist literature
1. Chief features
   a. Exploration of the irrational
   b. Uncertainty seen as desirable
   c. Positive view of conflict
   d. Formal manners discounted for
      contact with "reality"
2. Development of artistic bohemias
3. The armory show
4. Emphasis on the "new" in many
   facets of life
5. Role of Harriet Monroe
6. Chief American prophets of
   modernism
   a. Ezra Pound
   b. T. S. Eliot
   c. Gertrude Stein
7. Expatriates
   a. F. Scott Fitzgerald
   b. Ernest Hemingway
      i. Cult of masculinity
      ii. Terse literary style

IV. Return of social significance
A. Impact of the depression
B. Allegiance to revolution
C. Novels of social significance
1. John Steinbeck
2. Richard Wright
D. The Southern Renaissance
1. Effect of Mencken's critique of the
   South
2. Novelists of note
   a. Thomas Wolfe
   b. William Faulkner
E. The rediscovery of American culture

KEY ITEMS OF CHRONOLOGY

Einstein's paper on the Theory of Relativity	1905
Organization of the NAACP	1910
Ratification of the Eighteenth Amendment (prohibition)	1919
Ratification of the Nineteenth Amendment (women's suffrage)	1920
Sinclair Lewis's *Babbitt*	1922
Scopes trial	1924
Hemingway's *The Sun Also Rises*	1926

Execution of Sacco and Vanzetti	1927
Heisenberg's Principle of Uncertainty stated	1927
Scottsboro case	1931
John Steinbeck's *The Grapes of Wrath*	1939
Richard Wright's *Native Son*	1940

TERMS TO MASTER

Listed below are some important terms or people with which you should be familiar after you complete the study of this chapter. Explain the significance of each name or term.

1. Sacco and Vanzetti
2. KKK
3. "monkey trial"
4. Sigmund Freud
5. Eighteenth Amendment
6. "Great Migration"
7. Marcus Garvey
8. NAACP
9. Theory of Relativity
10. Principle of Uncertainty
11. modernist movement
12. F. Scott Fitzgerald
13. Ernest Hemingway
14. John Steinbeck
15. Richard Wright
16. "The Sahara of the Bozart"
17. Thomas Wolfe
18. William Faulkner

VOCABULARY BUILDING

Listed below are some words used in this chapter. Look up each word in your dictionary.

1. sedition
2. nativism
3. visceral
4. anticlimactic
5. prescience
6. banality
7. sublimation
8. ephemeral
9. bohemia
10. expatriates

EXERCISES FOR UNDERSTANDING

When you have completed reading the chapter, answer each of the following questions. If you have difficulty, go back and reread the section of the chapter related to the question.

Multiple-Choice Questions

Select the letter of the response which best completes the statement.

1. In the United States, the end of World War I brought
   A. a renewed belief in the old values of glory, honor, and courage
   B. the optimistic conviction that the world was constantly improving
   C. disillusionment with modern civilization
   D. a greater appreciation of diversity and change in American life

2. Obstacles to prohibition included
   A. profits from bootlegging
   B. inadequate congressional support for enforcement
   C. public demand for alcohol
   D. all of the above

3. The immigration acts of the 1920s were designed to
   A. reduce immigration from all countries except England
   B. allow immigration only from Latin America
   C. reduce immigration from southern and eastern Europe
   D. increase immigration from England and Germany

4. The ideas of Sigmund Freud affected American attitudes about
   A. the Scopes trial in 1924
   B. sex and morality

C. efforts to start a Negro republic in Africa

D. the importance of quanta

5. The Harlem Renaissance, an artistic and literary blossoming, featured the works of

A. Claude McKay, Langston Hughes, and Countee Cullen

B. H. L. Mencken, Eugene O'Neill, and Sinclair Lewis

C. Thomas Wolfe, Ernest Hemingway, and the Fugitives

D. Albert Einstein, Sigmund Freud, and Marcus Garvey

6. The scientific work of Einstein, Heisenberg, and others

A. reinforced the traditional faith in reason and order

B. increased confidence in man's ability to fully understand the world

C. was incompatible with the disillusionment and despair of the postwar period

D. suggested that there is a limit to man's understanding of the universe

7. The features of modernist literature included *all but which one* of the following:

A. exploration of the irrational as an essential part of human nature

B. the view of the universe as operating on unchanging and stable principles.

C. the view that conflict was more fundamental than harmony

D. the view that freedom from convention was more important than following tradition.

8. John Steinbeck's *The Grapes of Wrath* is an example of

A. modernist writing

B. the Harlem Renaissance

C. social concerns in the depression

D. the Southern Renaissance

True-False Questions

Indicate whether each statement is true or false.

1. The Ku Klux Klan was directed against blacks, Jews, and Catholics.

2. John T. Scopes's conviction for a payroll robbery and murder in Indiana led to the downfall of the KKK.

3. Organized crime began during the depression.

4. The Nineteenth Amendment to the Constitution gave women the right to vote.

5. The NAACP's strategy stressed working through the legal system to achieve changes in race relations.

6. The chief American prophets of modernism in literature lived in Europe.

7. The leading black novelist during the depression was Richard Wright.

8. In varying the usual rhetorical strategies so that new insights would take the reader by surprise, William Faulkner was one of the most skilled modernist writers.

Essay Questions

1. In what ways were the 1920s a time of social and intellectual defensiveness and disillusionment?

2. Describe the "new morality" of the 1920s.

3. Compare and contrast the Harlem Renaissance and the Southern Renaissance.

4. Explain the contributions of Freud, Marx, Einstein, and Heisenberg to the new mood of the twenties.

5. What were the chief features of modernist literature? Show how those features were exhibited in the works of one of the authors mentioned in the text.

6. How did the depression transform the literary outlook of the twenties into that of the thirties?

DOCUMENT

Testimony about the Work of the Ku Klux Klan

These excerpts from testimony before a congressional inquiry give some insight into the work of the Ku Klux Klan in the 1920s.

Mr. Campbell. Mr. Wright, will you state your name to the stenographer?

Mr. Wright. C. Anderson Wright. . . . I was formerly a member of the New York klan, king kleagle, assigned as chief of staff of the invisible planet, Knights of the Air. . . .

Mr. Campbell. What were your instructions with respect to whom you should regulate and how, and how you were to serve the klan or uplift the community?

Mr. Wright. My instructions as a klansman were simply starting in and giving the Jews the dickens in New York. Their idea was this, as preached by Clarke and Hooper in my presence, with several other prospective members whom I brought up, that the Jew patronizes the Jew, if possible: therefore, we as klansmen, the only real 100 per cent Americans, will only patronize klansmen. Now, the idea was this, to simply organize everybody that was of their belief and religious belief into this order and they would practice not only moral clannishness but also practical clannishness; in other words a klansman would be compelled to buy from another klansman if possible. That was how it was explained to us by Hooper. He did not really know much about it at that time; he was simply out for the money he could make out of it, and that was also explained by Clarke. They said, "In New York City here we have all the Jews; they are controlling New York; we will get under here and when we have 10,000 members here, if we do not want a certain man to do a certain thing, if this man receives 10,000 letters or telegrams stating that he should not do this thing, he is not very apt to do it." In other words, if a member of the klan should be brought on trial before a certain judge or jury, if that judge or jury received 10,000 requests from New York to do a certain thing, they would be pretty apt to do it. That was their idea of gaining control of the courts.

Mr. Campbell. What, if anything, were you told about the wearing of the mask, or were you told it was important that you should do that.

Mr. Wright. You only wore the mask, according to imperial instructions, when you were in the klavern or klan, and then only when what they called the aliens or strangers or people to be initiated were present. Of course, in official parades it was up to the exalted cyclops. . . .

Mr. Kreider. What was the object to be accomplished, or what were the duties of the aerial service?

Mr. Wright. I will tell you what my idea is and what the ideas of the flyers of this country were. We saw that the Aero Club of America and other organizations were absolutely going out of existence: they were decaying; and we felt that we should get a fraternal order together of flyers to promote commercial aviation and give the boys a chance to fly. We are all reserve officers, or some of us are, and since we have been out of the Army we have never seen an airplane. If we take our reserve documents and go to a field to fly we are told there are no ships available, and we have to go through a certain medical examination, which is ridiculous, but we can not fly. So we got several together. . . .

Mr. Kreider. Did all the members of this organization, known as the Knights of the Air, have to be members of the Ku-Klux Klan?

Mr. Wright. No, sir, but here is where the hitch came, as decided by Clarke; he said, "No man can become an officer of the Knights of the Air who is not a klansman; we will absolutely control the Knights of the Air through having only klansmen as officers." That was the first thing; and then Clarke decided that the equipment that the klan got should be placed in his name and not in the name of the Knights of the Air, his idea being to absolutely control it with an iron hand. As I say, out there it was talked over for two days what we were going to do, and he was very visionary, and he saw Edward Young Clarke controlling the air in America, without question or belief. . . .

Mr. Kreider. Was this organization to be used later on or at any time to terrorize men?

Mr. Wright. Oh, no. The Knights of the Air was simply started into being with the flyers as something to get us together, and was capitalized by Clarke as a money-making plan; that is all. I afterwards saw letters, after I left Atlanta, being sent out under the name of Mr. Cherry, who was a klansman, and an assistant over in the office, who had never seen an airplane, I think, to all the aero clubs and flyers throughout the country, saying what a great thing the Knights of the Air was; in fact, after I left there, there was nobody that I know of that was a flyer or a reserve officer in the Army. It was simply a case of Clarke's ideas being absolutely so that no man could conscientiously go into it as a reserve officer in the United States Army. There is no question about it. The whole Ku-Klux Klan is simply based on treason against the country, in this way, that they have planned and schemed and would have, if not publicly exposed, gotten control of practically every seat of government through their tremendous voting power. In the State of Texas to-day I venture to say that practically all the smaller cities are absolutely controlled by the klan from the mayor on down. Texas should be the headquarters of the Ku-Klux Klan and not Georgia, because in Georgia they all look upon it more as a joke—the Atlanta people. . . .

Mr. Fess. What is the purpose of the parades we hear about?

Mr. Wright. The parades?

Mr. Fess. Yes; we have had statements about terrorizing.

Mr. Wright. Well, the idea is this, which I can prove and will be very glad to file before the committee, by their own semiofficial organ, the Searchlight—the idea was simply to terrorize people by showing their strength. To cite an instance of that, in Dallas, Tex., they were having trouble there with a certain class of the building trades—I do not know just exactly what it was—and the klan decided they would hold a parade to show their strength. So it seems like it was all arranged with the city authorities and the parade was held in Dallas, and they marched down the street in full regalia, and about the time they appeared the lights were all extinguished, and the next day the people were back at work. This is cited in their semiofficial organ and in the press throughout the country. . . .

Mr. Snell. What induced you to disclose the secrets of the klan?

Mr. Wright. Why did I?

Mr. Snell. Yes, anything special?

Mr. Wright. Yes, sir. My reason was simply this: I have nothing against the mass of klansmen. They go into it in ignorance, and I knew that. My idea was not to expose so much race hatred, which would drive lots of people into the klan. In other words, there are enough narrow-minded people who would be glad enough to join an order against the Jews, Catholics, foreign born, and Negroes; but if you can show a man where he was simply taken in and made a goat of in order to get money out of him by selling all these mystic contrivances and show him how his money went and the men it was making wealthy and the women who was behind the whole thing and show him where the man at the head of the order was not receiving any money or the imperial treasury was not receiving any money, I figures the klansmen should know that and would be glad to know that, whether they had done any violence or anything else. In other words, I think to-day the more the papers preach on the Ku-Klux Klan as preaching racial hatred, the more members they are going to get, because there are so many narrow-minded people who will join, but when you can show them where their money goes and what a fool he is made and the character of the people getting it, then I think the klansmen of the country will realize and wake up to what they have gone into.

[The Ku Klux Klan, Committee on Rules, House of Representatives, 67th Cong., 1st sess., pp. 15–27, quoted in *Looking for America*, edited by Stanley I. Kutler (New York: W. W. Norton, 1979), 2: 352–356]

Questions for Reflection

Why does Wright say that the Klan was engaged in treason? What were the prospects for the Klan's success? How did the conditions of America in the twenties help to develop the Klan's attitudes as shown in this document?

ANSWERS TO MULTIPLE-CHOICE AND TRUE-FALSE QUESTIONS

Multiple-Choice Questions

1-C, 2-D, 3-C, 4-A, 5-B, 6-D, 7-B, 8-C

True-False Questions

1-T, 2-F, 3-F, 4-T, 5-T, 6-T, 7-T, 8-T

26

REPUBLICAN RESURGENCE
AND DECLINE, 1920–1932

CHAPTER OBJECTIVES

After you complete the reading and study of this chapter you should be able to

1. Describe the effects of the Harding presidency upon the nation.
2. Explain the new prosperity of the twenties.
3. Describe the features of the economy in the New Era decade.
4. Explain Hoover's policies for the nation and indicate their effects.
5. Account for the stock market crash of 1929.
6. Describe the status of farmers during the twenties.
7. Describe the status of labor unions during the 1920s.

CHAPTER OUTLINE

I. The fate of progressivism in the twenties
  A. Causes for the dissolution of the progressive coalition in Congress
    1. Disaffection with the war and the war's aftermath
    2. Administration and labor
    3. Farmers' concerns
    4. Intellectuals' disillusionment

5. Middle class preoccupation with business
  B. Survivals of progressivism in the twenties
    1. Domination of Congress
    2. Strong pressure at local levels for "good government" and public services
    3. Reform impulse transformed into the drive for moral righteousness

II. The election of 1920
  A. Mood of the country
  B. Republican shift to the right
  C. Democratic nomination
  D. Results

III. The Harding administration
  A. The Harding appointments
  B. Nature of the Harding presidency
  C. Efforts for economy
    1. Tax cuts
    2. Spending cuts
    3. Tariffs
  D. Deemphasis on regulating agencies
  E. Corruption in the administration
    1. Veterans Bureau
    2. Harry Daugherty
    3. Teapot Dome
    4. Role of Harding
  F. Harding's death
  G. Assessment

IV. The Coolidge years
   A. Character of the man
   B. The election of 1924
     1. Coolidge's control of the
       Republican Party
     2. Dissension among the Democrats
     3. Emergence of the Progressive
       Party
     4. Results of the election
   C. Aspects of the New Era
     1. The consumption ethic
     2. Growth of advertising
     3. Development of the movies
     4. Growth of radio
     5. Growth of aviation
     6. Impact of the automobile
   D. Hoover's role
     1. His concept of voluntary
       cooperation
     2. Growth of the Commerce
       Department
     3. Promotion of trade associations
     4. The acquiescence of the Supreme
       Court
   E. Problems in agriculture
     1. Reasons for the agricultural slump
     2. Mechanization of farms
     3. New farm organizations
       a. Marketing associations
       b. Formation of the Farm Bloc in
         Congress
     4. Legislation favorable to agriculture
       a. Early acts
       b. The McNary-Haugen scheme
   F. Setbacks for unions
     1. Earnings in industry

     2. Efforts to forestall unions
   G. The election of 1928
     1. The Republican position
     2. The Democratic choice
     3. Issues of the election
     4. Results
V. The Hoover presidency
   A. The prospects for success
   B. Hoover's general policies
   C. His support for agriculture
     1. Aids for cooperative marketing
     2. Tariff increases
   D. The speculative mania
     1. The Florida real estate bubble
     2. Development of the Great Bull
       Market
     3. Efforts to curb the market
   E. The crash
     1. Description of the crash
     2. Immediate effects
     3. Causes for the crash
   F. Efforts for recovery
     1. Advocates of laissez-faire
     2. Hoover's exhortations
     3. Public works and credit
     4. Democratic victory in 1930
     5. International complications
   G. Congressional initiatives
     1. The RFC and its role
     2. Help for financial institutions
     3. Plans for relief
   H. Plight of the farmers and veterans
     1. Means of farmer protest
     2. The Bonus Expeditionary Force
   I. Mood of the nation

KEY ITEMS OF CHRONOLOGY

First radio commercial	1922
Death of Harding	1923
Florida real estate collapse	1926
Lindbergh flight	May 1927
McNary-Haugen bills passed Congress	1927, 1928
Stock market crash	October 1929
Smoot-Hawley Tariff	1930
Hoover's moratorium on war-debt payments	1931
Creation of RFC	1932
Attack on the Bonus Expeditionary Force	July 1932

TERMS TO MASTER

Listed below are some important terms or people with which you should be familiar after you complete the study of this chapter. Explain the significance of each name or term.

1. normalcy
2. Andrew Mellon
3. Teapot Dome affair
4. Robert M. La Follette
5. Calvin Coolidge
6. Charles A. Lindbergh, Jr.
7. Herbert Hoover
8. associationalism
9. marketing cooperatives
10. McNary-Haugen scheme
11. "yellow dog" contract
12. Alfred E. Smith
13. Agricultural Marketing Act
14. margin buying
15. Reconstruction Finance Corporation
16. Federal Home Loan Bank Act
17. Bonus Expeditionary Force

VOCABULARY BUILDING

Listed below are some words used in this chapter. Look up each word in your dictionary.

1. nostrums
2. impropriety
3. exult
4. cornucopia
5. therapeutic
6. trifling
7. parity
8. portentous
9. exacerbate
10. debacle

EXERCISES FOR UNDERSTANDING

When you have completed reading the chapter, answer each of the following questions. If you have difficulty, go back and reread the section of the chapter related to the question.

Multiple-Choice Questions

Select the letter of the response which best completes the statement.

1. The major issue in the 1920 campaign was
   A. the League of Nations
   B. prohibition
   C. the Teapot Dome scandal
   D. none of the above

2. The Teapot Dome scandal involved
   A. kickbacks to the president
   B. oil leases in Wyoming
   C. Harding's affair with Nan Britton
   D. tariffs on products from the Orient, especially tea

3. The year 1920 marked the arrival of the first
   A. motion picture
   B. solo airplane flight over the Atlantic
   C. talking movie
   D. regular radio programs

4. Mass production in the automobile industry was the creation of
   A. Henry Ford
   B. Walter E. Flanders
   C. F. W. Taylor
   D. all of the above (each contributed in part)

5. As secretary of commerce, Herbert Hoover promoted
   A. keen competition among corporations
   B. standardization of products (tires, bricks, etc.)
   C. a vigorous trustbusting campaign
   D. federal ownership of the radio and airline industries

6. The most important proposal in the 1920s to aid farmers was
   A. the "American Plan"
   B. McNary-Haugenism
   C. the Volstead Act
   D. the Smoot-Hawley Tariff

7. In the 1928 election, Alfred E. Smith represented
   A. the supporters of prohibition
   B. farmers
   C. conservative business interests
   D. urban immigrants

8. Hoover's approach to recovery placed an emphasis on
A. government construction of housing
B. voluntary efforts of the people
C. assistance to European trade
D. government aid to the unemployed

True-False Questions

Indicate whether each statement is true or false.

1. Presidents Harding and Coolidge were leading progressives in the 1920s.
2. During the 1920s, government expenditures declined, the national debt decreased, and tax rates dropped.
3. Sen. Robert La Follette of Wisconsin was the Democratic opponent of Coolidge in the 1924 election.
4. American agriculture prospered during the 1920s.
5. *Real* wages of labor *increased* in the decade of the 1920s.

6. Buying stocks on margin helped restrain speculation in the stock market.
7. Excessively high wages for labor in the 1920s helped cause the stock market crash in 1929.
8. The Reconstruction Finance Corporation assisted farmers, homeowners, and labor unions.

Essay Questions

1. What happened to progressivism in the 1920s?
2. Were the Harding and Coolidge administrations on the whole successful or not? Explain.
3. Which best describes the 1920s: "normalcy" or "the New Era"? Why?
4. What was Hoover's conception of the role of the federal government and how did he apply it in the 1920s?
5. Evaluate the efforts of both Hoover and Congress to revive the American economy in the late 1920s.

DOCUMENT

Hoover's "Philosophy of Rugged Individualism" Speech

Herbert Hoover wound up his successful 1928 campaign for the presidency in New York City on October 22, 1928, with the speech that follows. In it he clearly explains the social philosophy of the Republicans in the 1920s, and of his campaign in particular.

This campaign now draws near a close. The platforms of the two parties defining principles and offering solutions of various national problems have been presented and are being earnestly considered by our people. . . .

In my acceptance speech I endeavored to outline the spirit and ideals by which I would be guided in carrying that platform into administration. Tonight I will not deal with the multitude of issues which have been already well canvassed. I intend rather to discuss some of those more fundamental principles and ideals upon which I believe the government of the United States should be conducted. . . .

After the war, when the Republican party assumed administration of the country, we were faced with the problem of determination of the very nature of our national life. During one hundred and fifty years we have builded up a form of self-government and a social system which is peculiarly our own. It differs essentially from all others in the world. It is the American system. It is just as definite and positive a political and social system as has ever been developed on earth. It is founded upon a particular conception of self-government in which decentralized local responsibility is the very base. Further than this, it is founded upon the conception that only through ordered liberty, freedom, and equal opportunity to the individual will his initiative and enterprise spur on the march of progress. And in our insistence upon equality of opportunity has our system advanced beyond all the world.

During the war we necessarily turned to the government to solve every difficult economic problem. The government having absorbed every energy of our people for war, there was no other solution. For the preservation of the state the Federal Government became a centralized despotism which undertook unprecedented responsibilities, assumed autocratic powers, and took over the business of citizens. To a large degree we regimented our whole people temporarily into a socialistic state. However justified in time of war, if continued in peace-time it would destroy not only our American system but with it our progress and freedom as well.

When the war closed, the most vital of all issues both in our own country and throughout the world was whether governments should continue their wartime ownership and operation of many instrumentalities of production and distribution. We were challenged with a peace-time choice between the American system of rugged individualism and a European philosophy of diametrically opposed doctrines—doctrines of paternalism and state socialism. The acceptance of these ideas would have meant the destruction of self-government through centralization of government. It would have meant the undermining of the individual initiative and enterprise through which our people have grown to unparalleled greatness.

The Republican Party from the beginning resolutely turned its face away from these ideas and these war practices. . . . When the Republican Party came into full power it went at once resolutely back to our fundamental conception of the state and the rights and responsibilities of the individual. Thereby it restored confidence and hope in the American people, it freed and stimulated enterprise, it restored the government to its position as an umpire instead of a player in the economic game. For these reasons the American people have gone forward in progress while the rest of the world has halted, and some countries have even gone backwards. If anyone will study the causes of retarded recuperation in Europe, he will find much of it due to stifling of private initiative on one hand, and overloading of the government with business on the other.

There has been revived in this campaign, however, a series of proposals which, if adopted, would be a long step toward the abandonment of our American system and a surrender to the destructive operation of governmental conduct of commercial business. Because the country is faced with difficulty and doubt over certain national problems—that is prohibition, farm relief, and electrical power—our opponents propose that we must thrust government a long way into the businesses which give rise to these problems. In effect, they abandon the tenets of their own party and turn to state socialism as a solution for the difficulties presented by all three. It

is proposed that we shall change from prohibition to the state purchase and sale of liquor. If their agricultural relief program means
anything, it means that the government shall directly or indirectly
buy and sell and fix prices of agricultural products. And we are to
go into the hydroelectric power business. In other words, we are
confronted with a huge program of government in business.

There is, therefore, submitted to the American people a question
of fundamental principle. That is: shall we depart from the principles of our American political and economic system, upon which we
have advanced beyond all the rest of the world, in order to adopt
methods based on principles destructive of its very foundations?
And I wish to emphasize the seriousness of these proposals. I wish
to make my position clear; for this goes to the very roots of American life and progress. . . .

I do not wish to be misunderstood in this statement. I am defining
a general policy. It does not mean that our government is to part
with one iota of its national resources without complete protection
to the public interest. I have already stated that where the government is engaged in public works for purposes of flood control, of
navigation, of irrigation, of scientific research or national defense,
or in pioneering a new art, it will at times necessarily produce
power or commodities as a by-product. But they must be a by-
product of the major purpose, not the major purpose itself.

Nor do I wish to be misinterpreted as believing that the United
States is free-for-all and devil-take-the-hindmost. The very essence
of equality of opportunity and of American individualism is that
there shall be no domination by any group or combination in this
republic, whether it be business or political. On the contrary, it
demands economic justice as well as political and social justice. It
is no system of laissez faire.

I feel deeply on this subject because during the war I had some
practical experience with governmental operation and control. I
have witnessed not only at home but abroad the many failures of
government in business. I have seen its tyrannies, its injustices, its
destructions of self-government, its undermining of the very instincts which carry our people forward to progress. I have witnessed
the lack of advance, the lowered standards of living, the depressed
spirits of people working under such a system. My objection is based
not upon theory or upon a failure to recognize wrong or abuse, but
I know the adoption of such methods would strike at the very roots
of American life and would destroy the very basis of American
progress.

Our people have the right to know whether we can continue to
solve our great problems without abandonment of our American
system. I know we can. . . .

And what have been the results of the American system? Our
country has become the land of opportunity to those born without
inheritance, not merely because of the wealth of its resources and
industry but because of this freedom of initiative and enterprise.
Russia has natural resources equal to ours. Her people are equally
industrious, but she has not had the blessings of one hundred and
fifty years of our form of government and our social system.

By adherence to the principles of decentralized self-government, ordered liberty, equal opportunity, and freedom to the individual, our American experiment in human welfare has yielded a degree of well-being unparalleled in all the world. It has come nearer to the abolition of poverty, to the abolition of fear of want, than humanity has ever reached before. Progress of the past seven years is the proof of it. This alone furnishes the answer to our opponents, who ask us to introduce destructive elements into the system by which this has been accomplished. . . .

I have endeavored to present to you that the greatness of America has grown out of a political and social system and a method of control of economic forces distinctly its own—our American system—which has carried this great experiment in human welfare farther than ever before in all history. We are nearer today to the ideal of the abolition of poverty and fear from the lives of men and women than ever before in any land. And I again repeat that the departure from our American system by injecting principles destructive to it which our opponents propose, will jeopardize the very liberty and freedom of our people, and will destroy equality of opportunity not alone to ourselves but to our children. . . .

[From *The New Day: Campaign Speeches of Herbert Hoover* (Stanford, Calif.: Stanford University Press, 1928), p. 149*ff*]

Questions for Reflection

To support his arguments for "rugged individualism," Hoover cites economic "progress of the past seven years." How would you assess the health of the American economy in the mid to late 1920s? Do you agree or disagree with Hoover on this point?

Is Hoover fair in his characterization of the Democratic program? How would you describe the philosophy of the Democrats in 1928? Do you agree with Hoover that the government should be "an umpire instead of a player in the economic game"?

ANSWERS TO MULTIPLE-CHOICE AND TRUE-FALSE QUESTIONS

Multiple-Choice Questions

1-D, 2-B, 3-D, 4-D, 5-B, 6-B, 7-D, 8-B

True-False Questions

1-F, 2-T, 3-F, 4-F, 5-T, 6-F, 7-F, 8-F

27

FRANKLIN D. ROOSEVELT
AND THE NEW DEAL

CHAPTER OBJECTIVES

*After you complete the reading and study
of this chapter you should be able to*

1. Describe the character and appeal of FDR.
2. Describe the sources of New Deal legislation.
3. Explain the New Deal approaches to the problems of recovery in industry and agriculture.
4. Describe the criticisms made of the New Deal by the left and the right.
5. Describe New Deal efforts to deal with unemployment and welfare.
6. Assess the changes in the United States wrought by the New Deal.

CHAPTER OUTLINE

I. The election of 1932
   A. The candidates
   B. The Roosevelt background and character
   C. The campaign contrasts
   D. Results of the election

II. The early New Deal
   A. Mood of the inauguration
   B. Willingness to experiment

C. Action for banks, the economy, and beer
D. Overview of the Hundred Days
E. Measures to improve financial institutions
   1. Extension of farm credit
   2. Help for home mortgages
   3. Action to protect banks and security purchases
   4. Abandonment of the gold standard
F. Relief measures
   1. Civilian Conservation Corps (CCC)
   2. Federal Emergency Relief Administration (FERA)
   3. Civilian Works Administration (CWA)
   4. Works Progress Administration (WPA)

III. Recovery through regulation and planning
   A. Aid for agriculture
      1. Wide variety of options within the Agricultural Adjustment Administration (AAA)
      2. Creation of the Commodity Credit Corporation
      3. General effects on farm income and farmers
      4. Supreme Court negates the processing tax of AAA

5. Soil Conservation Act: provisions
   and effects
6. Second AAA
B. Efforts for the recovery of industry
   1. The Public Works Administration
      (PWA)
   2. The National Recovery
      Administration (NRA)
      a. Two primary aims
      b. Nature of the NRA operation
      c. Objections to the NRA codes
      d. Enduring impact of the NRA
C. Regional planning: Tennessee
   Valley Authority (TVA)
   1. Historical basis
   2. Nature of the legislation
   3. Impact of the TVA
   4. Creation of the Rural
      Electrification Association (REA)

IV. Critics left and right
   A. Increased support for FDR in 1934
   B. Conservatives launch the American
      Liberty League
   C. Thunder on the left
      1. Huey Long's threat
      2. Francis Townsend's program
      3. Father Coughlin's role
      4. Potential threat of the left
   D. Pressure on FDR to restore
      competition
   E. Roadblocks from the Supreme Court

V. The Second New Deal
   A. The Wagner Act for workers
   B. The Social Security Act
      1. Old Age and Survivors' Insurance
      2. Unemployment Insurance
      3. Public Assistance Programs
      4. Limitations
   C. The Wealth Tax Act
   D. Right-wing criticisms of the New Deal

VI. The election of 1936
   A. Contribution of Eleanor Roosevelt
   B. Republicans choose progressive
      Landon

C. Republican strategy
D. The new Roosevelt coalition
E. Results of the election

VII. Second-term developments
   A. The court-packing plan
      1. FDR's view of the election
      2. Effects of Court rulings
      3. The court-packing plan
      4. Events blunt the plan
      5. Impact of the fight
   B. Stirrings among labor
      1. Impetus to unionization
      2. Rise of industrial unions
      3. Intense conflict with management
         a. Techniques used by
            management
         b. The sitdown strike
         c. CIO victories
         d. Growing power for organized
            labor
   C. Reaction to a new depression
      1. Course of the 1937 slump
      2. Administration's reaction
      3. The battle over policy
         a. Fear of the unbalanced budget
         b. A move from regulation to
            antitrust action
      4. Roosevelt's call for spending
      5. Reforms of 1937 and 1938
         a. Housing legislation
         b. Assistance for tenant farmers
         c. Fair Labor Standards Act
   D. Setbacks to the New Deal
      1. Emergence of an opposition
         a. Defection of the southerners
         b. Victories of the opposition in
            1938
      2. Roosevelt's 1938 purge
      3. Results of the 1938 elections
      4. Limited legislation in 1939

VIII. Impact of the New Deal
   A. Some enduring changes
   B. A course between extremes
   C. Creation of the "broker state"

KEY ITEMS OF CHRONOLOGY

Roosevelt's administrations	1933–April 1945
The Hundred Days	March 4–June 16, 1933
Second New Deal initiatives	1935
Court-packing plan presented	1937

TERMS TO MASTER

Listed below are some important terms or people with which you should be familiar after you complete the study of this chapter. Explain the significance of each name or term.

1. The Hundred Days
2. brain trust
3. Securities and Exchange Commission
4. Civilian Conservation Corps
5. Agricultural Adjustment Administration
6. *United States v. Butler*
7. Soil Conservation Act
8. Public Works Administration
9. Tennessee Valley Authority
10. Huey Long
11. *Schechter Poultry Corp. v. United States*
12. Wagner Act
13. Social Security Act
14. court-packing plan
15. CIO
16. John L. Lewis
17. Fair Labor Standards Act
18. broker state

VOCABULARY BUILDING

Listed below are some words used in this chapter. Look up each word in your dictionary.

1. ebullient
2. requisite
3. sallow
4. dole
5. purge
6. consummate
7. panacea
8. galvanized
9. surrogate
10. malevolent

EXERCISES FOR UNDERSTANDING

When you have completed reading the chapter, answer each of the following questions. If you have difficulty, go back and reread the section of the chapter related to the question.

Multiple-Choice Questions

Select the letter of the response which best completes the statement.

1. Before becoming president, Franklin Roosevelt had
   A. suffered from polio
   B. never run for national political office
   C. served as a U. S. Senator
   D. all of the above

2. In 1933 the New Deal immediately attacked problems in
   A. race relations
   B. banking and finance
   C. labor
   D. diplomacy with Germany

3. The Share Our Wealth program was the creation of
   A. John Davis and Al Smith
   B. Francis E. Townsend
   C. Charles E. Coughlin
   D. Huey P. Long

4. The National Industrial Recovery Act provided for
   A. $3.3 billion in spending through the PWA
   B. codes of fair practice for industries
   C. the right of workers to form unions
   D. all of the above

5. The New Deal's "cornerstone" and "supreme achievement," according to FDR, was
   A. Social Security
   B. the Wagner Labor Relations Act
   C. the Tennessee Valley Authority
   D. the PWA and WPA

6. Eleanor Roosevelt helped her husband most by
   A. remaining discreetly noncontroversial
   B. maintaining ties to blacks and labor
   C. pulling him toward more conservative policies
   D. going on diplomatic missions to Asia and Africa

7. The Supreme Court packing plan was defeated in part because of
   A. Democratic losses in 1936
   B. its violation of the Constitution
   C. a change in the Court's direction in rulings on key measures
   D. all of the above

8. The momentum of FDR and the New Deal was hurt by
   A. the election of 1936
   B. the failure of CIO efforts in the auto and steel industries
   C. a second attack of polio
   D. the recession of 1937

True-False Questions

Indicate whether each statement is true or false.

1. In his 1932 campaign, FDR spelled out in detail his plans for fighting the depression.
2. The U.S. abandoned the gold standard for its money in 1933.
3. The AAA of 1933 tried to help farmers by getting them to reduce production.
4. FDR preferred work-relief to the dole.
5. The Social Security tax did "soak the rich."
6. The GOP candidate in 1936 was a longtime opponent of the entire New Deal.
7. Perhaps the most enduring voting change brought by FDR was the shift of the farm vote to the Democratic Party.
8. An innovation in labor unions in the 1930s involved organizing workers in entire industries into the same union.

A Match of New Deal Agencies

The New Deal period witnessed the creation of a plethora of new government agencies which became known as the alphabet agencies because they were referred to by their initials. To help you focus on major agencies and to test your grasp of the material, match the description or statement on the right with the agencies or act on the left. Some of the agencies or acts may match with more than one description. Answers are at the end of this chapter.

Essay Questions

1. What special qualities did Franklin Roosevelt bring to the presidency?
2. How did the "first" and "second" New Deals differ? How were they similar?
3. Compare and contrast the New Deal's policies toward labor and agriculture.
4. What were the three or four most important programs of the New Deal? Explain your choices.
5. What factors in 1937 and 1938 contributed to a decline of the New Deal?
6. Evaluate the long-term significance of the New Deal.

DOCUMENT

Excerpts from the Federal Writers Project Interviews with Depression Victims

Through the efforts of New Deal agencies Americans learned much about themselves in the 1930s. The Federal Writers Project, for instance, published poignant accounts of the lives of people in some southern states.

The excerpts below come from those accounts. You may wish to compare them with the accounts in Chapter 20 of industrial workers in Illinois in the 1880s.

From the Account of a White Brick-Plant Worker and His Washer-Woman Wife

"Hub's hired solid time and has been for two years. He works every day from six in the morning till six at night in Mr. Hunter's brick plant across the tracks. Some days more'n that—twenty-four hours on a stretch. That's over-time, but it don't mean no extra pay. It's forty dollars a month straight, no matter what."

Agency or Act	Description
1. FDIC	a. created a regional rehabilitation of a river basin
2. FERA	b. investigated the concentration of economic power in the United States
3. Economy Act	c. set minimum wages and maximum hours for certain industries in interstate commerce
4. First AAA	d. provided a variety of methods for increasing farm income
5. Civilian Conservation Corps	e. provided insurance for bank deposits
6. PWA	f. provided $3.3 billion for jobs on major building projects
7. TVA	g. established a stopgap plan for aiding the unemployed from 1933 to 1935
8. NRA	h. provided loans to rural cooperatives to run electrical lines to remote farms
9. REA	i. established a plan to cut wages of veterans and federal employees
10. Wagner Act	j. provided jobs for young men in the nation's parks
11. Social Security Act	k. regulated the sale of stocks and bonds
12. Wealth Tax Act	l. allowed industries to collaborate together to limit production of goods and raise wages
13. SEC	m. provided farmers payments to conserve soil by not planting crops
14. TNEC	n. created a committee to oversee elections for unions
15. Farm Security Administration	o. established the welfare system for mothers and dependent children
16. Soil Conservation Act	p. greatly increased income taxes
17. Fair Labor Standards Act	q. provided a tax on incomes to ensure retirement benefits

Agency or Act	Description
18. WPA	r. placed a tax on farm products when first processed for market
	s. provided loans to help farm tenants buy their land
	t. established a long-term federal program to provide jobs, including in symphony orchestras, and in artistic and theater projects
	u. provided aid to the states for work projects as well as a dole
	v. built dams to produce and sell electricity
	w. a counterpart to NRA, this agency provided jobs on major construction projects

Rena Murray—small, stooped, hollow-chested—put her whole ninety pounds behind the heavy flatiron. Collar and cuffs came from under the heat, stiff and slick. She lifted the shirt from the board for final inspection.

"Hub fires the boiler most of the time. Then when they're drying bricks, he has to run the fan for twenty-four hours. They couldn't make out in that kiln unless Hub was there.

"He ought to git more for the work he puts out. Forty dollars a month just ain't enough for us to live on. Me and Hub and the three children. We have to pay four dollars out every month for this shack. Mr. Hunter makes the hands live close by the plant. And he gits ahold of that four dollars for rent before we ever see a cent of Hub's wages. This shack ain't worth four dollars a month, neither. Mr. Hunter won't do nothing toward fixing it up. If a window pane's broke, we do the putting in. Leak done ruint the paper and it's up to us to see to new paper."

Rena stooped to the tub of sprinkled clothes. She shook out a rolled-up bundle and slipped another shirt over the narrow end of the home-made ironing board. She settled the board again between the center table and the lard bucket set in a backless kitchen chair.

"I take in washing or do what I can to help out."

"We ain't been to church for years. I was taught working on Sunday was wrong. Folks that holds out against working on Sunday don't have to hire others to work for 'em if they don't show up. Hub had to pay a dollar and a quarter yesterday to git a man to turn the fan so's he could see after his sister. She's about to die. Dirty shame for a man to have to pay to go see his own die. I sure wish he could find hisself a better job."

"What he aims to do is to turn over every stone he can to git back on the WPA. We got along a lot better on the WPA. We had our check regular and had good warm clothes for the girls. And they give Hub clothes, too, because his work kept him in the open. I didn't git none but I could manage all right when the others was gitting all they did. Whenever one of us would git down, the WPA would send a doctor and medicine. They give us food, too. Things that are supposed to be healthy for eating such as prunes and raisins. We can't buy 'em now."

"Burial insurance is a good thing. I wish I had a policy on me and every one of the children. That's just wishing. It pinches us plumb to death to keep Hub's going. We was always behind in dues till he got put on solid time. I couldn't git no insurance noways on account of my bad health. I've had the pneumonia since we've been here. Down three months. There wasn't a Hunter had feeling enough to set foot in this shack. Mrs. Hunter has spoke to me times since, but Mr. Hunter don't trouble about speaking to them that slaves for him. My mammy taught me a dog was good enough to be nice to."

From the Account of a Young Shoe-Factory Worker

"My work is hard all right. It's hard on me because I ain't but only seventeen and ain't got my full growth yet. It's work down in the steam room which they call it that because it's always full of steam which sometimes when you go in it you can't hardly see. You steam leather down there and that steam soaks you clean to the skin. It makes me keep a cold most of the time because when I go out doors I'm sopping wet. Another thing that's hard about it is having so much standing up to do. My hours is from seven o'clock in the morning till four in the evening. And it's stand on my feet the whole time. When noon time comes and I'm off an hour, why I just find me somewheres to set and I sure set there. You couldn't pay me to stand up during lunch time.

"I'm on piecework now and I can't seem to get my production up to where I make just a whole lot. You get paid by the production hour and it takes fifty pair of shoes to make that hour. You get forty-two cents for the hour. Highest I ever made in one week was eleven dollars and the lowest was seven dollars and forty-two cents. I usually hit in between and make eight or nine dollars.

"Now and then somebody will say, 'We ought to have us a union here of some sort.' That kind of talk just makes me mad all over. Mr. Pugh is a Christian man. He brought his factory here to give us some work which we didn't have any before. We do pretty well, I think, to just stay away from that kind of talk. All but the sore-heads and trouble-makers is satisfied and glad to have work.

"I don't blame Mr. Pugh a bit the way he feels about the unions. The plant manager knows Mr. Pugh mighty well and he told my foreman what Mr. Pugh said. Mr. Pugh said, 'If the union ever comes in here and I have to operate my plant under a union, why I'll just close the plant down and move it away from Hancock so quick it'll make your head swim.' That's his word on it and I don't blame him none. I'd hate to see a union try here. No plant and no jobs for anybody. They just operate these unions out of Wall Street, anyhow, trying to ruin people like Mr. Pugh. . . .

"My money has to go a long way. I've got to pay eight dollars a month rent and I have to buy coal and stove wood. I got to buy clothes for the family and something to eat for them. Then twice a month there's that five dollar ambulance bill which it's to take my brother that's got the T.B. to the City Hospital in Memphis where they take and drain his lungs. Sure charge you for an ambulance, don't they? Now, some people say if you just take one trip in an ambulance, the undertaker won't ask a cent for it. Figures he'll get your custom if you pass on. But they sure charge me for my brother.

"Well, I'm always glad when it's quitting time. I like to work there, but you can't help getting tired. I go on home. I walk four blocks and I'm there. Usually I have to wait a while for supper so I just set at the window. I like to watch and see if maybe something will come along the street and I can watch it. Sometimes there's a new funny paper there and I will look it over—specially if it's Tarzan. That's the best thing in a funny paper, the Tarzan part. Nobody ever gets it over old Tarzan, do they? Most times, though, I like to just set there and watch."

"I work steady but I'm most always financially in need of money. It takes a lot to keep a family going. My little sister needs glasses but they cost too much. All of my family has weak eyes but we can't afford to wear glasses.

"So I haven't the money for running around. I wouldn't if I had the money, either. The Bible is against running around and playing cards and seeing the moving pictures. People should study their Bible more and we'd have more Christian men like Mr. Pugh and more jobs. So me and a young lady I know of go to church and Sunday School instead of running around. My family belongs to the Baptist Church, but this certain young lady is a Nazarene and that's where we go.

"You know, when you're blue and down at the mouth and don't see any use anyhow, a good sermon just lifts you up. You haven't got a thing to lose by living a Christian life. Take Mr. Pugh. He lives it and look where he is now. And if you don't make out that way, if you're poor all your life, then you get a high place in the Kingdom. Just do the best you know how and the Lord will take care of you either here or hereafter. It sure is a comfort."

From the Account of a Young Man in Charge of a WPA Supply Room

"The way I look at it is this. This is a rich country. I figger it ain't going to hurt the government to feed and clothe them that needs it. Half of 'em can't get work, or just ain't fixed to handle work if they get it. I imagine this country's worth near on to ten billion dollars. We've got the money. Plenty of it. No sense in the big fellows kicking about a little handout to the poor. Matter's not if some ain't deserving.

"I'll admit there's some don't deserve a nickel of the government's money. Lot of them that comes here, why I'd sooner give them a kick in the pants than shove 'em out supplies. But you got to take the good with the bad. Or bad with the good, whichever way you've a mind to put it. Most that comes here are poor and can't help it. Needs help. Needs it just same I need this job. Always going to be more poor folks than them that ain't poor. Now take me. I've always been poor and I guess I always will be. I ain't saying that's the government's fault. It's just a downright truth, that's all.

"There's a lot of things I'd like different in the world. But I can't say I got so much to complain of. If I'd had more education like as not I'd be getting more pay. Maybe, I wouldn't. Not getting no schooling is my own fault. Poor or rich, humans is faulty one way or the next. Time I got to the seventh grade I got the making of money in my head. Wages looked to be about the best thing in the world. Well, I had a run of good jobs. Made fair money for a year or two driving trucks. Took a turn at auto fixing, too, around a filling station. Just first one thing and another. Jobs was easy to get then. That's before women got set on going to work. That's what caused all this depression business. I'm not saying that the women don't need jobs now. They does. But they got themselves to thank for the fix the world's in. They started out taking jobs from men when there wasn't no sense in them working. Them men lost out on good jobs and dropped right down and took ours. Just wasn't no jobs left for poor folks.

"Folks that ain't never been poor just don't know nothin' a-tall about doing on nothing. I get so all-fired full of laugh when some of these women from the higher ups comes down to the Welfare Department. Nice ladies, but it ain't a salt spoon of sense about poor folks in their heads. Pretty little thing come last week to tell the women come here about cooking. Before she started spieling, she seen them cans of salmon I took from the big case and put on that shelf back there. That give her a start. She aimed to tell them how to make up a pot dish from salmon. We ain't really got no salmon here. Just a cheap grade of canned mackerel. She sailed in. 'Brush the baking dish with melted butter,' says she. If she hadn't been so pretty and so young, I'd liked to asked right off—'Where they going to get the butter? Ain't two in the room's got butter for their bread. You'll have to shift to a skillet for the cooking. That's about the best they got for greasing up.' Of course I didn't say no such to her. She was just plumb wore out time she got that salmon out of her head and into the cook stove. When she come to tail part of the talk giving them leave to ask her questions, she looked to me about ready to fall off the box I'd drug out for her to speak from. It's a blessing the Lord made it easy for some. A blessing. And I'm glad He done it."

"Asides from groceries and rent and clothes there's ten dollars a week wages. I figger our spending, all told, about twenty dollars a month. Things we got to have that ain't give us is bought on the installment plan. Cost more that way. But what you going to do when things got to be got and there's no spot cash to hand! We's pulling long through debt right well. Just fifteen dollars owing on the furniture and about twenty-five on the washing machine. Lord, that washing machine's worth ever cent we paid for it. I told Ella if I ever seen another thing that'd be as big help to her I'd buy it if I had to bust a bank. It don't take her half the time used to to get all them youngun's clothes did and the house things and such. Ella keep everthing from the kids to the kivers clean as a pin. House the same. We keep our kids close to home. Don't let them run round with just any trash. I got the last one of ours insured for burial— except sister. I'll get her fixed time she's year old. I pay twenty cents a week on me and Ella. Ten cents for the two oldest boys, five cents for the others.

"Thing that worries me most about a large family is the feeding of them right. I know ours don't have what they's supposed to. Not if half's right I hear them ladies who come here to talk says. We can't manage the milk we should for them. If we get Grade A they ain't enough for more than a cup around. I guess that cheap canned milk's good enough for cooking. We uses what they give us. Them things concocted for the place of butter ain't as cheap as you'd think. I ain't strong like I used to be. And with all this talk I hear floating round I wonder if its the things I ain't had to eat that'd done it."

From the Account of a CCC Boy

"I ain't never been much to school. Jist went to the second grade, that's all, excepting what I learned here in the CCC. I could have gone, I guess, but for some reason didn't keer nothing about it. Jist didn't want to go. I would have went if I wanted to. They didn't make me not go. We jist didn't none of us go. I got one brother that went to the second grade, too, and my sister she went to the first. Then she quit. We jist wasn't a family that like school.

"I quit that old second grade when I was fourteen. I left home and went to work. Been on my own ever since. I went down here to Woolard and went to work on a farm. The man he was sick and not able to work and had to have somebody to help him. That's why I got to work so long, and even got the job at all. Got twenty dollars a month."

I asked, "Would you go on to school and finish now if you had the chance?"

"Don't know whether I could or not. I would really like to learn." He flushed and scowled. "The boys they make fun of us when we can't read the funnies nor nothing. I look at pictures in books, and things like that in the recreation hall, so they won't laugh at me. I wish I had gone on to school now and would go as far as I could if I git the chance. Guess I couldn't git much learning now though, could I? I'm too old most to learn now."

I asked if he wanted to stay with the CCC.

"Yes'm, as long as I kin, because I git plenty to eat here. I didn't always at home, not the same kind of stuff, anyhow. Guess we had plenty, such as it was, at home, but it jist wasn't good like this, nor enough of it for the kind it was. I git to go more, git to see more. I'm learning too. I watch the others, and then, I have more clothes and can keep cleaner too."

"Do I go to church?

"Well, no'm. Not now. But while in the C's I do. The chaplain preaches to us two times a month, and I like to hear him. He makes tears come in my eyes, too. I quit drinking all on account of him. I'm a good boy now. I don't go to church at town much because I'm afraid they'll laugh at me. My mother she's a Baptist, but I jist go to any of them. I always give some money when I have it to give.

"Down home it's different. I've rambled all over that place and they ain't got no churches down there. I been there two years and ain't ever seen no church yet. Some of my little brothers ain't never seen no church yet."

[From *These Are Our Lives* (1939), as told to and written by members of the Federal Writers' Project of the W.P.A. (New York: W. W. Norton & Co., 1975), pp. 224–228, 231–235, 366–368, 412–414]

Questions for Reflection

Compare the wages and expenses of these workers. Which one seems to be better situated financially? What role does religion play in the lives of these people? How do they feel about their "bosses" and others in positions superior to them? Whom do they blame for their financial difficulties? What was the attitude of the shoe-factory worker toward labor unions? One of the benefits of the New Deal was improved public education on nutrition. What evidence do you find in these accounts of nutritional awareness? What evidence is there that the advice of government social workers to the poor was impractical?

How do these accounts of workers' lives compare with those of the 1880s Illinois workers in Chapter 20?

ANSWERS TO MULTIPLE-CHOICE, TRUE-FALSE, AND MATCHING QUESTIONS

Multiple-Choice Questions

1-A, 2-B, 3-C, 4-D, 5-A, 6-B, 7-C, 8-D

True-False Questions

1-F, 2-T, 3-T, 4-T, 5-F, 6-F, 7-F, 8-T

Matching Questions

1-e, 2-q,u, 3-i, 4-d,r, 5-j, 6-f,w, 7-a,v, 8-l,
9-h, 10-n, 11-o,q, 12-p, 13-k, 14-b, 15-s,
16-m, 17-c, 18-t

28

FROM ISOLATION TO GLOBAL WAR

CHAPTER OBJECTIVES

*After you complete the reading and study
of this chapter you should be able to*

1. Explain and account for the foreign
   policy pursued by the United States in
   the interwar period.
2. Describe the aggressions of Japan, Italy,
   and Germany in the decade of the
   1930s.
3. Account for American efforts at
   neutrality in the face of aggression and
   assess the effectiveness of neutrality in
   preventing war.
4. Describe the election of 1940.
5. Explain American support of Britain and
   Russia prior to the United States's entry
   into the war.
6. Explain and account for the effectiveness
   of the attack on Pearl Harbor.

CHAPTER OUTLINE

I. Postwar isolationism
   A. Evidences of isolationist sentiment
   B. Counteractions of world involvement
   C. Relations with the League
   D. The war-debt tangle
      1. Problems with repayment of debts
      2. Linkage of debts to reparations
      3. Depression and debt cancellation
   E. Efforts toward disarmament
      1. A substitute for League membership
      2. Strained Japanese-American
         relations
      3. The Washington Armaments
         Conference
         a. Hughes's initiative
         b. Agreements made at the
            conference
         c. Effects of the treaties
      4. The movement to outlaw war
         a. Development of the
            Kellogg-Briand Pact
         b. Effect of the pact
   F. The Good-Neighbor Policy
      1. Early efforts to improve relations
         with Latin America
      2. Hoover and the Clark Memorandum
      3. Further improvements under FDR

II. War clouds
   A. Japanese incursion in China
      1. Chinese weaknesses
      2. Japanese occupation of Manchuria
      3. Reactions to occupation
         a. League condemnation
         b. Japan's withdrawal from the
            League
   B. Mussolini's rise to power
   C. Hitler's rise to power
   D. American recognition of the Soviet
      Union

E. Aggression in Asia and Europe
  1. Italian invasion of Ethiopia, 1935
  2. Hitler's occupation of the Rhineland, 1936
  3. Spanish Civil War, 1936
  4. Japanese invasion of China, 1937
  5. Hitler's *Anschluss* with Austria, 1938
  6. The Munich Agreement, 1938
  7. War began over Poland, 1939

III. American efforts for neutrality
  A. The Nye Committee investigations
  B. Congressional effort to avoid World War I
  C. The first Neutrality Act, 1935
    1. Sale of arms to belligerents forbidden
    2. Travel discouraged on belligerent ships
  D. Reaction to the invasion of Ethiopia
  E. The second Neutrality Act: loans to belligerents forbidden
  F. Extension of the Neutrality Act to cover civil wars
  G. Further neutrality provisions
  H. Reactions to Japanese action in China
    1. Lack of use of neutrality laws
    2. Quarantine speech
  I. Reactions to war in Europe
    1. Change to cash-and-carry arms sales
    2. Extension of war zone

IV. The storm in Europe
  A. Hitler's *Blitzkrieg*
  B. American aid to embattled Britain

  1. Growth of U.S. defense effort
  2. Sales of arms to Britain
  C. Other defense measures
  D. The destroyer-bases deal
  E. Peacetime conscription
  F. Polarization of public opinion
    1. Committee to Defend America
    2. America First Committee

V. The election of 1940
  A. The choice of Willkie
  B. The choice of FDR
  C. Nature of the campaign
  D. Results of the election

VI. The arsenal of democracy
  A. The Lend-Lease program
  B. Further Axis gains
  C. Reaction to the invasion of the Soviet Union
  D. The Atlantic Charter
  E. Conflict with the Germans in the Atlantic

VII. The storm in the Pacific
  A. Japanese aggression in Southeast Asia
  B. Tripartite Pact
  C. Negotiations between Japan and the United States
  D. Warlords gain control in Japan
  E. Attack on Pearl Harbor
    1. Extent of U.S. foreknowledge
    2. Errors in warning
    3. Damage from the attack
    4. Other Japanese aggression in the Pacific
  F. Declaration of war

KEY ITEMS OF CHRONOLOGY

Washington Disarmament Conference	1921–1922
Mussolini took power in Italy	1925
Kellogg-Briand Pact	1928
Japanese invasion of Manchuria	1931
Hitler took power in Germany	1933
London Economic Conference	1933
Nye Committee	1934–1937
Italy's invasion of Ethiopia	1935
Japan's invasion of China	1937
Quarantine Speech	1937
World War II began	September 1, 1939
First peacetime draft	1940

Fall of France	June 1940
Lend-Lease program began	1941
Germany's invasion of Russia	June 1941
Japanese extend protectorate over Indochina	July 1941
Attack on Pearl Harbor	December 7, 1941

TERMS TO MASTER

Listed below are some important terms or people with which you should be familiar after you complete the study of this chapter. Explain the significance of each name or term.

1. World Court
2. Washington Armaments Conference
3. reparations
4. Five-Power Treaty
5. Kellogg-Briand Pact
6. Good-Neighbor Policy
7. Stimson Doctrine
8. London Naval Conference
9. Cordell Hull
10. Reciprocal Trade Agreements
11. Nye Committee
12. Neutrality Acts
13. cash and carry
14. *Blitzkrieg*
15. America First Committee
16. Wendell Willkie
17. Lend-Lease program
18. Four Freedoms
19. Atlantic Charter

VOCABULARY BUILDING

Listed below are some words used in this chapter. Look up each word in your dictionary.

1. reparations
2. encroachments
3. partition
4. allay
5. abrogate
6. incursion
7. fascist
8. ludicrous
9. brazenly
10. embargo

EXERCISES FOR UNDERSTANDING

When you have completed reading the chapter, answer each of the following questions. If you have difficulty, go back and reread the section of the chapter related to the question.

Multiple-Choice Questions

Select the letter of the response which best completes the statement.

1. America's involvement with the rest of the world was assured in the 1920s by
   A. the wordwide connections of American business
   B. American investments and loans abroad
   C. United States possessions in the Pacific
   D. all of the above

2. The naval armaments race after World War I came in response to
   A. the rise of Hitler
   B. British expansion in East Asia and the Pacific
   C. the Harding administration's commitment to a big navy
   D. the growing power of Japan

3. In the early 1930s Roosevelt's foreign policy included
   A. advocacy of U.S. membership in the League of Nations
   B. proposals to deal with the depression on an international scale
   C. reciprocal trade agreements
   D. all of the above

4. The Nye Committee investigations seemed to prove that
   A. the United States entered World War I to permit the munitions manufacturers to make greater profits

B. the United States should back down
from its dispute with Japan over
China
C. the only way to end the war was with
a treaty
D. the United States was not responsible
for the success of the attack by Japan
5. The Neutrality Act of 1939
A. prohibited all trade with belligerents
B. allowed trade with only one side in a
war
C. kept U.S. ships from war zones but
approved cash-and-carry trade even
for arms
D. permitted nonmilitary trade in
American ships only
6. In the summer of 1940
A. the United States and Britain
swapped destroyers for naval and air
bases
B. Congress appropriated $4 billion for a
two-ocean navy
C. the first peacetime draft became law
D. all of the above occurred
7. The Atlantic Charter of 1941
A. declared British-American war aims
B. ordered German U-boats out of the
Atlantic
C. ended U.S. neutrality on the seas and
led to conflict with Germany
D. reaffirmed the Kellogg-Briand Pact
8. The Japanese attack on Pearl Harbor
A. was a complete success
B. sunk or severely damaged all U.S.
aircraft carriers in the Pacific
C. killed 25,000 Americans
D. missed vital shore installations and oil
tanks

True-False Questions

Indicate whether each statement is true or false.

1. America's allies in World War I had paid
all their war debts by 1924.
2. The Kellogg-Briand Pact provided for
multinational attacks on any nation
which started a war.
3. The Clark Memorandum attacked the
Japanese invasion of Korea.
4. The United States gave diplomatic .
recognition to the Soviet Union in 1933.
5. The United States tried to avoid World
War II by outlawing the supposed causes
of World War I.
6. The America First Committee advocated
aid to Great Britain.
7. In 1941 the Lend-Lease program
concentrated on stopping Italian
conquests in Eastern Europe.
8. The United States declaration of war in
1941 passed the Congress unanimously.

Essay Questions

1. Was the United States more isolationist
in its foreign policy during 1920–1929 or
1930–1939? Explain.
2. Describe American efforts to achieve
peace and disarmament during the
1920s.
3. Describe American efforts to improve
relations with Latin America from 1921
through 1940.
4. How did the United States and the
Allied nations react to Axis aggressions in
the 1930s? Why?
5. Why did the United States seek to
remain neutral in the 1930s?
6. Explain the importance of foreign policy
issues in the election of 1940.
7. Account for the attack on Pearl Harbor
in 1941 and assess its consequences.

DOCUMENTS

Document 1. Roosevelt's Quarantine Speech, 1937

In the wake of the rearmament of
Germany, the Italian invasion of Ethiopia,
the Spanish Civil War, and finally the
Japanese invasion of China, Roosevelt visited
Chicago, the heart of isolationist sentiment
in America, on October 5, 1937, to make

what has generally been dubbed his Quarantine Speech. Look carefully in the following excerpts for the promises or pledges that the president sought to exact on the issues of peace and war.

I am glad to come once again to Chicago and especially to have the opportunity of taking part in the dedication of this important project of civic betterment. . . .

Without a declaration of war and without warning or justification of any kind, civilians, including women and children, are being ruthlessly murdered with bombs from the air. In times of so-called peace ships are being attacked and sunk by submarines without cause or notice. Nations are fomenting and taking sides in civil warfare in nations that have never done them any harm. Nations claiming freedom for themselves deny it to others. . . .

The peace-loving nations must make a concerted effort in opposition to those violations of treaties and those ignorings of humane instincts which today are creating a state of international anarchy and instability from which there is no escape through mere isolation or neutrality. . . .

There is a solidarity and interdependence about the modern world, both technically and morally, which makes it impossible for any nation completely to isolate itself from economic and political upheavals in the rest of the world, specially when such upheavals appear to be spreading and not declining.

It seems to be unfortunately true that the epidemic of world lawlessness is spreading.

When an epidemic of physical disease starts to spread, the community approves and joins in a quarantine of the patients in order to protect the health of the community against the spread of the disease.

War is a contagion, whether it be declared or undeclared. It can engulf states and peoples remote from the original scene of hostilities. . . . We are adopting such measures as will minimize our risk of involvement, but we cannot have complete protection in a world of disorder in which confidence and security have broken down.

If civilization is to survive the principles of the Prince of Peace must be restored. Shattered trust between nations must be revived.

Most important of all, the will for peace on the part of peace-loving nations must express itself to the end that nations that may be tempted to violate their agreements and the rights of others will desist from such a cause. There must be positive endeavors to preserve peace.

America hates war. America hopes for peace. Therefore, America actively engages in the search for peace.

[U.S. Department of State, *Peace and War: United States Foreign Policy, 1931–1941* (Washington, D.C.: U.S. Government Printing Office, 1943), pp. 384–387]

Document 2. Roosevelt's "Four Freedoms" Speech, 1941

The "Four Freedoms," formulated in Roosevelt's annual message to Congress on January 6, 1941, have come to be accepted as the most succinct statement of the things for which the American people were prepared to fight.

To the Congress of the United States:

I address you, the Members of the Seventy-Seventh Congress, at a moment unprecedented in the history of the Union. I use the word "unprecedented," because at no previous time has American security been as seriously threatened from without as it is today. . . .

It is true that prior to 1914 the United States often had been disturbed by events in other Continents. We had even engaged in two wars with European nations and in a number of undeclared wars in the West Indies, in the Mediterranean and in the Pacific for the maintenance of American rights and for the principles of peaceful commerce. In no case, however, had a serious threat been raised against our national safety or our independence.

What I seek to convey is the historic truth that the United States as a nation has at all times maintained opposition to any attempt to lock us in behind an ancient Chinese wall while the procession of civilization went past. Today, thinking of our children and their children, we oppose enforced isolation for ourselves or for any part of the Americas.

Even when the World War broke out in 1914, it seemed to contain only small threat of danger to our own American future. But, as time went on, the American people began to visualize what the downfall of democratic nations might mean to our own democracy.

We need not over-emphasize imperfections in the Peace of Versailles. We need not harp on failure of the democracies to deal with problems of world deconstruction. We should remember that the Peace of 1919 was far less unjust than the kind of "pacification" which began even before Munich, and which is being carried on under the new order of tyranny that seeks to spread over every continent today. The American people have unalterably set their faces against that tyranny.

Every realist knows that the democratic way of life is at this moment being directly assailed in every part of the world—assailed either by arms, or by secret spreading of poisonous propaganda by those who seek to destroy unity and promote discord in nations still at peace. During sixteen months this assault has blotted out the whole pattern of democratic life in an appalling number of independent nations, great and small. The assailants are still on the march, threatening other nations, great and small.

Therefore, as your President, performing my constitutional duty to "give to the Congress information of the state of the Union," I find it necessary to report that the future and the safety of our country and of our democracy are overwhelmingly involved in events far beyond our borders.

Armed defense of democratic existence is now being gallantly waged in four continents. If that defense fails, all the population and all the resources of Europe, Asia, Africa and Australasia will be dominated by the conquerors. The total of those populations and their resources greatly exceeds the sum total of the population and resources of the whole of the Western Hemisphere—many times over.

In times like these it is immature—and incidentally untrue—for anybody to brag that an unprepared America, single-handed, and with one hand tied behind its back, can hold off the whole world.

No realistic American can expect from a dictator's peace international generosity, or return of true independence, or world disarmament, or freedom of expression, or freedom of religion—or even good business. Such a peace would bring no security for us or for our neighbors. "Those, who would give up essential liberty to purchase a little temporary safety, deserve neither liberty nor safety." As a nation we may take pride in the fact that we are soft-hearted; but we cannot afford to be soft-hearted. We must always be wary of those who with sounding brass and a tinkling cymbal preach the "ism" of appeasement. We must especially beware of that small group of selfish men who would clip the wings of the American eagle in order to feather their own nests.

I have recently pointed out how quickly the tempo of modern warfare could bring into our very midst the physical attack which we must expect if the dictator nations win this war.

There is much loose talk of our immunity from immediate and direct invasion from across the seas. Obviously, as long as the British Navy retains its power, no such danger exists. Even if there were no British Navy, it is not probable that any enemy would be stupid enough to attack us by landing troops in the United States from across thousands of miles of ocean, until it had acquired strategic bases from which to operate. But we learn much from the lessons of the past years in Europe—particularly the lesson of Norway, whose essential seaports were captured by treachery and surprise built up over a series of years. The first phase of the invasion of this Hemisphere would not be the landing of regular troops. The necessary strategic points would be occupied by secret agents and their dupes—and great numbers of them are already here, and in Latin America.

As long as the aggressor nations maintain the offensive, they—not we—will choose the time and the place and the method of their attack. That is why the future of all American Republics is today in serious danger. That is why this Annual Message to the Congress is unique in our history. That is why every member of the Executive branch of the government and every member of the Congress face great responsibility—and great accountability.

The need of the moment is that our actions and our policy should be devoted primarily—almost exclusively—to meeting this foreign peril. For all our domestic problems are now a part of the great emergency. Just as our national policy in internal affairs has been based upon a decent respect for the rights and dignity of all our fellowmen within our gates, so our national policy in foreign affairs has been based on a decent respect for the rights and dignity of all nations, large and small. And the justice of morality must and will win in the end.

Our national policy is this.

First, by an impressive expression of the public will and without regard to partisanship, we are committed to all-inclusive national defense.

Second, by an impressive expression of the public will and without regard to partisanship, we are committed to full support of all those resolute peoples, everywhere, who are resisting aggression and are thereby keeping war away from our Hemisphere. By this support, we express our determination that the democratic cause shall prevail; and we strengthen the defense and security of our own nation.

Third, by an impressive expression of the public will and without regard to partisanship, we are committed to the proposition that principles of morality and considerations for our own security will never permit us to acquiesce in a peace dictated by aggressors and sponsored by appeasers. We know that enduring peace cannot be bought at the cost of other people's freedom.

In the recent national election there was no substantial difference between the two great parties in respect to that national policy. No issue was fought out on this line before the American electorate. Today, it is abundantly evident that American citizens everywhere are demanding and supporting speedy and complete action in recognition of obvious danger. Therefore, the immediate need is a swift and driving increase in our armament production. . . .

Our most useful and immediate role is to act as an arsenal for them as well as for ourselves. They do not need man power. They do need billions of dollars worth of the weapons of defense. . . .

Let us say to the democracies: "We Americans are vitally concerned in your defense of freedom. We are putting forth our energies, our resources and our organizing powers to give you the strength to regain and maintain a free world. We shall send you, in ever-increasing numbers, ships, planes, tanks, guns. This is our purpose and our pledge." In fulfillment of this purpose we will not be intimidated by the threats of dictators that they will regard as a breach of international law and as an act of war our aid to the democracies which dare to resist their aggression. Such aid is not an act of war, even if a dictator should unilaterally proclaim it so to be. When the dictators are ready to make war upon us, they will not wait for an act of war on our part. They did not wait for Norway or Belgium or the Netherlands to commit an act of war. Their only interest is in a new one-way international law, which lacks mutuality in its observance, and, therefore, becomes an instrument of oppression.

The happiness of future generations of Americans may well depend upon how effective and how immediate we can make our aid felt. No one can tell the exact character of the emergency situations that we may be called upon to meet. The Nation's hands must not be tied when the Nation's life is in danger. We must all prepare to make the sacrifices that the emergency—as serious as war itself— demands. Whatever stands in the way of speed and efficiency in defense preparations must give way to the national need.

A free nation has the right to expect full cooperation from all groups. A free nation has the right to look to the leaders of business, of labor, and of agriculture to take the lead in stimulating effort, not among other groups but within their own groups. The best way of dealing with the few slackers or trouble makers in our midst is, first, to shame them by patriotic example, and, if that fails, to use the sovereignty of government to save government.

As men do not live by bread alone, they do not fight by armaments alone. Those who man our defenses, and those behind them who build our defenses, must have the stamina and courage which come from an unshakable belief in the manner of life which they are defending. The mighty action which we are calling for cannot be based on a disregard of all things worth fighting for.

The Nation takes great satisfaction and much strength from the things which have been done to make its people conscious of their individual stake in the preservation of democratic life in America. Those things have toughened the fibre of our people, have renewed their faith and strengthened their devotion to the institutions we make ready to protect. Certainly this is no time to stop thinking about the social and economic problems which are the root cause of the social revolution which is today a supreme factor in the world.

There is nothing mysterious about the foundations of a healthy and strong democracy. The basic things expected by our people of their political and economic systems are simple. They are: equality of opportunity for youth and for others; jobs for those who can work; security for those who need it; the ending of special privilege for the few; the preservation of civil liberties for all; the enjoyment of the fruits of scientific progress in a wider and constantly rising standard of living.

These are the simple and basic things that must never be lost sight of in the turmoil and unbelievable complexity of our modern world. The inner and abiding strength of our economic and political systems is dependent upon the degree to which they fulfill these expectations.

Many subjects connected with our social economy call for immediate improvement. As examples: We should bring more citizens under the coverage of old age pensions and unemployment insurance. We should widen the opportunities for adequate medical care. We should plan a better system by which persons deserving or needing gainful employment may obtain it.

I have called for personal sacrifice. I am assured of the willingness of almost all Americans to respond to that call. . . .

In the future days, which we seek to make secure, we look forward to a world founded upon four essential human freedoms.

The first is freedom of speech and expression—everywhere in the world.

The second is freedom of every person to worship God in his own way—everywhere in the world.

The third is freedom from want—which, translated into world terms, means economic understandings which will secure to every nation a healthy peace time life for its inhabitants—everywhere in the world.

The fourth is freedom from fear—which, translated into world terms, means a worldwide reduction of armaments to such a point and in such a thorough fashion that no nation will be in a position to commit an act of physical aggression against any neighbor—anywhere in the world.

That is no vision of a distant millenium. It is a definite basis for a kind of world attainable in our own time and generation. That kind of world is the very antithesis of the so-called new order of tyranny which the dictators seek to create with the crash of a bomb.

To that new order we oppose the greater conception—the moral order. A good society is able to face schemes of world domination and foreign revolutions alike without fear.

Since the beginning of our American history we have been engaged in change—in a perpetual peaceful revolution—a revolution which goes on steadily, quietly adjusting itself to changing conditions—without the concentration camp or the quick-lime in the ditch. The world order which we seek is the cooperation of free countries, working together in a friendly, civilized society.

This nation has placed its destiny in the hands and heads and hearts of its millions of free men and women; and its faith in freedom under the guidance of God. Freedom means the supremacy of human rights everywhere. Our support goes to those who struggle to gain those rights or keep them. Our strength is in our unity of purpose.

To that high concept there can be no end save victory.

[From *The Public Papers and Addresses of Franklin D. Roosevelt* (New York: Macmillan, 1940), 9:663*ff*]

Questions for Reflection

What actions did Roosevelt ask of the United States or other powers in his 1937 Quarantine Speech? What actions *seemed* to be *implied?* Why do you think this speech caused a great outcry of opposition from those groups who did not want the United States to become involved in the affairs of other nations?

What, specifically, did Roosevelt propose that the United States do, in his 1941 speech? Was Roosevelt able to stake out a position between isolation and intervention? How would you assess his leadership in this crisis?

ANSWERS TO MULTIPLE-CHOICE AND TRUE-FALSE QUESTIONS

Multiple-Choice Questions

1-D, 2-D, 3-C, 4-A, 5-C, 6-D, 7-A, 8-D

True-False Questions

1-F, 2-F, 3-F, 4-T, 5-T, 6-F, 7-F, 8-F

29

THE WORLD AT WAR

CHAPTER OBJECTIVES

After you complete the reading and study of this chapter you should be able to

1. Describe the major military strategies in both the European and Pacific theaters.
2. Explain the problems relating to mobilization and financing of the war.
3. Describe the impact of the war on the economy.
4. Assess the impact of the war on women, blacks, and Japanese-Americans.
5. Explain the decisions made at the Yalta Conference.
6. Account for the decision to use the atomic bomb and discuss its consequences.

CHAPTER OUTLINE

I. America's early battles
  A. Retreat in the Pacific
    1. Collapse along the Pacific
    2. Surrender of the Philippines
    3. Japanese strategy
    4. Battle of the Coral Sea (May 1942)
  B. Midway: a turning point
  C. Early setbacks in the Atlantic
    1. Devastation from German submarines
    2. Strategy of small patrol vessels

II. Mobilization at home
  A. Preparedness and mobilization
  B. Economic conversion to war
    1. War Production Board
    2. Role of the Office of Scientific Research and Development
    3. Effects of wartime spending
  C. Financing the war
    1. Roosevelt's effort to raise taxes
    2. Congressional reaction to taxation
    3. Sale of bonds
  D. Impact of the war on the economy
    1. Personal incomes
    2. Efforts to control prices
    3. Efforts to control wages and farm prices
    4. Seizure of industries
  E. Social effects of the war on women
    1. Women in the civilian workforce and the military
    2. Changing attitudes toward sex roles
  F. Social effects of the war on blacks
    1. Problems of the segregated armed forces
    2. Role of blacks in war industries
      a. The March on Washington Movement
      b. Impact of black militancy
    3. Challenges to other forms of discrimination
    4. Militant white counterreaction
  G. Impact of the war on Japanese-Americans

1. General record of the war on civil
   liberties
2. Internment of the Nisei
H. Evidences of domestic conservatism
   1. Congressional elections of 1942
   2. Abolition of New Deal agencies
   3. Actions against labor
I. Congressional reaction to the war

III. The war in Europe
   A. Initial decisions
      1. Basis for moving against Germany
         first
      2. Aspects of joint conduct of the war
      3. The formulation of the decision for
         the North African invasion
   B. The North Africa campaign
   C. Agreements at Casablanca
   D. Sicily and Italy
      1. Invasion of Sicily
      2. Italian surrender
      3. German control of northern Italy
      4. The battle for Rome
   E. Strategic bombing of Europe
      1. British and American cooperation
      2. Impact of the bombing
   F. Decisions of the Teheran Conference
   G. The D-Day invasion
      1. Development and implementation
         of "Overlord"
      2. German reaction
      3. Invasion of the French
         Mediterranean coast
      4. Slowing momentum of the drive
         on Germany

IV. The war in the Pacific
   A. Guadalcanal offensive
   B. MacArthur's sweep up the West
      Pacific

1. Approval for the MacArthur plan
2. The technique of "leapfrogging"
C. Nimitz's moves in the Central Pacific
D. The naval battle of Leyte Gulf

V. The election of 1944
   A. Republican strategy
   B. Democratic vice-presidential choice
   C. Campaign and results

VI. Closing on Germany
   A. The German counteroffensive
   B. Allied moves

VII. The Yalta Conference
   A. Nature of the decisions
   B. Call for a United Nations
   C. Occupation of Germany
   D. Decisions about eastern Europe
   E. An assessment of the Yalta decisions

VIII. Collapse of the Third Reich
   A. Roosevelt's death
   B. Collapse of Germany
   C. Discovery of the Nazi Holocaust

IX. The grinding war in the Pacific
   A. Japanese resistance in the Philippines
   B. Occupation of Iwo Jima and Okinawa
   C. Impact of these victories on the
      conduct of the war

X. The atomic bomb
   A. Manhattan Project
   B. The decision to use the bomb
   C. Effect of dropping two bombs
   D. Negotiation for surrender

XI. The final ledger of the war
   A. Estimates of death and destruction
   B. Impact on the United States and the
      USSR

KEY ITEMS OF CHRONOLOGY

Battle of Midway	June 1942
American troops invade North Africa	November 1942
Imposition of payroll tax deduction	1943
Casablanca Conference	January 1943
Teheran Conference	November– December 1943
Smith v. Allwright	1944
D-Day invasion	June 6, 1944

Yalta Conference	February 1945
Roosevelt's death and Truman's accession	April 12, 1945
V-E Day	May 8, 1945
Potsdam Conference	July 1945
Atomic bomb dropped on Hiroshima	August 6, 1945
Japan's surrender	September 2, 1945

TERMS TO MASTER

Listed below are some important terms or people with which you should be familiar after you complete the study of this chapter. Explain the significance of each name or term.

1. War Production Board
2. Office of Price Administration
3. rationing
4. "Rosie the Riveter"
5. FEPC
6. War Relocation Camps
7. Smith-Connally Act
8. Winston Churchill
9. second front
10. unconditional surrender
11. Gen. Dwight D. Eisenhower
12. Operation "Overload"
13. "leapfrogging"
14. Gen. Douglas MacArthur
15. Battle of Leyte Gulf
16. Yalta Conference
17. Nazi Holocaust
18. Hiroshima

VOCABULARY BUILDING

Listed below are some words used in this chapter. Look up each word in your dictionary.

1. seismic
2. cryptanalysts
3. watershed
4. vexations
5. pincers
6. strategic
7. expedite
8. holocaust
9. latent
10. labyrinth

EXERCISES FOR UNDERSTANDING

When you have completed reading the chapter, answer each of the following questions. If you have difficulty, go back and reread the section of the chapter related to the question.

Multiple-Choice Questions

Select the letter of the response which best completes the statement.

1. The Battle of Midway was the turning point of the war in the Pacific because that battle
   A. stopped the eastward advance of the Japanese
   B. destroyed most of what was left of the American fleet after Pearl Harbor
   C. destroyed the Japanese fleet so that they were unable to pursue naval war after this
   D. placed the United States Air Force close enough to the mainland of Japan to carry out bombing raids there

2. The wartime powers of the federal government expanded to include
   A. control of wages and prices
   B. rationing of scarce materials
   C. seizure of some businesses
   D. all of the above

3. Blacks during World War II achieved
   A. an end to segregation in the military
   B. equal employment opportunities in the government and industry
   C. a court ruling outlawing white primaries
   D. social and political equality in the South

4. From the start, British and American leaders completely agreed
   A. to defeat Japan first
   B. to attack Germany only indirectly through Africa
   C. to strike directly at Germany across the English Channel
   D. on none of the above

5. Strategic bombing of Germany in 1943
   A. cut German production by at least 25 percent
   B. broke German morale
   C. involved British and American planes
   D. failed because of a lack of planes

6. The Battle of Leyte Gulf was
   A. a prime example of the "leapfrogging" strategy
   B. the largest naval battle in history
   C. the Allies' worst defeat in the Pacific
   D. the key to Allied success in Sicily and Italy

7. The decisions made at the Yalta Conference did *not* include agreement that
   A. Russia would have three votes in the U.N. General Assembly
   B. Russia would have an occupation zone in the nonindustrialized area of East Germany as well as in part of Berlin
   C. free elections would be held in Poland to select a government
   D. both Russia and the United States would reduce their armaments by half after the war ended

8. American officials were slow to aid Jewish refugees because
   A. they feared anti-Semitism in the United States
   B. their experience with wartime propaganda created doubts about reports of the Holocaust
   C. reported evidence of genocide seemed beyond belief
   D. of all of the above

True-False Questions

Indicate whether each statement is true or false.

1. In the first half of 1942 German submarines sank several hundred ships just off the U.S. coast.
2. To finance World War II, FDR preferred deficits instead of higher taxes.
3. During the war, most working women for the first time were married women.
4. During World War II, Congress readily renewed and extended such New Deal programs as the National Youth Administration.
5. FDR, Churchill, and Stalin first met together in Teheran in 1943.
6. The major matter of dispute in the Democratic convention of 1944 was the selection of a vice-presidential nominee.
7. The War Refugee Board was amazingly successful at rescuing Jews from Europe.
8. The Manhattan Project developed the atomic bomb.

Essay Questions

1. Outline America's major strategy in the war against both Germany and Japan. Explain why this strategy was chosen.
2. What effects did World War II have on the power of the federal government? Be specific in your response.
3. Explain the major decisions made at Casablanca, Teheran, and Yalta.
4. How did the war affect the respective status of blacks, women, and Japanese-Americans?
5. What innovations, technical and tactical, helped the Allies win the war?
6. Russia continually called for a second front in Europe but the United States refused to oblige until June 1944. Why?

DOCUMENT

The Effects of the Atomic Bomb on Hiroshima

The United States military conducted extensive investigations of the effects the atomic bomb had on the populations of Hiroshima and Nagasaki. Excerpted here are selections from that survey. Note the physical destruction, the human casualties, and the effects on morale wrought by the bomb.

A single atomic bomb, the first weapon of its type ever used against a target, exploded over the city of Hiroshima at 0815 on the morning of 6 August 1945. Most of the industrial workers had already reported to work, but many workers were enroute and nearly all the school children and some industrial employees were at work in the open on the program of building removal to provide firebreaks and disperse valuables to the country. The attack came 45 minutes after the "all clear" had been sounded from a previous alert. Because of the lack of warning and the populace's indifference to small groups of planes, the explosion came as an almost complete surprise, and the people had not taken shelter. Many were caught in the open, and most of the rest in flimsily constructed homes or commercial establishments.

The bomb exploded slightly northwest of the center of the city. Because of this accuracy and the flat terrain and circular shape of the city, Hiroshima was uniformly and extensively devastated. Practically the entire densely or moderately built-up portion of the city was leveled by blast and swept by fire. A "fire-storm," a phenomenon which has occurred infrequently in other conflagrations, developed in Hiroshima: fires springing up almost simultaneously over the wide flat area around the center of the city drew in air from all directions. The inrush of air easily overcame the natural ground wind, which had a velocity of only about 5 miles per hour. The "fire-wind" attained a maximum velocity of 30 to 40 miles per hour 2 to 3 hours after the explosion. The "fire-wind" and the symmetry of the built-up center of the city gave a roughly circular shape to the 4.4 square miles which were almost completely burned out.

The surprise, the collapse of many buildings, and the conflagration contributed to an unprecedented casualty rate. Seventy to eighty thousand people were killed, or missing and presumed dead, and an equal number were injured. The magnitude of casualties is set in relief by a comparison with the Tokyo fire raid of 9–10 March 1945, in which, though nearly 16 square miles were destroyed, the number killed was no larger, and fewer people were injured.

The impact of the atomic bomb shattered the normal fabric of community life and disrupted the organizations for handling the disaster. In the 30 percent of the population killed and the additional 30 percent seriously injured were included corresponding proportions of the civil authorities and rescue groups. A mass flight from the city took place, as persons sought safety from the conflagration and a place for shelter and food. Within 24 hours, however, people were streaming back by the thousands in search of relatives and friends and to determine the extent of their

property loss. Road blocks had to be set up along all routes leading into the city, to keep curious and unauthorized people out.
The bulk of the dehoused population found refuge in the surrounding countryside; within the city the food supply was short
and shelter virtually nonexistent. . . .

The status of medical facilities and personnel dramatically illus-
trates the difficulties facing authorities. Of more than 200 doctors
in Hiroshima before the attack, over 90 percent were casualties and
only about 30 physicians were able to perform their normal duties
a month after the raid. Out of 1,780 nurses, 1,654 were killed or
injured. Though some stocks of supplies had been dispersed, many
were destroyed. Only three out of 45 civilian hospitals could be
used, and two large Army hospitals were rendered unusable. Those
within 3,000 feet of ground zero were totally destroyed, and the
mortality rate of the occupants was practically 100 percent.

1. *Casualties.*—The most striking result of the atomic bombs was
the great numbers of casualties. The exact number of dead and
injured will never be known because of the confusion after the
explosions. Persons unaccounted for might have been burned beyond recognition in the falling buildings, disposed of in one of the
mass cremations of the first week of recovery, or driven out of the
city to die or recover without any record remaining. No sure count
of even the preraid populations existed. . . . In this uncertain situation, estimates of casualties have generally ranged between 100,000
and 180,000 for Hiroshima, and between 50,000 and 100,000 for
Nagasaki. The Survey believes the dead at Hiroshima to have been
between 70,000 and 80,000, with an equal number injured; at
Nagasaki over 35,000 dead and somewhat more than that injured
seems the most plausible estimate.

Most of the immediate casualties did not differ from those
caused by incendiary or high-explosive raids. The outstanding
difference was the presence of radiation effects, which became
unmistakable about a week after the bombing. At the time of impact, however, the causes of death and injury were flash burns,
secondary effects of blast and falling debris, and burns from blaz-
ing buildings. . . .

The seriousness of . . . radiation effects may be measured by
the fact that 95 percent of the traced survivors of the immediate
explosion who were within 3,000 feet suffered from radiation disease. . . .

. . . Some of the dead were said by survivors to have had their
abdomens ruptured and intestines protruding; others were reported to have protruding eyes and tongues, and to have looked as
if they had drowned. Thorough check by Allied investigators dis-
credited these stories as evidence of direct blast effects; the normal
effects of blast are internal hemorrhage and crushing. These external signs point to injuries from debris rather than blast.

Injuries produced by falling and flying debris were much more
numerous, and naturally increased in number and seriousness
nearer the center of the affected area. . . .

There is no doubt that the bomb was the most important influence among the people of these areas in making them think that defeat was inevitable. . . .

Admiration for the bomb was more frequently expressed than anger. Over one-fourth of the people in the target cities and surrounding area said they were impressed by its power and by the scientific skill which underlay its discovery and production.

. . . The two raids were all-Japan events and were intended so: The Allied Powers were trying to break the fighting spirit of the Japanese people and their leaders, not just of the residents of Hiroshima and Nagasaki. . . .

The reactions found in the bombed cities appeared in the country as a whole—fear and terror, anger and hatred against the users, admiration for the scientific achievement—though in each case with less intensity.

[The United States Strategic Bombing Survey, *The Effects of Atomic Bombs on Hiroshima and Nagasaki* (Washington, D.C.: U.S. Government Printing Office, 1946), pp. 3, 6, 15, 17–18, 21]

Questions for Reflection

How do you react to reading about the physical and human destruction wrought by the bomb? How do the reactions of the Japanese people to the impact of the bomb compare with what you would have expected their reactions to have been? How would you compare the use of the atomic bomb to the use of conventional weapons in war? What has been the legacy of Hiroshima and Nagasaki?

ANSWERS TO MULTIPLE-CHOICE AND TRUE-FALSE QUESTIONS

Multiple-Choice Questions

1-A, 2-D, 3-C, 4-D, 5-C, 6-B, 7-D, 8-D

True-False Questions

1-T, 2-F, 3-T, 4-F, 5-T, 6-T, 7-F, 8-T

30

THE FAIR DEAL AND CONTAINMENT

CHAPTER OBJECTIVES

After you complete the reading and study of this chapter you should be able to

1. Analyze the problems of demobilization and conversion to peacetime production.
2. Account for Truman's troubles with Congress and assess the measure of accomplishment that he achieved.
3. Explain the policy of containment and trace its development to 1950.
4. Account for Truman's reelection in 1948.
5. Assess the strength of McCarthyism in the United States.
6. Explain the origins of the Korean War and trace its major developments.

CHAPTER OUTLINE

I. Demobilization under Truman
   A. The Truman style
      1. Truman's background and character
      2. Domestic proposals of 1945
   B. Demobilization
      1. Rapid reduction of armed forces
      2. Escalation of birth rate
      3. Efforts for economic stabilization
   C. Efforts to control inflation
      1. Demands for wage increases
      2. A wave of strikes
      3. Truman's response to strikes
      4. Efforts to control prices
      5. The end of controls
   D. Congressional elections of 1946

II. Record of the Republican Congress
   A. Taft-Hartley Act
   B. Efforts for tax reduction
   C. Governmental reorganization
      1. Features of the National Security Act
      2. Changes in presidential succession
      3. Twenty-second Amendment

III. Development of the Cold War
   A. Creating the United Nations
      1. Background to the U.N.
      2. Scheme of its operations
      3. U.S. ratification of U.N. membership
   B. Differences with the Soviets
      1. Problems relating to Eastern Europe
      2. Development of the peace treaties
      3. Proposals to control atomic energy
   C. Development of the containment policy
      1. Kennan's theory
      2. Problems in Iran, Turkey, and Greece
      3. The Truman Doctrine
      4. Greek-Turkish Aid
      5. The Marshall Plan
         a. The proposal
         b. European response
         c. Work of the ERP

6. Division of Germany
    a. Merger of Allied zones
    b. Berlin Blockade
    c. Berlin Airlift
    d. Creation of West and East
       Germany
7. Development of NATO
8. Establishment of Israel

IV. Truman's domestic politics
    A. Democratic divisions
    B. Truman's game plan
    C. Efforts for civil rights for blacks
    D. The 1948 election
        1. The Republican position
        2. Democratic battle over civil rights
        3. Creation of the Dixiecrats
        4. Wallace's Progressive Party
        5. Nature of the campaign
        6. Election results
        7. Assessment of the results
    E. The fate of the Fair Deal

V. The Cold War heats up
    A. Point Four Program
    B. China's fall to communism
        1. History of the movement in China
        2. Assessment of the Communist
           victory

C. Soviet atomic bomb
D. Work on the hydrogen bomb
E. NSC-68

VI. The Korean War
    A. Background to conflict
    B. Response to the invasion
    C. Military developments
        1. Rout of the U.N. forces
        2. Counterattack
        3. The decision to invade the North
        4. Entry of the Chinese Communists
    D. The dismissal of MacArthur
        1. Reasons for the action
        2. Reactions to the firing
    E. Negotiations for peace

VII. Another red scare
     A. Evidences of espionage
     B. The Truman loyalty program
     C. The Alger Hiss case
     D. Conviction of spies
     E. McCarthy's witch-hunt
         1. The emergence of Senator
            McCarthy
         2. Assessment of his tactics
     F. The McCarran Internal Security Act

VIII. Assessing the Cold War

KEY ITEMS OF CHRONOLOGY

FDR dies	April 1945
Taft-Hartley Act	1947
Truman Doctrine	1947
Marshall Plan launched	1947
Berlin Blockade and Berlin Airlift	June 1948–May 1949
Creation of Israel	1948
Hiss case	1948–1950
Establishment of NATO	April 1949
China became communist	1949
Sen. Joseph McCarthy's speech in Wheeling, West Virginia, citing communists in the State Department	February 1950
Korean War	June 1950–July 1953
MacArthur dismissed	April 1951

TERMS TO MASTER

Listed below are some important terms or people with which you should be familiar after you complete the study of this chapter. Explain the significance of each name or term.

1. Servicemen's Readjustment Act
2. Henry A. Wallace
3. Taft-Hartley Act
4. National Security Act, 1947
5. CIA
6. Twenty-second Amendment
7. United Nations
8. "iron curtain"
9. George F. Kennan
10. containment
11. Truman Doctrine
12. Cold War
13. Marshall Plan
14. Berlin Blockade
15. NATO
16. Dixiecrats
17. Fair Deal
18. Douglas MacArthur
19. Alger Hiss
20. Joseph R. McCarthy
21. McCarran Act

VOCABULARY BUILDING

Listed below are some words used in this chapter. Look up each word in your dictionary.

1. credence
2. bipartisan
3. *realpolitik*
4. reparations
5. brandish
6. charnel
7. partition
8. intractable
9. censure
10. ploy

EXERCISES FOR UNDERSTANDING

When you have completed reading the chapter, answer each of the following questions. If you have difficulty, go back and reread the section of the chapter related to the question.

Multiple-Choice Questions

Select the letter of the response which best completes the statement.

1. Enacted in 1944, the G.I. Bill of Rights
   A. guaranteed constitutional rights to soldiers
   B. organized postwar demobilization
   C. provided federal funds for veterans' education, job training, and housing
   D. established standard procedures for the Allies prior to the Normandy invasion

2. After World War II, the American economy
   A. never reverted to peacetime production because of the Cold War
   B. suffered from some inflation
   C. plunged into a depression
   D. maintained wage and price controls for more than eight years

3. Congress passed *over Truman's veto*
   A. the Marshall Plan
   B. the Taft-Hartley Act
   C. the Twenty-second Amendment
   D. all of the above

4. Postwar disagreements between the United States and the Soviet Union especially concerned
   A. the formation of the United Nations
   B. governments in Eastern Europe
   C. the reconstruction of Japan
   D. the Nuremberg trials

5. The Marshall Plan was designed to
   A. help Western European nations rebuild their armies
   B. subvert communist nations into the capitalist camp
   C. lend money to Western European nations
   D. help all European nations, including communist ones, to rebuild their war-torn economies

6. An important new issue in the 1948 presidential election was
   A. civil rights
   B. organized labor
   C. agricultural policy
   D. the regulation of business
7. Alger Hiss was convicted of
   A. belonging to the Communist Party
   B. passing atomic secrets to the Soviets
   C. lying under oath
   D. nothing—he was acquitted
8. After 1950, the leader of the red scare was
   A. Richard Nixon
   B. Owen Lattimore
   C. Alger Hiss
   D. Joseph McCarthy

True-False Questions

Indicate whether each statement is true or false.

1. Harry S. Truman ended most New Deal programs.
2. The Taft-Hartley Act outlawed unions at any plant that paid at least the minimum wage.
3. The National Security Act of 1947 created the Central Intelligence Agency.
4. Aid to Greece and Turkey came before the Marshall Plan.

5. The new state of Israel was created by formal action of the U.N. General Assembly.
6. The Dixiecrat candidate in 1948 was Henry A. Wallace.
7. The communists gained control of China, the Soviets exploded an atomic device, and the Korean War started—all in 1949.
8. More than a dozen countries sent troops to fight alongside Americans in Korea.

Essay Questions

1. How successful was President Truman in achieving his domestic goals?
2. Account for the onset of the Cold War.
3. Compare and contrast the aid provided under the Truman Doctrine and under the Marshall Plan.
4. Why was Harry Truman reelected in 1948?
5. Was America's entry into the Korean War a success? Explain.
6. Why did Truman fire MacArthur? Was his action justified? What reactions did it bring?
7. What was the basis for Joe McCarthy's appeal to the American people? Assess the importance of his anticommunist crusade.

READINGS

Reading 1. Arthur Schlesinger Explains the Origins of the Cold War

The origin of the Cold War is one of today's complex and controversial historiographical problems. The issues involve which side was responsible for the hostility that developed after World War II between the United States and the Soviet Union. In the article excerpted here, Arthur M. Schlesinger, Jr., a prominent historian and adviser to President Kennedy, takes a position somewhat more centrist than that of the revisionists who place the blame for the Cold War on the United States. Writing in 1967 just after he had broken with the Johnson administration over the Vietnam War, Schlesinger here attempts to show just how complex the development of the Cold War was.

The orthodox American view, as originally set forth by the American government and as reaffirmed until recently by most American scholars, has been that the Cold War was the brave and essential response of free men to communist aggression. Some have gone back well before the Second World War to lay open the sources of Russian expansionism. Geopoliticians traced the Cold War to imperial Russian strategic ambitions which in the nineteenth century led to the Crimean War, to Russian penetration of the Balkans and the Middle East and to Russian pressure on Britain's "lifeline" to India. Ideologists traced it to the Communist Manifesto of 1848 ("the violent overthrow of the bourgeoisie lays the foundation for the sway of the proletariat"). Thoughtful observers (a phrase meant to exclude those who speak in Dullese about the unlimited evil of godless, atheistic, militant communism) concluded that classical Russian imperialism and Pan-Slavism, compounded after 1917 by Leninist messianism, confronted the West at the end of the Second World War with an inexorable drive for domination.

The revisionist thesis is very different. In its extreme form, it is that, after the death of Franklin Roosevelt and the end of the Second World War, the United States deliberately abandoned the wartime policy of collaboration and, exhilarated by the possession of the atomic bomb, undertook a course of aggression of its own designed to expel all Russian influence from Eastern Europe and to establish democratic-capitalist states on the very border of the Soviet Union. As the revisionists see it, this radically new American policy—or rather this resumption by Truman of the pre-Roosevelt policy of insensate anti-communism—left Moscow no alternative but to take measures in defense of its own borders. The result was the Cold War. . . .

. . . Any honest reappraisal of the origins of the Cold War requires the imaginative leap—which should in any case be as instinctive for the historian as it is prudent for the statesman—into the adversary's viewpoint. We must strive to see how, given Soviet perspectives, the Russians might conceivably have misread our signals, as we must reconsider how intelligently we read theirs.

Nor can the historian forget the conditions under which decisions are made, especially in a time like the Second World War. These were tired, overworked, aging men: in 1945, Churchill was 71 years old, Stalin had governed his country for 17 exacting years, Roosevelt his for 12 years nearly as exacting. . . . All—even Stalin, behind his screen of ideology—had become addicts of improvisation, relying on authority and virtuosity to conceal the fact that they were constantly surprised by developments. . . . None showed great tactical consistency, or cared much about it; all employed a certain ambiguity to preserve their power to decide big issues; and it is hard to know how to interpret anything any one of them said on any specific occasion. . . .

Peacemaking after the Second World War was not so much a tapestry as it was a hopelessly raveled and knotted mess of yarn. Yet, for purposes of clarity, it is essential to follow certain threads. One theme indispensable to an understanding of the Cold War is the contrast between two clashing views of world order: the "universalist" view, by which all nations shared a common interest in all the affairs of the world, and the "sphere-of-influence" view, by which each great power would be assured by the other great powers of an acknowledged predominance in its own area of special interest. The universalist view assumed that national security would be guaranteed by an international organization. The sphere-of-interest view assumed that national security would be guaranteed by the balance of power. While in practice these views have by no means been incompatible (indeed, our shaky peace has been based on a combination of the two), in the abstract they involved sharp contradictions.

The tradition of American thought in these matters was universalist. . . .

The Kremlin, on the other hand, thought *only* of spheres of interest; above all, the Russians were determined to protect their frontiers, and especially their border to the west, crossed so often and so bloodily in the dark course of their history. . . .

It is now pertinent to inquire why the United States rejected the idea of stabilizing the world by division into spheres of influence and insisted on an East European strategy. . . .

The first reason is that they regarded this solution as containing within itself the seeds of a third world war. The balance-of-power idea seemed inherently unstable. . . .

. . . the second objection: that the sphere-of-influence approach would, in the words of the State Department in 1945, "militate against the establishment and effective functioning of a broader system of general security in which all countries will have their part." The United Nations, in short, was seen as the alternative to the balance of power. . . .

Third, the universalists feared that the sphere-of-interest approach would be what Hull termed "a haven for the isolationists," who would advocate America's participation in Western Hemisphere affairs on condition that it did not participate in European or Asian affairs. . . .

Fourth, the sphere-of-interest solution meant the betrayal of the principles for which the Second World War was being fought—the Atlantic Charter, the Four Freedoms, the Declaration of the United Nations. . . .

Fifth, the sphere-of-influence solution would create difficult domestic problems in American politics. Roosevelt was aware of the six million or more Polish votes in the 1944 election. . . .

Sixth, if the Russians were allowed to overrun Eastern Europe without argument, would that satisfy them? . . .

But the great omission of the revisionists—and also the fundamental explanation of the speed with which the Cold War escalated—lies precisely in the fact that the Soviet Union was not a traditional national state. The Soviet Union was a phenomenon very different from America or Britain: it was a totalitarian state, endowed with an all-explanatory, all-consuming ideology, committed to the infallibility of government and party, still in a somewhat messianic mood, equating dissent with treason, and ruled by a dictator who, for all his quite extraordinary abilities, had his paranoid moments.

Marxism-Leninism gave the Russian leaders a view of the world according to which all societies were inexorably destined to proceed along appointed roads by appointed stages until they achieved the classless nirvana. . . .

A revisionist fallacy has been to treat Stalin as just another Real-politik statesman, as Second World War revisionists see Hitler as just another Stresemann or Bismarck. But the record makes it clear that in the end nothing could satisfy Stalin's paranoia. His own associates failed. Why does anyone suppose that any conceivable American policy would have succeeded?

The difference between America and Russia in 1945 was that some Americans fundamentally believed that, over a long run, a modus vivendi with Russia was possible; while the Russians, so far as one can tell, believed in no more than a short-run modus vivendi with the United States.

In retrospect, if it is impossible to see the Cold War as a case of American aggression and Russian response, it is also hard to see it as a pure case of Russian aggression and American response. . . .
    The Cold War could have been avoided only if the Soviet Union had not been possessed by convictions both of the infallibility of the communist word and of the inevitability of a communist world. These convictions turned an impasse between national states into a religious war, a tragedy of ability into one of necessity. One might wish that America had preserved the poise and proportion of the first years of the Cold War and had not succumbed to its own forms of self-righteousness. But the most rational American policies could hardly have averted the Cold War. Only if Russia began to recede from its messianic mission and to accept, in fact if not yet in principle, the permanence of the world of diversity, only then did the hope flicker that this long, dreary, costly contest may at last be taking forms less dramatic, less obsessive and less dangerous to the future kind.
    [Arthur Schlesinger, Jr., "Origins of the Cold War," *Foreign Affairs* 46 (October 1967): 22–52]

Reading 2. Barton Bernstein Presents a Revisionist View

Barton Bernstein has been one of the leading revisionists in the controversy over the origins of the Cold War. The excerpt below will introduce the reader to the essentials of that view.

Despite some dissents, most American scholars have reached a general consensus on the origins of the Cold War. As confirmed internationalists who believe that Russia constituted a threat to America and its European allies after World War II, they have endorsed their nation's acceptance of its obligations as a world power in the forties and its desire to establish a world order of peace and prosperity. Convinced that only American efforts prevented the Soviet Union from expanding past Eastern Europe, they have generally praised the containment policies of the Truman Doctrine, the Marshall Plan, and NATO as evidence of America's acceptance of world responsibility. While chiding or condemning those on the right who opposed international involvement (or had even urged preventive war), they have also been deeply critical of those on the left who have believed that the Cold War could have been avoided, or that the United States shared substantial responsibility for the Cold War.

Despite the widespread acceptance of this interpretation, there has long been substantial evidence (and more recently a body of scholarship) which suggests that American policy was neither so innocent nor so nonideological; that American leaders sought to promote their conceptions of national interest and their values even at the conscious risk of provoking Russia's fears about her security. In 1945 these leaders apparently believed that American power would be adequate for the task of reshaping much of the world according to America's needs and standards.

By overextending policy and power and refusing to accept Soviet interests, American policy-makers contributed to the Cold War. There was little understanding of any need to restrain American political efforts and desires. Though it cannot be proved that the United States could have achieved a *modus vivendi* with the Soviet Union in these years there is evidence that Russian policies were reasonably cautious and conservative, and that there was at least a basis for accommodation. But this possibility slowly slipped away as President Harry S. Truman reversed Roosevelt's tactics of accommodation. As American demands for democratic governments in Eastern Europe became more vigorous, as the new administration delayed in providing economic assistance to Russia and in seeking international control of atomic energy, policy-makers met with increasing Soviet suspicion and antagonism. Concluding that Soviet-American cooperation was impossible, they came to believe that the Soviet state could be halted only by force or the threat of force....

. . . It is clear that Truman was either incapable or unwilling to reexamine his earlier assumption (or decision) of using the bomb. Under the tutelage of Byrnes and Stimson, Truman had come to assume by July that the bomb should be used, and perhaps he was incapable of reconsidering this strategy because he found no compelling reason not to use the bomb. Or he may have consciously rejected the options because he wanted to use the bomb. Perhaps he was vindictive and wished to retaliate for Pearl Harbor and other atrocities. (In justifying the use of the bomb against the Japanese, he wrote a few days after Nagasaki, "The only language they seem to understand is the one we have been using to bombard them. When you have to deal with a beast you have to treat him as a beast.") Or, most likely, Truman agreed with Byrnes that using the bomb would advance other American policies: It would end the war before the Russians could gain a hold in Manchuria, it would permit the United States to exclude Russia from the occupation government of Japan, and it would make the Soviets more manageable in Eastern Europe. It would enable the United States to shape the peace according to its own standards.

At minimum, then, the use of the bomb reveals the moral insensitivity of the President—whether he used it because the moral implications did not compel a reexamination of assumptions, or because he sought retribution, or because he sought to keep Russia out of Manchuria and the occupation government of Japan, and to make her more manageable in Eastern Europe. In 1945 American foreign policy was not innocent, nor was it unconcerned about

Russian power, nor did it assume that the United States lacked the power to impose its will on the Russian state, nor was it characterized by high moral purpose or consistent dedication to humanitarian principles.

While the Soviet Union would not generally permit in Eastern Europe conditions that conformed to Western ideals, Stalin was pursuing a cautious policy and seeking accommodation with the West. He was willing to allow capitalism but was suspicious of American efforts at economic penetration which could lead to political dominance. Though by the autumn of 1945 the governments in Russia's general area of influence were subservient in foreign policy, they varied in form and in degree of independence—democracy in Czechoslovakia (the only country in this area with a democratic tradition), free elections and the overthrow of the Communist party in Hungary, a Communist-formed coalition government in Bulgaria, a broadly based but Communist-dominated government in Poland, and a Soviet-imposed government in Rumania (the most anti-Russian of these nations). In all of these countries Communists controlled the ministries of interior (the police) and were able to suppress anti-Soviet groups, including anti-communist democrats.

Those who have attributed to Russia a policy of inexorable expansion have often neglected this immediate postwar period, or they have interpreted it simply as a necessary preliminary (a cunning strategy to allay American suspicions until the American Army demobilized and left the continent) to the consolidation and extension of power in east-central Europe. From this perspective, however, much of Stalin's behavior becomes strangely contradictory and potentially self-defeating. If he had planned to create puppets rather than an area of "friendly governments," why (as Isaac Deutscher asks) did Stalin "so stubbornly refuse to make any concessions to the Poles over their eastern frontiers"? Certainly, also, his demand for reparations from Hungary, Rumania, and Bulgaria would have been unnecessary if he had planned to take over these countries. (America's insistence upon using a loan to Russia to achieve political goals, and nearly twenty-month delay after Russia first submitted a specific proposal for assistance, led Harriman to suggest in November that the loan policy "may have contributed to their [Russian] avaricious policies in the countries occupied or liberated by the Red Army.")

Russian sources are closed, so it is not possible to prove that Soviet intentions were conservative; nor for the same reason is it possible for those who adhered to the thesis of inexorable Soviet expansion to prove their theory. But the available evidence better supports the thesis that these years should be viewed not as a cunning preliminary to the harshness of 1947 and afterward, but as an attempt to establish a *modus vivendi* with the West and to protect "socialism in one country." This interpretation explains more adequately why the Russians delayed nearly three years before ending dissent and hardening policies in the countries behind their own military lines. It would also explain why the Communist parties in France and Italy were cooperating with the coalition governments until these parties were forced out of the coalitions in 1947. . . .

If the Russian policy was conservative and sought accommodation (as now seems likely), then its failure must be explained by looking beyond Russian actions. Historians must reexamine this period and reconsider American policies. Were they directed toward compromise? Can they be judged as having sought adjustment? Or did they demand acquiescence to the American world view, thus thwarting real negotiations?

There is considerable evidence that American actions clearly changed after Roosevelt's death. Slowly abandoning the tactics of accommodation, they became even more vigorous after Hiroshima. The insistence upon rolling back Soviet influence in Eastern Europe, the reluctance to grant a loan for Russian reconstruction, the inability to reach an agreement on Germany, the maintenance of the nuclear monopoly—all of these could have contributed to the sense of Russian insecurity. The point, then, is that in 1945 and 1946 there may still have been possibilities for negotiations and settlements, for accommodations and adjustments, if the United States had been willing to recognize Soviet fears, to accept Soviet power in her areas of influence, and to ease anxieties.

[Barton J. Bernstein, "American Foreign Policy and the Origins of the Cold War," in *Politics and Policies of the Truman Administration*, edited by Barton J. Bernstein (Chicago: Quadrangle Books, 1970), pp. 15–49]

Questions for Reflection

After reading both excerpts and answering the questions that follow, attempt to write in a few paragraphs your own view of the origins of the Cold War.

What is the orthodox view of the origins of the Cold War? The revisionist view? What special considerations should be taken into account in attempting to explain the Cold War? What important theme does Schlesinger want the reader to consider in explaining the development of Cold War events? What does he think the revisionists have omitted in their analysis of the Cold War?

How does Bernstein's initial description of the consensus view of Cold War origins compare with Schlesinger's view above? Needless use of the atomic bomb is one of the central themes of revisionist history. How does Bernstein deal with this matter? How does he argue that the United States acted incorrectly in Eastern Europe? How do we know Russia's motives after World War II? What limitation does that place on historians?

ANSWERS TO MULTIPLE-CHOICE AND TRUE-FALSE QUESTIONS

Multiple-Choice Questions

1-C, 2-B, 3-B, 4-B, 5-D, 6-A, 7-C, 8-D

True-False Questions

1-F, 2-F, 3-T, 4-T, 5-F, 6-F, 7-F, 8-T

31

THROUGH THE PICTURE WINDOW:
SOCIETY AND CULTURE, 1945–1960

CHAPTER OBJECTIVES

After you complete the reading and study of this chapter you should be able to

1. Account for the emergence of a consumer culture in the prosperous postwar era.
2. Describe the growth of suburban America after World War II.
3. Illustrate the widespread conformity in American culture in the 1950s.
4. Understand the ideas of the major critics of conformity.
5. Explain the artistic and literary dissent beginning in the 1950s.

CHAPTER OUTLINE

I. Postwar economy
   A. Growth and prosperity
      1. Military spending
      2. International trade dominance
      3. Technological innovation
      4. "Baby boom" and consumer demand
   B. Consumer culture
      1. Television
      2. Marketing and packaging
      3. Credit cards
      4. Shopping malls
   C. Growth of suburbs
      1. Rural-to-urban migration
      2. Levittowns
      3. Automobiles and roads
      4. "White flight"

II. Postwar conformity
   A. Corporate life
      1. Large corporations
      2. Managerial personality
   B. Women and cult of domesticity
   C. Religion
      1. Growth in church membership
         a. Religious revival
         b. Patriotism
         c. Marketing of religion
      2. Rev. Norman Vincent Peale and "positive thinking"
      3. Neo-orthodoxy
         a. Critical of religiosity
         b. Reinhold Niebuhr

III. Social critics of conformity
   A. John Kenneth Galbraith's *The Affluent Society*
   B. *The Crack in the Picture Window*
   C. David Riesman and *The Lonely Crowd*

IV. Alienation in the arts
   A. Drama

    1. Oppressiveness of mass culture
    2. Arthur Miller's *Death of a Salesman*
    3. Tennessee Williams and Edward Albee
  B. The novel
    1. The individual's struggle for survival
    2. J. D. Salinger's *Catcher in the Rye*
    3. *From Here to Eternity* by James Jones
    4. Saul Bellow, Ralph Ellison, Joseph Heller, Norman Mailer, Joyce Carol Oates, et al.
  C. Painting
    1. Edward Hopper and desolate loneliness

    2. Abstract expressionism
      a. Violent and chaotic modern society
      b. Jackson Pollock
      c. William de Kooning, Mark Rothko, et al.
  D. The Beats
    1. Liberation of self-expression
    2. Greenwich Village background
    3. William Burrough's *Naked Lunch*
    4. *Howl* by Allen Ginsberg
    5. Jack Kerouac's *On the Road*
    6. Influences
      a. Mort Sahl
      b. Lenny Bruce
      c. Bob Dylan

KEY ITEMS OF CHRONOLOGY

Dr. Benjamin Spock's *Common Sense Book of Baby and Child Care*	1946
The first Levittown in New York	1947
Arthur Miller's *Death of a Salesman*	1949
David Riesman's *The Lonely Crowd*	1950
J. D. Salinger's *Catcher in the Rye*	1951
"one Nation under God" added to the Pledge of Allegiance	1954
Allen Ginsberg's *Howl*	1956
Jack Kerouac's *On the Road*	1957
John Kenneth Galbraith's *The Affluent Society*	1958
Vance Packard's *The Waste Makers*	1960

TERMS TO MASTER

Listed below are some important terms or people with which you should be familiar after you complete the study of this chapter. Explain the significance of each name or term.

1. baby-boom generation
2. suburbs
3. William Levitt
4. "white flight"
5. white collar
6. cult of domesticity
7. "in God we trust"
8. Norman Vincent Peale
9. neo-orthodoxy
10. Reinhold Niebuhr
11. "other-directed"
12. *Death of a Salesman*
13. Holden Caulfield
14. abstract expressionism
15. Jackson Pollock
16. The Beats

VOCABULARY BUILDING

Listed below are some words used in this chapter. Look up each word in your dictionary.

1. prolific
2. wean
3. obsolescence
4. discretionary
5. orthodoxy
6. harangue
7. religiosity
8. inculcate
9. vaunted
10. stupefy
11. kaleidoscopic

EXERCISES FOR UNDERSTANDING

When you have completed reading the chapter, answer each of the following questions. If you have difficulty, go back and reread the section of the chapter related to the question.

Multiple-Choice Questions

Select the letter of the response which best completes the statement.

1. Nine out of ten American homes had a television set by
   A. 1940
   B. 1950
   C. 1960
   D. 1970

2. William Levitt was a leading
   A. suburban home builder
   B. Beat poet
   C. radio and television minister
   D. critic of conformity in the 1950s

3. The ideal for a middle-class woman in the 1950s was to be
   A. an independent white-collar professional
   B. a wife and mother
   C. employed outside the home
   D. none of the above

4. The religious revival of the 1950s was spurred by
   A. the Cold War
   B. television
   C. a mobile population's need for community
   D. all of the above

5. Norman Vincent Peale urged Americans to
   A. buy his homes in the suburbs
   B. "stop worrying and start living"
   C. give up all worldly possessions
   D. realize that pain was part of real peace

6. John Keats's *The Crack in the Picture Window* was a stinging critique of
   A. the quality of housing in the suburbs
   B. television
   C. modern art
   D. suburban life

7. A leading abstract expressionist painter was
   A. Gregory Corso
   B. Ralph Ellison
   C. Jackson Pollock
   D. Reinhold Niebuhr

8. A "pack of oddballs who celebrate booze, dope, sex, and despair" was *Time*'s description of
   A. C. Wright Mills, John Kenneth Galbraith, and John Keats
   B. the Beat writers, poets, painters, and musicians
   C. abstract expressionists
   D. white-collar residents of suburbs

True-False Questions

Indicate whether each statement is true or false.

1. Defense spending was the most important contributor to economic growth after World War II.
2. Consumer debt declined in the prosperous 1950s.
3. The baby boom began in the late 1950s.
4. "In God We Trust" was put on all American currency starting in 1955.
5. The leading exponent of "positive thinking" was Reinhold Niebuhr.

6. According to David Riesman, the "inner-directed" person lives according to a set of basic values similar to the Protestant work ethic.

7. The author of *Catcher in the Rye* was J. D. Salinger.

8. Allen Ginsberg's autobiography was *On the Road.*

Essay Questions

1. What factors contributed to the economic growth and prosperity of the postwar period?

2. Who was William Levitt and why was his work important?

3. Describe some of the drawbacks of suburban living in the 1950s.

4. Compare and contrast the ideas of Norman Vincent Peale and Reinhold Niebuhr.

5. How did many important postwar novels reinforce the image of Americans as "a lonely crowd"? Refer to specific examples.

6. Who were the Beats and what were their concerns?

DOCUMENT

Betty Friedan Describes the Attitude of the "Bored Housewife"

As the text shows, the ideal American woman in the 1950s was the housewife-mother. In the following excerpt from her influential work *The Feminine Mystique* (1963), Betty Friedan analyzes this "ideal" and explores how it came about.

In the early 1960's *McCall's* has been the fastest growing of the women's magazines. The image of woman that emerges from this big, pretty magazine is young and frivolous, almost childlike; fluffy and feminine; passive; gaily content in a world of bedroom and kitchen, sex, babies, and home. The magazine surely does not leave out sex; the only passion, the only pursuit, the only goal a woman is permitted is the pursuit of a man. It is crammed full of food, clothing, cosmetics, furniture, and the physical bodies of young women, but where is the world of thought and ideas, the life of the mind and spirit? In the magazine image, women do no work except housework and work to keep their bodies beautiful and to get and keep a man.

This was the image of the American woman in the year Castro led a revolution in Cuba and men were trained to travel into outer space; the year that the African continent brought forth new nations, and a plane whose speed is greater than the speed of sound broke up a Summit Conference; the year artists picketed a great museum in protest against the hegemony of abstract art; physicists explored the concept of anti-matter; astronomers, because of new radio telescopes, had to alter their concepts of the expanding universe; biologists made a breakthrough in the fundamental chemistry of life; and Negro youth in Southern schools forced the United States, for the first time since the Civil War, to face a moment of democratic truth. But this magazine, published for over 5,000,000 American women, almost all of whom have been through high school and nearly half to college, contained almost no mention of the world beyond the home. In the second half of the twentieth century in America, woman's world was confined to her own body and beauty, the charming of man, the bearing of babies, and the physical care and serving of husband, children, and home. And this was no anomaly of a single issue of a single women's magazine.

I sat one night at a meeting of magazine writers, mostly men, who work for all kinds of magazines, including women's magazines. . . . [We] spent an hour listening to Thurgood Marshall on the inside story of the desegregation battle, and its possible effect on the presidential election. "Too bad I can't run that story," one editor said. "But you just can't link it to woman's world."

As I listened to them, a German phrase echoed in my mind—*"Kinder, Kuche, Kirche,"* the slogan by which the Nazis decreed that women must once again be confined to their biological role. But this was not Nazi Germany. This was America. The whole world lies open to American women. Why, then, does the image deny the world? Why does it limit women to "one position, one role, one occupation"? Not long ago, women dreamed and fought for equality, their own place in the world. What happened to their dreams; when did women decide to give up the world and go back home?

I sat for many days in the New York Public Library, going back through bound volumes of American women's magazines for the last twenty years. I found a change in the image of the American woman, and in the boundaries of the woman's world, as sharp and puzzling as the changes revealed in the cores of ocean sediment.

In 1939, the heroines of women's magazine stories were not always young, but in a certain sense they were younger than their fictional counterparts today. They were young in the same way that the American hero has always been young: they were New Women, creating with a gay determined spirit a new identity for women—a life of their own. There was an aura about them of becoming, of moving into a future that was going to be different from the past. The majority of heroines in the four major women's magazines (then *Ladies' Home Journal, McCall's, Good Housekeeping, Woman's Home Companion*) were career women—happily, proudly, adventurously, attractively career women—who loved and were loved by men. And the spirit, courage, independence, determination—the strength of character they showed in their work as nurses, teachers, artists, actresses, copywriters, saleswomen—were part of their charm. There was a definite aura that their individuality was something to be admired, not unattractive to men, that men were drawn to them as much for their spirit and character as for their looks.

These were the mass women's magazines—in their heyday. The stories were conventional: girl-meets-boy or girl-gets-boy. But very often this was not the major theme of the story. These heroines were usually marching toward some goal or vision of their own, struggling with some problem of work or the world, when they found their man. And this New Woman, less fluffily feminine, so independent and determined to find a new life of her own, was the heroine of a different kind of love story. She was less aggressive in pursuit of a man. Her passionate involvement with the world, her own sense of herself as an individual, her self-reliance, gave a different flavor to her relationship with the man.

These stories may not have been great literature. But the identity of their heroines seemed to say something about the housewives who, then as now, read the women's magazines. These magazines were not written for career women. The New Woman heroines were the ideal of yesterday's housewives; they reflected the dreams, mirrored the yearning for identity and the sense of possibility that existed for women then. And if women could not have these dreams for themselves, they wanted their daughters to have them. They wanted their daughters to be more than housewives, to go out in the world that had been denied them.

As for not earning any money, the argument goes, let the housewife compute the cost of her services. Women can save more money by their managerial talents inside the home than they can bring into it by outside work. As for woman's spirit being broken by the boredom of household tasks, maybe the genius of some women has been thwarted, but "a world full of feminine genius, but poor in children, would come rapidly to an end. . . . Great men have great mothers."

The feminine mystique says that the highest value and the only commitment for women is the fulfillment of their own femininity. It says that the great mistake of Western culture, through most of its history, has been the undervaluation of this femininity. It says this femininity is so mysterious and intuitive and close to the creation and origin of life that man-made science may never be able to understand it. But however special and different, it is in no way inferior to the nature of man; it may even in certain respects be superior. The mistake, says the mystique, the root of women's troubles in the past is that women envied men, women tried to be like men, instead of accepting their own nature, which can find fulfillment only in sexual passivity, male domination, and nurturing maternal love.

But the new image this mystique gives to American women is the old image: "Occupation: housewife." The new mystique makes the housewife-mothers, who never had a chance to be anything else, the model for all women; it presupposes that history has reached a final and glorious end in the here and now, as far as women are concerned. Beneath the sophisticated trappings, it simply makes certain concrete, finite, domestic aspects of feminine existence—as it was lived by women whose lives were confined, by necessity, to cooking, cleaning, washing, bearing children—into a religion, a pattern by which all women must now live or deny their femininity.

Fulfillment as a woman had only one definition for American women after 1949—the housewife-mother. As swiftly as in a dream, the image of the American woman as a changing, growing individual in a changing world was shattered. Her solo flight to find her own identity was forgotten in the rush for the security of togetherness. Her limitless world shrunk to the cozy walls of home.

The end of the road, in an almost literal sense, is the disappearance of the heroine altogether, as a separate self and the subject of her own story. The end of the road is togetherness, where the woman has no independent self to hide even in guilt; she exists only for and through her husband and children.

Coined by the publishers of *McCall's* in 1954, the concept

"togetherness" was seized upon avidly as a movement of spiritual significance by advertisers, ministers, newspaper editors. For a time, it was elevated into virtually a national purpose. But very quickly there was sharp social criticism, and bitter jokes about "togetherness" as a substitute for larger human goals—for men. Women were taken to task for making their husbands do housework, instead of letting them pioneer in the nation and the world. Why, it was asked, should men with the capacities of states-men, anthropologists, physicists, poets, have to wash dishes and diaper babies on weekday evenings or Saturday mornings when they might use those extra hours to fulfill larger commitments to their society?

But forbidden to join man in the world, can women be people? Forbidden independence, they finally are swallowed in an image of such passive dependence that they want men to make the decisions, even in the home. The frantic illusion that togetherness can impart a spiritual content to the dullness of domestic routine, the need for a religious movement to make up for the lack of identity, betrays the measure of women's loss and the emptiness of the image. Could making men share the housework compen-sate women for their loss of the world? Could vacuuming the liv-ing-room floor together give the housewife some mysterious new purpose in life?

In 1956, at the peak of togetherness, the bored editors of *McCall's* ran a little article called "The Mother Who Ran Away." To their amazement, it brought the highest readership of any article they had ever run. "It was our moment of truth," said a former editor. "We suddenly realized that all those women at home with their three and a half children were miserably unhappy."

But by then the new image of American woman, "Occupation: housewife," had hardened into a mystique, unquestioned and per-mitting no questions. . . .

By the time I started writing for women's magazines, in the fifties, it was simply taken for granted by editors, and accepted as an immutable fact of life by writers, that women were not interested in politics, life outside the United States, national issues, art, science, ideas, adventure, education, or even their own communities, except where they could be sold through their emotions as wives and mothers.

Politics, for women, became Mamie's clothes and the Nixons' home life. Out of conscience, a sense of duty, the *Ladies' Home Journal* might run a series like "Political Pilgrim's Progress," show-ing women trying to improve their children's schools and play-grounds. But even approaching politics through mother love did not really interest women, it was thought in the trade. Everyone knew those readership percentages. An editor of *Redbook* inge-niously tried to bring the bomb down to the feminine level by showing the emotions of a wife whose husband sailed into a con-taminated area.

"Women can't take an idea, an issue, pure," men who edited the mass women's magazines agreed. "It had to be translated in terms they can understand as women." This was so well understood by those who wrote for women's magazines that a natural childbirth expert submitted an article to a leading woman's magazine called "How to Have a Baby in a Atom Bomb Shelter." "The article was not well written," an editor told me, "or we might have bought it." According to the mystique, women, in their mysterious femininity, might be interested in the concrete biological details of having a baby in a bomb shelter, but never in the abstract idea of the bomb's power to destroy the human race.

Such a belief, of course, becomes a self-fulfilling prophecy. In 1960, a perceptive social psychologist showed me some sad statistics which seemed to prove unmistakably that American women under thirty-five are not interested in politics. "They may have the vote, but they don't dream about running for office," he told me. "If you write a political piece, they won't read it. You have to translate it into issues they can understand–romance, pregnancy, nursing, home furnishings, clothes. Run an article on the economy, or the race question, civil rights, and you'd think that women had never heard of them."

This is the real mystery: why did so many American women, with the ability and education to discover and create, go back home again, to look for "something more" in housework and rearing children? For, paradoxically, in the same fifteen years in which the spirited New Woman was replaced by the Happy Housewife, the boundaries of the human world have widened, the pace of world change has quickened, and the very nature of human reality has become increasingly free from biological and material necessity.

[From Betty Friedan, *The Feminine Mystique* (New York: W. W. Norton & Co., 1974; originally published 1963), pp. 36, 37, 38, 40, 42, 43–44, 47–48, 50–51, 67]

Questions for Reflection

What effects do the images depicted in magazines (and on television) have on readers (and viewers)? Discuss this with specific regard to the images of women in the 1950s. What does Friedan see as "the feminine mystique," and what does she think of it? How appropriate is "the feminine mystique" as a guideline for women today?

ANSWERS TO MULTIPLE-CHOICE AND TRUE-FALSE QUESTIONS

Multiple-Choice Questions

1-C, 2-A, 3-B, 4-D, 5-B, 6-D, 7-C, 8-B

True-False Questions

1-T, 2-F, 3-F, 4-T, 5-F, 6-T, 7-T, 8-F

32

CONFLICT AND DEADLOCK:
THE EISENHOWER YEARS

CHAPTER OBJECTIVES

After you complete the reading and study of this chapter you should be able to

1. Describe the Eisenhower style and his approach to the nation's problems.
2. Assess the nature of modern Republicanism in relation to New Deal liberalism, focusing especially on Eisenhower's stance on key domestic legislation.
3. Assess the early performance of Dulles's diplomacy, especially as compared to the policy of containment.
4. Explain the origins of the Indochina War and assess Eisenhower's response to it.
5. Describe the developments in civil rights in the Eisenhower era and assess his responses to them.
6. Explain the Suez Crisis and the Hungarian revolt, their interrelations and their consequences.
7. Assess the impact of Sputnik.

CHAPTER OUTLINE

I. Rise of Eisenhower
   A. Election of 1952

   1. Appeal of Ike
   2. Adlai Stevenson
   B. Ike's background and personality
   1. Army career
   2. Warm and unpretentious

II. The early Eisenhower administration
   A. Appointments
   B. Dynamic conservatism
   1. Some New Deal programs cut
      a. Reconstruction Finance Corporation
      b. Wage and price controls
   2. Some New Deal programs extended
      a. Social security
      b. Minimum wage
      c. Health care
      d. Housing
   C. Public works
   1. St. Lawrence Seaway
   2. Interstate highways
   D. Armistice in Korea
   1. Ike's bold stand
   2. Reasons for settlement
   E. End to McCarthyism
   1. McCarthy's tactics
   2. McCarthy and the army
   3. Senate condemnation
   F. Internal security worries
   G. Dulles and foreign policy
   1. Dulles's background

2. Idea of liberation
3. Covert action and Allen Dulles
4. Massive retaliation
5. Brinksmanship
H. Problems of Indochina
    1. Background to war
        a. Nationalism in Asia
        b. French control
        c. Ho Chi Minh and independence
    2. First Indochina war
        a. Outbreak of fighting
        b. American aid
        c. Ike's domino theory
    3. Geneva Accords
        a. French defeat
        b. Provisions of the agreement
    4. Creation of SEATO
    5. Government of Diem
        a. Need for reform
        b. Opposition suppressed

III. Stirrings in civil rights
A. Ike's stance on civil rights
B. *Brown v. Board of Education*
    1. Court's decision
    2. Reactions
        a. Eisenhower's reluctance
        b. Token compliance
        c. Massive resistance
C. Montgomery bus boycott
    1. Cause for action
    2. Role of Martin Luther King, Jr.
    3. Strategy of nonviolence
    4. Results
D. Civil rights legislation

E. Little Rock
IV. Election of 1956
A. Eisenhower's health
B. Stevenson defeated again

V. A season of troubles
A. The Suez crisis
    1. Eisenhower's Middle East policy
    2. Rise of Nasser in Egypt
    3. Offer and withdrawal of loan
    4. Nasser's seizure of Suez
    5. Israeli invasion
    6. Resolution of crisis
B. The Hungarian revolt
C. Sputnik
    1. The Russian feat
    2. American reactions
        a. U.S. space effort
        b. Deployment of missiles
        c. Creation of NASA
        d. National Defense Education Act
D. Corruption in administration
E. Other foreign problems
    1. Eisenhower doctrine
    2. Marines to Lebanon
    3. The Berlin problem
    4. The U-2 affair
        a. Spy plane downed
        b. Collapse of summit
    5. Castro's Cuba
        a. Castro's takeover
        b. American responses
VI. Assessing the Eisenhower years
A. Accomplishments
B. Farewell address

KEY ITEMS OF CHRONOLOGY

Fall of Dien Bien Phu	May 1954
Brown v. Board of Education	May 1954
Geneva Accords signed	July 1954
SEATO created	September 1954
McCarthy condemned by the Senate	December 1954
Montgomery bus boycott	December 1955– December 1956
Suez crisis (and Hungarian revolt)	October 1956
Little Rock High School crisis	September 1957
Sputnik launched	October 1957
U-2 incident	May 1960

TERMS TO MASTER

Listed below are some important terms or people with which you should be familiar after you complete the study of this chapter. Explain the significance of each name or term.

1. Adlai Stevenson
2. "dynamic conservatism"
3. St. Lawrence Seaway
4. Interstate Highway System
5. Earl Warren
6. "liberation"
7. "massive retaliation"
8. Ho Chi Minh
9. Dien Bien Phu
10. Geneva Accords
11. SEATO
12. *Brown v. Board of Education*
13. Martin Luther King, Jr.
14. Suez crisis
15. Sputnik
16. U-2 incident

VOCABULARY BUILDING

Listed below are some words used in this chapter. Look up each word in your dictionary.

1. incumbent
2. egghead
3. syntax
4. renege
5. armistice
6. splenetic
7. capricious
8. sonorous
9. scurrilous
10. acclamation

EXERCISES FOR UNDERSTANDING

When you have completed reading the chapter, answer each of the following questions. If you have difficulty, go back and reread the section of the chapter related to the question.

Multiple-Choice Questions

Select the letter of the response which best completes the statement.

1. The Eisenhower administration
   A. reduced farm subsidies
   B. extended Social Security benefits
   C. started the Interstate Highway System
   D. did all of the above

2. Senator McCarthy met his downfall as a result of a direct conflict with
   A. Eisenhower, whom he called a Communist
   B. the FBI
   C. the State Department
   D. the United States Army

3. Eisenhower once said the "biggest damnfool mistake I ever made" was
   A. retiring from the army and entering politics
   B. appointing Earl Warren to the Supreme Court
   C. not attacking China with atomic weapons
   D. using federal troops in Little Rock, Arkansas

4. The Geneva Accords involving Southeast Asia
   A. were signed by the United States
   B. neutralized Vietnam
   C. divided Laos and Cambodia at the 38th Parallel
   D. called for elections to unify Vietnam

5. In *Brown v. Board of Education,* the Supreme Court ruled that
   A. racial segregation was constitutional
   B. "separate but equal" in public education was unconstitutional
   C. all children under the age of eighteen had to attend school
   D. Kansas must provide free education for Indian children

6. The Civil Rights Act of 1957
   A. was supported by Eisenhower and Lyndon Johnson
   B. established the Civil Rights Commission
   C. focused on voting rights for blacks
   D. did all of the above

7. In the Suez crisis of 1956, the United States was on the same side as
   A. the Soviet Union
   B. France and Great Britain
   C. Israel
   D. Hungary
8. Eisenhower's Farewell Address dealt with
   A. the need for greater military spending
   B. the dangers of a military-industrial complex
   C. how to solve problems of civil rights
   D. the need for a better highway system

True-False Questions

Indicate whether each statement is true or false.

1. Eisenhower's chief rival for the 1952 nomination was Sen. Joseph McCarthy of Ohio.
2. The Eisenhower administration was especially strong in its denunciation of U.S. policy commitments made at Yalta.
3. Under Secretary of State Dulles, American policy radically changed from the containment followed by Truman and Acheson.
4. SEATO was exactly like NATO except in Southeast Asia.

5. Eisenhower thought that laws could quickly and easily provide equal rights for blacks.
6. The leader of the Montgomery bus boycott was Martin Luther King, Jr.
7. The NDEA was a United States response to the launching of Sputnik.
8. Eisenhower always worked with solid Republican majorities in Congress.

Essay Questions

1. How did Ike's administrative style, philosophy, and programs differ from those of the New Deal?
2. What factors contributed to the fall of Senator McCarthy?
3. How did the Eisenhower administration try to "contain" communism?
4. Assess America's involvement in Indochina during the Eisenhower administration.
5. Describe the first developments in the civil rights movement.
6. Account for the United States position in both the Suez crisis and the Hungarian revolt of 1956.
7. What was the U-2 and how did it affect American foreign policy?

DOCUMENT

Eisenhower's Farewell Address, January 17, 1961

Eisenhower's farewell address, below, includes his famous warning about the growing influence of "the military-industrial complex."

> *My fellow Americans:*
> Three days from now, after half a century in the service of our country, I shall lay down the responsibilities of office as, in traditional and solemn ceremony, the authority of the Presidency is vested in my successor. . . .
> We now stand ten years past the midpoint of a century that has witnessed four major wars among great nations. Three of them involved our own country. Despite these holocausts America is today the strongest, the most influential and most productive nation in the world. Understandably proud of this pre-eminence we yet realize that America's leadership and prestige depend, not merely

upon our unmatched material progress, riches and military strength, but on how we use our power in the interests of world peace and human betterment.

Throughout America's adventure in free government, our basic purposes have been to keep the peace; to foster progress in human achievement, and to enhance liberty, dignity and integrity among people and among nations. To strive for less would be unworthy of a free and religious people. Any failure traceable to arrogance, or our lack of comprehension or readiness to sacrifice would inflict upon us grievous hurt both at home and abroad.

Progress toward these noble goals is persistently threatened by the conflict now engulfing the world. It commands our whole attention, absorbs our very beings. We face a hostile ideology—global in scope, atheistic in character, ruthless in purpose, and insidious in method. Unhappily the danger it poses promises to be of indefinite duration. To meet it successfully, there is called for, not so much the emotional and transitory sacrifices of crisis, but rather those which enable us to carry forward steadily, surely, and without complaint the burdens of a prolonged and complex struggle—with liberty the stake. Only thus shall we remain, despite every provocation, on our charted course toward permanent peace and human betterment. . . .

A vital element in keeping the peace is our military establishment. Our arms must be mighty, ready for instant action, so that no potential aggressor may be tempted to risk his own destruction.

Our military organization today bears little relation to that known by any of my predecessors in peacetime, or indeed by the fighting men of World War II or Korea.

Until the latest of our world conflicts, the United States had no armaments industry. American makers of plowshares could, with time and as required, make swords as well. But now we can no longer risk emergency improvisation of national defense; we have been compelled to create a permanent armaments industry of vast proportions. Added to this, three and a half million men and women are directly engaged in the defense establishment. We annually spend on military security more than the net income of all United States corporations.

This conjunction of an immense military establishment and a large arms industry is new in the American experience. The total influence—economic, political, even spiritual—is felt in every city, every statehouse, every office of the federal government. We recognize the imperative need for this development. Yet we must not fail to comprehend its grave implications. Our toil, resources, and livelihood are all involved; so is the very structure of our society.

In the councils of government, we must guard against the acquisition of unwarranted influence, whether sought or unsought, by the military-industrial complex. The potential for the disastrous rise of misplaced power exists and will persist.

We must never let the weight of this combination endanger our liberties or democratic processes. We should take nothing for granted. Only an alert and knowledgeable citizenry can compel the proper meshing of the huge industrial and military machinery of defense with our peaceful methods and goals, so that security and liberty may prosper together.

Akin to, and largely responsible for the sweeping changes in our industrial-military posture, has been the technological revolution during recent decades.

In this revolution, research has become central; it also becomes more formalized, complex, and costly. A steadily increasing share is conducted for, by, or at the direction of, the federal government. . . .

The prospect of domination of the nation's scholars by federal employment, project allocations, and the power of money is ever present—and is gravely to be regarded.

Yet, in holding scientific research and discovery in respect, as we should, we must also be alert to the equal and opposite danger that public policy could itself become the captive of a scientific-technological elite.

It is the task of statesmanship to mold, to balance, and to integrate these and other forces, new and old, within the principles of our democratic system—ever aiming toward the supreme goals of our free society.

Another factor in maintaining balance involves the element of time. As we peer into society's future, we—you and I, and our government—must avoid the impulse to live only for today, plundering, for our own ease and convenience, the precious resources of tomorrow. We cannot mortgage the material assets of our grandchildren without risking the loss also of their political and spiritual heritage. We want democracy to survive for all generations to come, not to become the insolvent phantom of tomorrow.

Down the long lane of the history yet to be written America knows that this world of ours, ever growing smaller, must avoid becoming a community of dreadful fear and hate, and be, instead, a proud confederation of mutual trust and respect.

Such a confederation must be one of equals. The weakest must come to the conference table with the same confidence as do we, protected as we are by our moral, economic, and military strength. That table, though scarred by many past frustrations, cannot be abandoned for the certain agony of the battlefield.

Disarmament, with mutual honor and confidence, is a continuing imperative. Together we must learn how to compose differences, not with arms, but with intellect and decent purpose. Because this need is so sharp and apparent I confess that I lay down my official responsibilities in this field with a definite sense of disappointment. As one who has witnessed the horror and the lingering sadness of war—as one who knows that another war could utterly destroy this civilization which has been so slowly and painfully built over thousands of years—I wish I could say tonight that a lasting peace is in sight.

Happily, I can say that war has been avoided. Steady progress toward our ultimate goal has been made. But, so much remains to be done. As a private citizen, I shall never cease to do what little I can to help the world advance along that road. . . .

[From *Public Papers of the Presidents: Dwight D. Eisenhower*, 1960–1961 (Washington, D. C.: U. S. Government Printing Office, 1961), no. 421, pp. 1035–1040]

Questions for Reflection

Describe the conflict that Eisenhower sees as "now engulfing the world." Why does Eisenhower consider it significant that the United States for the first time had a permanent armaments industry? What dangers does he think the "military-industrial complex" poses? Explain whether or not you agree with Eisenhower's analysis.

ANSWERS TO MULTIPLE-CHOICE AND TRUE-FALSE QUESTIONS

Multiple-Choice Questions

1-D, 2-D, 3-B, 4-D, 5-B, 6-D, 7-A, 8-B

True-False Questions

1-F, 2-F, 3-F, 4-F, 5-F, 6-T, 7-T, 8-F

33   ✑

INTO THE MAELSTROM: THE SIXTIES

CHAPTER OBJECTIVES

After you complete the reading and study of this chapter you should be able to

1. Describe Kennedy's style and compare it to the style of his predecessor and successor.
2. Assess Kennedy's domestic legislative achievements.
3. Assess the Kennedy record in foreign affairs.
4. Describe and account for LBJ's legislative accomplishments.
5. Explain why the Vietnam War became a quagmire for the United States and why LBJ changed his policy there in 1968.
6. Trace the transformation of the civil rights movement into the black power movement.

CHAPTER OUTLINE

I. The 1960 election
  A. Nixon's experience
  B. Kennedy's background
  C. Campaign
    1. Televised debates
    2. Results

II. The New Frontier

  A. Start of the administration
    1. Appointments
    2. Inaugural address
  B. Legislative achievements
    1. Urban renewal, minimum wage, social security
    2. Alliance for Progress
    3. Peace Corps
    4. Trade Expansion Act
  C. Civil rights
    1. Kennedy's commitment
    2. Martin Luther King, Jr.
    3. Students and sit-ins
    4. CORE freedom rides
    5. Crisis at Ole Miss
    6. Birmingham
    7. Wallace and the University of Alabama
    8. March on Washington
  D. Warren Court
    1. School prayer
    2. Rights of defendants

III. Kennedy and foreign affairs
  A. Early setbacks
    1. Bay of Pigs disaster
    2. Vienna summit
    3. Berlin
  B. Cuban missile crisis
    1. Causes of crisis
    2. Kennedy's action
    3. Resolution of crisis
    4. Aftereffects

C. Vietnam
    1. Neutrality for Laos
    2. Problems with Diem
    3. Kennedy's reluctance to escalate
    4. Overthrow of Diem

IV. Assassination of President Kennedy

V. Lyndon Johnson and the Great Society
    A. Background and personality
    B. War on poverty
        1. *The Other America*
        2. 1964 tax cut
        3. Economic Opportunity Act
    C. Election in 1964
        1. Goldwater—choice not echo
        2. LBJ appeals to consensus
        3. Johnson landslide
    D. Landmark legislation
        1. Health insurance
        2. Aid to education
        3. Appalachian redevelopment
        4. Housing and urban development
    E. Shortcomings of Great Society

VI. From civil rights to black power
    A. Civil Rights Act of 1964
    B. Voting Rights Act of 1965
        1. The Selma march
        2. Provisions of the act
    C. Development of black power
        1. Race riots of 1965 and 1966
        2. Plight of urban blacks

        3. Call for black power
           a. Stokely Carmichael
           b. Black Panther party
           c. Malcolm X
        4. Assessment of black power

VII. The tragedy of Vietnam
    A. Dimensions of war
        1. Troop commitments
        2. Cost of fighting
    B. Escalation
        1. Gulf of Tonkin Resolution
        2. Bombing and combat troops in
           1965
    C. Context for policy
        1. Containment theory
        2. Not an accident
        3. Erosion of support for war
        4. Unity of North Vietnamese
    D. Turning point of the war
        1. Tet offensive
        2. Presidential primaries
        3. LBJ decides not to run

VIII. The crescendo of the sixties
    A. Assassinations in 1968
        1. Martin Luther King, Jr.
        2. Robert F. Kennedy
    B. Election of 1968
        1. Chicago and Miami
        2. George Wallace
        3. Election of Nixon

KEY ITEMS OF CHRONOLOGY

Kennedy administration	1961–63
Bay of Pigs invasion	April 1961
Freedom rides	May 1961
Cuban missile crisis	October 1963
Overthrow of Ngo Dinh Diem	November 1963
Kennedy assassination	November 1963
Civil Rights Act (public accommodations)	July 1964
Gulf of Tonkin Resolution	August 1964
Voting Rights Act	1965
Tet offensive	January–February 1968
Assassinations of King and Robert Kennedy	1968

TERMS TO MASTER

Listed below are some important terms or people with which you should be familiar after you complete the study of this chapter. Explain the significance of each name or term.

1. New Frontier
2. Peace Corps
3. Martin Luther King, Jr.
4. SNCC
5. Freedom rides
6. Bay of Pigs invasion
7. Berlin Wall
8. Cuban missile crisis
9. Nuclear Test Ban Treaty
10. Ngo Dinh Diem
11. Great Society
12. *The Other America*
13. Medicare and Medicaid
14. Barry Goldwater
15. Watts riot
16. black power
17. Malcolm X
18. Gulf of Tonkin Resolution
19. Vietcong
20. Tet offensive
21. Eugene McCarthy
22. Robert Kennedy

VOCABULARY BUILDING

Listed below are some words used in this chapter. Look up each word in your dictionary.

1. maelstrom
2. pundits
3. chameleon
4. scurrilous
5. infidelity
6. desegregate
7. sublime
8. debacle
9. immolate
10. poignant

EXERCISES FOR UNDERSTANDING

When you have completed the reading of the chapter, answer each of the following questions. If you have difficulty, go back and reread the section of the chapter related to the question.

Multiple-Choice Questions

Select the letter of the response which best completes the statement.

1. By 1960 John F. Kennedy had
   A. a long and distinguished political career
   B. a great reputation as an able legislator
   C. charm, good looks, wit, and wealth
   D. all of the above

2. Congress blocked Kennedy's proposals for
   A. a tax cut
   B. federal aid to education
   C. health insurance for the elderly
   D. all of the above

3. In the Cuban missile crisis, President Kennedy ordered
   A. surgical air strikes of Cuba
   B. a quarantine of Cuba
   C. the Bay of Pigs invasion
   D. removal of U.S. missiles from Turkey

4. By the end of 1963, the United States had sent to Vietnam
   A. only 2,000 military advisers
   B. more than 15,000 military advisers
   C. 25,000 fighting troops
   D. over 100,000 fighting troops

5. *The Other America* aroused concern about
   A. aid to South America
   B. poverty
   C. rights of blacks
   D. the women's movement

6. In 1964 Lyndon Johnson defeated
   A. Richard Nixon
   B. Nelson Rockefeller
   C. Barry Goldwater
   D. Robert Taft

7. Discrimination in hotels and restaurants
was outlawed by
   A. the Supreme Court's *Brown* decision
   in 1954
   B. Martin Luther King's "I Have a
   Dream" speech
   C. presidential order of Kennedy
   D. the Civil Rights Act of 1964
8. Johnson sought to deescalate the
Vietnam War because
   A. the Tet offensive showed that we
   could not win
   B. political challengers showed the high
   level of public opposition to the war
   C. key national leaders called on him to
   end the war
   D. of all of the above

True-False Questions

*Indicate whether each statement is true or
false.*

1. Nixon's 1960 campaign benefited from
his televised debate with Kennedy.
2. Planning for the Bay of Pigs invasion
began in the Eisenhower administration.
3. Kennedy supported neutrality for Laos.

4. The effects of the 1964 tax cut helped
finance the war on poverty.
5. Goldwater opposed the nuclear test ban
and the Civil Rights Act.
6. Martin Luther King, Jr., was the head of
the SNCC.
7. The first American combat troops went
to Vietnam in 1966.
8. The Tet offensive had a great effect on
American public opinion.

Essay Questions

1. How did John Kennedy personify the
"New Frontier"?
2. Assess the successes and failures of JFK's
foreign policy.
3. Compare and contrast the achievements
of the New Frontier and the Great
Society.
4. What were the major milestones in the
Vietnam conflict between 1961 and
1986?
5. How effective was the civil rights
movement of the 1960s?
6. Account for the election of Richard
Nixon in 1968.

DOCUMENT

Johnson's Speech on Vietnam, 1965

The speech that follows, given at Johns
Hopkins University on April 7, 1965,
contains President Johnson's rationale for a
critical buildup of American forces in South
Vietnam. That year, 1965, proved to be a
fateful year for American involvement in
Vietnam.

. . . Over this war, and all Asia, is the deepening shadow of Communist China. The rulers in Hanoi are urged on by Peking. This is a regime which has destroyed freedom in Tibet, attacked India, and been condemned by the United Nations for aggression in Korea. It is a nation which is helping the forces of violence in almost every continent. The contest in Vietnam is part of a wider pattern of aggressive purpose.

Why are these realities our concern? Why are we in South Vietnam? We are there because we have a promise to keep. Since 1954 every American President has offered support to the people of South Vietnam. We have helped to build, and we have helped to defend. Thus, over many years, we have made a national pledge to help South Vietnam defend its independence. And I intend to keep our promise.

To dishonor that pledge, to abandon this small and brave nation to its enemy, and to the terror that must follow, would be an unforgivable wrong.

We are also there to strengthen world order. Around the globe, from Berlin to Thailand, are people whose well-being rests, in part, on the belief that they can count on us if they are attacked. To leave Vietnam to its fate would shake the confidence of all these people in the value of American commitment, the value of America's word. The result would be increased unrest and instability, and even wider war.

We are also there because there are great stakes in the balance. Let no one think for a moment that retreat from Vietnam would bring an end to conflict. The battle would be renewed in one country and then another. The central lesson of our time is that the appetite of aggression is never satisfied. To withdraw from one battlefield means only to prepare for the next. We must say in Southeast Asia, as we did in Europe, in the words of the Bible: "Hitherto shalt thou come, but no further."

There are those who say that all our effort there will be futile, that China's power is such it is bound to dominate all Southeast Asia. But there is no end to that argument until all the nations of Asia are swallowed up.

There are those who wonder why we have a responsibility there. We have it for the same reason we have a responsibility for the defense of freedom in Europe. World War II was fought in both Europe and Asia, and when it ended we found ourselves with continued responsibility for the defense of freedom.

Our objective is the independence of South Vietnam, and its freedom from attack. We want nothing for ourselves, only that the people of South Vietnam be allowed to guide their own country in their own way.

We will do everything necessary to reach that objective. And we will do only what is absolutely necessary.

In recent months, attacks on South Vietnam were stepped up. Thus it became necessary to increase our response and to make attacks by air. This is not a change of purpose. It is a change in what we believe that purpose requires.

We do this in order to slow down aggression.

We do this to increase the confidence of the brave people of South Vietnam who have bravely borne this brutal battle for so many years and with so many casualties.

And we do this to convince the leaders of North Vietnam, and all who seek to share their conquest, of a very simple fact:

We will not be defeated.

We will not grow tired.

We will not withdraw, either openly or under the cloak of a meaningless agreement. . . .

Once this is clear, then it should also be clear that the only path for reasonable men is the path of peaceful settlement.

Such peace demands an independent South Vietnam securely guaranteed and able to shape its own relationships to all others, free from outside interference, tied to no alliance, a military base for no other country.

These are the essentials of any final settlement.

We will never be second in the search for such a peaceful settlement in Vietnam.

There may be many ways to this kind of peace: in discussion or negotiation with the governments concerned; in large groups or in small ones; in the reaffirmation of old agreements or their strengthening with new ones.

We have stated this position over and over again fifty times and more, to friend and foe alike. And we remain ready, with this purpose, for unconditional discussions.

And until that bright and necessary day of peace we will try to keep conflict from spreading. We have no desire to see thousands die in battle, Asians or Americans. We have no desire to devastate that which the people of North Vietnam have built with toil and sacrifice. We will use our power with restraint and with all the wisdom we can command. But we will use it. . . .

We will always oppose the effort of one nation to conquer another nation.

We will do this because our own security is at stake.

But there is more to it than that. For our generation has a dream. It is a very old dream. But we have the power and now we have the opportunity to make it come true.

For centuries, nations have struggled among each other. But we dream of a world where disputes are settled by law and reason. And we will try to make it so.

For most of history men have hated and killed one another in battle. But we dream of an end to war. And we will try to make it so.

For all existence most men have lived in poverty, threatened by hunger. But we dream of a world where all are fed and charged with hope. And we will help to make it so.

The ordinary men and women of North Vietnam and South Vietnam—of China and India—of Russia and America—are brave people. They are filled with the same proportions of hate and fear, of love and hope. Most of them want the same things for themselves and their families. Most of them do not want their sons ever to die in battle, or see the homes of others destroyed. . . .

Every night before I turn out the lights to sleep, I ask myself this question: Have I done everything that I can do to unite this country? Have I done everything I can to help unite the world, to try to bring peace and hope to all the peoples of the world? Have I done enough?

Ask yourselves that question in your homes and in this hall tonight. Have we done all we could? Have we done enough? . . .

[*Department of State Bulletin,* April 26, 1965 (Washington, D. C.: U. S. Government Printing Office, 1940–)]

Questions for Reflection

Compare Lyndon Johnson's address to Franklin Roosevelt's speech of January 1941 in Chapter 28. To what extent were they concerned about the same kinds of threats? Was Johnson correct in drawing parallels between events in Vietnam and events in Europe before World War II? What similarities and differences do you see? What is your view of the policy Johnson outlines here?

ANSWERS TO MULTIPLE-CHOICE AND TRUE-FALSE QUESTIONS

Multiple-Choice Questions

1-C, 2-D, 3-B, 4-B, 5-B, 6-C, 7-D, 8-D

True-False Questions

1-F, 2-T, 3-T, 4-T, 5-T, 6-F, 7-F, 8-T

34

REBELLION AND REACTION:
THE NIXON YEARS

CHAPTER OBJECTIVES

After you complete the reading and study of this chapter you should be able to

1. Account for the rise and decline of New Left protests.
2. Describe the counterculture and its impact.
3. Trace the reform movements for women, Hispanics, Indians, and the environment.
4. Explain Nixon's aims in Vietnam.
5. Assess the impact of the Vietnam War on American society, military morale, and later foreign policy.
6. Explain Nixon's goals in domestic policy and account for his limited accomplishment.
7. Explain the problems plaguing the United States economy in the decade of the 1970s, and describe the various cures Nixon tried.
8. Describe Nixon's foreign policy triumphs in China and the Soviet Union, and explain their significance.
9. Discuss the Watergate coverup and account for the difficulty in unraveling it.

CHAPTER OUTLINE

I. Fissures in the consensus
II. Youth revolt
   A. Baby-boomers as young adults
   B. Sit-ins and end of apathy
III. New Left
   A. Students for a Democratic Society
      1. Port Huron Statement
      2. Participatory democracy
   B. Free Speech movement
      1. Berkeley
      2. Quality of campus life
   C. Antiwar protests
   D. Growing militance
   E. 1968
      1. Columbia University uprising
      2. Democratic convention in Chicago
      3. Fracturing of SDS
IV. Counterculture
   A. Descendants of the Beats
   B. Contrasted with New Left
   C. Drugs, communes, hedonism
   D. Rock music
      1. Woodstock
      2. Altamont
   E. Cooptation and failure

V. Feminism
  A. Betty Friedan's *The Feminine Mystique*
  B. National Organization of Women
  C. Federal actions
    1. Affirmative action
    2. *Roe v. Wade*
    3. Equal Rights Amendment's failure
  D. Divisions and reactions

VI. Minorities
  A. Hispanics
    1. United Farm Workers
    2. Chicanos, Puerto Ricans, Cubans
    3. Political power
  B. American Indians
    1. Emergence of Indian rights
    2. American Indian Movement
    3. Legal actions

VII. "Silent majority"

VIII. Nixon and Vietnam
  A. The policy of gradual withdrawal
  B. Movement on three fronts
    1. Insistance on Communist withdrawal from South Vietnam
    2. Efforts to undercut unrest in the United States
      a. Troop reductions
      b. Lottery and volunteer army
    3. Expanded air war
  C. Impact of the war on military morale
    1. Military disobedience
    2. Fraggings
    3. Drug problems
  D. Occasions for public outcry against the war
    1. My Lai massacre
    2. Cambodian "incursion"
      a. Campus riots
      b. Public reaction
    3. *Pentagon Papers*
      a. Method of disclosure
      b. Revelations of the papers
      c. Supreme Court ruling
  E. American withdrawal
    1. Kissinger's efforts before the 1972 election
    2. The Christmas bombings
    3. Final acceptance of peace
    4. U.S. withdrawal in March 1973
  F. Ultimate victory of the North: March–April 1975

  G. Assessment of the war
    1. Communist control
    2. Failure to transfer democracy
    3. Erosion of respect for the military
    4. Drastic division of the American people
    5. Impact on future foreign policy

IX. Nixon and Middle America
  A. A reflection of Middle American values
  B. Domestic affairs
    1. Continuance of civil rights progress
      a. Voting Rights Act continued over a veto
      b. Courts uphold integration
        i. In Mississippi
        ii. School busing
        iii. Limitation on busing
        iv. The *Bakke* decision
    2. Revenue sharing
    3. Other domestic legislation
  C. The economic malaise
    1. The causes of stagflation
    2. Nixon's efforts to improve the economy
      a. Reducing the federal deficit
      b. Reducing the money supply
      c. Wage and price controls
  D. The environmental movement
    1. Recognition of the limits of growth
    2. Environmental Protection Agency
    3. Impact of the energy crisis
    4. Opposition to environmental reform

X. Nixon's foreign triumphs
  A. Rapprochement with China
  B. Détente with the Soviet Union
    1. The visit to Moscow
    2. The SALT agreement
  C. Kissinger's shuttle diplomacy in the Middle East

XI. The election of 1972
  A. Removal of the Wallace threat
  B. The McGovern candidacy
  C. Results of the election

XII. Watergate
  A. Unraveling the coverup
    1. Judge Sirica's role
    2. Nixon's personal role
    3. The development of illegal tactics

4. April resignations
5. Discovery of the tapes
6. The Saturday Night Massacre
7. The Court decides against the
   president
8. Articles of impeachment
9. The resignation

B. The aftermath of Watergate
   1. Ford's selection
   2. The Nixon pardon
   3. Resiliency of American institutions
   4. War Powers Act
   5. Campaign financing legislation
   6. Freedom of Information Act

KEY ITEMS OF CHRONOLOGY

Port Huron Statement	1962
Betty Friedan's *The Feminine Mystique*	1963
N.O.W. founded	1966
My Lai massacre	1968
Woodstock Music Festival	1969
Cambodian "incursion"	April 1970
Swann v. Charlotte-Mecklenburg Board of Education	1971
Pentagon Papers published	June 1971
Roe v. Wade	1972
Nixon's visit to China	February 1972
SALT agreement signed	May 1972
Watergate break-in occurred	June 1972
Last American troops left Vietnam	March 1973
War Powers Act	1973
Nixon's resignation	Aug. 9, 1974
South Vietnam fell to the North	April 1975
Bakke v. Board of Regents of California	1978

TERMS TO MASTER

Listed below are some important terms or people with which you should be familiar after you complete the study of this chapter. Explain the significance of each name or term.

1. New Left
2. SDS
3. participatory democracy
4. Free Speech movement
5. Weathermen
6. counterculture
7. Betty Friedan
8. N.O.W.
9. Equal Rights Amendment
10. "silent majority"
11. *Pentagon Papers*
12. *Swann v. Charlotte-Mecklenburg Board of Education*
13. *Bakke v. Board of Regents of California*
14. revenue sharing
15. Spiro Agnew
16. OPEC
17. SALT
18. George McGovern
19. Watergate
20. Saturday Night Massacre
21. Henry Kissinger
22. War Powers Act

VOCABULARY BUILDING

Listed below are some words used in this chapter. Look up each word in your dictionary.

1. estranged
2. odious
3. nihilistic
4. mesmerize
5. hedonism
6. karma
7. assuage
8. poignant
9. ignoble
10. tenor
11. détente
12. lamentation
13. incriminating
14. impeach

EXERCISES FOR UNDERSTANDING

When you have completed reading the chapter, answer each of the following questions. If you have difficulty, go back and reread the section of the chapter related to the question.

Multiple-Choice Questions

Select the letter of the response which best completes the statement.

1. The leaders of the New Left included
   A. Tom Hayden and Mark Rudd
   B. Abbie Hoffman and Cesar Chavez
   C. Richard Daley and Spiro Agnew
   D. Timothy Leary and Richie Havens

2. The counterculture declined because of
   A. the violence at Altamont
   B. cooptation by conventional commercialism
   C. its own impracticality and naïveté
   D. all of the above

3. Betty Friedan launched the women's movement with claims that women
   A. were too educated to dabble in politics
   B. deserved equality with men in all areas

C. should be permitted to serve in the armed forces
D. were bored with housework and child care

4. In *Roe v. Wade* the Supreme Court ruled that
   A. busing for school integration was unconstitutional
   B. Indians were to receive four million acres in Wyoming
   C. abortion in the first three months of pregnancy was legal
   D. the Watergate coverup was sufficient to impeach Nixon

5. Nixon sought to lessen criticism of the Vietnam War by
   A. slowly reducing the number of American troops there
   B. creating a lottery to determine who would be drafted
   C. using more air strikes rather than ground warfare
   D. all of the above methods

6. Nixon's chief link to Middle America was
   A. Daniel Moynihan
   B. Robert Finch
   C. Spiro Agnew
   D. Henry Kissinger

7. Stagflation in the 1970s was caused by
   A. tax increases to pay for the Vietnam War
   B. rising OPEC oil prices
   C. rapid expansion of the American workforce
   D. all of the above

8. During the Watergate crisis, Nixon was *not* accused of
   A. obstructing justice through paying witnesses to remain silent
   B. defying Congress by withholding the tapes
   C. using federal agencies to deprive citizens of their rights
   D. stealing funds from the reelection campaign

True-False Questions

Indicate whether each statement is true or false.

1. Campus turmoil in 1968 reached a peak at Columbia University.
2. Spiro Agnew urged hippies to "Tune in, turn on, drop out."
3. Cesar Chavez was the leader of the United Farm Workers.
4. The Cambodian "incursion" led to widespread rioting on American college campuses.
5. Two years after the Vietnam War ended, North Vietnam took control of the South.
6. As Nixon had hoped, the Burger Court opposed further school integration.
7. Nixon used wage and price controls to stem inflation.
8. The War Powers Act requires a president to withdraw troops sent abroad after sixty days unless Congress specifically authorizes a longer stay.

Essay Questions

1. Compare and contrast the New Left and the counterculture.
2. Evaluate the accomplishments of the women's movement in the 1960s and 1970s.
3. How did Nixon's Vietnam War policies compare with Johnson's?
4. Discuss the impact of the Vietnam War on American society.
5. How did Nixon try to appeal to the "silent majority" with his domestic policies? Did he succeed?
6. How important were Nixon's diplomatic achievements with China and Russia? Could a Democrat have achieved the same gains? Explain.
7. Explain the Watergate controversy and Nixon's involvement in it.

DOCUMENTS

Document 1. The Charges against Nixon

When the House Judiciary Committee completed its investigation and voted the impeachment of Nixon in July 1974, three articles obtained a majority vote of the committee. Those three articles are excerpted here.

Article I. In his conduct of the office of President of the United States, Richard M. Nixon, in violation of his constitutional oath faithfully to execute the office of President of the United States and, to the best of his ability, preserve, protect, and defend the Constitution of the United States, and in violation of his constitutional duty to take care that the laws be faithfully executed, has prevented, obstructed, and impeded the administration of justice, . . . Richard M. Nixon, using the powers of his high office, engaged personally and through his subordinates and agents, in a course of conduct or plan designed to delay, impede, and obstruct the investigation of such unlawful entry; to cover up, conceal and protect those responsible; and to conceal the existence and scope of other unlawful covert activities. . . .

Article II. . . . Richard M. Nixon . . . has repeatedly engaged in conduct violating the constitutional rights of citizens, impairing the due and proper administration of justice and the conduct of lawful inquiries, or contravening the laws governing agencies of the executive branch and the purpose of these agencies. . . .

Article III. Richard M. Nixon, contrary to his oath faithfully to execute the office of President of the United States . . . has failed without lawful cause or excuse to produce papers and things as directed by duly authorized subpoenas issued by the Committee on the Judiciary of the House of Representatives on April 11, 1974, May 15, 1974, May 30, 1974, and June 24, 1974, and willfully disobeying such subpoenas. . . . In refusing to produce these papers and things, Richard M. Nixon, substituting his judgment as to what materials were necessary for the inquiry, interposed the powers of the Presidency against the lawful subpoenas of the House of Representatives, thereby assuming to himself functions and judgments necessary to the exercise of the sole power of impeachment vested by the Constitution in the House of Representatives.

[U.S. Congress, House of Representatives, *Report of the Committee on the Judiciary*, 93rd Cong., 2d sess., 1974.]

Document 2. Senator Sam Ervin Explains the Meaning and Consequences of Watergate

Prior to the report quoted above, the Ervin Committee of the Senate had throughout the summer of 1973 treated the American public to weeks of televised hearings at which various Watergate conspirators had testified about the labyrinthine developments of the Watergate affair. In June 1974, shortly before the House Judiciary Committee moved to impeach Nixon, the Ervin Committee made its report. Accompanying the report was a statement from Senator Ervin in which he tried to summarize the Watergate episode in a few paragraphs. Because the report was made prior to the House committee's decision to move toward impeachment of the president, Ervin began his report with a disclaimer to indicate that he was not trying to pass judgment on the president's guilt in the matter. His report is a succinct statement of the Watergate affair and a comment on its implications for the future.

I am not undertaking to usurp and exercise the power of impeachment, which the Constitution confers upon the House of Representatives alone. As a consequence, nothing I say should be construed as an expression of an opinion in respect to the question of whether or not President Nixon is impeachable in connection with the Watergate or any other matter. . . .

I shall also refrain from making any comment on the question of whether or not the President has performed in an acceptable manner his paramount constitutional obligation "to take care that the laws be faithfully executed."

Watergate was not invented by enemies of the Nixon administration or even by the news media. On the contrary, Watergate was perpetrated upon America by White House and political aides, whom President Nixon himself had entrusted with the management of his campaign for reelection to the Presidency, a campaign which was divorced to a marked degree from the campaigns of other Republicans who sought election to public office in 1972. I note at this point without elaboration that these White House and political aides were virtually without experience in either Government or politics apart from their association with President Nixon.

5. Watergate was without precedent in the political annals of America in respect to the scope and intensity of its unethical and

illegal actions. To be sure, there had been previous milder political scandals in American history. That fact does not excuse Watergate. Murder and stealing have occurred in every generation since Earth began, but that fact has not made murder meritorious or larceny legal.

What Was Watergate?

Watergate was a conglomerate of various illegal and unethical activities in which various officers and employees of the Nixon reelection committee and various White House aides of President Nixon participated in varying ways and degrees to accomplish these successive objectives:

1. To destroy, insofar as the Presidential election of 1972 was concerned, the integrity of the process by which the President of the United States is nominated and elected.

2. To hide from law enforcement officers, prosecutors, grand jurors, courts, the news media, and the American people the identities and wrongdoing of those officers and employees of the Nixon reelection committees, and those White House aides who had undertaken to destroy the integrity of the process by which the President of the United States is nominated and elected.

To accomplish the first of these objectives. . . .

1. They exacted enormous contributions—usually in cash—from corporate executives by impliedly implanting in their minds the impressions that the making of the contributions was necessary to insure that the corporations would receive governmental favors, or avoid governmental disfavors, while President Nixon remained in the White House. A substantial portion of the contributions were made out of corporate funds in violation of a law enacted by Congress a generation ago.

2. They hid substantial parts of these contributions in cash in safes and safe deposits to conceal their sources and the identities of those who had made them.

3. They disbursed substantial portions of these hidden contributions in a surreptitious manner to finance the bugging and the burglary of the offices of the Democratic National Committee in the Watergate complex in Washington. . . .

4. They deemed the departments and agencies of the Federal Government to be the political playthings of the Nixon administration rather than impartial instruments for serving the people, and undertook to induce them to channel Federal contracts, grants, and loans to areas, groups, or individuals so as to promote the reelection of the President rather than to further the welfare of the people.

5. They branded as enemies of the President individuals and members of the news media who dissented from the President's policies and opposed his reelection, and conspired to urge the Department of Justice, the Federal Bureau of Investigation, the Internal Revenue Service, and the Federal Communications Commission to pervert the use of their legal powers to harass them for so doing.

6. They borrowed from the Central Intelligence Agency disguises which E. Howard Hunt used in political espionage operations, and photographic equipment which White House employees known as

the "Plumbers" and their hired confederates used in connection with burglarizing the office of a psychiatrist which they believed contained information concerning Daniel Ellsberg which the White House was anxious to secure.

7. They assigned to E. Howard Hunt, who was at the time a White House consultant occupying an office in the Executive Office Building, the gruesome task of falsifying State Department documents which they contemplated using in their altered state to discredit the Democratic Party by defaming the memory of former President John Fitzgerald Kennedy, who as the hapless victim of an assassin's bullet had been sleeping in the tongueless silence of the dreamless dust for 9 years.

8. They used campaign funds to hire saboteurs to forge and disseminate false and scurrilous libels of honorable men running for the Democratic Presidential nomination in Democratic Party primaries.

During the darkness of the early morning of June 17, 1972, James W. McCord, the security chief of the John Mitchell committee, and four residents of Miami, Fla., were arrested by Washington police while they were burglarizing the offices of the Democratic National Committee in the Watergate complex to obtain political intelligence. . . .

The arrest of McCord and the four residents of Miami created consternation in the Nixon reelection committees and the White House. . . . various White House aides undertook to conceal from law enforcement officers, prosecutors, grand jurors, courts, the news media, and the American people the identities and activities of those officers and employees of the Nixon reelection committee and those White House aides who had participated in any way in the Watergate affair. . . .

1. They destroyed the records of the Nixon reelection committee antedating the bugging and the burglary.

2. They induced the Acting Director of the FBI, who was a Nixon appointee, to destroy the State Department documents which E. Howard Hunt had been falsifying.

3. They obtained from the Acting Director of the FBI copies of the scores of interviews conducted by the FBI agents in connection with their investigation of the bugging and the burglary, and were enabled thereby to coach their confederates to give false and misleading statements to the FBI.

4. They sought to persuade the FBI to refrain from investigating the sources of the campaign funds which were used to finance the bugging and the burglary.

5. They intimidated employees of the Nixon reelection committees and employees of the White House by having their lawyers present when these employees were being questioned by agents of the FBI, and thus deterred these employees from making full disclosures to the FBI.

6. They lied to agents of the FBI, prosecutors, and grand jurors who undertook to investigate the bugging and the burglary, and to Judge Sirica and the petit jurors who tried the seven original Watergate defendants in January, 1973.

7. They persuaded the Department of Justice and the prosecutors to take out-of-court statements from Maurice Stans, President Nixon's chief campaign fundraiser, and Charles Colson, Egil Krogh, and David Young, White House aides, and Charles Colson's secretary, instead of requiring them to testify before the grand jury investigating the bugging and the burglary in conformity with established procedures governing such matters, and thus denied the grand jurors the opportunity to question them.

8. They persuaded the Department of Justice and the prosecutors to refrain from asking Donald Segretti, their chief hired saboteur, any questions involving Herbert W. Kalmbach, the President's personal attorney, who was known by them to have paid Segretti for dirty tricks he perpetrated upon honorable men seeking the Democratic Presidential nomination. . . .

9. They made cash payments totaling hundreds of thousands of dollars out of campaign funds in surreptitious ways to the seven original Watergate defendants as hush money to buy their silence. . . .

10. They gave assurances to some of the original seven defendants that they would receive Presidential clemency after serving short portions of their sentences if they refrained from divulging the identities and activities of the officers and employees of the Nixon reelection committees and the White House aides who had participated in the Watergate affair.

11. They made arrangements by which the attorneys who represented the seven original Watergate defendants received their fees in cash from moneys which had been collected to finance President Nixon's reelection campaign.

12. They induced the Department of Justice and the prosecutors of the seven original Watergate defendants to assure the news media and the general public that there was no evidence that any persons other than the seven original Watergate defendants were implicated in any way in the Watergate-related crimes.

13. They inspired massive efforts on the part of segments of the news media friendly to the administration to persuade the American people that most of the members of the Select Committee named by the Senate to investigate the Watergate were biased and irresponsible men motivated solely by desires to exploit the matters they investigated for personal or partisan advantage. . . .

One shudders to think that the Watergate conspiracies might have been effectively concealed and their most dramatic episode might have been dismissed as a "third-rate" burglary conceived and committed solely by the seven original Watergate defendants had it not been for the courage and penetrating understanding of Judge Sirica, the thoroughness of the investigative reporting of Carl Bernstein, Bob Woodward, and the other representatives of the free press, the labors of the Senate Select Committee and its excellent staff, and the dedication and diligence of Special Prosecutors Archibald Cox and Leon Jarworski and their associates.

Why Was Watergate?

Unlike the men who were responsible for Teapot Dome, the Presidential aides who perpetrated Watergate were not seduced by the love of money, which is sometimes thought to be the root of all evil. On the contrary, they were instigated by a lust for political power, which is at least as corrupting as political power itself. . . .

They knew that the power they enjoyed would be lost and the policies to which they adhered would be frustrated if the President should be defeated.

As a consequence of these things, they believed the President's reelection to be a most worthy objective, and succumbed to an age-old temptation. They resorted to evil means to promote what they conceived to be a good end.

Their lust for political power blinded them to ethical considerations and legal requirements; to Aristotle's aphorism that the good of man must be the end of politics; and to Grover Cleveland's conviction that a public office is a public trust.

They had forgotten, if they ever knew, that the Constitution is designed to be a law for rulers and people alike at all times and under all circumstances; and that no doctrine involving more pernicious consequences to the commonweal has ever been invented by the wit of man than the notion that any of its provisions can be suspended by the President for any reason whatsoever.

On the contrary, they apparently believed that the President is above the Constitution, and has the autocratic power to suspend its provisions if he decides in his own unreviewable judgment that his action in so doing promotes his own political interests or the welfare of the Nation. . . .

The Antidote for Future Watergates

Is there an antidote which will prevent future Watergates? If so, what is it? . . .

Candor compels the confession . . . that law alone will not suffice to prevent future Watergates. . . .

Law is not self-executing. Unfortunately, at times its execution rests in the hands of those who are faithless to it. And even when its enforcement is committed to those who revere it, law merely deters some human beings from offending, and punishes other human beings for offending. It does not make men good. This task can be performed only by ethics or religion or morality. . . .

When all is said, the only sure antidote for future Watergates is understanding of fundamental principles and intellectual and moral integrity in the men and women who achieve or are entrusted with governmental political power.

[U.S. Congress, Senate, Select Committee on Presidential Campaign Activities, *Final Report,* 93rd Cong., 2d sess., 1974, pp. 1097–1103]

Questions for Reflection

The United States Constitution in Article II, Section 4, states that the president "shall be removed from office on impeachment for, and on conviction of, treason, bribery, or other high crimes and misdemeanors." Do you consider the crimes of which Nixon was accused impeachable offenses? Why or why not?

Why was Ervin so careful to disavow any indictment of the president in his report? Based on the charges of the House Rules Committee in Document 1, which of the actions attributed to others by Ervin might have been charged to the president also?

Who benefited from the Watergate crimes? Were monetary considerations at the heart of the Watergate crimes? Is a president who is dutifully exercising his responsibilities "above the Constitution" with the power to suspend its provisions when he needs to do so? Explain.

What and/or who does Ervin credit with bringing the Watergate conspirators to justice? What does the case suggest about the need for an independent judiciary and a free press? How do you react to Ervin's prescription for preventing future Watergates?

ANSWERS TO MULTIPLE-CHOICE AND TRUE-FALSE QUESTIONS

Multiple-Choice Questions

1-A, 2-D, 3-D, 4-C, 5-D, 6-C, 7-D, 8-D

True-False Questions

1-T, 2-F, 3-T, 4-T, 5-T, 6-F, 7-T, 8-T

35

RETRENCHMENT: FORD TO REAGAN

CHAPTER OBJECTIVES

After you complete the reading and study of this chapter you should be able to

1. Describe the brief presidency of Gerald Ford.
2. Assess the Carter administration's successes and failures.
3. Explain the popular appeal of Ronald Reagan.
4. Discuss the economic programs of the Reagan administration.
5. Examine the foreign policies of the United States under Reagan.
6. Suggest the significance of the Reagan presidency.

CHAPTER OUTLINE

I. Ford and Carter presidencies
  A. Ford administration
    1. Drift at the end of Nixon administration
    2. Battle with the economy
    3. Diplomatic accomplishments
  B. Election of 1976
    1. Ford's nomination
    2. Rise of Jimmy Carter
    3. Carter's victory
  C. Carter presidency

    1. Early domestic moves
      a. Appointments
      b. Amnesty for draft dodgers
      c. Environmental legislation
      d. Energy crisis
      e. Crisis of confidence
    2. Foreign policy initiatives
      a. Human rights
      b. Panama Canal treaties
      c. Camp David Agreement
    3. Troubles
      a. Stagflation
      b. SALT II treaty
      c. Afghanistan invasion
    4. Iranian crisis
      a. Background
      b. Efforts to aid hostages
      c. End of 444-day crisis

II. Background of Reagan
  A. Hollywood
    1. Actor
    2. Spokesman for GE
    3. Liberal to conservative
  B. Conservative governor of California
  C. Political rise of Reagan
    1. Demographic changes
      a. Older population
      b. Growth of Sunbelt
    2. Religious revival
      a. Fundamentalism
      b. "Moral Majority"
      c. Traditional values

D. Election of 1980
   1. Carter's decline
   2. Reagan's promises
   3. Reagan victory

III. Reagan's domestic policies
  A. Opulent inauguration
  B. Reaganomics
    1. Supply-side economics
    2. Tax cut in 1981
    3. Budget cuts and deficits
    4. Tax increase in 1982
    5. Deregulation
  C. Ethical misconduct
    1. In EPA
    2. Deaver and Nofziger
    3. "Sleaze factor"
  D. Effects of social policies
    1. Labor unions
    2. Feminism
    3. Minorities

IV. Foreign affairs in the 1980s
  A. Reagan's anticommunism
  B. Military buildup
  C. Emphasis on Central America
    1. El Salvador
    2. Nicaragua
      a. Sandinistas
      b. Contras
      c. Arias peace plan
  D. Middle East

    1. Iran-Iraq War
    2. Lebanon, PLO, Israel
  E. Grenada

V. Reagan's second term
  A. Election of 1984
    1. Economic recovery
    2. Mondale and taxes
    3. Landslide and its dangers
  B. Tax reform of 1986
  C. Arms control
    1. Obstacle of "Star Wars"
    2. Meetings with Gorbachev

VI. Twilight of the Reagan presidency
  A. Reagan's continued popularity
  B. Iran-Contra scandal
    1. Arms for hostages
    2. Profits to Contras
    3. North, Poindexter, McFarlane, Casey
    4. Congressional investigation
    5. Tower Commission
    6. Special prosecutor
  C. Conservative criticisms
  D. Social crises and scandals
    1. AIDS
    2. Gary Hart
    3. Ivan Boesky and Wall Street corruption
  E. Stock market collapse
  F. INF arms agreement
  G. Reagan legacy

KEY ITEMS OF CHRONOLOGY

Ford pardons Nixon	September 8, 1974
Camp David Agreement	1978
Seizure of Americans in Teheran	November 1979
Iran-Iraq War	1980–1988
Reagan administration	1981–1988
Economic Recovery Tax Act	1981
Bombing of marines in Beirut	October 23, 1983
Deficit Reduction Act	1984
Tax Reform Act	1986
Shuttle *Challenger* explosion	January 28, 1986
Iran-Contra scandal emerges	November 1986
Stock market crash	October 19, 1987
INF treaty signed	December 9, 1987

TERMS TO MASTER

Listed below are some important terms or people with which you should be familiar after you complete the study of this chapter. Explain the significance of each name or term.

1. WIN button
2. Anwar Sadat
3. Camp David Agreement
4. SALT II
5. Ayatollah Khomeini
6. supply-side economics
7. Economic Recovery Tax Act
8. "sleaze factor"
9. Sandra Day O'Connor
10. Contras
11. PLO
12. Grenada
13. Geraldine Ferraro
14. Tax Reform Act of 1986
15. S.D.I.
16. Mikhail Gorbachev
17. AIDS
18. Lt.-Col. Oliver North

VOCABULARY BUILDING

Listed below are some words used in this chapter. Look up each word in your dictionary.

1. rapprochement
2. dint
3. amnesty
4. flay
5. malaise
6. effigy
7. fervid
8. beguiling
9. chagrin
10. euphemism

EXERCISES FOR UNDERSTANDING

When you have completed reading the chapter, answer each of the following questions. If you have difficulty, go back and reread the section of the chapter related to the question.

Multiple-Choice Questions

Select the letter of the response which best completes the statement.

1. Jimmy Carter's 1976 victory can be attributed to
   A. his strong support among southern blacks
   B. the traditional Democratic sweep of the West
   C. his long career as a national politician
   D. the large voter turnout in the election

2. Carter's most significant accomplishment in foreign policy was
   A. retaining complete control over the Panama Canal
   B. an agreement with OPEC on oil prices
   C. opposition to Soviet invasion of Afghanistan
   D. a treaty between Israel and Egypt

3. The new political right in the 1970s
   A. advocated teaching creationism
   B. supported abortions
   C. endorsed the Equal Rights Amendment
   D. did all of the above

4. Reagan's economic program succeeded in 1981 in
   A. balancing the federal budget
   B. cutting deficit spending
   C. slashing personal income taxes
   D. tightening the regulation of business

5. The "sleaze factor" in the Reagan administration involved
   A. George Bush and the B-1 bomber
   B. Caspar Weinberger and $659 ashtrays
   C. James Watt's profits from land sales
   D. Michael Deaver's exploitation of his White House connections

6. In Nicaragua, the United States under Reagan supported
   A. Anastasio Somoza
   B. the Sandinistas
   C. the Contras
   D. none of the above

7. In 1973 the United States successfully rescue Americans in
   A. Lebanon
   B. Grenada
   C. Afghanistan
   D. Iran
8. A major accomplishment of the second Reagan administration was
   A. tax reform
   B. signing SALT II in 1986
   C. balancing the 1986 budget
   D. helping the Sandinistas in El Salvador

True-False Questions

Indicate whether each statement is true or false.

1. Gerald Ford called the fight against inflation "the moral equivalent of war."
2. Carter stressed a foreign policy of pragmatism rather than supporting a policy based on fixed principle.
3. The Shah's secret police masterminded the seizure of Americans in Teheran in 1979.
4. Before becoming president, Ronald Reagan had never held elective office.

5. Reagan always opposed raising taxes to balance the budget.
6. Reagan supported the ERA.
7. In 1984 Walter Mondale lost to Reagan in a landslide.
8. Geraldine Ferraro was the first woman appointed to the Supreme Court.

Essay Questions

1. What were the shortcomings and weaknesses of Jimmy Carter and his administration?
2. Why was Ronald Reagan elected in 1980? What factors contributed to his victory?
3. What was "Reaganomics," and was it a success? Why or why not?
4. How did Reagan's strong anticommunist beliefs guide his foreign policies in Central America and the Middle East?
5. Describe the ethical scandals that plagued the Reagan administration.
6. Explain the issues raised in the Iran-Contra scandal.
7. Will Ronald Reagan be considered a successful president? Explain with specific examples.

DOCUMENTS

Document 1. Ronald Reagan's First Inaugural Address, 1981

In his inaugural address in 1981 Ronald Reagan outlined the economic ills of the nation and promised an administration which would begin to reverse these ills. Read carefully his description of the problems and his promised solutions.

These United States are confronted with an economic afflication of great proportions. We suffer from the longest and one of the worst sustained inflations in our national history. It distorts our economic decisions, penalizes thrift, and crushes the struggling young and the fixed-income elderly alike. It threatens to shatter the lives of millions of our people.

Idle industries have cast workers into unemployment, human misery, and personal indignity. Those who do work are denied a fair return for their labor by a tax system which penalizes successful achievement and keeps us from maintaining full productivity.

But great as our tax burden is, it has not kept pace with public spending. For decades we have piled deficit upon deficit, mortgaging our future and our children's future for the temporary convenience of the present. To continue this long trend is to guarantee tremendous social, cultural, political, and economic upheavals.

You and I, as individuals, can, by borrowing, live beyond our means, but for only a limited period of time. Why, then, should we think that collectively, as a nation, we're not bound by that same limitation? We must act today in order to preserve tomorrow. And let there be no misunderstanding: We are going to begin to act, beginning today.

In this present crisis, government is not the solution to our problem; government *is* the problem. From time to time we've been tempted to believe that society has become too complex to be managed by self-rule, that government by an elite group is superior to government for, by, and of the people. Well, if no one among us is capable of governing himself, then who among us has the capacity to govern someone else? All of us together, in and out of government, must bear the burden. The solutions we seek must be equitable, with no one group singled out to pay a higher price.

It is my intention to curb the size and influence of the Federal establishment and to demand recognition of the distinction between the powers granted to the Federal Government and those reserved to the States or to the people. All of us need to be reminded that the Federal Government did not create the States; the States created the Federal Government.

Now, so there will be no misunderstanding, it's not my intention to do away with government. It is rather to make it work—work with us, not over us; to stand by our side, not ride on our back. Government can and must provide opportunity, not smother it; foster productivity, not stifle it.

[From *Messages and Papers of Ronald Reagan,* 1981, 1:1–2]

Document 2. Ronald Reagan's Second Inaugural Address, 1985

By the time of his second inauguration in 1985 Reagan had the opportunity to begin acting on the promises he had made in 1981. His address makes claims of accomplishment and indicates continued challenges. In the final rhetorical flourish one can see evidence of the orator who had mesmerized audiences with "the speech" as he wound his way from actor and television host to president.

Four years ago, I spoke to you of a New Beginning, and we have accomplished that. But in another sense, our New Beginning is a continuation of that beginning created two centuries ago when, for the first time in history, government, the people said, was not our master, it is our servant; its only power that which we the people allow it to have.

That system has never failed us, but for a time we failed the system. We asked things of government that government was not equipped to give. We yielded authority to the National Government that properly belonged to States or to local governments or to the people themselves. We allowed taxes and inflation to rob us of our earnings and savings and watched the great industrial machine that had made us the most productive people on Earth slow down and the number of unemployed increase.

A dynamic economy, with more citizens working and paying taxes, will be our strongest tool to bring down budget deficits. But an almost unbroken 50 years of deficit spending has finally brought us to a time of reckoning. We've come to a turning point, a moment for hard decisions. I have asked the Cabinet and my staff a question and now I put the same question to all of you. If not us, who? And if not now, when? It must be done by all of us going forward with a program aimed at reaching a balanced budget. We can then begin reducing the national debt.

I will shortly submit a budget to the Congress aimed at freezing government program spending for the next year. Beyond this, we must take further steps to permanently control government's power to tax and spend. We must act now to protect future generations from government's desire to spend its citizens' money and tax them into servitude when the bills come due. Let us make it unconstitutional for the Federal Government to spend more than the Federal Government takes in.

History is a ribbon, always unfurling. History is a journey. And as we continue our journey, we think of those who traveled before us. We stand again at the steps of this symbol of our democracy—well, we would have been standing at the steps if it hadn't gotten so cold. [*Laughter*] Now we're standing inside this symbol of our democracy, and we see and hear again the echoes of our past: a general falls to his knees in the hard snow of Valley Forge; a lonely President paces the darkened halls and ponders his struggle to preserve the Union; the men of the Alamo call out encouragement to each other; a settler pushes west and sings a song, and the song echoes out forever and fills the unknowing air.

It is the American sound. It is hopeful, big-hearted, idealistic, daring, decent, and fair. That's our heritage, that's our song. We sing it still. For all our problems, our differences, we are together as of old. We raise our voices to the God who is the Author of this most tender music. And may He continue to hold us close as we fill the world with our sound—in unity, affection, and love—one people under God, dedicated to the dream of freedom that He has placed in the human heart, called upon now to pass that dream on to a waiting and hopeful world.

God bless you, and God bless America.

[From *Weekly Compilation of Presidential Documents,* 21, no. 4 (January 28, 1985): 67–68, 70]

Questions for Reflection

What economic ills did Reagan say afflicted the nation when he took office? What was his solution for these problems? In the first inaugural Reagan made reference to the deficit; to what extent was he successful in dealing with that problem? What was his method for solving the problem?

What new and specific promises did he make in 1985? In light of deficit spending during times of national crisis, how wise was Reagan's proposal for a constitutional amendment to prohibit deficit spending? What is your assessment of the conclusion of Reagan's speech?

ANSWERS TO MULTIPLE-CHOICE
AND TRUE-FALSE QUESTIONS

Multiple-Choice Questions

1-A, 2-D, 3-A, 4-C, 5-D, 6-C, 7-B, 8-A

True-False Questions

1-F, 2-F, 3-F, 4-F, 5-F, 6-F, 7-T, 8-F